世界遗产概论

JNTRODUCTION TO THE WORLD HERJTAGE

韩嫣薇 杨凡 等编著

浙江工商大学出版社

图书在版编目(CIP)数据

世界遗产概论 / 韩嫣薇,杨凡等编著. — 杭州 :浙江工商大学出版社,2014.6(2020.8 重印)

ISBN 978-7-5178-0508-3

Ⅰ. ①世… Ⅱ. ①韩… ②杨… Ⅲ. ①文化遗产—概况—世界 Ⅳ. ①K103

中国版本图书馆 CIP 数据核字(2014)第 128665 号

世界遗产概论

韩嫣薇　杨　凡 等 编著

责任编辑	王黎明
封面设计	包建辉
责任印制	包建辉
出版发行	浙江工商大学出版社
	(杭州市教工路 198 号　邮政编码 310012)
	(E-mail:zjgsupress@163.com)
	(网址:http://www.zjgsupress.com)
	电话:0571 - 88904980,88831806(传真)
排　版	杭州朝曦图文设计有限公司
印　刷	广东虎彩云印刷有限公司绍兴分公司
开　本	787mm×1092mm　1/16
印　张	22.5
字　数	534 千
版印次	2014 年 6 月第 1 版　2020 年 8 月第 4 次印刷
书　号	ISBN 978-7-5178-0508-3
定　价	49.00 元

本书编委会

主　编　韩嫣薇　杨　凡

编委会　史钰军　于静波　王慧中

　　　　郭　宁　钟　玮

PREFACE 前言

　　根据联合国教科文组织的定义,世界遗产是属于全人类的具有突出的普遍价值的文物古迹和自然景观。自 1978 年第一批世界遗产诞生以来,已有 981 处遗产被列入《世界遗产名录》。通过几十年的发展,世界遗产保护的观念日益深入人心,其理念和准则改变了世界文化与自然资源的保护格局,有力地推动了世界各国的遗产保护实践。

　　中国是历史悠久的文明古国,文化传统悠久,历史遗迹众多。同时,我国地域广袤,地理形态各异,拥有许多神奇的自然地貌。自 1985 年我国加入《保护世界文化和自然遗产公约》以来,截至 2013 年,经联合国教科文组织审核、批准,列入《世界遗产名录》的世界遗产已达 45 处,世界遗产总量位居世界第二,仅次于意大利。

　　随着世界遗产数量的增加,我国已经成为遗产大国,但是想要成为世界遗产强国,实现遗产资源的可持续保护和开发,进一步扩大我国自然与文化遗产在世界上的影响力,还需要大力推进国内相关的研究和教育工作。这就需要该领域的研究者和学习者拥有国际化的眼界、掌握第一手的资料。经过三十多年的研究和积累,我国在这一领域已经出版了不少译介的资料和研究成果,但是系统介绍世界遗产的英语资料仍然比较匮乏。本书的编写正是出于填补空缺的目的,以纯正的英文文献,为读者系统介绍遍布于五大洲的世界各国的自然和文化遗产资源,为这一领域的研究者和学习者提供可靠的研究和学习资料。

　　本书以世界遗产的地理分布为经线,以遗产类别为纬线,纵横交织出人类文明与自然造化的斑斓画卷,引领读者进入原汁原味的世界遗产阅读之旅。全书分六章。第一章为绪论,提纲挈领地介绍了世界遗产的由来,《保护世界文化和自然遗产公约》的核心内容,相关国际组织的职能和运作,世界遗产的定义与分类,世界遗产的评定标准,以及中国的世界遗产概述。第二章至第六章各由四个小节组成,分别介绍了每个大洲最有代表性的文化遗产、自然遗产、双重遗产、文化景观遗产。每个遗产地既有简要介绍,也有精选英语文献,并配有相关的专项练习。

　　本书在编写过程中参阅了大量的出版文献和网络资料,因篇幅有限,现已将主要的参考资料列明。在此,谨向所有的作者表示至深至诚的感谢!

　　本书的编写集合了众位编者的智慧和努力,由浙江工商大学的韩嫣薇和杨凡任主编,拟定纲要并汇总修改,浙江工商大学的史钰军、于静波、郭宁、钟玮及杭州师范大学的王慧中参与本书的具体编写。具体分工如下:钟玮、杨凡编写第一章;郭宁、钟玮等编写第二章;杨凡等编写第三章;韩嫣薇、于静波等编写第四章;于静波等编写第五章;史钰军、于静波等编写第六章;杭州师范大学王慧中教授编写了本书中有关湿地、生态和植物等方面的内容。由于编写者能力和水平的局限,书中难免有疏漏之处,敬请各位专家学者不吝指正。

编　者

2014 年 6 月于杭州

CONTENTS
目录

1

北美洲

第五章 北美洲的世界遗产

大洋洲

第六章 大洋洲的世界遗产

世界遗产概论

第一章 绪 论

Introduction to the World Heritage

世界遗产是全人类共同拥有的宝贵财富,它是大自然慷慨的赐予和人类数百万年辛勤劳作的结晶。世界遗产不仅仅是历史的珍贵遗存,更是对今天和将来具有重要作用的、可持续发展的事物,具有社会价值、经济价值、美学价值和科学价值等完整的价值体系。自 20 世纪 70 年代创设了世界遗产的评选、管理和保护体系以来,该体系获得了快速的发展和长足的进步,其蓬勃的生机便是世界遗产卓越价值的体现与明证。

自《保护世界文化和自然遗产公约》诞生以来的四十多年间,世界遗产的评选、管理和保护等实践工作的规模日益扩大,其广度和深度获得了前所未有的发展。关于世界遗产包含的类型,人们开始日益关注工业遗产、文化线路、农业遗产,甚至是军事遗产;关于世界遗产的管理,人们开始日益重视法律的重要性和遗产地社区居民的参与度;关于世界遗产的保护,人们对原真性和完整性等原则的理解和认识越来越深入和富有创新性。世界遗产已经摆脱了简单意义上的著名旅游景点的定位,它的社会意义、文化意义已被社会公众广泛认可。世界遗产已被越来越多的人视为人类文明脉络延续的最高层次的体现与载体。

第一节　世界遗产的由来

随着人类社会的不断发展,特别是工业化、全球化的快速推进,人类的文化遗产和自然遗产受到日益严重的威胁,一方面是自然因素所致,另一面人为因素正在不断造成更加致命的损害和破坏。战争、灾害等因素经常会对这些人类共享的文明财富造成极大的威胁。随着社会的发展,不少有识之士指出:如果再不重视对人类文明的保护,未来的人们可能再也看不到现代人还能欣赏到的精彩世界。尤其是 20 世纪上半期的两次世界大战,在重创了人类社会的同时,也让人们产生了要建立一个平等、和平世界的愿望。联合国应运而生,宣告了全球化时代的到来。联合国的存在,不仅使得国际合作成为可能,而且使得各国分享文明成果和技术进步成为可能。散落于世界各地的人类文明遗产也成为这一国际组织的得益者,现在它们不仅属于它们所在地的国家和人民,也属于全世界,为全人类所共享和关注,每个人都担负起保护世界遗产的责任。

1954 年,联合国教科文组织(UNESCO)通过了《武装冲突情况下保护文化财产公约》,该公约认为,"对任何民族文化财产的损害即是对全人类文化遗产的损害",人类需要承担"共同的责任"。

持续 20 年的努比亚遗址的救援和宣传活动,是催生《保护世界文化和自然遗产公约》出世的直接诱因,也是对其实施的初期检验。1959 年,为发展当地经济、消除水患、发挥水电效能,埃及政府决定,在南部阿斯旺地区拦腰切断尼罗河,修建纳赛尔水库。这项工程中必须修建的一道高坝,抬高了水位,使努比亚遗址受到了严重威胁。当河水行将淹没努比亚遗址的时候,埃及和苏丹两国向联合国教科文组织提出了请求,希望得到国际社会的帮助,以拯救受到威胁的努比亚遗址。

对这一请求的回应,是联合国教科文组织保护人类文化遗产的第一次国际行动。联合国教科文组织的努力得到了大约 50 个国家的支持。各个国家及国际组织捐款达 8 000 万美元。从 1964 年开始，用了整整 10 年时间，阿布辛拜勒的两座神庙被完整切割、异地重建。

在针对努比亚遗址开展的保护工作中，人们开始认识到，随着世界各国经济的发展和现代化建设步伐的加快，许多文化遗产和自然遗产正面临严重的威胁，如不及时采取有效的保护和拯救措施，它们都将遭到毁灭性的破坏。保护和拯救那些历经数千年甚至数万年之久而形成的重要文化遗产和自然遗产，单靠其所在国家的力量往往难以完成，特别是小国和穷国更是如此，需要各国伸出援助之手。这种保护和拯救，还必须以国际公约的法律形式予以确认，从而对缔约国产生约束力，使人类遗产的保护真正到位。

各个民族或国家的文化财富应该被视为人类共同的遗产，国际上的几次精诚合作显然可以证明"世界遗产"的理念已经渐渐在世界范围内得到认可。然而，为了使全人类真正达成保护世界遗产的共识，仍需要形成一种世界范围内的管理和合作机制，以及一些大家都能够接受的原则性规定。

1964 年签署的《威尼斯宪章》，是针对历史建筑和遗址进行保护的文件，标志着当代全新的文化遗产保护理论和技术标准的形成。《威尼斯宪章》特别强调了对历史建筑及遗址的历史价值的保护，因为这些历史建筑和遗址所传递的信息说明了人类的发展历史，记录了人类社会成长的历程，有助于我们更好地解读自身历史。

在 1965 年华盛顿会议上，联合国教科文组织建议成立"世界遗产信托基金"。1968 年世界自然保护联盟（IUCNNR）向"世界遗产信托基金"提出加入该基金，使得人类历史上第一次将自然遗产和文化遗产结合在一起进行保护成为可能。

联合国教科文组织 1968 年在巴黎召开第一次政府间环境会议，议题是各国共同利用和保护地球生物圈，制订"人和生物圈计划"。1972 年联合国在斯德哥尔摩举行关于人类环境问题的会议。在会议上，国际社会强调迫切需要采取措施来保护自然环境及人类创造的杰出成果。会议还确认了各国要对处于危险中的环境集体负责这一观念。

到 20 世纪 60 年代末 70 年代初，世界各国的公众开始真正意识到，各国各民族所拥有的文化遗产，以及长期以来他们居住和生活的自然环境应该受到充分的尊重和保护。他们强调这些文明成果是他们祖先的杰出创造，而不同的自然环境使各民族的文化得到了最充分的发展，这两者正是他们民族文化特殊性最实际的，也往往是最高的体现。他们还认为，除了依靠每个国家来维护自己的文化特殊性之外，以国际集体责任的名义参加保护工作，也应是所有国家义不容辞的责任。

在这样的背景下，联合国教科文组织和一个非政府组织——国际遗迹遗址理事会（ICOMOS）——就保护文化遗产起草了一个公约。与此同时，美国积极参与了自然遗产部分的起草工作。它与另一个非政府国际组织——世界自然保护联盟合作，对自然遗产的保护进行归纳，并提议将保护自然遗产和文化遗产放在同一个法律文件中。1972 年，联合国在瑞典斯德哥尔摩召开的联合国人类环境大会上对提议进行了讨论，最后决定，由联合国教科文组织正式拟定一个公约，来规范全世界文化遗产和自然遗产的保护工作。

1972 年 10 月至 11 月，在巴黎召开的联合国教科文组织第 17 届全体会议，对于世界遗产保护来说，是一个重要的时刻。这次会议正式通过了全球性保护世界遗产方面最重要的国际公约：《保护世界文化和自然遗产公约》。主要规定了文化遗产和自然遗产的定义、文化和自然遗产的国家保护及国际保护措施等条款;规定了各缔约国可自行确定本国领土内的文化和自然遗产,并向世界遗产委员会(World Heritage Committee)递交其遗产清单,由世界遗产大会审核和批准。凡是被列入世界文化和自然遗产的项目,都将由其所在国家依法严格予以保护。根据该《公约》,还设立了联合国教科文组织的世界遗产委员会和世界遗产基金(World Heritage Fund)。世界遗产委员会是《保护世界文化和自然遗产公约》的管理机构,该委员会于 1976 年成立,并同时建立了《世界遗产名录》。

《世界遗产名录》的编制和世界遗产委员会等相关机构的成立为全球合作保护世界遗产提供了重要的前提条件,之后的《实施世界遗产公约的操作指南》(简称《操作指南》)更为保证保护工作的权威性和可操作性提供了有力的后盾,标志着人类共同保护文化成就和自然财富的崭新时代的来临。

第二节 《保护世界文化和自然遗产公约》

联合国教科文组织大会(General Conference of UNESCO)于 1972 年 10 月 17 日至 11 月 21 日在巴黎举行第 17 届全体会议,原来只是想制定一项国际协议,以推动相互援助进行保护古迹和建筑物这类文化遗产的工作。后来由于形势的发展和舆论的推动,大会经过认真讨论,终于在 11 月 16 日通过了《保护世界文化和自然遗产公约》(*Convention Concerning the Protection of the World Cultural and Natural Heritage*)(以下简称《世界遗产公约》或《公约》)。11 月 23 日,会议主席和教科文组织总干事在两个正式文本上签字。

《公约》正文前的缘起部分叙述制定本《公约》的背景、必要性和紧迫性。近年来,文化遗产和自然遗产越来越受到被破坏的威胁,它所造成的损害或破坏现象更加难以治理。而且,这种损害或破坏现象,对世界各国遗产造成的有害影响往往难以挽回。现在许多国家保护遗产的工作不够完善,而且经济、科学和技术力量也不充分具备。有些文化遗产和自然遗产具有突出的重要性,因而需要作为全人类遗产的一部分加以保存。国际社会有责任通过提供集体援助,来参与保护具有突出和普遍价值的文化遗产和自然遗产。这种援助尽管不能代替有关国家采取的行动,但可以是它的有效补充。鉴于以上原因,有必要制定一项《公约》,建立一个按现代方法组织的而且永久有效的制度,以便集体保护这些遗产。

《公约》正文有 8 个部分,共 38 条。

第一部分是文化遗产和自然遗产的定义。

《公约》将文化遗产分为三类,即文物古迹、建筑群和遗址。就文物古迹和建筑群而言,它在历史、艺术或科学方面应当有突出的普遍价值。就遗址而言,它在历史、审美、人种学或人类学角度应当是具有突出的普遍价值的人类工程或自然与人的联合工程及考古地址。

《公约》将自然遗产分为自然景观、地质与地文结构(从审美或科学角度看具有突出的普遍价值的由物质和生物结构或这类结构群组成的自然面貌)、动物与植物生态区(从科学或保护角度看具有突出的普遍价值的地质和自然地理结构及明确划为受威胁的动物和植物生境区)、天然名胜和自然区域(从科学、保护或自然美角度看具有突出的普遍价值的天然名胜或明确划分的自然区域)。这些都是在审美、科学、保护或自然美方面应当有突出的普遍价值,或者已被明确划分为受到威胁的区域。

《公约》认为,缔约国都可以自行确定和划分上面所提及的本国领土内的文化遗产和自然遗产。

第二部分是文化遗产和自然遗产的国家保护和国际保护。

缔约国要承认确定、保护、保存、展出本国领土内的文化遗产和自然遗产,并将它传给后代,这些主要是本国的责任,要尽力而为。在适当的时候利用能获得的国际援助与合作。缔约国还要承认这类遗产是世界遗产的一部分,因此,在最大限度地利用本国资源的基础上,必要时应取得国际的援助和合作,特别是财政、艺术、科学及技术方面的援助和合作。整个国际社会有责任进行合作,予以保护。缔约国承诺不故意损害其他国家的文化遗产和自然遗产。

为了实现《公约》提出的这个宗旨,需要建立一个国际合作和援助体制。《公约》各缔约国应视本国具体情况尽力做到以下几点:

1. 通过一项旨在使文化和自然遗产在社会生活中起一定作用并把遗产保护工作纳入全面规划的总政策。

2. 如本国内尚未建立负责文化和自然遗产的保护、保存和展出的机构,则应建立一个或几个此类机构,配备适当的工作人员和为履行其职能所需的手段。

3. 开展科学和技术研究,并制定出能够抵抗威胁本国文化或自然遗产的危险的实际方法。

4. 采取为确定、保护、保存、展出和恢复这类遗产所需的适当的法律、科学、技术、行政和财政措施。

5. 促进建立或发展有关保护、保存、展出文化和自然遗产的国家或地区培训中心,并鼓励这方面的科学研究。

第三部分是保护世界文化遗产和自然遗产政府间委员会(简称世界遗产委员会)的介绍。这一部分有三项内容。

第一项是世界遗产委员会的组成。它由缔约国大会选出的21个国家组成,即自当选之应届大会常会结束时起至应届大会后第三次常会闭幕时止,通常为6年,每届改选1/3的成员国。成员国应选派在文化遗产或自然遗产方面有资历的人担任代表。委员会委员的选举须保证均衡地代表世界的不同地区和不同文化。另外有三个非政府的国际组织,即国际文物保护与修复研究中心(ICCROM)、国际古迹遗址理事会(ICOMOS)和世界自然保护联盟(IUCN)可以各派一名代表,以咨询者身份出席委员会会议。除此之外,应联合国教科文组织大会常会期间举行大会的本《公约》缔约国提出的请求,其他具有类似目标的政府或非政府组织的代表亦可以咨询者身份出席委员会的会议。

第二项是《世界遗产名录》(*List of World Heritage*)的制定。各国应尽力向世界遗产委员会递交本国适宜列入世界遗产名录的文化遗产和自然遗产预备名单,这份预备名录要尽量齐全,它应包括有关遗产的所在地及其意义的文献资料。委员会按照本《公约》

规定的遗产定义和要求，经过一定的程序，及时制定、更新并公布《世界遗产名录》。一份最新目录应至少每两年分发一次。委员会还要制定一份《濒危世界遗产名录》(List of World Heritage in Danger)，将受到严重威胁的遗产列入其中。为制定《世界遗产名录》，委员会要确定可操作的文化遗产和自然遗产入选标准。

第三项是国际援助。委员会要接受并研究缔约国就本国遗产要求国际援助的申请。国际援助要按实际情况排出顺序。

第四部分是保护世界文化遗产和自然遗产基金。

《公约》规定设立世界遗产基金(World Heritage Fund)。资金来自以下各方面：缔约国义务捐款和自愿捐款；其他国家政府、联合国系统的组织或其他政府间组织捐款、赠款；团体或个人捐款、赠款或遗赠；基金款所得利息；募捐的资金、募款活动收入和世界遗产委员会拟定的基金条例所认可的所有其他资金。缔约国应考虑设立本国的类似的基金会或者协会。缔约国应对在联合国教科文组织赞助下为世界遗产基金所组织的国际募款运动给予援助，提供便利。

第五部分是国际援助的条件和安排。

缔约国均可要求对本国领土内具有突出的普遍价值的文化或自然遗产给予国际援助。申请援助要提供必要的文件、资料和专家报告。对于因自然灾害或灾难而提出的申请，委员会应立即优先审议，委员会也应掌握一笔应急储备金。

国际援助大体分三类：第一类是世界遗产的保护、保存、展出或恢复，这包括已列入名录的和可能适于列入名录的，还包括鉴定缔约国提请研究审定的遗产；第二类是培训遗产鉴定、保护、保存、展出和恢复方面的各级工作人员和专家；第三类是向自行培训这类人员的国家提供援助。世界遗产委员会提供援助的形式有：研究名录中所列世界遗产的艺术、科学和技术性问题；为已批准的工程提供专家、技术人员和熟练工人；提供紧缺的设备；提供长期偿还的低息或无息贷款；在例外并有特殊原因的情况下提供无偿补助金。对于提供大规模国际援助，要先进行周密的科学、经济和技术研究，并考虑采用最先进的技术，还要合理利用当事国的现有资源。国际社会只担负必要工程的部分费用，受益国家要承担主要费用。

第六部分是教育计划。

缔约国要通过各种手段，特别是教育和宣传，努力在以下三方面使公众增强认识：对世界遗产的了解、赞赏和尊重；广泛了解当前有哪些危险因素对世界遗产造成威胁，广泛了解国际社会和本国政府为履行本《公约》进行的各项活动；国际援助的受益国要使人们了解受援助的遗产的重要性和国际援助所发挥的作用。

第七部分是报告工作。

缔约国要向联合国教科文组织报告本国政府为实施公约通过的立法和行政规定，以及采取的其他行动的情况，并要详细叙述取得的经验。还应提请世界遗产委员会注意这些报告。委员会应在联合国教科文组织大会的每届常会上递交一份关于其活动的报告。

第八部分是最后条款。主要包括：

条约文本：本《公约》以阿拉伯文、英文、法文、俄文和西班牙文拟定，五种文本具有同等效力。

会员国的批准或接受：本《公约》应由联合国教科文组织会员国根据各自的宪法程序

予以批准或接受。

条约生效：就任何其他国家而言，本《公约》应在这些国家交存其批准书、接受书或加入书的三个月之后生效。

退约和废约：缔约国均可通告废除本《公约》，废约通告应以一份书面文件交存联合国教科文组织的总干事。《公约》的废除应在接到废约通告书一年后生效。废约在生效日之前不得影响退约国承担的财政义务。

修订：本《公约》可由联合国教科文组织大会修订。任何修订对《公约》缔约国均具有约束力。

按照《联合国宪章》第 102 条，本《公约》须应联合国教科文组织总干事的要求在联合国秘书处登记。《公约》于 1972 年 11 月由联合国教科文组织大会通过后，美国于 1973 年 12 月率先加入《公约》，到 1975 年有法定的 20 个国家加入，《公约》于是生效。截止到 2003 年，已经有 170 个国家加入《公约》，至此，联合国教科文组织成员中只有个别成员还没有加入《公约》，《公约》已经成为世界遗产保护领域最具普遍性的国际法律文书。《公约》认为某些文化和自然遗产具有突出的普遍价值，首次正式提出了"人类共同遗产"的概念，具有划时代意义。

第三节　与世界遗产相关的国际组织

与世界遗产相关的国际组织主要有联合国教科文组织、联合国教科文组织世界遗产委员会及世界遗产中心、世界自然保护联盟、国际古迹遗址理事会、国际文物保护与修复研究中心等，它们在世界遗产的保护和管理中起到了重要的作用。

1. 联合国教科文组织（United Nations Educational, Scientific and Cultural Organization, UNESCO）是联合国专门机构之一。该组织于 1946 年 11 月 4 日成立，同年 12 月成为联合国专门机构之一，总部设在巴黎。其宗旨是促进成员国在教育、科学及文化方面的国际合作，从而加强对联合国宪章所规定的正义、法律，以及对不分种族、性别、语言、宗教的全人类应该拥有的人权和基本自由的广泛尊重，有利于各国人民相互了解，维护世界和平。

联合国教科文组织在其主管的教育、科学、文化、传播与信息等业务范围内设立了十多个政府间机构及大型合作计划，以推动国际智力合作，其中主要有：国际教育局、人与生物圈计划、国际地质对比计划、国际水文计划、政府间海洋学委员会、社会变革管理计划、世界遗产委员会、促使文化财产归还原主国或归还非法占有文化财产政府间委员会、世界版权公约政府间委员会、国际传播发展计划、综合信息计划、政府间信息学计划、政府间体育运动委员会等。联合国教科文组织大会选举产生的各执行理事机构负责规划和管理各计划的活动，并建立各自的国际或地区合作网络，如"国际生物圈保护区网络"和《世界遗产名录》等。此外，联合国教科文组织还同世界上三百多个在教育、科学、文化等领域有重要地位和影响的非政府国际组织建立了正式（协作类、咨询类）关系或业务关系。

联合国教科文组织给予会员国的援助主要通过智力合作的方式来体现,如派遣专家、组织召开大型或专业国际会议/研讨会,开展人员培训,参与会员国在相关领域的能力建设,制定国际准则性文件,提出或倡导新思想新理念等。它是开展多边外交和教育、科学、文化、传播等领域国际交往的重要窗口和阵地。该组织在全民教育、扫盲、高等教育、遗产保护及生物多样性、海洋、水文、地质等领域成绩显著,并产生了巨大的社会和经济效益。

发展教育是联合国教科文组织的工作重心。它在教育领域的计划旨在实现所有级别持续一生的全民教育目标。事实上,教育对个人发展、经济增长和社会团结至关重要。这也是在与贫困做斗争和维持可持续发展中起决定性作用的一项工作。联合国教科文组织通过国际教育局、国际教育论坛、世界全民教育大会、国际职业技术教育大会等形式普及初级教育和消除两性间在受教育方面的不平等现象。

联合国教科文组织在科学领域涉猎广泛,除基础科学、工程科学外,主要精力放在当前人类面临的主要问题上,如可持续发展问题、生命伦理问题、人类安全问题、水资源管理问题等。为此,联合国教科文组织专门设立了如下重点计划项目。

(1)国际水文计划。作为一个以水科学研究和教育为重点的计划,它进行一系列的国际性、全球性的水科学研究,并进行水科学的国际培训和知识传播,以期提高各国政府决策人、科技人员和一般群众对水科学的认识,重点放在将水文学应用于水资源的调查评价、开发利用、管理保护及人类活动对水资源和水环境的影响,最终目的是帮助解决重大的水资源问题和与水有关的社会经济发展问题。

(2)政府间海洋学委员会(简称海委会)。海委会的宗旨是促进海洋科学调查并提供相关服务,以便通过会员国的一致行动,了解海洋的性质和海洋资源状况,帮助各国尤其是发展中国家提高海洋科研能力。海委会正从一个单纯的侧重海洋科研调查的国际机构转变为包括海洋调查、海洋服务、海洋与海岸带管理、海洋法律与政策制定在内的全方位的海洋国际机构,在国际海洋界发挥着日益重要的作用。除了协调联合国各机构外,它还负责长期监测海洋的情况,以改进气象预报,预告厄尔尼诺现象的出现,并且在发生海啸或飓风的情况下能够提前足够长的时间发出预警。该委员会参与建立全球海洋观测系统,该系统将确保浮标、船只和专用卫星提供的数据之间的联系,以便更好地了解洋流与气候之间的联系。

(3)人与生物圈计划(Man and the Biosphere Programme,简称 MAB)。这是联合国教科文组织科学部门于 1971 年发起的一项政府间跨学科的大型综合性的研究计划。生物圈保护区是 MAB 的核心部分,具有保护、可持续发展、提供科研教学、培训、监测基地等多种功能。其宗旨是通过自然科学和社会科学的结合,基础理论和应用技术的结合,科学技术人员、生产管理人员、政治决策者和广大人民的结合,对生物圈不同区域的结构和功能进行系统研究,并预测人类活动引起的生物圈及其资源的变化,以及这种变化对人类本身的影响。为合理利用和保护生物圈的资源、保存遗传基因的多样性、改善人类同环境的关系提供科学依据和理论基础,以寻找有效地解决人口、资源、环境等问题的途径。

(4)国际地质比对计划。此项计划旨在赞助与促进全球规模的各项基础地质问题的合作研究。还涉及管理和勘探矿物资源及解决各类环境问题,近些年来将减灾、抗灾及提高人们对自然灾害的认识作为重点。支持各国建立由"联合国教科文组织支持的世界地质公园"。

联合国教科文组织在文化领域的活动涉及文化政策、文化多样性、艺术、版权、物质和非物质遗产、文化间对话、历史、文化与青年、文化与妇女及性别平等诸多方面。

在人文社科领域，联合国教科文组织的作用是确保知识、标准、智力合作的进步，以促进保障正义、自由和人类宽容等世界性价值标准得到巩固的社会转变。主要使命可以归结为以下几点：研究现实（通过社会科学和人文科学领域基于经验的研究）；预见在这一现实中可能会发生什么（通过哲学和观察研究）；查清被推测为现实的东西（通过伦理和人权）。其目的是缩小现实与更美好的现实之间的差距，如社会变革管理计划。

文化领域，联合国教科文组织发起成立了世界文化和发展委员会，着手研究文化与发展的关系；组织创建了全球文化多样性联盟，通过了《保护世界文化和自然遗产公约》，建立了世界遗产委员会。

保护世界文化和自然遗产是联合国教科文组织发起的一项深受各国欢迎的国际合作活动。该活动的主要目的是确认符合标准的世界遗产并对缔约国境内的具有"突出意义和普遍价值"的文物古迹和自然景观/资源加以保护。1972 年，该组织的第 17 届大会通过了《保护世界文化和自然遗产公约》，迄今为止，世界上已有 190 个国家批准或加入了该《公约》。全球共有 981 处遗产地被列入《世界遗产名录》。

1985 年我国加入《保护世界文化和自然遗产公约》，截至 2013 年底，我国共有 45 处文化和自然遗产被批准列入《世界遗产名录》。

保护非物质文化遗产是联合国教科文组织在近些年来逐渐完善的一个优先计划。非物质文化包括所有传统和民间文化的表达形式，如口传文化传统、习俗、语言、音乐、舞蹈、宗教仪式、节日、传统医学和药典、烹调艺术及所有与物质文化（如工具和聚居地等）相关的特殊技能。

2001 年，经过各国提名和专家委员会的评审，联合国教科文组织公布了第一批"人类口头和非物质遗产代表作"，中国的昆曲名列其中。第二批"代表作"已于 2003 年公布，中国古琴顺利入选。按照规定，"代表作"每两年公布一次。截至 2011 年 11 月底，我国入选联合国教科文组织世界非物质类文化遗产名录项目总数已达 36 项，成为世界上入选"非遗"项目最多的国家。

记忆遗产反映了语言、民族和文化的多样性，它是世界的一面镜子，同时也是世界的记忆。但是，这种记忆是脆弱的，每天都有濒危的重要记忆在消失。因此，联合国教科文组织发起了世界记忆计划，以防止集体记忆的丧失，并且呼吁保护宝贵的文化遗产和馆藏文献，并让它们的价值在世界范围内广泛传播。目前共有 100 个国家的 299 份具有世界意义的文献和文献集合入选了《世界记忆名录》。其中我国已有 9 份古文献遗产入选《世界记忆名录》。

2. 联合国教科文组织世界遗产委员会（World Heritage Committee，WHC）成立于1976 年 11 月，由 21 名成员组成，负责《保护世界文化和自然遗产公约》的实施。委员会每年召开一次会议，主要决定哪些遗产可以列入《世界遗产名录》，对已列入名录的世界遗产的保护工作进行监督指导。委员会成员每届任期 6 年，每两年改选其中的 1/3。委员会内由 7 名成员构成世界遗产委员会主席团，主席团每年举行两次会议，筹备委员会的工作。

世界遗产委员会承担的任务：

（1）在缔约国提名的基础上，将国际上认为具有突出的普遍价值的文物古迹和自然遗产列入《世界遗产名录》并受《保护世界文化和自然遗产公约》保护。在挑选录入《世界遗产名录》的文化和自然遗产地时，负责对世界遗产的定义进行解释。在完成这项任务时，该委员会得到国际古迹遗址理事会（ICOMOS）和世界自然保护联盟（IUCN）的帮助。这两个组织仔细审查各缔约国对世界遗产的提名项目，并针对每一项提名项目写出评估报告。国际文物保护与修复研究中心（ICCROM）也对该委员会提出建议，例如文化遗产方面的培训和文物保护技术的建议。

（2）对已列入《世界遗产名录》的项目的保护和管理状况进行监督，使其得到有效的保护。审查世界遗产保护状况报告。当遗产得不到恰当的处理和保护时，该委员会让缔约国采取特别性保护措施。

（3）在紧急需要的情况下，决定将《世界遗产名录》的遗产列入《濒危世界遗产名录》（仅限那些需要进行大规模保护行动的遗产地和按照《保护世界文化和自然遗产公约》要求提出援助的遗产地）。

（4）管理世界遗产基金（保护世界文化和自然遗产基金）。决定世界遗产基金的资源以何种方法及在何种条件下最有效地帮助缔约国，审定各缔约国提出的援助申请，对为保护遗产而申请援助的国家给予技术和财力援助，以使其保护好那些杰出和举世公认的遗产。

截至2002年，在全球范围内，共有175个国家或地区加入《保护世界文化和自然遗产公约》，成为缔约国，是目前加入缔约国最多的公约之一。中国自1985年成为《保护世界文化和自然遗产公约》缔约国以来，与联合国教科文组织在世界遗产保护领域有着良好的合作关系。

世界遗产大会，是联合国教科文组织世界遗产委员会的例会，每年召开一次，会议审批列入《世界遗产名录》的项目，并对已列入名录的世界遗产的保护工作进行监督指导。

迄今，世界遗产大会已举行过37届。第28届大会于2004年7月在中国苏州举行。会议通过了"苏州决定"，要求从2006年起，《保护世界文化和自然遗产公约》每个缔约国每年申报的世界遗产项目为2项，其中至少包括1项自然遗产提名。会议还发表了《世界遗产青少年教育苏州宣言》。苏州会议上，有34项遗产地入选《世界遗产名录》。

世界遗产大会历届主办国一览表

会议	年	日　　　期	主办城市	国　　家
1	1977年	6月27日—7月1日	巴黎	法国
2	1978年	9月5日—8日	华盛顿哥伦比亚特区	美国
3	1979年	10月22日—26日	开罗和卢克索	埃及
4	1980年	9月1日—5日	巴黎	法国
5	1981年	10月26日—30日	悉尼	澳大利亚
6	1982年	12月13日—17日	巴黎	法国
7	1983年	12月5日—9日	佛罗伦萨	意大利
8	1984年	10月29日—11月2日	布宜诺斯艾利斯	阿根廷
9	1985年	12月2日—6日	巴黎	法国

会议	年	日　　　期	主办城市	国　　家
10	1986 年	11 月 24 日—28 日	巴黎	法国
11	1987 年	12 月 7 日—11 日	巴黎	法国
12	1988 年	12 月 5 日—9 日	巴西利亚	巴西
13	1989 年	12 月 11 日—15 日	巴黎	法国
14	1990 年	12 月 7 日—12 日	班芙	加拿大
15	1991 年	12 月 9 日—13 日	迦太基	突尼斯
16	1992 年	12 月 7 日—14 日	圣菲	美国
17	1993 年	12 月 6 日—11 日	卡塔赫纳	哥伦比亚
18	1994 年	12 月 12 日—17 日	普吉	泰国
19	1995 年	12 月 4 日—9 日	柏林	德国
20	1996 年	12 月 2 日—7 日	梅里达	墨西哥
21	1997 年	12 月 1 日—6 日	那不勒斯	意大利
22	1998 年	11 月 30 日—12 月 5 日	京都	日本
23	1999 年	11 月 29 日—12 月 4 日	马拉喀什	摩洛哥
24	2000 年	11 月 27 日—12 月 2 日	凯恩斯	澳大利亚
25	2001 年	12 月 11 日—16 日	赫尔辛基	芬兰
26	2002 年	6 月 24 日—29 日	布达佩斯	匈牙利
27	2003 年	6 月 30 日—7 月 5 日	巴黎	法国
28	2004 年	6 月 28 日—7 月 7 日	苏州	中国
29	2005 年	7 月 10 日—17 日	德班	南非
30	2006 年	7 月 8 日—16 日	维尔纽斯	立陶宛
31	2007 年	6 月 23 日—7 月 3 日	基督城	新西兰
32	2008 年	7 月 2 日—10 日	魁北克市	加拿大
33	2009 年	6 月 22 日—30 日	塞维利亚	西班牙
34	2010 年	7 月 25 日—8 月 3 日	巴西利亚	巴西
35	2011 年	6 月 19 日—29 日	巴黎	法国
36	2012 年	6 月 24 日—7 月 6 日	圣彼得堡	俄罗斯
37	2013 年	6 月 17 日—6 月 27 日	金边	柬埔寨

3. 联合国教科文组织世界遗产中心，又称为"公约执行秘书处"，该中心协助缔约国具体执行《世界遗产公约》，对世界遗产委员会提出建议，执行世界遗产委员会的决定。

世界遗产中心主要负责《世界遗产公约》的日常管理招待情况。包括组织世界遗产局和世界遗产委员会的年会;在遗产提名的准备工作中为各国政府提供咨询;根据各国政府的申请提供技术援助,调整遗产状况报告;当遗产受到威胁时采取紧急措施;负责世界遗产基金的管理工作;等等。

4. 世界自然保护联盟(International Union for Conservation of Nature and Natural Resources,IUCN),1948 年在联合国教科文组织的支持下成立的国际非政府组织,拥有来自 125 个国家的 800 余名成员,总部设在瑞士格兰德。宗旨是谋求完整性和自然多样性的保存,以及自然资源利用的平衡性和生态发展的可持续性。作为世界遗产委员会的合作伙伴,它负责对所有被提议参评的世界自然遗产、文化与自然双重遗产、文化景观遗产进行评估;就已有的世界自然遗产地的保护状况向世界遗产委员会提供报告;对自然遗产的保护人员进行培训。

世界自然保护联盟是国际自然保护组织的带头人,它本着造福大众的宗旨,在可持续发展的前提下,通过下设的 6 个专家委员会开展工作。这些委员会是世界上最大的环境专家网络,参加专家委员会工作的各国科学家无偿地为自然保护和发展做出贡献,许多中国科学家是委员会或其下属专家组的成员。

IUCN 在自然保护的传统领域处于领先地位。IUCN 的主要使命为:影响、鼓励和帮助全世界的科学家去保护自然资源的完整性和多样性,包括拯救濒危的植物和动物物种,建立国家公园和自然遗产保护地,评估物种和生态系统的保护现状等。

中国野生动物保护协会是 IUCN 的非政府组织会员之一。

世界自然保护联盟作为《世界遗产公约》的自然遗产评选和评估的官方技术咨询机构,对自然遗产提名项目能否列入《世界遗产名录》具有举足轻重的作用。我国的一些世界自然遗产和文化与自然双重遗产,如黄山、泰山、武夷山、丹霞地貌、三江并流、澄江化石地等项目,均接受该机构专家的评审。

5. 国际古迹遗址理事会(International Council on Monuments and Sites,ICOMOS),1965 年在波兰华沙成立,总部设在法国巴黎,是世界上唯一从事文化遗产保护理论、方法、科学技术研究的国际非政府组织,是世界遗产委员会的专业咨询机构,拥有来自 100 多个国家的 6000 余名成员。作为世界遗产委员会的合作伙伴,它负责对所有被提名进入《世界遗产名录》的文化遗产进行评估,并在评估文化与自然双重遗产和文化景观遗产工作中与世界自然保护联盟紧密配合。我国于 1993 年加入 ICOMOS,成立了国际古迹遗址理事会中国委员会(ICOMOS China),即中国古迹遗址保护协会。

6. 国际文物保护与修复研究中心(International Centre for the Study of the Preservation and Restoration of Cultural Property,ICCROM),成立于 1959 年,是联合国教科文组织创设的一个独立的国际科学机构。它通过教育培训、信息交流、调查研究技术合作及舆论宣传等方式致力于文化遗产的保护工作,作为咨询机构,向世界遗产委员会提供技术性建议。

第四节　世界遗产的定义与分类

世界遗产,是指经联合国教科文组织世界遗产委员会确认的、具有突出的普遍价值的自然景观与文物古迹,是人类珍稀的且无法取代的财产。世界遗产分为文化遗产、自然遗产、文化与自然双重遗产和文化景观四大类。

截至 2013 年 6 月第 37 届世界遗产大会,载入《世界遗产名录》的世界遗产总数达到 982 处,其中包括文化遗产 759 处、自然遗产 193 处及文化和自然双重遗产 29 处。

1. 文化遗产。

《保护世界文化和自然遗产公约》规定,属于下列内容之一者,可列为文化遗产。

文物:从历史、艺术或科学角度看,具有突出、普遍价值的建筑物、雕刻和绘画,具有考古意义的成分或结构,铭文、洞穴、住区及各类文物的综合体,如:美国的自由女神像,印度的泰姬陵。

建筑群:从历史、艺术或科学角度看,因其建筑的形式、同一性及其在景观中的地位,具有突出、普遍价值的单独或相互联系的建筑群,如:摩洛哥的阿伊特·本·哈杜杜,马耳他的巨石庙。

遗址:从历史、美学、人种学或人类学角度看,具有突出、普遍价值的人造工程或人与自然的共同杰作及考古遗址地带,如:叙利亚的帕尔米拉古城遗址,巴基斯坦的塔克希拉。

有些遗产可能满足以上多条定义,比如可能同时既是文物也是建筑群。

凡提名列入《世界遗产名录》的文化遗产项目,必须符合下列一项或几项标准方可获得批准:

标准 1:代表人类创造性的天才杰作。(人类创造性智慧)

标准 2:展示出一定时期内或世界某一文化区域内,在建筑或技术、纪念物艺术、城镇规划或景观设计等领域的发展上人类价值的重要交融。(价值的交融)

标准 3:能为一种现存或已消逝的文化传统、文明提供独一无二或至少是特殊的(突出的)见证。(文化传统的见证)

标准 4:作为一种类型的建筑物、建筑或科技的组合或景观的杰出典范,代表一种或几种文化,或者代表人与环境的相互作用(尤其在不可逆转的变化影响下显得易受侵害时)。(传统的人类居住地)

标准 5:作为传统的人类居住地或土地利用、海洋利用的杰出典范,代表一种或几种文化,或者代表人与环境的相互作用(尤其在不可逆转的变化影响下变得易受侵害时)。(传统的人类居住地)

标准 6:与具有普遍意义的重要事件或现行传统、思想、信仰或文学艺术作品有直接或实质的联系(世界遗产委员会认为,该项标准应该配合其他标准一起使用,才能成为列入《世界遗产名录》的理由)。(与具有普遍意义的事件相关联)

2. 自然遗产。

《保护世界文化和自然遗产公约》给自然遗产下的定义是符合下列规定之一者：

从美学或科学角度看，具有突出的普遍价值的由地质和生物结构或这类结构群组成的自然面貌，如：中国南方的喀斯特，俄罗斯的堪察加火山群。

从科学或保护角度看，具有突出的普遍价值的地质和自然地理结构及明确划定的濒危动植物物种生态区，如：刚果的霍加皮野生生物保护区，法国的新喀里多尼亚环礁。

从科学、保护或自然美角度看，具有突出的普遍价值的天然名胜或明确划定的自然地带，如：美国的大峡谷国家公园，越南的下龙湾。

列入《世界遗产名录》的自然遗产项目必须符合下列一项或几项标准方可获得批准：

标准 7：包含最显著的自然现象或具有突出自然美和美学重要性的区域。（自然现象或自然美）

标准 8：作为地球演化史中重要阶段的突出例证，包括生命的记录、地貌变迁时期持续的重要地质过程或重要的自然地理地貌特征。（地球历史中的重要阶段）

标准 9：在陆地、淡水、沿海及海洋生态系统，以及动植物群落的演化和发展时期，作为重要的生态过程和生物演化过程的突出例证。（重要的生态过程和生物演化过程）

标准 10：包含生物多样性原址保护的最重要和突出的自然栖息地，包括那些从科学或保护角度看，存在突出的普遍价值的濒危动植物的栖息地。（具有生物多样性的重要的自然栖息地）

3. 文化和自然双重遗产。

同时符合《保护世界文化和自然遗产公约》中第一条和第二条中对于文化遗产和自然遗产所设的部分或全部定义的遗产地，如：危地马拉的蒂卡尔国家公园，阿尔及利亚的塔西利·恩·阿耶。

4. 文化景观及其他。

文化景观是文化遗产的一种特例。1992 年 12 月在美国圣菲召开的第 16 届世界遗产大会上，文化景观的概念首次被正式确认，文化景观由于其独特的价值，成为世人瞩目的世界遗产新概念。

根据《实施世界遗产公约的操作指南》中的相关定义，文化景观代表"自然与人类的共同作品"。文化景观的最大价值特征是表现了人与自然不同类型的良性互动关系。这不仅是文化景观区别于其他遗产类型的关键，也是它可以被"概念性"地分为设计类、有机演进类及关联性三大类型的基础。

一般来说，文化景观有以下类型：

（1）由人类有意设计和建筑的景观。包括出于美学原因建造的园林和公园景观，它们经常（但并不总是）与宗教或其他纪念性建筑物或建筑群有联系。

例如：英国伦敦皇家植物园邱园（其人与自然的互动主要体现在园内 18 至 20 世纪间一系列重要的景观设计和建筑的发展）、葡萄牙的辛特拉文化景观和波兰的瓦利泽布日多夫斯津朝圣园。

（2）有机进化的景观。按照《实施世界遗产公约的操作指南》的定义，这类景观"产生于最初始的一种社会、经济、行政及宗教需要，并通过与周围自然环境的相联系或相适应而发展到目前的形式"。这类景观在所有文化景观遗产中所占比重最大，其下又包括两个子类别：一是残迹、残遗物或化石类景观，代表一种过去某段时间已经完成的进化过程，包括其中突发的或是渐进的。它们之所以具有突出的普遍价值，是因为其显著特点依然体现在实物上，这也是它们之所以具有突出、普遍价值的原因。此类景观主要为保持较好的大规模考古遗址，具体包括城镇、聚落、墓群、农业遗址等类型。由于生产力、技术水平等方面因素的制约，古代人的生产与生活往往要在合适的自然环境中进行，而考古遗址则往往能对此加以较完整的记录与保存。但与一般考古遗址不同的是，此类景观所记录的人类对自然的依赖与利用较为突出与明显，具有突出的普遍价值。例如：意大利的帕埃斯图姆和韦利亚考古遗址，阿富汗的巴米扬山谷的文化景观和考古遗迹，巴布亚新几内亚的库科早期农业遗址。二是持续性景观，它在当今与传统生活方式相联系的社会中，保持一种积极的社会作用，而且其自身演变过程仍在进行之中，同时又展示了历史上其演变发展的物证。这类景观突出人类与自然环境的持续性互动过程，以及在其中形成和演变的生活方式和传统。例如：法国的卢瓦尔河谷沿岸分布着大量的历史名镇和村庄与雄伟的古堡，以及几个世纪以来人类开垦的耕地。

（3）关联性文化景观。根据《实施世界遗产公约的操作指南》的定义，"这类景观以自然因素、强烈的宗教、艺术或文化关联性为特征，而不是以文化物为特征，后者对它来说是没有意义的，甚至是可以忽略的"。此类文化景观中人与自然的互动已经从景观设计、土地利用、生活传统等方面上升到精神层面，如宗教与艺术等。如富勒所言，该类景观的推出正是为了使人们能够自由思考"理念型景观"。关联性文化景观主要具有以下几个特点：

第一，该类景观具有显著的自然元素，尤其是高山或巨石。山石元素在此类景观中的突出性不是偶然的，而是和其固有的自然与文化属性密不可分的。由于山的巍峨与雄伟，在人类文明的初期，它往往被认为是神秘、永恒的，并具有沟通宇宙苍穹或神祇与祖先的神圣性，并由此衍生出历代不息的祭祀与信仰传统，成为人与自然密切关联最典型的一类例证。例如马达加斯加的皇家蓝山行宫，津巴布韦的马托博山等。

第二，到目前为止，该类景观所关联的非物质价值主要体现在强烈的宗教性上，比如新西兰的汤加里罗国家公园与澳大利亚的乌卢鲁-卡塔曲塔国家公园均反映了当地原住民传统的原始宗教信仰，纪伊山地则反映了日本的神道教与佛教传统。该类景观关联的其他非物质价值有以中国庐山为代表的国家的传统文化①，以及以冰岛的平位利尔为代表的国家身份的象征。

第三，该类景观亦可具有价值突出的文化物证。虽然根据关联性景观的定义，它们"不是以文化物证为特征，后者对它来说是没有意义的，甚至是可以忽略的"，而且该类景观的最早的两个例证——新西兰的汤加里罗国家公园与澳大利亚的乌卢鲁-卡塔曲塔国家公园——也几乎没有任何文化物证，但此后的申报实践显示，该类遗产也可具有突出的文化物证。如在庐山，山上分布着丰富的考古遗迹、碑文、历史建筑和中外别墅，而吉尔吉斯斯坦的苏莱曼圣山也拥有大量的与祭祀有关的神坛和岩石壁画及后期的清真寺。因此，文化物证与该类遗产的突出的普遍价值并不矛盾，而是有助于证实与传达这种价值。

---

① 在1996年的世界遗产委员会决议中，委员会指出，"根据标准2,3,4和6,将庐山作为具有杰出美学价值和与中国精神和文化生活有着强大关联性的文化景观入选《世界遗产名录》。"

近 20 年的实践证明,这种"概念性而非功能性"的分类方式高屋建瓴,具有很大的灵活性,较准确地涵盖了文化景观的各种类型,已成为文化景观研究、申报与评估的基石之一。[①] 不同价值内涵使文化景观遗产在评估时适用不同的 OUV 标准,其中设计类景观反映其人与自然互动价值符合的主要是标准 4,对于有机演进类景观来说主要是标准 3、4、5,标准 6 则是评估关联性景观互动价值最重要的标准。[②]

第五节　世界遗产的评定

一项文化或自然遗产要申报《世界遗产名录》,所在国家首先必须是《世界遗产公约》的缔约国;非缔约国的文化或自然遗产,不能申报《世界遗产名录》。所以,加入《世界遗产公约》,成为《公约》缔约国,是申报世界遗产的前提条件。具体的申报和评定程序,大体可以归纳为以下三个步骤。

第一个步骤是提交提名清单,包括英文的申报文本、图纸、图片、幻灯片、录像带等。申报文本要写明遗产的准确名称、地理位置、法律地位、从属关系;要对保护现状和申报理由做出详细的描述和论证,包括可能的国内外比较研究;要划定保护区和缓冲区,并注明各区域内的居民人口;要就保护法规和措施及遗产面临的压力和威胁做出详细说明;还须介绍日常管理制度和监测措施。

第二个步骤是实地考察,世界遗产中心收到申报文本后,要组织国际专家进行考察评估。考察的专家不能来自申请国。考察的重点在于遗产地的管理状况,对遗产价值的评估主要是以通讯的形式征求各领域权威学者的意见,最后汇总成为评估报告。

第三个步骤是材料处理。由联合国教科文组织世界遗产中心对申报文本和专家报告进行综合处理,提交当年召开的世界遗产委员会大会审议。由于审查非常严格,从正式申报到完成各项批准,通常需要不少于一至两年的时间,从而确保被列入《世界遗产名录》的遗产真正具有"突出的普遍价值"。

1. 世界遗产申报的具体过程。

(1)申报国。

签字承认《世界遗产公约》,成为《保护世界文化和自然遗产公约》缔约国,承担和进行本国自然和文化遗产的保护工作。

(2)缔约国。

①制定世界遗产申报的预备名单,将本国未来 5—10 年拟申报为世界遗产的项目列入《世界遗产预备清单》,通报世界遗产中心备案。

②提出将遗产列入《世界遗产名录》的建议。

---

① 中国古迹遗址保护协会:《〈文化景观遗产研究报告〉成果汇报》,国家文物局:《世界遗产与可持续发展》,文物出版社 2012 年版,第 82 页。

② 同上,第 81 页。

③每年7月1日前，按统一格式和内容，将本国自认为条件已经完全成熟的预备项目向联合国教科文组织世界遗产中心提出正式申报文件。申报文件统一使用世界遗产委员会的标准表格，主要内容包括：

确切地点：国家、省、市、遗产名称，标明遗产地点和地理坐标的地图和平面图。

法律资料：遗产所有权、有关本遗产保护和管理的法律和条例、开放程度、管理机构和组织。

说明材料：遗产描述和图表、照片及影片资料、历史状况、文献资料。

保存状况：现状描述、保护管理机构、此前的保管过程、保护措施、当地的开放计划。

提议列入名录的理由：符合哪些标准的规定，在与其他同类地点比较的前提下评估本地点的保护状况、遗产的真实性。

提名建筑群或遗址群所需的特殊材料：不同范围内容和比率尺的地图、地形图和平面图、多种照片、幻灯片和光盘、有关本遗产研究成果的论著和相关机构的资料、有关保护的法律资料、各级管理机构的资料。

（3）联合国教科文组织世界遗产中心。

①审核申报文件。

②将申报文件提交下列组织：文化遗产提交给国际古迹遗址理事会（ICOMOS），自然遗产提交给世界自然保护联盟（IUCN）；双重遗产或文化景观遗产，同时呈递给以上两个组织（ICOMOS & IUCN）。

（4）国际古迹遗址理事会及世界自然保护联盟。

①向申报单位派遣专家，对申报项目进行评估，准备申请报告。

②根据《世界遗产公约》对所申报的文物进行审核。

③将评估报告附以推荐材料呈递世界遗产中心。

（5）世界遗产中心（世界遗产委员会秘书处）。

①审核文件。

②向申报国索要补充材料。

③向世界遗产委员会进行推荐。

（6）世界遗产委员会。

①列入《世界遗产名录》之前，向申报国索要补充材料。

②做出入选、推迟入选或拒绝的决定，入选的即可列入《世界遗产名录》。

2. 世界遗产评定的发展趋势。

由于"世界遗产"头衔给所在国与所在区域带来的巨大效益，申请世界遗产越来越为各缔约国重视，每年申报的国家和项目越来越多。如何平衡各国的申报需求成为一个日益重要的课题。

世界遗产委员会于1978年确定了首批12处世界遗产列入《世界遗产名录》，《世界遗产公约》自此开始发挥作用。从1978年起，世界遗产委员会每年都审议遗产提名。每年审议通过的遗产数目不等，20世纪70年代和80年代数目相对均衡，每年约20处。进入20世纪90年代，每年通过的遗产数目增多。1997年世界遗产委员会大会在意大利召开，当年通过列入《世界遗产名录》的意大利遗产就有10处，是各年度一个国家的遗产被列入名录的最高纪录。后来由于《世界遗产名录》中的遗产数目增加过快，而且各国遗产数目差别较大,于是在 2000 年澳大利亚凯恩斯举行的第 24 届大会上通过了《凯恩斯决议》,其核心内容是:限制已有较多世界遗产的国家申报,一国一年只能申报一项;尚没有遗产的和遗产少的国家可以不受这项决定的约束,而且可以得到特别支持;世界遗产委员会每年受理的遗产项目最多不超过 30 个。会议还决定这项决议试行两年后再审议是否修订。这项决议意味着:遗产数目已经较多的国家应当减缓申请新的遗产。原定 2003 年 7 月在我国苏州举行的第 27 届大会,当年因为"非典"在我国部分地区流行而改在巴黎举行,大会通过新列入《世界遗产名录》的遗产数减少到 24 处,有 4 个国家是首次有遗产列入名录,分别是冈比亚、哈萨克斯坦、蒙古和苏丹。

2004 年 6 月末至 7 月初,第 28 届世界遗产委员会大会在我国苏州举行,中国作为东道国相对有优势,按规定,这届会议也应再次审核《凯恩斯决议》。会议期间,中国代表联合阿根廷等国代表提出,《凯恩斯决议》并不能有效解决世界遗产战略所期望的代表性和平衡性,也不利于保护更多的世界遗产,建议修改。最后大会决定修改《凯恩斯决议》,通过了《苏州决定》,主要变动是:原定一国每年只能申报一项世界遗产的规定,改为可以申报两项,但其中至少有一项是自然遗产;世界遗产委员会每年受理的新申报项目从以前的 30 个增加到 45 个。不过,原来曾有的遗产扩展项目、推迟项目、跨国申报项目、紧急申报项目和补充材料等都要计算在各国申请的数目中。大会通过的决定指出,这一修订仍然是一个"试验性和过渡性"的措施,也有两年的试行期,将来还要再审议。

第六节　中国的世界遗产

中国作为一个历史悠久、文化璀璨的国家,创造了独特的文明成果,累积了众多的名胜古迹,拥有众多雄伟的古代建筑、壮观的名山奇峰、纵横交错的河流,遗产资源非常丰富。

中国政府一贯重视对文化与自然遗产的保护,并积极参与联合国教科文组织和世界遗产委员会关于保护世界文化与自然遗产的活动。

1985 年 12 月 12 日,中国成为《保护世界文化和自然遗产公约》缔约方,同年 12 月 22 日,经第六届全国人民代表大会常务委员会第 13 次会议审批批准加入该《公约》,成为该《公约》的第 89 个缔约国。

1986 年,中国开始向联合国教科文组织申报世界遗产项目,提交了包括长城在内的 28 项遗产预备名单。

1987 年,中国拥有了第一批世界遗产,其中文化遗产 5 项,即周口店北京人遗址、长城、故宫、敦煌莫高窟、秦始皇陵;自然和文化双重遗产 1 项,即泰山。

1991 年 10 月,在世界遗产委员会第 11 次大会上,中国首次当选为世界遗产委员会成员。1992 年、1993 年中国两次当选为世界遗产委员会副主席,从而连续 3 年进入世界遗产委员会主席团。

1999 年 10 月 29 日,中国再次当选为世界遗产委员会成员,在世界遗产的保护事业中发挥着重要的作用。

为了加强世界遗产的申报、管理和保护工作,2002 年国务院授权国家文物局设立了世界遗产处。

我国的文化遗产一般由国家文物局负责提出,自然遗产由建设部负责提出,报国务院批准后,再由联合国教科文组织中国委员会向总部申报。

2014 年 3 月,中国土司遗产正式向世界遗产中心提交申遗文本,国家文物局确定:由湖南永顺土司城遗址、湖北唐崖土司城遗址、贵州播州海龙屯遗址联合代表中国土司遗产作为中国 2015 年申报世界文化遗产的项目。

中国是拥有世界遗产类别最齐全的国家之一,包括文化遗产、自然遗产、文化和自然双重遗产、文化景观遗产。截至 2013 年底,我国已有 45 项遗产被列入《世界遗产名录》,其中文化遗产 31 处,自然遗产 10 处,双重遗产 4 处。

我国现已拥有 4 项世界文化和自然双重遗产,这在《世界遗产公约》缔约国中名列第一。我国拥有的双重遗产是泰山、黄山、峨眉山-乐山大佛、武夷山。其他国家最多只拥有两项双重遗产。

世界文化遗产的评选标准共有 6 条。迄今,全球只有 3 项世界文化遗产是以符合文化遗产的全部 6 条标准而被确认的。它们是意大利的威尼斯、中国的敦煌莫高窟和泰山。

目前的世界遗产中只有两项遗产是以符合 7 条标准进入名录的,一项为澳大利亚的塔斯马尼亚公园群,另一项为中国的泰山。泰山不仅符合文化遗产的 6 条标准,同时还符合自然遗产中的 1 条标准。

北京拥有故宫、周口店北京人遗址、长城、天坛、颐和园和十三陵等 6 项世界遗产,是世界上拥有世界遗产项最多的城市。

中国政府在文化遗产的保护方面提出了保护为主、合理利用为辅的指导思想。在自然遗产方面提出了保护放在首位、合理开发利用、加强管理的方针。这与世界遗产委员会制定的规则是一致的。但随着中国改革开放和经济发展,中国的世界遗产正面临市场经济错位开发的严重威胁。许多早已过度开发的世界遗产地,还在大兴土木、开山伐木、滥建索道、商店、宾馆和娱乐场所,导致世界遗产地,尤其是核心地段的过分人工化、商业化和城市化,使珍贵遗产的真实性和完整性遭到严重的破坏。

到目前为止,中国还没有专门的世界遗产系统管理体制,对于世界遗产的管理大多沿用属地管理体制。管理的主要法律依据是国务院颁布的《风景名胜区管理暂行条例》。管理模式主要分为行政管理模式和市场管理模式两类,前者主要靠政府部门,管理的目的是保护资源,资金主要来源是国家财政拨款。后者的管理主体是企业,目的是开发利用资源,经费主要来源于开发利用的市场。目前国内两种管理模式并存,行政管理由于条块分割、政府部门的缺位与越位等弊端而备受争议;市场管理模式又因急功近利、重开发轻保护等问题而饱受诟病。

附 录

一、中国现有的世界遗产共计 45 项（截至 2013 年 12 月 31 日）

	Cultural Heritage（27）	Inscription	Ref	Criteria
1	The Great Wall	1987	438	(i),(ii),(iii),(iv),(vi)
2	Imperial Palaces of the Ming and Qing Dynasties in Beijing and Shenyang	1987, Ext. 2004	439	(i),(ii),(iii),(iv)
3	Mogao Caves	1987	440	(i),(ii),(iii),(iv),(v),(vi)
4	Mausoleum of the First Qin Emperor	1987	441	(i),(iii),(iv),(vi)
5	Peking Man Site at Zhoukoudian	1987	449	(iii),(vi)
6	Mountain Resort and Its Outlying Temples, Chengde	1994	703	(ii),(iv)
7	Temple and Cemetery of Confucius and the Kong Family Mansion in Qufu	1994	704	(i),(iv),(vi)
8	Ancient Building Complex in the Wudang Mountains	1994	705	(i),(ii),(vi)
9	Historic Ensemble of the Potala Palace，Lhasa	1994 Ext. 2000,2001	707ter	(i),(iv),(vi)
10	Ancient City of Ping Yao	1997	812	(ii),(iii),(iv)
11	Classical Gardens of Suzhou	1997	813	(i),(ii),(iii),(iv),(v)
12	Old Town of Lijiang (*Minor modification inscribed year*：2012)	1997 2012 *	811	(ii),(iv),(v)
13	Temple of Heaven	1998	881	(i),(ii),(iii)
14	Summer Palace	1998	880	(i),(ii),(iii)
15	Dazu Rock Carvings	1999	912	(i),(ii),(iii)
16	Mount Qingcheng and the Dujiangyan Irrigation System	2000	1001	(ii),(iv),(vi)
17	Ancient Villages in Southern Anhui—Xidi and Hongcun	2000	1002	(iii),(iv),(v)
18	Longmen Grottoes	2000	1003	(i),(ii),(iii)
19	Imperial Tombs of the Ming and Qing Dynasties	2000 Ext. 2003, 2004	1004	(i),(ii),(iii),(iv),(vi)

Cultural Heritage (27)		Inscription	Ref	Criteria
20	Yungang Grottoes	2001	1039	(i)，(ii)，(iii)，(iv)
21	Capital Cities and Tombs of the Ancient Koguryo Kingdom	2004	1135	(i)，(ii)，(iii)，(iv)，(v)
22	Historic Centre of Macao	2005	1110	(ii)，(iii)，(iv)，(vi)
23	Yin Xu	2006	1114	(ii)，(iii)，(iv)，(vi)
24	Kaiping Diaolou and Villages	2007	1112	(ii)，(iii)，(iv)
25	Fujian Tulou	2008	1113	(iii)，(iv)，(v)
26	Historic Monuments of Dengfeng in "The Centre of Heaven and Earth"	2010	1305	(iii)，(vi)
27	Site of Xanadu	2012	1389	(ii)，(iii)，(iv)，(vi)

Natural Heritage (10)		Inscription	Ref	Criteria
1	Jiuzhaigou Valley Scenic and Historic Interest Area	1992	637	(vii)
2	Huanglong Scenic and Historic Interest Area	1992	638	(vii)
3	Wulingyuan Scenic and Historic Interest Area	1992	640	(vii)
4	Three Parallel Rivers of Yunnan Protected Areas	2003	1083bis	(vii)，(viii)，(ix)，(x)
5	Sichuan Giant Panda Sanctuaries—Wolong, Mt Siguniang，and Jiajin Mountains	2006	1213	(x)
6	South China Karst	2007	1248	(vii)，(viii)
7	Mount Sanqingshan National Park	2008	1292	(vii)
8	China Danxia	2010	1335	(vii)，(viii)
9	Chengjiang Fossil Site	2012	1388	(viii)
10	Xinjiang Tianshan	2013	1414	(vii)，(ix)

Mixed Heritage (4)		Inscription	Ref	Criteria
1	Mount Taishan	1987	437	(i)，(ii)，(iii)，(iv)，(v)，(vi)，(vii)
2	Mount Huangshan	1990	547bis	(ii)，(vii)，(x)

	Mixed Heritage (4)	Inscription	Ref	Criteria
3	Mount Emel Scenic Area, including Leshan Giant Buddha Scenic Area	1996	779	(iv), (vi), (x)
4	Mount Wuyi	1999	911	(iii), (vi), (vii), (x)

	Cultural Landscape (4)	Inscription	Ref	Criteria
1	Lushan National Park	1996	778	(ii), (iii), (iv), (vi)
2	Mount Wutai	2009	1279	(ii), (iii), (iv), (vi)
3	West Lake Cultural Landscape of Hangzhou	2011	1334	(ii), (iii), (vi)
4	Cultural Landscape of Honghe Hani Rice Terraces	2013	1111	(iii), (v)

二、中国的预备名单

(一)国家文物局制定的文化遗产预备名单

《中国世界文化遗产预备名单》(2012 年 9 月更新)共 45 项

1. 北京中轴线(含北海)(北京市)

2. 大运河(北京市、天津市、河北省、江苏省、浙江省、安徽省、山东省、河南省)

3. 中国白酒老作坊:杏花村汾酒老作坊(山西省汾阳市)、成都水井街酒坊(四川省成都市)、泸州老窖作坊群(四川省泸州市)、古蔺县郎酒老作坊(四川省泸州市)、剑南春酒坊及遗址(四川省绵竹市)、宜宾五粮液老作坊(四川省宜宾市)、红楼梦糟房头老作坊(四川省宜宾市)、射洪县泰安作坊(四川省射洪县)

4. 辽代木构建筑:应县木塔(山西应县)、义县奉国寺大雄殿(辽宁义县)

5. 关圣文化建筑群(山西省运城市)

6. 山陕古民居:丁村古建筑群(山西省襄汾县)、党家村古建筑群(陕西省韩城市)

7. 阴山岩刻(内蒙古自治区巴彦淖尔市)

8. 辽代上京城和祖陵遗址(内蒙古自治区赤峰市)

9. 红山文化遗址:牛河梁遗址(辽宁省朝阳市);红山后遗址、魏家窝铺遗址(内蒙古自治区赤峰市)

10. 中国明清城墙:兴城城墙(辽宁省兴城市)、南京城墙(江苏省南京市)、临海台州府城墙(浙江省临海市)、寿县城墙(安徽省寿县)、凤阳明中都皇城城墙(安徽省凤阳县)、荆州城墙(湖北省荆州市)、襄阳城墙(湖北省襄阳市)、西安城墙(陕西省西安市)

11. 侵华日军第七三一部队旧址(黑龙江省哈尔滨市)

12. 金上京遗址(黑龙江省哈尔滨市)

13. 扬州瘦西湖及盐商园林文化景观(江苏省扬州市)

14. 无锡惠山祠堂群(江苏省无锡市)

15. 江南水乡古镇：甪直（江苏省苏州市）、周庄（江苏省昆山市）、千灯（江苏省昆山市）、锦溪（江苏省昆山市）、沙溪（江苏省太仓市）、同里（江苏省吴江市）、乌镇（浙江省桐乡市）、西塘（浙江省嘉善县）、南浔（浙江省湖州市）、新市（浙江省德清县）

16. 丝绸之路（河南省、陕西省、甘肃省、青海省、宁夏回族自治区、新疆维吾尔自治区）；海上丝绸之路（江苏省南京市、扬州市，浙江省宁波市，福建省泉州市、福州市、漳州市，山东省蓬莱市，广东省广州市，广西壮族自治区北海市）

17. 良渚遗址（浙江省杭州市）

18. 青瓷窑遗址（浙江省慈溪市、龙泉市）

19. 闽浙木拱廊桥（浙江省泰顺县、景宁县、庆元县；福建省寿宁县、周宁县、屏南县、政和县）

20. 鼓浪屿（福建省厦门市）

21. 三坊七巷（福建省福州市）

22. 闽南红砖建筑（福建省厦门市、南安市）

23. 赣南围屋（江西省赣州市）

24. "明清皇家陵寝"扩展项目：潞简王墓（河南省新乡市）

25. 黄石矿冶工业遗产（湖北省黄石市）

26. 土司遗址：唐崖土司遗址（湖北省咸丰县）、容美土司遗址（湖北省鹤峰县）；老司城遗址（湖南省永顺县）；海龙屯遗址（贵州省遵义市）

27. 凤凰区域性防御体系（湖南省凤凰县）

28. 侗族村寨（湖南省通道侗族自治县、绥宁县，广西壮族自治区三江县，贵州省黎平县、榕江县、从江县）

29. 南越国遗迹（广东省广州市）

30. 灵渠（广西壮族自治区兴安县）

31. 花山岩画文化景观（广西壮族自治区崇左市）

32. 白鹤梁题刻（重庆市涪陵区）

33. 钓鱼城遗址（重庆市合川区）

34. 蜀道：金牛道广元段（四川省广元市）

35. 古蜀文明遗址：金沙遗址、古蜀船棺合葬墓（四川省成都市），三星堆遗址（四川省广汉市）

36. 藏羌碉楼与村寨（四川省甘孜藏族自治州、阿坝藏族羌族自治州）

37. 苗族村寨（贵州省台江县、剑河县、榕江县、丛江县、雷山县、锦屏县）

38. 万山汞矿遗址（贵州省铜仁市）

39. 哈尼梯田（云南省元阳县）

40. 普洱景迈山古茶园（云南省澜沧拉祜族自治县）

41. 芒康盐井古盐田（西藏自治区芒康县）

42. 统万城（陕西省靖边县）

43. 西夏陵（宁夏回族自治区银川市）

44. 坎儿井（新疆维吾尔自治区吐鲁番地区）

45. 志莲净苑与南莲园池（香港特别行政区）

（二）住房和城乡建设部制定的《中国国家自然遗产、国家自然与文化双遗产预备名录》

《中国国家自然遗产、国家自然与文化双遗产预备名录》（以下简称《预备名录》），理论上是推荐列入《世界自然遗产、自然与文化双遗产预备名单》的候选名录。根据原建设部《关于做好建立〈中国国家自然遗产、国家自然与文化双遗产预备名录〉工作的通知》，《预备名录》项目被推荐列入《世界自然遗产、自然与文化双遗产预备名单》后，将不在《预备名录》中保留，但在实际运作中却存在差异现象，主要表现于：

在第一批《预备名录》于 2006 年公布前有关名录中的许多项目实际早已列入《世界自然遗产、自然与文化双遗产预备名单》，如五台山等；

在第二批《预备名录》于 2009 年公布前有关名录中的部分项目实际提前列入《世界自然遗产、自然与文化双遗产预备名单》，如恒山和冠豸山风景名胜区等。

1. 第一批中国国家自然遗产、国家自然与文化双遗产预备名录

①国家自然遗产预备名录（17 处）：

黑龙江：五大连池风景名胜区

吉林：长白山植被垂直景观及火山地貌景观

福建：海坛风景名胜区

江西：三清山风景名胜区；武功山风景名胜区

河南：云台山风景名胜区

湖南：崀山风景名胜区

重庆：天坑地缝风景名胜区；金佛山风景名胜区

四川：贡嘎山风景名胜区；若尔盖湿地

贵州：织金洞风景名胜区；马岭河峡谷风景名胜区；平塘省级风景名胜区

云南：澄江动物化石群保护地

青海：青海湖风景名胜区

新疆：喀纳斯自治区级风景名胜区

②国家自然与文化双遗产预备名录（13 处）：

山西：五台山风景名胜区

安徽：九华山风景名胜区

福建：清源山风景名胜区

江西：龙虎山风景名胜区；高岭-瑶里风景名胜区

河南：嵩山风景名胜区

湖南：南岳衡山风景名胜区；紫鹊界-梅山龙宫风景名胜区

贵州：黄果树风景名胜区及屯堡文化

云南：大理苍山与南诏历史文化遗存

陕西：华山风景名胜区

甘肃：麦积山风景名胜区

宁夏：贺兰山-西夏王陵风景名胜区

2. 第二批中国国家自然遗产、国家自然与文化双遗产预备名录

①国家自然遗产预备名录（18 处）：

北京：房山岩溶洞穴及峰丛地貌

河北：承德丹霞地貌

山西：壶口风景名胜区

黑龙江：扎龙自然保护区

辽宁：本溪水洞风景名胜区

浙江：方岩风景名胜区

福建：冠豸山风景名胜区；太姥山风景名胜区

江西：鄱阳湖湿地

湖南：万佛山-侗寨省级风景名胜区

四川：佛宝-蜀南竹海风景名胜区；光雾山-诺水河风景名胜区

贵州：兴义锥状喀斯特

西藏：纳木错；格拉丹东-长江源；土林-古格

新疆：天山天池风景名胜区；赛里木湖风景名胜区

②国家自然与文化双遗产预备名录（8处）：

山西：恒山风景名胜区；芦芽山省级风景名胜区

黑龙江：兴凯湖省级风景名胜区

江苏：南京中山陵

安徽：天柱山风景名胜区

江西：井冈山风景名胜区

山东：济南名泉

四川：剑门蜀道风景名胜区

参考文献

［1］MARSHALL D．Preparing World Heritage Nominations［M/OL］．2nd ed．Paris：United Nations Educational，Scientific and Cultural Organization，（2011-10-16）［2012-08-16］．http://whc.unesco.org/ uploads/ activities/documents/activity-643-1.pdf.

［2］STOLTON，S，D N．Managing Natural World Heritage［M/OL］．Paris：United Nations Educational，Scientific and Cultural Organization，（2012-08-20）［2012-08-24］．http://whc.unesco.org/uploads/activities/documents/activity-703-1.pdf.

［3］晁华山．世界遗产［M］．北京：北京大学出版社，2009.

［4］费尔登·贝纳德．世界文化遗产地管理指南［M］．刘永孜，刘迪，等，译．上海：同济大学出版社，2008.

［5］国家文物局．世界遗产与可持续发展［M］．北京：文物出版社，2012.

［6］联合国教育、科学及文化组织．世界遗产大全［M］．陈培，尚凤梅，季舒琳，等，译．合肥：安徽科学技术出版社，2011.

［7］刘红婴. 世界遗产法［M］. 北京：北京大学出版社,2008.

［8］刘世锦. 中国文化遗产事业发展报告（2010）［M］. 北京：社会科学文献出版
社,2010.

［9］刘新静. 世界遗产教程［M］. 上海：上海交通大学出版社,2012.

［10］骆文伟. 浙江省保护和申报世界遗产战略研究［J］. 宁波大学学报：人文科学
版，2010,23(1).

［11］单霁翔. 走进文化景观遗产的世界［M］. 天津：天津大学出版社,2010.

［12］孙克勤. 世界文化与自然遗产概论（第 2 版）［M］. 武汉：中国地质大学出版社,
2012.

［13］熊康宁,肖时珍,陈浒,等. 世界遗产与赤水丹霞景观［M］. 北京：高等教育出版
社,2012.

世界遗产概论

第二章 欧洲的世界遗产

Introduction to the World Heritage

第一节　欧洲的世界文化遗产

Acropolis，Athens
雅典卫城

⇨ **简介**

所属国家：希腊（Greece）

入选时间：1987

入选标准：(i)(ii)(iii)(iv)(vi)

The Acropolis is located on a rocky promontory 156 m above the valley of Ilissos; it covers a surface area of less than 3 ha. From the 2nd millennium BC it was a fortress protecting place of worship and royal palaces. The Acropolis of Athens and its monuments are universal symbols of the classical spirit and civilization and form the greatest architectural and artistic complex bequeathed by Greek Antiquity to the world. In the second half of the fifth century BC，Athens，following the victory against the Persians and the establishment of democracy，took a leading position amongst the other city-states of the ancient world. In the age that followed，as thought and art flourished，an exceptional group of artists put into effect the ambitious plans of Athenian statesman Pericles and，under the inspired guidance of the sculptor Pheidias，transformed the rocky hill into a unique monument of thought and art. The most important monuments were built during that time：the Parthenon，built by Ictinus，the Erechtheon，the Propylaea，the monumental entrance to the Acropolis，designed by Mnesicles and the small temple Athena Nike.

The Athenian Acropolis is the supreme expression of the adaptation of architecture to a natural site. This grand composition of perfectly balanced massive structures creates a monumental landscape of unique beauty consisting of a complete series of masterpieces of the 5th century BC. The monuments of the Acropolis have exerted an exceptional influence，not only in Graeco-Roman antiquity，a time when in the Mediterranean world they were considered exemplary models，but in contemporary times as well.

雅典卫城建于海拔 156 米的山崖之上,俯瞰伊利索斯山谷,占地 3 公顷。自公元前 2000 年起,这里就是保卫神殿和皇家宫殿的堡垒。雅典卫城及古迹是人类共同的古典精神和文明的象征,是古希腊留给世界最伟大的建筑和艺术综合体。公元前 5 世纪后半叶,雅典在战胜波斯人并建立民主城邦后,确立了其在世界各个城邦中的领导地位。之后,随着思想和艺术的蓬勃发展,一批优秀的艺术家使雅典政治家伯里克利雄心勃勃的计划得以实施,在雕刻家菲迪亚斯的启发指导下,他们把岩石山变成了一座独一无二的思想艺术丰碑。雅典卫城包括希腊古典艺术最伟大的四大杰作——伊克蒂诺建造的帕提侬神庙、厄瑞克修姆庙、姆奈西克里设计的卫城入口和雅典娜胜利神庙。

雅典卫城是人类建筑与周边自然环境完美融合的杰出代表。这片宏伟的建筑群构成了一幅独特壮丽的美景,其中每一座建筑都是公元前5世纪的经典之作。雅典卫城在世界上有极其深远的影响,在古希腊、古罗马时期,它就被奉为地中海地区的建筑典范,直到现在,它仍散发着耀眼的光芒。

Vocabulary

1. promontory *n.* 岬;海角

A stark, rocky promontory towered over a stand of majestic pines.

一片悬崖高耸在一片巍巍的松树之上。

2. bequeath *v.* 遗赠;留下;把……传下去

It is true that colonialism did not bequeath much to Africa.

殖民主义给非洲确实没有留下多少东西。

3. antiquity *n.* 古时;古物;年代悠久

The statue was brought to Rome in antiquity.

这座雕像是古时运到罗马的。

4. exert *v.* 施加(影响、压力等);行使,运用(权威等);尽力;努力

Consumers will exert a measure of influence over the market economy.

消费者会对市场经济产生一定程度的影响。

5. contemporary *adj.* 当代的,现代的;同时期的

She wrote a lot of contemporary music for people like Whitney Houston.

她给像惠特尼·休斯顿这样的人创作了很多当代音乐作品。

扩展阅读

The Acropolis of Athens Greece

The word "Acropolis" means city by the edge, and there are many acropolises all over Greece. They were always situated on a high spot, and were often used as a place for shelter and defence against various enemies. The one in Athens is the best known of them all, and is therefore often referred to as "The Acropolis". Towering over the capital, it is a very impressive sight, and walking around on its grounds, it gives the visitor a feeling of awe and a true sense of the greatness of the ancient Greeks.

Mythology

The founder of Athens and Greek civilizations was King Cecrops, according to mythology. He had been born out of the earth and was half man half snake. He taught the people many crafts, as well as the burial customs, and decided which god would protect the city.

There were two candidates: the goddess Athena and the god Poseidon. In order to prove their worth, and perhaps bribe the people, they each presented the city with a gift. Poseidon struck his trident into the rock of the Acropolis, and out sprang a well. The people ran to the well to drink its water, but had to spit it out since the water was salt, Poseidon being a sea god. Then Athena touched the ground, and an olive tree grew out. This proved to be a much more useful present, so Cecrops decided that Athena would be the patron of the city—thus giving it her name as well. The wooden statue of Athena which originally stood on the Acropolis was believed to have fallen out of the sky.

History of the Acropolis

The Acropolis is believed to have been inhabited since at least the 7th Millennium BC. During the Mycenaean civilization walls were built around it and there is evidence that there was a Mycenaean palace here as well. The tomb of Cecrops also lay here, and the Athenians might have kept a snake here—symbolizing their first king. There were also other tombs and temples here, all connected to kings, heroes and gods that had to do with Athens.

In the 6th century BC the Acropolis had changed quite significantly. It was no longer a place for palaces, but had turned more into a sanctuary than anything else. Every year a huge procession to the Acropolis took place, and the wooden statue of Athena was dressed and sacrificed to. The Panathenean games were also very important. The games included both athletic and musical competitions and the winner would receive an amphora filled with olive oil—the olive tree being the sacred tree of Athena. During the Persian wars in the 5th century the Athenians started building the Parthenon, but the Persians burnt the Acropolis and all focus was put on the battles. It was during Pericles era, the so called Golden Age, when the Acropolis got the structure we see today. Started in the middle of the 5th century, the Parthenon, the Propylaea and a huge bronze statue of Athena was made. It is said that Pericles used unemployed Athenians for workers, and that it was thanks to this initiative, every Athenian had food on his table. The Parthenon was made by the architects Ictinus and Callicrates, and the statue by Phidias. Towards the end of the 5th century BC the Erechteion was built, as well as the temple of Athena Nike.

When the Romans conquered Greece in the 2nd century BC, many of the sanctuaries were looted. Statues and other works of art were taken back to Rome from Olympia and Delphi for example, but the Acropolis was pretty much left alone. Some of the emperors did make a few additions, though. In the 2nd century Herodes Atticus had his great theatre built, and to this day, Athenians are enjoying concerts and ballets here.

During the Middle Ages several of the temples on the Acropolis were converted into Christian churches. Quite characteristic is the fact that the Parthenon, which had been a temple to the virgin goddess Athena, now became a church to the virgin saint Mary.

When the Turks came towards the end of the 16th century, they turned the Parthenon into a mosque. Until the 17th century the temple was relatively unharmed, but in 1687 the Venetians bombarded the Acropolis, and a projectile hit the Parthenon, which the Turks used as a storage room for gunpowder. The temple exploded and this is why the temple does not have a roof today.

In the beginning of the 19th century the English lord Elgin was allowed by the sultan to take with him various objects from the Acropolis. It was he took the famous Parthenon marbles, which until today is a matter of controversy since they are housed in the British Museum despite the Greeks plea to get them back.

Despite all that the Acropolis has been through, it is really the pollution in modern Athens that is its worst enemy. The problem has been known for many decades now, but still no real solution has been found.

（资料来源：http://www. in2greece. com/english/places/historical/mainland/acropolis. htm）

Questions

1. According to ancient Greek methology, how did Athens get its name?
2. How did the functions of the Acropolis change in different stages of history?

Historic Centre of Florence
佛罗伦萨历史中心

简介

所属国家：意大利（Italy）

入选时间：1982

入选标准：(i)(ii)(iii)(iv)(vi)

Built on the site of an Etruscan settlement, Florence, the symbol of the Renaissance, rose to economic and cultural pre-eminence under the Medici in the 15th and 16th centuries. Starting from the 15th century, Florence exerted a powerful influence on the development of architecture and the monumental arts, first in Italy, and then throughout Europe. Its 600 years of extraordinary artistic activity can be seen above all in the 13th-century cathedral (Santa Maria del Fiore), the Church of Santa Croce, the Uffizi and the Pitti Palace, the work of great masters such as Giotto, Brunelleschi, Botticelli and Michelangelo.

The historic centre of Florence may best be described as a treasure chest of works of art and architecture. The spiritual focus of the city is the Cathedral Piazza of Santa Maria del Fiore, with Giotto's campanile on one side and the Baptistry of St. John in front, with the Gates of Paradise by Lorenzo Ghiberti. Going north from here, one comes across the Palazzo Medici-Riccardi by Michelozzo and St. Lawrence's Basilica by Brunelleschi with the sacristies inside designed by Donatello and Michelangelo. Further on are the Museum of St. Mark's, with Fra Angelico's masterpieces, the Galleria dell'Accademia with Michelangelo's *David* (1501—1504) and the Santissima Annunziata Piazza with the Lodge of the Holy Innocents by Brunelleschi. On the south side of the cathedral is the political/cultural centre of Florence, with the Palazzo Vecchio and the Galleria degli Uffizi nearby. Close to these are the Museo del Bargello and the Basilica of the Holy Cross. Across the Ponte Vecchio is the Oltrarno quarter, with the Pitti Palace and Boboli Gardens. Still in the Oltrarno, mention must be made of the Holy Ghost Basilica by Filippo Brunelleschi and the Carmelite Church, with its frescoes by Masolino, Masaccio and Filippino Lippi. To the west of the cathedral are the imposing Strozzi Palace and the Basilica of Santa Maria Novella, its facade designed by Leon Battista Alberti.

佛罗伦萨是在意大利古国伊特鲁里亚的定居点上建立起来的。作为文艺复兴的象征,在15世纪和16世纪的美第奇家族时代,佛罗伦萨达到它在经济和文化上的顶峰。自15世纪开始,佛罗伦萨对意大利乃至整个欧洲的建筑业和建筑艺术发展产生了深远的影响。600年来佛罗伦萨的艺术活动异常活跃,这首先从它13世纪的圣母百花大教堂中就可以看出,当然也包括圣十字教堂、乌菲齐宫、皮蒂宫,以及乔托、布鲁内莱斯基、博蒂切利和米开朗琪罗等大师的杰作等。

佛罗伦萨历史中心可谓艺术品和建筑的宝库。其宗教中心是圣母百花大教堂的比萨大教堂广场,与之毗邻的是乔托钟楼,前方是圣若望洗礼堂和洛伦佐·吉贝尔蒂设计的天堂之门。从比萨大教堂广场往北,是米开罗佐设计的美第奇-里卡迪宫,和布鲁内莱斯基设计建造的圣洛伦佐教堂,其内的圣器室由多纳泰罗和米开朗琪罗设计。再往北是圣马可博物馆,内有弗拉·安杰利科的许多代表作;还有收藏了米开朗琪罗名作《大卫雕像》(创作于1501—1504年)的艺术学院美术馆,和圣母领报广场(其育婴堂由布鲁内莱斯基设计)。比萨大教堂广场南面是佛罗伦萨的政治与文化中心,毗邻韦奇奥宫(佛罗伦萨的市政厅)和乌菲兹美术馆,周围还有巴杰罗美术馆和圣十字圣殿(世界上最大的方济各会教堂)。穿过阿诺河上的维奇奥桥(意大利现存最古老的石造封闭拱肩圆弧拱桥)就到了奥特拉诺区,皮蒂宫和波波里庭院(享誉世界的古代罗马园艺花园)均坐落于该区。提到奥特拉诺区,值得一提的还有菲利波·布鲁内莱斯基设计的圣灵大教堂,以及内有马索利诺、马萨乔和菲利皮诺·利皮所绘湿壁画的卡尔米内圣母大殿(又名圣衣大教堂)。教堂西面是壮观的斯特罗齐宫和新圣母大殿,其正立面是由莱昂·巴蒂斯塔·阿尔伯蒂设计的。

Vocabulary

1. pre-eminence *n.* 卓越;杰出

For those under 40 the pre-eminence of post-war US literature goes unquestioned.

对于那些不到40岁的人来说,战后的美国文学无疑是最杰出的。

2. campanile *n.* 钟楼;钟塔

The Italian campanile could either be attached to a church or freestanding.

意大利的钟楼既可以附属于教堂,也可作为独立建筑物而矗立。

3. sacristy *n.* (教堂的)圣器收藏室,圣职人员更衣室,祭衣间

He even entered the cathedral one night, and despoiled the sacristy.

他甚至于黑夜闯入天主堂,卷走圣衣库中的东西。

4. fresco *n.* 湿壁画

This is a masterpiece in fresco.

这是一幅湿壁画杰作。

5. facade *n.* 建筑物的正面;(虚假的)外观;假象

That is the ornate facade of the palace.

那是宫殿装饰华丽的正面。

扩展阅读

Focus on Florence

The Renaissance was a rebirth that occurred throughout most of Europe. However, the changes that we associate with the Renaissance first occurred in the Italian city of Florence and continued to be more pervasive there than anywhere else. The city's economy and its writers, painters, architects, and philosophers all made Florence a model of Renaissance culture.

Fifteenth-century Florence was an exciting place to be. In 1425 the city had a population of 60,000 and was a self-governed, independent city-state. Twelve artist guilds that regulated the trades were the basis of Florence's commercial success. Members of the guilds, who were wealthy and held positions in government, were some of Florence's most influential people in society and politics. Because of its strong economy and a political philosophy that was dedicated to the welfare of the city, Florence thrived.

The most powerful guilds were those that represented textile workers. Much of Florence's wealth was dependent on the manufacture or trade of cloth, primarily wool. Wool of superior quality was often purchased unfinished and untreated from England and Iberia. Florentine textile workers then cleaned, carded, spun, dyed, and wove the wool into cloth of excellent quality. They sold the finished material in Italy, northern European cities, and even in eastern countries. Other textile experts purchased inferior cloth from northern cities and refinished it to create a superior product.

Because Florence was not a port city like Venice, sea trade was not a primary source of its income. Banking, however, was. Many families of Florence, beginning in the thirteenth century, were successful bankers. The Florentine gold coin known as the florin was of such reliable purity that it was the standard coinage throughout Europe. Florentine bankers were known throughout Europe as well, for they established banking houses in other important cities such as London, Geneva, and Bruges (Belgium).

The Palazzo Vecchio, constructed in 1299, was the home of the Florentine guilds. Then, as well as today, it functioned as the seat of municipal government and the heart of Florentine culture. It was here that the city's 5,000 guild members, who had the power of the vote, gathered to discuss and determine city issues. In addition to textile workers and bankers, the guild members included masons and builders, sculptors, lawyers, and solicitors.

Florentine life

The humanist movement was prevalent in Florence. Cosimo de Medici, Florence's wealthiest and most influential citizen, studied the works of ancient authors and collected manuscripts of classical writings. His delight in discussing humanist issues led him to organize the Plato Academy, where intellectuals would gather to discuss ideas concerning the classics. The academy continued even after Cosimo's death.

The Florentines enjoyed many pleasurable diversions from business and intellectual life. Lorenzo de Medici, Cosimo's grandson who was known as "the Magnificent", influenced the types of entertainment and often sponsored the activities. Mystery plays, based on the theme of the Passion (the sufferings of Jesus), were regularly staged for the enjoyment and edification of the citizens. To celebrate the feast day of St John, Florence's patron saint, Florentines held a horse race that ran throughout the city. And festivals held during the season before Lent—called Carnival—were grand productions, especially in the late fifteenth century.

Savonarola and spiritual concerns

Although the humanist movement in Florence was very prevalent, Florentines were also concerned about their spiritual lives. Thus, amidst their prosperity, a preacher named Savonarola was able to change the thinking of many citizens. Savonarola was concerned about what he considered abuses by the church and about people's excessive interest in material goods. He preached against the accumulation of worldly possessions and called for a "bonfire of the vanities" in which people were to burn "immoral" paintings, cosmetics, and such entertainment-related items as musical instruments and playing cards.

Savonarola was successful in convincing many Florentines to return to a more spiritual way of life. However, his condemnation of church abuses of wealth led to his downfall. The Pope restricted Savonarola from preaching; when he continued to do so, he was excommunicated. Soon after, Florentines turned against him for what they saw as his role in an unfavorable political climate. He was publicly executed in 1498.

Michelangelo and botticelli

Several of the greatest artists of the age studied or worked in Florence, including Michelangelo and Botticelli. Michelangelo began to study painting in Florence with Ghirlandaio and later learned sculpture under the patronage of Lorenzo the Magnificent. It was for the Florence Cathedral that Michelangelo created his famous sculpture of *David*. The Renaissance aesthetic is apparent in the careful and accurate depiction of the human body and its representation as a nude.

The painter Botticelli was a friend of both Michelangelo and Leonardo da Vinci, and the principal painter of the Medici family. His works represent Renaissance style in his use of classical subject matter and in the effect of motion that he achieves. It was for the home of a Medici that he created his two most famous works: *Primavera* and *The Birth of Venus*. In both works Botticelli uses figures from antiquity, such as the goddess Venus and the three Graces. He balances his figures in nearly symmetrical groupings, yet never loses a feeling of motion and lightness.

Renaissance style in art, exemplified in works from Florentine artists, flourished largely because of the patronage, or financial support, of wealthy citizens and the church. By purchasing numerous works of art, Renaissance men and women provided a livelihood for many painters, sculptors, and architects. It was also the Renaissance humanist desire to imitate and revive the beauty of ancient Greece, and to have that beauty surround them in their daily lives, that produced the wealth of superb art that is one of the hallmarks of Renaissance culture.

（资料来源：http://www. learner. org/interactives/renaissance/florence. html）

Questions

1. What led to the prosperity of Florence in the 15th century?
2. How did the Florentines influence the Renaissance?

Banks of the Seine, Paris
巴黎塞纳河畔

⟶ **简介**

所属国家：法国（France）

入选时间：1991

入选标准：(i)(ii)(iv)

The banks of the Seine are studded with a succession of masterpieces. From the Louvre to the Eiffel Tower, from the Place de la Concorde to the Grand and Petit Palais, the evolution of Paris and its history can be seen from the River Seine. A number of them, such as Notre Dame and the Sainte Chapelle, were definitive references in the spread of Gothic construction, while the Place de la Concorde or the vista at the Invalides exerted influence on the urban development of European capitals. The Marais and the Île St-Louis have coherent architectural ensembles, with highly significant examples of Parisian construction of the 17th and 18th centuries. Haussmann's wide squares and boulevards influenced late 19th and 20th century town planning the world over.

Paris is a river town. Ever since the first human settlements, the Seine has played both a defensive and an economic role. The present historic city, which developed between the 16th century and the 20th century (and particularly the 17th century), translates the evolution of the relationship between the river and the people: defence, trade, promenades, etc.

The site and the river were gradually brought under control with the articulation of the two islets, the Île de la Cité and the Île St-Louis with the bank, the creation of north-south thoroughfares, installations along the river course, construction of quays, and the channelling of the river. Similarly, although the successive walls of the city have disappeared, their traces may be read in the difference in size and spacing of the buildings: closer together in the Marais and the Île St-Louis, more open after the Louvre, beyond which are a greater number of major classic constructions laid along three perpendicular axes: the Palais Bourbon-the Place de la Concorde-the Place de la Madeleine, the Invalides-the Grand and Petit Palais, the Champ-de-Mars-the École Militaire-the Palais de Chaillot. The ensemble must be regarded as a geographical and historic entity. Today it constitutes a remarkable example of urban riverside architecture, where the strata of history are harmoniously superposed.

Haussmann's urbanism, which marks the western part of the city, inspired the construction of the great cities of the New World, in particular in Latin America. The Eiffel Tower and the Palais de Chaillot are living testimony of the great universal exhibitions, which were of such great importance in the 19th and 20th centuries.

塞纳河两岸散布着众多建筑杰作。从罗浮宫到埃菲尔铁塔,从协和广场到大小王宫,巴黎的历史变迁从塞纳河可见一斑。其中,巴黎圣母院、圣礼拜堂,是哥特式建筑传播的绝佳范例;协和广场和巴黎荣军院的建筑风格对欧洲国家首都的发展产生了影响;玛莱区和圣路易岛的建筑群浑然一体,是 17、18 世纪巴黎建筑的重要典范;奥斯曼男爵兴建的宽阔广场和林荫道则影响着 19 世纪末和 20 世纪全世界的城市规划。

巴黎是个河滨城市。自人类开始在此居住以来,塞纳河就在防御和经济两方面都发挥着作用。如今的历史名城巴黎是于 16 世纪到 20 世纪间(尤其是 17 世纪)发展起来的。它体现了塞纳河与人类之间关系的演进:塞纳河从最早的被用于防御,到后来用于发展贸易,如今的河岸则是人们休闲散步的好去处。

历史上,政府对该地和塞纳河进行了一系列建设,以便控制管理,如:西岱岛、圣路易岛和塞纳河岸连接起来了;修建了贯通南北的大道;沿河道配备了各种设施;修建了一些码头;疏通河道;等等。同样,虽然巴黎的城墙已经不复存在,但从建筑物的大小和间距的变化仍能看出城墙的踪迹:玛莱区和圣路易岛的建筑间距较密,罗浮宫后面的区域则较开阔。罗浮宫外面,沿三条垂直轴线,有很多重要的古典建筑:一条线上是波旁宫、协和广场和玛德莲广场,一条线上有荣军院和小皇宫,还有一条线则是战神广场、军事学院和夏佑宫。这一建筑群在地理和历史意义上是一个整体,它和谐地展现了历史的层次,如今是城市沿河建筑的杰出典范。

奥斯曼男爵的城市规划是巴黎西部的标志,为美洲(尤其是拉丁美洲)许多大城市的建设提供了灵感。埃菲尔铁塔和夏佑宫则是 19、20 世纪巴黎主办的重要世界博览会留下的丰碑。

Vocabulary

1. studded *adj*. 布满……的；有很多……的；用类似饰钉物装饰的；带饰钉的

The sky was studded with twinkling stars.

天空布满闪烁的星星。

2. ensemble *n*. 整体；总体；全体；合唱组；乐团；全体演员；舞蹈团

The state is an ensemble of political and social structures.

国家是一个政治结构和社会结构的组合体。

3. promenade *n*. 散步，闲逛；人行道；散步场所

We took a promenade along the canal after Sunday dinner.

星期天晚饭后我们沿着运河散步。

4. articulation *n*. 连接，联系，相互关系；（思想或感情的）表达；清楚的咬字（或发音）

The social formations reflect the interaction, or articulation of different modes of production.

这些社会结构反映了不同形式的生产方式之间的互动，或者说相互联系。

5. perpendicular *adj*. 垂直的；笔直的；垂直（于）的；成90度角的

It takes courage and strength to climb up the perpendicular cliff.

攀上这悬崖峭壁需要勇气和力量。

6. axes *n*. 轴；轴线；核心

This choice of axes simplifies the analysis of the particular problem.

这样选坐标轴，可简化这个特殊问题的分析。

7. entity *n*. 独立存在体；实体

As a separate legal entity, the corporation must pay taxes.

作为一个独立的法律实体，公司必须纳税。

8. strata *n*. (stratum 的名词复数)社会阶层；岩层

We can also observe them in certain Strata of our own society, especially in show business and among the very wealthy.

我们也可以在社会的一些阶层中观察到它们，特别在演艺界和非常富有的人群中。

扩展阅读

The River Seine

While it's common knowledge that the Notre Dame Cathedral is the technical epicenter of Paris, the real essence of the city is captured by the River Seine.

Almost any city situated near water is changed by that relationship between the static and the constantly moving. On a metaphysical level, the water is a type of mirror in which the city finds its own reflection. For centuries, poets, painters, philosophers, novelists, architects, lovers, suicides, and finally, tourists, have understood this powerful attraction. The River Seine flows right through the heart of Paris bordering 10 of the 20 arrondisements. It was no accident that the city evolved around this gigantic avenue for commerce and transportation, or that the early Parisi tribes on the river's island were attacked and overthrown by the Romans. This early coup took place on what was later to become some very prime real estate. At that time the river was called by its Latin name: Sequana. The river is still the chief commercial waterway and half of the water used in Paris still comes from the Seine. Don't think about that when you look at the sick green water flowing under the bridge, or when your waiter brings you a glass of tap water.

Tourists are often confused about the terms "right bank" and "left bank" and spend hours on street corners with crumpled maps trying to orient themselves and figure out which side of the riverbank they are standing on. The system is very simple and was devised because the river's curvy nature often does make orientation difficult. The trick is to remember when you face Downriver the left bank is on your left and the right bank is on your right. If you can't tell left from right at this point you should not travel alone. If you can't figure out which way the water is flowing (Don't look at the boats; they go upstream too!) drop a potato chip or look for some debris and see which way it's floating. Then you will be able to make it to the Cafe Les Deux Magots on time, and not end up at La Defense.

There are 32 bridges on the river in Paris; some of them are more impressive than others. The oldest bridge is the Pont Neuf which has been immortalized by artists and poets and even 20th century films. There is a beautiful little island crossed by the bridge which the riverboat tours now used as a docking station. In the spring or summer it's a wonderful place to hang out on a bench under the willow trees, or sunbathe on the slanted stone embankments near the tended gardens in its center. To get there, simply make your way toward the equestrian statue of Henri V and find the steps leading down toward the docks. If you are the kind of person who likes watching boats this is a great spot. Actually it is one of the nicest places to hang out in all of Paris.

Another popular bridge is the Pont Des Arts, which differs from many other bridges in that it is constructed of metal and is entirely pedestrian. With one of the most stunning views in all of Paris this is a top hang-out and pick-me-up zone in good weather. Some people bring wine and picnics, others bring guitars and the atmosphere is almost always festive. Below the bridge on the left and right quays you will see hundreds of sunbathers, cyclists, strollers, joggers and anything else you could hope for, making use of the elegant stone quays. The quays run along the entire length of the river as it bisects the city, parts merging into riverside highways and others into pedestrian walkways and bicycle paths. A section of the pedestrian bank has been designated the "Paris Beach" by the new mayor, and has become the summer attraction in the city. Thousands of tons of sand are imported along with full size palm trees, beach chairs and chaise-lounges to create what may be the only artificial "beach" in Europe. It's bizarre, but the French love it. Whether you like it or not, it's a good chance to see some scantily clad Parisians.

The riverbanks are worth exploring. There are floating restaurants, discos, cafes for those who can afford it, and free benches for all those travelers who are just as happy to enjoy the same view with their own wine, bread and cheese from a local grocer. Houseboats can be examined close up on the right bank near the Orangerie, and the stone walls of the quays are a type of code language for the river's past. If you look carefully you can see the various water levels form past floods, the giant iron rings used to tie river barges to the docks, the odd iron grate or doorway leading to an underground passage, an ancient sewer system, metro portals, an unknown catacomb? These stone embankments are now protected by UNESCO as World Heritage sites. The best way to get the feel of the river is of course by boat. There are many boat tour operators in Paris offering various levels of service form taxi-boats to private dining experiences. The most famous are still the Bateaux-Mouches. There are also lunch and dinner cruises which begin by the Musee Dorsay run by Marina de Paris. There is another sightseeing cruise that sails the Canal St. Martin. From the Paris Arsenal Marina to the Parc de la Villette or the other way around the trip takes around two and a half hours.

Beyond the mere technical facts surrounding the river and its environs is a deeper and more inexplicable attraction. The water speaks to us of a past we will never experience but nevertheless find ourselves linked to by association. Staring at the murky river from a old bridge in a Parisian winter it is impossible not to think of Paul Celan, the tormented poet of the holocaust, who plunged to his death in those same waters, or the less known victims of French Revolution when hundreds of bodies were dredged from the depths, or simply the unnamed and uncelebrated who also met their ends at the river bottom. This is not to say the river represents a cult of death, but it's interesting to conceive of it as part of the full cycle of life. Great triumphs and great tragedies have occurred near the river which less aware tourists view as the background to their photo collection.

（资料来源：http://www. aparisguide. com/seine）

Questions

1. What do you know about Paris and the Seine? According to the article, what's the relationship between the river and the city?

2. What are the attractions along the riverbanks? How can visitors distinguish the right bank from the left bank?

Tower of London
伦敦塔

⇨ 简介

所属国家：英国(The United Kingdom of Great Britain and Northern Ireland)

入选时间：1988

入选标准：（ii）（iv）

The massive White Tower is a typical example of Norman military architecture of the late 11th century, whose influence was felt throughout the kingdom. It was built on the Thames by William the Conqueror to protect London and assert his power. The Tower of London—an imposing fortress with many layers of history, which has become one of the symbols of royalty—was built around the White Tower.

Built during the 1080s and modified over the centuries, the White Tower, as it is now called, became the centrepiece of the complex of fortifications, courtyards and other buildings which extends over 7.3 ha. As the most complete survival of an 11th-century fortress palace remaining in Europe, the White Tower, and its later 13th and 14th century additions, belong to a series of edifices which were at the cutting edge of military building technology internationally. They represent the apogee of a type of sophisticated castle design, which originated in Normandy and spread through Norman lands to England and Wales.

The London Tower has been the setting for some of the most momentous events in European and British history. Its role as a stage upon which history is enacted is one of the key elements which have contributed towards the tower's status as an iconic structure. The imprisonments in the tower, of Edward V and his younger brother in the 15th century, and then in the 16th century of four English queens, three of them executed on Tower Green—Anne Boleyn, Catherine Howard and Jane Grey—with only Elizabeth I escaping, shaped English history. The tower also helped shape the Religious Reformation in England, as both Catholic and Protestant prisoners (those that survived) recorded their experiences and helped define the tower as a place of torture and execution.

宏伟的白塔是 11 世纪末诺曼军事建筑的典型，对整个英国的建筑风格产生了巨大影响。伦敦塔是威廉一世沿泰晤士河建造的，目的是保护伦敦，并占领领土。伦敦塔围绕白塔而建，是一个具有悠久历史的堡垒，也是王室权力的象征。

白塔建于 11 世纪 80 年代，随后的几百年间不断改建，以其为中心逐渐形成一处包括堡垒、庭院及其他建筑的建筑群，总面积达 7.3 公顷。白塔是欧洲现存最完整的 11 世纪堡垒和宫殿，它和 13、14 世纪的扩建部分形成一系列大型建筑，体现了当时处于国际领先地位的军事建筑技术。这些建筑所体现的城堡设计精密复杂，堪称巅峰之作，这种设计源于诺曼底，后来普及到诺曼地区和英格兰、威尔士。

伦敦塔是欧洲史、英国史上许多重大事件的发生地。它是历史上演的舞台，这也是伦敦塔成为标志性建筑的原因之一。在这儿，15 世纪关押过爱德华五世和他的弟弟，16 世纪关押过四位英格兰女王，其中三位（安妮・博林、凯瑟琳・霍华德和琴・格蕾）被处死于格林塔，只有一位（伊丽莎白一世）逃脱，这些事件影响了英国历史的发展。伦敦塔还影响了英格兰的宗教改革运动，运动中被关押在此的，无论是天主教徒还是新教徒，如能幸存，所述经历都把伦敦塔描述成充满酷刑和死刑的毛骨悚然之地。

Vocabulary

1. fortress *n.* 堡垒;防御阵地;要塞

After a long fight, they managed to take the fortress.

经过长时间的战斗,他们终于攻占了那座要塞。

2. edifice *n.* 大厦;雄伟的建筑物;(信仰或传统制度的)体系,结构

He surveyed the edifice from the outside and admired greatly.

他从外边打量着大厦,对它赞不绝口。

3. apogee *n.* 顶峰;顶点;最高点

The markets recovered quickly and the dotcom bubble reached its apogee.

金融市场很快恢复元气,而互联网泡沫则达到其最高点。

4. iconic *adj.* 偶像的;圣像的;似圣像的

The ads helped the firm to achieve iconic status.

这些广告帮助该公司成就了其偶像地位。

5. execute *v.* 将……处死;执行;实施;贯彻

The general gave the word to execute the deserters.

将军下令处决逃兵。

扩展阅读

Famous Tower of London Prisoners

If the stones of the tower's many walls could talk, what stories they could tell! Within the first 900 years of its existence, the Tower of London was the scene for many gruesome executions and deaths. Several English rulers met with unfortunate deaths in the tower.

One king, named Richard Ⅱ, was only ten years old when he became King of England. When he was fourteen, a group of overtaxed farmers stormed the tower. This revolt became known as the Peasants' Revolt. Although Richard was safely hidden, other royal leaders were not so lucky and lost their lives after being captured. Many years later Richard was thrown into a tower dungeon. He became the first English King prisoner in the tower.

Some famous prisoners who died in the Tower were guilty of interesting crimes. Read about some of their crimes below and what happened to them. What do you think would happen to these people today?

1441—Eleanor, Duchess of Gloucester, wife of the King's uncle Humphry. She was charged and killed for trying to kill the King by melting a wax image of him before a fire.

1483—Edward Ⅴ and Richard, Duke of York. These two young princes were the sons of King Edward Ⅳ. When King Edward died, their uncle Richard, Duke of Gloucester, wanted to become king. However, the boys were next in line for the throne. Richard plotted to take the throne for himself. He probably had the boys murdered in the Garden Tower. This tower is today known as the Bloody Tower.

1535—Ann Boleyn. She was King Henry Ⅷ's second wife. She was charged with being unfaithful to her husband and was beheaded. However, her real crime was giving birth to a daughter rather than a son, a future King of England.

1618—Sir Walter Raleigh. He was an explorer known for his expeditions to the Americas. He lost his head after he failed to find gold in South America and returned empty-handed.

1941—Rudolf Hess. This German spy was the last prisoner to stay at the Tower of London. He was Deputy Fuhrer of Nazi Germany during World War Ⅱ and was held captive and executed in May 1941.

Yeomen warders

Since the foundations for the tower were laid in 1078, there have been men appointed to guard the prisoners and attend the gates. Today men still serve as keepers of security for the tower. They are called Yeomen Warders. The Yeomen Warders originated during the reign of King Henry Ⅶ. These men still wear the costumes of that period. Their striking outfits include a red tunic with purple and gold lace trim, red knee breeches and red stockings, a ruff, a plumed hat, a steel gilt spear and battle ax with a red-and-gold tassel, and an ornamental sword. Today there are thirty-eight established Yeomen Warder posts. They are recruited from the Royal Marines, the Army, and the Royal Air Force. These men are responsible for the security of the tower and its visitors. They conduct public guided tours of the tower during the day. Each evening, a Ceremony of the Keys is held. The outer gates of the fortress are locked and the keys are taken to the Resident Governor. All Yeomen Warders are required to live on the grounds of the tower with their families. They live in private houses. Each evening, after the gates are locked, the tower becomes a separate, safe community for its permanent residents.

Legend of the ravens

By tradition, there have been ravens at the Tower of London for many centuries. The ravens are protected by an old legend which says that should the ravens ever leave the Tower of London, the White Tower will crumble and a great disaster shall befall England.

Strangely, the only recorded time there were no ravens at the tower was in 1946. At that time, World War Ⅱ had just ended, and England had come very close to falling. Do you think there is something ture of the legend?

There are six main resident ravens at the tower plus two alternate ravens. They live in nesting boxes in the tower grounds near the Wakefield Tower. They are cared for by one of the Yeomen Warders, called the Ravenmaster. This is a very important Yeomen Warder position.

Ravens are similar in appearance to the common crow. The wings of the tower's ravens are clipped so they cannot fly away. Ravens live an average of twenty-five years. If one dies, a young raven replaces it. The ravens can be seen at four areas within the Tower of London. One area is called the Tower Green. This is an old execution site. Ravens of the time would have witnessed the executions of Ann Boleyn, Walter Raleigh, and many other prisoners.

(资料来源：http://www.everycastle.com/Tower-of-London.html)

Questions

1. Why is the Tower of London also known as the Bloody Tower?

2. Who are Yeomen Warders? What are their responsibilities?

3. Where can visitors find ravens in the tower? Why are these ravens kept in the tower and taken care of?

Venice and Its Lagoon
威尼斯及其潟湖

⇨ 简介

所属国家：意大利（Italy）

入选时间：1987

入选标准：(i)(ii)(iii)(iv)(v)(vi)

Venice is a city in northeastern Italy, sited on a group of 118 small islands separated by canals and linked by bridges. It is located in the marshy Venetian Lagoon which stretches along the shoreline between the mouths of the Po and the Piave Rivers. The city seems to float on the waters of the lagoon and is renowned for the beauty of its setting, its architecture and its artworks. Venice possesses an incomparable series of architectural ensembles illustrating the age of its splendour. The whole city is an extraordinary architectural masterpiece in which even the smallest building contains works by some of the world's greatest artists such as Giorgione, Titian, Tintoretto, Veronese and others. It presents a complete typology whose exemplary value goes hand-in-hand with the outstanding character of an urban setting which had to adapt to the special requirements of the site. Venice was described as "undoubtedly the most beautiful city built by man" and one of Europe's most romantic cities.

In this lagoon, nature and history have been so closely linked since the 5th century AD when Venetian populations, to escape barbarian raids, found refuge on the sandy islands of Torcello, Iesolo and Malamocco. These temporary settlements gradually became permanent and the initial refuge of the land-dwelling peasants and fishermen became a major maritime power during the Middle Ages and Renaissance. It was also a very important center of commerce (especially silk, grain, and spice) and art in the 13th century up to the end of the 17th century. This made Venice a wealthy city throughout most of its history. It is also known for its several important artistic movements, especially the Renaissance period. Venice has played an important role in the history of symphonic and operatic music, and it is the birthplace of Antonio Vivaldi.

威尼斯位于意大利东北部,由威尼斯潟湖的 118 个小岛构成,其间以众多水道、桥梁连成一体。该潟湖多沼泽,分布在波河与皮亚韦河之间的海岸线上。威尼斯城仿佛漂浮在潟湖水面之上,其环境之优美、建筑之独特、艺术品之丰富,享誉世界。一系列无与伦比的大型建筑群,是威尼斯昔日辉煌的写照。整个威尼斯城就是一幅非凡的建筑杰作,即便是城中最不起眼的建筑也可能是出自诸如焦尔焦内、提香、丁托列托、韦罗内塞等世界大师之手。这儿的建筑风格堪称典范,同时也体现了城市规划与当地自然环境特殊要求相适应的特点。威尼斯被誉为"毫无疑问最美丽的人造都市"、欧洲最浪漫的城市之一。

在威尼斯潟湖,自然和历史自公元 5 世纪就紧密联系在一起。当时,这儿的居民为逃避野蛮的侵略者,移居到托切洛、耶索洛和马拉莫科等沙地小岛。这些农夫和渔民的临时避难所逐渐变成固定居所,进而发展成中世纪和文艺复兴时期最主要的海上力量。13 世纪至 17 世纪末,威尼斯是非常重要的商业(尤其是丝绸、粮食与香料贸易)和艺术中心。威尼斯一直以来的繁荣富庶推动了文化的发展,值得一提的是文艺复兴时期威尼斯的几次重要文艺运动。威尼斯在交响乐史和歌剧音乐史上也有重要地位,安东尼奥·维瓦尔第(著名巴洛克音乐作曲家、小提琴演奏家)就出生在这儿。

Vocabulary

1. lagoon *n.* 潟湖;环礁湖

The lagoon was pullulated with tropical fish.

那个潟湖聚满了热带鱼。

2. marshy *adj.* 沼泽般的;湿软的;泥泞的

The surrounding land is low and marshy.

周围地势低洼而多沼泽。

3. typology *n.* 类型学,分类法

But Darwin replaced typology with the new concept of populations.

但达尔文用种群的新概念替代了类型学。

4. raid *n.* 突然袭击;突击搜查;抢劫

The rebels attempted a surprise raid on a military camp.

叛军试图突袭一处军营。

5. symphonic *adj.* 交响乐的;类似交响乐的

Nature's symphonic world was drowned by man's industrial cacophony.

大自然的和声世界被人类的工业噪音淹没了。

扩展阅读

How to Save Venice: Make It Float

Everyone knows that on a sinking ship, you want to pump water out. But what do you do with a sinking city? In this case, the plan might be to pump water in.

The city of Venice has long been valued for its unique character. Built in a lagoon along the coast of Italy, the scenic city is crisscrossed with canals. Its waterlogged nature draws a steady stream of visitors, but also makes it vulnerable to costly flooding. The region sometimes experiences unusually high tides, locally referred to as "acqua alta". The phenomenon is caused by winds that drive water to "pile up" on the north end of the long and narrow Adriatic Sea. When that coincides with a high tide, "the city of water" gets even wetter, and the water level can rise by 1—2 meters.

Two factors are exacerbating the flooding risk to the city: global sea level rise and subsidence. In short, the sea is rising and the city is sinking. Like other cities built on river deltas, the sediment beneath the city is compacting over time. In a natural setting, this compaction would be offset by the deposition of fresh sediment at the surface, but the rivers feeding the lagoon were diverted in the 1500s. As a result, the land surface is sinking, and the salt marshes are suffering for it.

The pumping of shallow groundwater in the mid-1900s also contributed to the problem. Water in the pores between grains of sediment provides pressure that bears some of the load. When pore pressure decreases, or water is removed completely, grains can be packed together more tightly by collapsing the pore spaces. As sediment is compacted, the land surface drops. While the effect was small (less than 15cm), Venice doesn't have much wiggle room.

A remarkable system of inflatable gates that could close off the lagoon during dangerously high tides, dubbed the MOSE Project, has been in the works for a while now. Funding issues and environmental concerns have plagued the initiative, but it continues to move forward.

Recently, another idea has been discussed. Just as withdrawing groundwater can cause subsidence, injecting water can reverse it. It's not entirely a two-way street— much of the pore space lost during compaction can't be recovered—but increased pore pressure can begin to unpack the sediment. Injection was used successfully in Long Beach, California in the late 1950s to halt subsidence caused by oil and gas extraction as well as groundwater usage. After the land surface dropped nearly 30 feet, injection stabilized the subsidence and a slight rebound in land surface elevation (a little over 30cm) was even seen in some spots. Early research indicated that a similar amount of uplift could be achieved in Venice, which could make a big difference for a city on the edge. The precision of those predictions was limited, however, by the lack of detailed knowledge about the layers of sediment beneath the city.

A new paper, published in *Water Resources Research*, adds that information and uses it to show that the idea really could work in Venice. Without boreholes around the city to provide observations of the stratigraphy, researchers have relied on data gathered by seismic surveys. Like the familiar sonar systems used by submarines, seismic surveys require a (much more powerful) signal to be generated so its return can be analyzed as it bounces off sediment in the subsurface. That's been difficult to pull off around Venice, though, as the lagoon is too shallow for large boats to be used. And, attempts to use potent air and water guns as seismic signal sources caused problems by kicking up large amounts of sediment.

Back in the 1980s, though, oil and gas companies hadn't yet been banned from using explosives in settings like this. The Italian National Research Council acquired a large amount of old, raw seismic data from an Italian oil company, and the researchers were able to use it to construct a high-quality, three-dimensional model of the stratigraphy below Venice. This allowed them to confirm the presence of a continuous layer of impermeable clay, below which injected water could increase pore pressure, rather than simply bubble up to the surface. It also allowed them to determine the thickness and extent of the various layers proposed to be used for the injection.

The group simulated the effects of 12 injection wells in a ring around the city. The results showed that, after 10 years of continuous seawater injection (a total of almost 150 million cubic meters of water), the city could be lifted 25—30 centimeters. That would greatly cut down on the frequency with which the MOSE floodgate system would have to be activated each year. That, in turn, decreases operational and maintenance costs, and reduces the ecological impact of the system. In addition, the uplift around the city would benefit the slowly-drowning salt marshes in the lagoon.

The study also shows that by varying the pumping rates at each of the 12 wells, a very uniform uplift can be maintained across the city. If some areas of the city rise faster than others, buildings could be damaged—a result that would be counterproductive to the entire enterprise. With careful management, the researchers say that the difference in uplift between two points 100 meters apart would be less than 1 millimeter.

While it may initially sound far-fetched, this could become part of Venice's plan to mitigate flooding issues, which will only worsen in coming decades. Battling "acqua alta" would be much easier if the city had the high ground.

（资料来源：http://www. wired. com/wiredscience/2011/12/save-sinking-venice-by-floating)

Questions

1. Why is flooding a serious problem for the city of Venice?

2. What is a possible way, according to the passage, to keep Venice away from the threat of flooding?

Works of Antoni Gaudí
安东尼·高迪的建筑作品

⇨ **简介**

所属国家：西班牙（Spain）

入选时间：2005

入选标准：(i)(ii)(iv)

Seven properties built by the architect Antoni Gaudí (1852—1926) in or near Barcelona testify to Gaudí's exceptional creative contribution to the development of architecture and building technology in the late 19th and early 20th centuries. These monuments represent an eclectic, as well as a very personal, style which was given free reign in the design of gardens, sculpture and all decorative arts, as well as architecture. The seven buildings are: Parque Güell; Palacio Güell; Casa Mila; Casa Vicens; Gaudí's work on the Nativity façade and Crypt of La Sagrada Familia; Casa Batlló; Crypt in Colonia Güell.

The works of Antoni Gaudí represent a series of outstanding examples of the building typology in the architecture of the early 20th century, residential as well as public. It is, furthermore, an outstanding and well-preserved example of the ideal garden cities dreamed of by the urbanists of the end of the 19th century. It exhibits an important interchange of values closely associated with the cultural and artistic currents of his time, as represented in El Modernisme of Catalonia. It anticipated and influenced many of the forms and techniques that were relevant to the development of modern construction in the 20th century.

在巴塞罗那市区及近郊的 7 处安东尼·高迪（1852—1926）的建筑作品，见证了他对 19 世纪末 20 世纪初建筑技术的杰出创意与贡献。圭尔公园、圭尔宫、米拉大楼、文生之家、高迪关于耶稣诞生门和圣家堂的作品、巴特里奥之家和克洛尼亚古埃尔宫都呈现了折中主义风格，非常人性化，这对花园、雕塑及所有装饰艺术和建筑的设计产生了极大影响。

安东尼·高迪的作品是 20 世纪初民用建筑和公用建筑的杰出典范，这些保存良好的建筑也是 19 世纪末的城市规划者所梦想的理想花园城市的绝佳范例。正如加泰罗尼亚现代主义所代表的，这些作品体现了与当时各种文化、艺术思潮紧密联系的不同价值观之间的交流，预见并影响了与 20 世纪现代建筑发展息息相关的多种理念和工艺。

Vocabulary

1. testify v. （在法庭上）作证，证明；证明；证实

Recent excavations testify to the presence of cultivated inhabitants on the hill during the Arthurian period.

最近几次发掘证实了亚瑟王时期这座山上有农耕人口居住过。

2. eclectic *adj.* 折中的；兼收并蓄的；五花八门的；不拘一格的

She has very eclectic tastes in literature.

她在文学方面的兴趣非常广泛。

3. reign *n.* （君主的）统治；支配；主宰

His reign has never been considered particularly noteworthy.

从没有人认为他统治的时期特别值得关注。

4. urbanist *n.* 城市规划专家；城市规划者

For the urbanist，there is a lively and growing multicultural scene linked by excellent public transport.

对城市规划者而言，这里有日益增加的多文化场景和极其便利的公共交通。

5. interchange *n.* （思想、信息等的）交换，交流；交换位置；交替

What made the meeting exciting was the interchange of ideas from different disciplines.

会议上令人兴奋的是来自不同学科的思想交流。

扩展阅读

Antoni Gaudí：God's Architect

All the great cathedrals have taken centuries to complete. The Cathedral of the Sagrada Familia (Holy Family) in Barcelona, Spain, is no exception. Begun in 1883, only half of this imposing church is now complete. Construction work, however, steadily continues as donations keep coming in to support the work. Architects estimate that the church will take at least another 40 years to complete. Some say it could take as many as 150 years.

Sagrada Familia is the most renowned building designed by Spanish architect Antoni Gaudí, whose cause for beatification was opened last year by the Cardinal Archbishop of Barcelona. The cathedral is a testament to the architect's faith. In some ways, Gaudí's Barcelona church resembles the great cathedrals of the Medieval age: Sagrada Familia was based on the plan of a Gothic basilica with five naves, a transept, an apse, and ambulatory.

It is designed with soaring towers, capped by spires, and is replete with dense symbolism throughout the structure. Gaudí, however, wanted to create a "20th century cathedral", a synthesis of all his architectural knowledge with a visual explication of the mysteries of faith. He designed façades representing the Nativity, Crucifixion, and Resurrection of Christ; and eighteen towers, symbolizing the twelve Apostles, the four Evangelists, the Virgin Mary and Christ. The Christ tower, the tallest, when completed will stand some 500 feet high. To date, eight of the eighteen towers are completed. Each is of a unique spiral-shape covered in patterns of Venetian glass and mosaic crowned by the Holy Cross.

God's Architect

"My client can wait," was Gaudí's genial response to his helpers when delays occurred due to his constant changes to the original plans. Gaudí always acknowledged that his ultimate client was God, whom he felt was in no hurry. The architect wanted the finest and most perfect sacred temple for his client. He truly worked ad majorem Dei gloriam, for the greater glory of God.

Gaudí, known as "neo-Medieval" in his day, developed a unique style of building. His work is characterized by the use of naturalistic forms, and his approach came to be known as the "biological style". Sagrada Familia is known for its conical spires, parabolic arched doorways and freely curving lines. As in most of his works, Gaudí has created the impression that the stone used was soft and modeled like clay or wax.

Gaudí directed the construction of the church from 1883 until his sudden death in 1926. He became so involved with the church that he set up residence in his onsite study and devoted the last 14 years of his life to this most important of all his projects. He regarded Sagrada Familia as a great mission. On June 7, 1926, Gaudí was hit by a street car. Three days later he died at the age of 74.

When he died, the people of Barcelona popularly proclaimed him a "saint". There was great commotion. Even though he lived in a reserved manner, removed from the world, rumor of his sanctity had already spread. No newspaper, not even the most virulently anti-Catholic, attacked him. The director of the Museum of the Barcelona Archdiocese wrote an article calling Gaudí "God's Architect". His architecture is an expression of his Christian commitment. From the very beginning of the 20th century Sagrada Familia has become an icon of the city of Barcelona, just as the Eiffel Tower is an icon of Paris. And after the architect's death, the people of Barcelona regarded him as a patron of their grand city.

There have even been documented conversions resulting from the architecture of Sagrada Familia. The most prominent involved two Japanese men. One is architect Kenji Imai. He arrived in Barcelona two months after Gaudí's death. He was traveling all over the world to meet the great architects of the day, but by the time he reached Barcelona Gaudí was dead and buried. Even so, Imai was not disappointed. Sagrada Familia made such an impression on him that, when he became a professor in Japan he gave several lectures on Gaudí and, finally, converted to Catholicism. The other convert is sculptor Etsuro Sotoo, who worked for years fashioning statues on Barcelona's cathedral, and ultimately became a Catholic.

The Works Continue

After Gaudí's death, works continued on the church until 1936. These were the days of the bloody Spanish Civil War. The Communists, who hated all things Catholic, set fire to Gaudí's study which held his notes and designs for Sagrada Familia. Many of these were destroyed，but the project resumed in 1952 using the surviving drawings and models to continue the work. Today，the constructed part is open to visitors as well as the small museum that exhibits Gaudí's original plans and models.

Later this year，Cardinal Ricard Maria Carles of Barcelona will inaugurate Sagrada Familia with a solemn mass on December 31，the feast of the holy family. The 150-foot-high central nave is scheduled to be totally roofed by that date. Referring to the Basilica's beauty，Cardinal Carles told a Spanish newspaper，"For me it transmits an evangelical message，very much Gaudí's style." Perhaps for that reason，Antoni Gaudí is regarded still as "God's Architect".

（资料来源：http://www. sacredarchitecture. org/articles/antoni＿gaudi＿gods＿architect）

Questions

1. From the passage，what can you learn about the Cathedral of the Sagrada Familia?

2. What are the characteristics of Gaudí's works?

第二节　欧洲的世界自然遗产

Danube Delta
多瑙河三角洲

➭ 简介

所属国家：罗马尼亚（Romania）

入选时间：1991

入选标准：（vii）（x）

The waters of the Danube，which flow into the Black Sea，form the largest and best preserved of Europe's deltas. The reserve is vast in European terms with numerous freshwater lakes interconnected by narrow channels featuring huge expanses of aquatic vegetation. This is the largest continuous marshland in Europe and the second-largest delta (the Volga being the largest)，which includes the greatest stretch of reedbeds in the world. The Danube Delta falls within east European steppe ecosystem，with Mediterranean influences. It represents a very favourable place for the development of highly diverse flora and fauna，unique in Europe，with numerous rare species. It hosts 23 natural ecosystems. The delta has been classified into 12 habitat types as follows：

aquatic, lakes covered with flooded reedbeds; "plaur", flooded islets; flooded reeds and willows; riverine forest of willows and poplars; cane-fields; sandy and muddy beaches; wet meadows; dry meadows (arid); human settlements; sandy and rocky areas; steep banks; and forests on high ground.

The Danube Delta is a remarkable alluvial feature constituting critical habitat for migratory birds and other animals. It is the major remaining wetland on the flyway between central and eastern Europe and the Mediterranean and Middle East and Africa. Situated on major migratory routes, and providing adequate conditions for nesting and hatching, the Danube Delta is a magnet for birds. Over 300 species of birds, have been recorded, of which over 176 species breed, the most important being cormorant, pygmy cormorant, white pelican and Dalmatian pelican. The delta is very important for fish, with 45 fresh water species present.

多瑙河奔流直下,汇入黑海,形成了欧洲面积最大、保存最完好的三角洲。对欧洲来说,该保护区地域广阔,众多的淡水湖由狭窄的水道相连,生长着大片的水生植被。这儿是欧洲最大的连绵沼泽地,也是第二大三角洲(仅次于伏尔加河三角洲),其中有世界上最大的芦苇丛。多瑙河三角洲属于受地中海影响的东欧草原生态系统,良好的自然条件使得该地动植物品种非常丰富,其中不乏许多稀有品种,这在欧洲是独一无二的。它包含23个自然生态系统。该三角洲可被分为12种栖息地类型:水生型(即被大量水中芦苇覆盖的湖泊)、水浸芦苇小岛、水浸芦苇和柳树、河岸边的柳树及杨树林、甘蔗田、沙泥滩、湿草地、干草地、人类居住区、沙石区、陡岸、高地森林。

多瑙河三角洲这一辽阔的冲积三角洲,是候鸟和其他动物的重要栖息地,是欧洲中东部和地中海、中东、非洲之间候鸟迁徙路线上现存的主要湿地区域。该三角洲位于鸟类的主要迁徙路线上,其自然环境为鸟类筑巢、孵化提供了充分的条件,因此吸引了大量鸟类。在此栖息的鸟类,已记录的有300多种,其中176种在此繁殖,重要的鸟类包括鸬鹚、俾格米鸬鹚、白鹈鹕和卷羽鹈鹕。该三角洲也是重要的鱼类栖息地,共有45种多瑙河及其支流中特有的鱼类在此生活。

Vocabulary

1. aquatic *adj.* 水栖的;水生的;与水有关的;水上的

The pond is quite small but can support many aquatic plants and fish.

池塘虽小,但能为许多水生植物和鱼类提供足够的养分。

2. steppe *n.* 大草原;干草原

Forest is replaced by other vegetation types such as the forest steppe or steppe.

森林将被其他植被类型(例如森林草原或草原)所替代。

3. ecosystem *n.* 生态系统

The ecosystem can be redefined as interlocking life systems.

生态系统可以再定义为相互关联的生命系统的综合。

4. flora *n.* 植物群落

The subtropical island has a remarkably rich native flora.

这个亚热带岛屿有相当丰富的乡土植物种类。

5. fauna *n.* 动物群

Wild fauna and flora are important integrants of ecosystem.

野生动植物是生态系统的重要组成部分。

扩展阅读

Crowd Cuckoo Land: The Danube Delta Is a Paradise for Iconic Birds—and for Naturalists

Cuckoo, cuckoo, cuckoo, cuckoo! As we glided along the narrow channels in our small boat, cuckoos called incessantly on every side, interrupted at intervals only by the loud drumming of huge black woodpeckers and the screeching of the elegant whiskered terns that followed us everywhere.

With no roads, and hardly a human, for hundreds of square miles around us, we were in a naturalists' paradise—a world of water lilies, reeds and willow trees. This is the Danube Delta on the Romanian coast, where the mighty River Danube ends its 1,770-mile journey from Germany's Black Forest to the Black Sea, meandering through Austria, Slovakia, Hungary, Croatia, Serbia and Bulgaria along the way.

And clearly, the delta is not just a paradise for naturalists—it's a paradise for cuckoos too.

The cuckoo has to be one of our most iconic birds. Any child can mimic its call. Yet how many children, especially in the south and east of England, have actually heard a real one calling? Not many, because the number of cuckoos breeding in the south and east has fallen dramatically over the past 20 years. Happily, Scotland, Wales and the north and west of England aren't—yet—affected, so the British Trust for Ornithology (BTO) is trying to find out what's happening to our southern cuckoos. I say "our" cuckoos, but cuckoos spend only just over two months in the UK (from late April to early July), calling, mating and laying their eggs in the nests of other species. Then they are off again.

It's quite possible, indeed probable, that some of the problems affecting southern cuckoos have been caused here in the UK. For example, the universal use of powerful pesticides has had a drastic effect on the insect population of the countryside, significantly reducing the number of caterpillars that form a major part of the cuckoo's diet.

But the BTO also wants to investigate whether cuckoos are experiencing problems on their migration or in their wintering grounds, so it needs to know exactly where our cuckoos go and how they get there.

Until very recently, gathering this information would have been a virtually impossible task. Suddenly, however, there has been a huge leap in technology and it is now possible to attach tiny transmitters to birds as small as cuckoos that regularly beam back location data. A limited pilot trial was carried out last year, and this autumn cuckoos from Scotland, Wales and east Anglia are being tracked southward on their migration down to Africa.

It's early days, but one of the things we've discovered so far is that not all of our cuckoos fly due south via France, Spain and Italy.

Some fly further east—a Welsh cuckoo has just passed through Slovakia and Montenegro, and it may be that others fly down the western coast of the Black Sea.

So at the end of May, I went to the Danube Delta in Romania to see for myself, among other things, how the cuckoo was doing down there, with none of the man-made pressures it has to cope with in England.

Ten of us from the UK travelled in a floating hotel. The hotel is accompanied by a much smaller, yet still comfortable, motor boat that is able to penetrate the intricate network of smaller channels threading through the reed-beds and willow clumps that make up the Danube Delta. So we ate, drank and slept on the floating hotel but went exploring, for the most part, in the motor boat.

What a wealth of wildlife there was. I've been lucky enough to visit many of the richest wildlife areas in Europe, but I've never experienced anything like this. We were all bowled over by the sheer quantity of spectacular birds wherever we looked, and what made it even better was that most of them seemed to be quite unconcerned at our presence.

As large flocks of white pelicans glided overhead, we would make our way along narrow channels—often with overhanging willow trees—and find ourselves almost within touching distance of truly astonishing birds such as the rainbow-coloured bee-eater and the startlingly skyblue and purple roller—birds you think of as belonging in flamboyant Africa rather than sober Europe.

Other birds that just looked at us as we passed by included pygmy cormorants, squacco herons and red-footed falcons, all rare in Europe as a whole but abundant in the Danube Delta.

Birds we were able to glide up to in our boat, having cut the motor, included penduline tits and bearded tits, kingfishers, the normally elusive little bittern and woodpeckers both black and grey-headed.

But the biggest surprise to me was the sheer number of cuckoos. They seemed to be everywhere. Their calls were constantly in the air and we would frequently pass beneath one calling on a willow branch. All of us agreed that, well travelled though we were, we had never seen or heard so many cuckoos anywhere.

So whatever the problem is with the cuckoos that breed in southern Britain, it's not affecting the cuckoos that breed in the Danube Delta. This seems to suggest that the trouble is not in the wintering grounds in Africa but here in England, and perhaps on the migration routes through western Europe. Hopefully, the BTO's current research will begin to provide the answers.

"Cuckoo, cuckoo." As the sun set, and the last cuckoo's calls rang across the water lilies, I resolved that the Danube Delta was somewhere I should not only return to again and again, but somewhere I should try to encourage others to visit—the more of us who get down there to enjoy it in an entirely sustainable way, the more likely it is that the Romanian government, in economic difficulty like the rest of Europe, will resolve that it's in the best interests of the country to resist pressure to drain and develop the delta—and to keep it as fabulous as it is today.

（资料来源：http://www.dailymail.co.uk/travel/article-2217584/The-Danube-Delta-paradise-iconic-birds—naturalists.html）

Questions

1. The cuckoo is said to be one of the most iconic birds in the UK, but the number of cuckoos breeding in the south and east has fallen dramatically over the past 20 years. What are the possible reasons?

2. The Danube Delta is a paradise for cuckoos and many other species. Why does the author want to attract more people to visit the place? What can we do to reduce the impact of human activities on the reserve?

Ilulissat Icefjord

伊路利萨特冰湾

⬡ 简介

所属国家：丹麦（Denmark）

入选时间：2004

入选标准：（vii）（viii）

Located on the west coast of Greenland, 250 km north of the Arctic Circle, Greenland's Ilulissat Icefjord (40,240 ha) is the sea mouth of Sermeq Kujalleq, one of the few glaciers through which the Greenland ice cap reaches the sea. Sermeq Kujalleq is one of the fastest (19 m per day) and most active glaciers in the world. It annually calves over 35 km^3 of ice, i.e. 10% of the production of all Greenland calf ice and more than any other glacier outside Antarctica. Studied for over 250 years, it has helped to develop our understanding of climate change and icecap glaciology. The combination of a huge ice-sheet and the dramatic sounds of a fast-moving glacial ice-stream calving into a fjord covered by icebergs makes for a dramatic and awe-inspiring natural phenomenon, which is only seen in Greenland and Antarctica. Ilulissat offers both scientists and visitors easy access for close view of the calving glacier front as it cascades down from the ice sheet and into the ice-choked fjord.

Greenland has been inhabited for 4,500 years, settlers migrating from Asia via the Bering Straits and north-west Greenland in three main waves, known as the Saqqaq, Dorset and from AD 1000, the Thule peoples. Norsemen inhabited south-west Greenland between AD 985 and 1450. During the 16th—18th centuries explorers followed by whalers inhabited the area. The nominated area includes the archaeologically valuable sites of Sermermuit, abandoned in 1850, and Qajaa on the south side of the fjord, abandoned earlier. The early settlers summered in tents but used stone and turf hovels in winter.

格陵兰的伊路利萨特冰湾（40240 公顷）位于格陵兰岛西岸,北极圈以北 250 千米,是通过格陵兰冰冠入海的少数几个冰河之一——瑟梅哥-库雅雷哥(Sermeq Kujalleq)的出海口。瑟梅哥-库雅雷哥是世界上流速最快(每天 19 米),也是最活跃的冰川之一,每年裂冰超过 35 立方千米,占格陵兰岛裂冰的 10%,比南极洲以外的任何其他冰河都多。人们对这条冰湾的研究超过 250 年,冰湾有利于我们对气候变化和冰河学的了解。巨大的冰盖,加上冰流迅速移动,在冰山覆盖的峡湾内崩裂发出的巨响,形成了仅存于格陵兰岛和南极洲的、令人敬畏的自然现象。冰川前沿崩裂时,从冰盖上倾泻而下,落入浮冰拥塞的峡湾,伊路利萨特冰湾为科学家和游客提供了近距离观察此等奇景的机会。

人类在格陵兰岛的居住历史可以回溯到 4500 年前,来自亚洲的三批移民通过白令海峡和格陵兰岛西北部来到这里,他们分别是萨卡克人、多尔塞特人和公元 1000 年左右的图勒人。公元 985—1450 年,诺斯曼人在格陵兰西南部定居。16—18 世纪,探险者和捕鲸者先后在此定居。伊路利萨特冰湾的世界遗产地区包括一些有着极高考古价值的遗迹,如赛麦穆于特(于 1850 年被遗弃)及位于冰湾南部、更早被遗弃的卡加。早期的定居者在帐篷里度过夏天,在小石屋和茅舍里度过冬天。

Vocabulary

1. glacier *n.* 冰川;冰河

The glacier scooped a canyon out of rocks.

冰河在礁石中冲出了一条河谷。

2. calve *v.* (冰川)崩解;使(冰川)崩解

The icebergs and glaciers are calving.

冰山和冰川在崩解。

3. cascade *v.* (水)飞流直下,倾泻而下;垂落;悬挂

A waterfall cascades down the cliff from the hills behind.

一处瀑布从身后山崖上飞流直下。

4. turf *n.* 草皮

He was busy laying turf.

他正忙着铺草皮。

5. hovel *n.* (尤指破败不堪的)小屋,茅舍;肮脏简陋的住处

It's very uncomfortable to live in a dirty hovel like ours.

像我们这样住在肮脏的破屋子里,太不舒服了。

扩展阅读

Ilulissat Icefjord

The icefjord and the glacier at Ilulissat make up a world-class area of outstanding natural beauty, as a result of which the fjord was added to UNESCO's World Heritage list in 2004.

One thing is official lists, however, quite another is a wish list of places that you love and would be happy to return to again and again. Ilulissat and the surrounding region rich in ice also feature high up on this list.

Thousands of visitors travel to Ilulissat every year in order to satisfy themselves at first hand that this natural phenomenon is indeed world class.

What makes the location so magnificent is Sermeq Kujalleq, the biggest glacier and biggest ice stream outside Antarctica. Here you'll find a very unusual ice flow, a huge icefjord and enormous icebergs.

The figures speak for themselves: The glacier is more than $3,000 \text{km}^2$ in the area and calves about 40 cubic kilometres of ice every year. The ice from the glaciers thus totally dominates the sea in large parts of Disko Bay and in the sea west of Greenland.

Just has to be experienced

However, facts and figures alone cannot account for what you experience when visiting this place. It just has to be seen, heard, smelt and felt—in other words, to be experienced!

With its enormous dimensions, distinctive beauty and tranquility, the fantastic ice landscape provokes a particular mood, where you realise that all your everyday worries fade into insignificance against the perspective of the centuries that have gone by in the creation of this ice. Billions and billions of snowflakes have fallen and been compressed into Greenland's Ice Sheet, after which they've flowed together towards the ice fjord and ended up calving and breaking off into large icebergs that continue their journey out to sea.

These natural forces have been active for millennia, driven by the sun, the weather systems and the force of gravity. It's geophysics in a huge, large-scale laboratory lying at your feet as you look out from the cliff.

The settlement at Sermermiut

Cultural remnants from the Eskimo culture can also be found at the icefjord. Just one kilometre outside Ilulissat at the end of the Sermermiut valley lies the settlement of Sermermiut. The settlement was inhabited until the middle of the 19th century and contains traces of all three of the immigrant cultures that have populated and continue to populate Greenland.

Here, among the ruins of turf houses and kitchen middens and against a backdrop of icebergs, it isn't difficult to imagine life as it's been played out over the millennia: On the sea the hunters—family fathers—are making their way home from the hunt; round about the turf houses children are playing with their toys, which are miniature versions of the men's hunting tools; whilst the women are flaying seals or making food.

Earlier generations preferred this place in the same way that it continues to attract people from all over the world today. World-class natural scenery!

Icebergs

You'll meet icebergs all over Greenland. They come in all shapes and sizes, and no two icebergs are exactly alike. In the north, icebergs can be up to 100 metres in size; they're considerably smaller in the south, yet they're still masterpieces.

In fact, they could also be considered to be genuine wonders. You can only see a small part of the huge mass of ice, since 7/8 of an iceberg remain below the surface of the sea, where its shape and colours are left to your imagination—or to divers.

They look magnificent as they slowly float out towards the open sea. They're given birth to by the Ice Sheet and created by compacted snow which is thousands of years old. Each year the Ice Sheet produces thousands of icebergs, where they calve particularly frequently in the central and north-western regions of the country and along Greenland's east coast.

As tall as a 15-storey building

On a sailing trip in Ilulissat and Uummannaq you get a convincing demonstration of the size of the icebergs as they tower over the boat; beautiful and intimidating at the same time. It's vital to have great respect for the inherent power that an iceberg can release. The skipper of the boat, however, is well aware of this, since the local population know the icebergs by their sounds and shapes and know when not to get too close.

Interplay of colours in blue, turquoise and the transparency of glass

In south Greenland the icebergs are smaller, but equally spectacular. They are often turquoise and appear in many different forms—and are a work of art in themselves. In south Greenland it's easier to walk out to the glacial edges of the Ice Sheet, where the icebergs are produced, from where they then drift south for many thousands of kilometres. During the summer, the icebergs are floating ice sculptures, whilst during the winter they are gripped by the ice in its frozen embrace.

Ice isn't just ice

In many ways ice is synonymous with Greenland. The Ice Sheet is one thing, but the country is also known for its field ice, which is sea ice formed in the Arctic Ocean north of Greenland. This ice drifts with the current down the east coast of the country, rounds Cape Farewell in the south and then moves up the west coast. Solid ice is formed in the fjords during the winter months, where it gets hold of the icebergs on the way out to sea and keeps them in suspended animation until spring arrives and the onset of warmer weather causes the white mass to disappear.

（资料来源：http://www.greenland.com/en/things-to-do/naturoplevelser）

Questions

1. What are some of the natural wonders one may find in Ilulissat Icefjord?

2. Why does the writer say "Ice isn't just ice"?

Swiss-Alps Jungfrau-Aletsch

少女峰-阿雷奇冰河-毕奇霍恩峰

⇨ **简介**

所属国家：瑞士（Switzerland）

入选时间：2007

入选标准：（vii）（viii）（ix）

The extension of the natural World Heritage property of Jungfrau-Aletsch-Bietschhorn (first inscribed in 2001), expands the site to the east and west, bringing its surface area up to 82,400ha, up from 53,900 ha. The site provides an outstanding example of the formation of the High Alps, including the most glaciated part of the mountain range and the largest glacier in Eurasia. It features a wide diversity of ecosystems, including successional stages due particularly to the retreat of glaciers resulting from climate change. The geology of the site derives from the "Helvetic nappe" (a large body of rock that was thrust over younger rock in Europe during the Miocene epoch). The folding and over-thrusting of rock layers during the formation of the Alps have produced very complex rock formations that have since been exposed by glacial activity. The physiography of the area is characterized by steep north-facing slopes and relatively gentle southern ones. The scenic and aesthetic appeal is one of the most dramatic in the Alps, as evidenced by the long history of international visitation. The impressive northern wall of the site with the panorama of the Eiger, Mönch and Jungfrau mountains provides a classic view of the north face of the High Alps. Vegetation and fauna are representative of the Alps and vary by slope, aspect and elevation. There is a marked difference in vegetation between the northern and southern slopes.

The site is of outstanding universal value both for its beauty and for the wealth of information it contains about the formation of mountains and glaciers, as well as ongoing climate change. It is also invaluable in terms of the ecological and biological processes it illustrates, notably through plan succession. Its impressive landscape has played an important role in European art, literature, mountaineering and Alpine tourism.

自然世界遗产少女峰-阿雷奇冰河-毕奇霍恩峰（最早于2001年被列入）从东部扩展到

西部,面积从 53900 公顷扩展到 82400 公顷。该遗址为阿尔卑斯高山(包括山脉最受冰河作用的部分和欧亚大陆山脉最大的冰川)的形成提供了一个杰出的实例。它以生态系统多样性为特点,包括特别受气候变化冰川融化而形成的演替阶段。该地区的地质状况源于"海尔维推覆",即欧洲中新世时期新老岩层的叠加。阿尔卑斯山脉的形成过程中,岩层的重叠和逆冲推覆形成了复杂的岩石构造,在冰川运动作用下形成各种奇美造型。自然形态上,朝北的山坡比朝南的山坡更为陡峭。这里拥有阿尔卑斯山脉最壮美的景观:一览无遗的艾格尔峰、门希峰和少女峰美景,是阿尔卑斯高地北部山屏的著名景观。历史上来自世界各国的游客络绎不绝。少女峰-阿雷奇冰河-毕奇霍恩峰的动植物种类随着山坡倾斜度、朝向和海拔的变化而不同。山峰南北两侧的植被有显著差异。

该地区因景色秀美,在山脉和冰川形成及正在发生的气候变化方面具有突出的全球价值。在它尤其通过植物演替所阐释的生态和生物过程方面,该遗址的价值无法衡量。其令人难忘的景观在欧洲艺术、文化、登山和阿尔卑斯山旅游中起着重要作用。

Vocabulary

1. derive v. 获得;取得;得到;(使)起源于;(使)来自

Mr Wilson is one of those happy people who derive pleasure from helping others.

威尔逊先生属于那种助人为乐的快活人。

2. thrust v. 猛推;猛塞;刺;挤;推;扎;露在外面;凸出来

A ray of sunlight thrust out through the clouds.

一缕阳光透过云层照射下来。

3. epoch n. 时代;纪元;(地质中的)世,纪,期

Two main glacial epochs affected both areas during the last 100 million years of Precambrian times.

在前寒武纪的最后 1 亿年中,两个主要的冰川时期对两个地区都产生了影响。

4. physiography n. 地文学,地相学

To locate the optimal drill site, the team had to conduct the first detailed characterisation of the physiography of a sub-glacial lake.

为了确定最佳的钻探点,研究小组首先要确定详细的冰河湖的地貌。

5. aesthetic adj. 美的;艺术的;美感的;审美的

The professor advanced a new aesthetic theory.

那位教授提出了新的美学理论。

6. panorama n. 全景;远景;概述;概论

As I opened the scroll, a panorama of the Yellow River unfolded.

我打开卷轴时,黄河的景象展现在眼前。

扩展阅读

An Alpine Kingdom of Rock and Ice

Featuring majestic peaks, sheer rock faces, and an immense tongue of ice, the Jungfrau-Aletsch UNESCO World Natural Heritage site is certainly impressive.

The protected area, which lies between the Bernese Oberland and northeastern Valais, covers more than 800 kilometres^2 and is the first site of its kind in the Alps.

Countless roads, trails, cableways, ski-lifts and mountain railways—the best known being the Jungfrau line—lead up to the protected area and, in some cases, breach its borders. A dense network of trails criss-crosses the outer fringes. But its inner core remains virtually inaccessible, except for eagles and mountaineers.

The site includes famous mountains such as the Jungfrau-Eiger-Mönch triad, the Bietschhorn, the Wetterhorn, the Schreckhorn and the Finsteraarhorn—the highest peak in the area at 4,274 metres. Nine mountains break the 4,000-metre barrier and a further fifty the 3,500-metre mark. An area of around 350km^2 is covered in glaciers.

The wild, inhospitable landscape has fascinated generations of artists and travellers in search of unspoilt natural scenery in an increasingly industrialised Europe.

However, some of the outer parts of the site bear witness to human intervention and are shaped by the work of farmers and the daily life of mountain communities.

Not just mountains

"For us it has always been important to include the surrounding cultural landscape in the Jungfrau-Aletsch area," said Beat Ruppen, director of the UNESCO management centre at Naters in Valais, as he showed us photographs of the steep sheep-tracks leading up to the Aletsch meadows and the Alpine irrigation channels used to water pastures.

More cultural areas were added to the site with UNESCO's approval in 2007 when protected area was extended eastward to the Grimsel Pass and Meiringen, and westward to Lake Öschinen (Kandersteg) and the lower part of the Lötschental.

But the long UNESCO application process was not without controversy, as local people feared that their region would be subject to too many environmental regulations.

The first proposal to register the Aletsch region as a World Natural Heritage site was put forward in the 1960s. The idea was met with widespread scepticism from the local population and the project ground to a halt.

In the 1980s more than 90 per cent of the area now included in the site was listed in the Swiss federal inventory of landscapes of national importance.

Border queries

This decision partly defused the fear of over-burdensome regulations, and in 1996 paved the way for a fresh application to UNESCO. In the event, UNESCO's regulations do not go beyond those already laid down by the federal authorities.

There were also lengthy negotiations on defining the boundaries of the site.

"We adopted a participatory model, involving the local community in the discussions. It was a long process, but it enabled people living in the area to grasp the importance of UNESCO registration," explained Ruppen.

Even so, most of the areas of economic interest were eventually excluded. Ruppen clearly understands the viewpoint of people living in the Alps. "Without the prospect of economic development, these regions are in danger of abandonment. And this can hardly be the objective of a UNESCO site," he said.

Living with UNESCO

The Jungfrau-Aletsch-Bietschhorn region was added to the UNESCO World Heritage list in 2001. Following its enlargement in 2007, the site was renamed Swiss-Alps Jungfrau-Aletsch. Since then, even the locals have discovered the advantages of UNESCO recognition.

"People are proud to live in a region considered to be part of the world's natural heritage. It has strengthened local identity," said Ruppen.

The UNESCO name and logo is on display everywhere. Even those who were initially sceptical now use it to advertise their activities.

The next challenge is to achieve a sustainable balance between environmental protection and economic development.

Global warming is placing more pressure on tourism in mountain regions. The municipalities responsible for the UNESCO site are therefore committed to promoting sustainable development.

In 2001 they signed up to an environmental charter in the hope that glaciers, mountains and humans will continue to coexist for centuries to come.

（资料来源：http://www. swissinfo. ch/eng/culture/unesco. html? cid＝7906248）

Questions

1. Briefly describe the natural and cultural attractions of the Jungfrau-Aletsch UNESCO World Natural Heritage site.

2. What was the controversy in the process to register the Aletsch region as a World Natural Heritage site? How was it solved?

Volcanoes of Kamchatka
堪察加火山

⇨ 简介

所属国家：俄罗斯（Russian Federation）

入选时间：2001

入选标准：（ii）（iii）（iv）（ix）（x）

The site comprises six distinct locations on the Kamchatka Peninsula, in the Russian Far East, in the central mountainous spine of the peninsula, and coastal locations facing east towards the Bering Sea. This is one of the most outstanding volcanic regions in the world, with a high density of active volcanoes, a variety of types, and a wide range of related features. The six sites included in the serial designation group together the majority of volcanic features of the Kamchatka Peninsula. The interplay of active volcanoes and glaciers forms a dynamic landscape of great beauty. The sites contain great species diversity, including the world's largest known variety of salmonoid fish and exceptional concentrations of sea otter, brown bear and Stellar's sea eagle.

The property represents the most pristine parts of the Kamchatka Peninsula and a remarkable collection of volcanic areas, characteristic of the "Pacific Volcanic Ring". This is the surface expression of the subduction of the Pacific Ocean Continental Plate under the Eurasia Plate at rates of 10 cm annually. The addition of Kluchevskoy Nature Park, an outstanding example of geological processes and landforms, further adds to the range of natural features.

More than 300 volcanoes are found in Kamchatka, 29 being currently active, including caldera, strata-volcano, somma-volcano and mixed types, the largest included in the World Heritage site being Kronotskaya Sopka (3,528 m). In addition there is a multitude of thermal and mineral springs, geysers and other phenomena of active vulcanism.

Surrounded by sea, the peninsula enjoys a moist and relatively mild climate leading to a lush vegetation cover. With only modest history of human exploitation, the vegetation is in largely pristine conditions. The region also contains an especially diverse range of Palaearctic flora (including a number of nationally threatened species and at least 16 endemic). The faunal complement is relatively low in diversity, with the Kamchatka Peninsula exhibiting some of the biogeographic qualities of an island.

堪察加火山位于俄罗斯远东的堪察加半岛上，由6个不同区域组成：其中1个位于堪察加半岛中部的山脊上，其他都是朝东对着白令海。堪察加火山是世界上最著名的火山区之一，它拥有高密度的活火山，而且类型和特征各不相同。指定考察的6个景点集中了堪察加半岛大多数的火山奇异景观。活火山与冰河相互作用造就了这里的生机和美景。景区内物种丰富，除世界现存的最大鲑鱼群外，还集中了大量的海獭、棕熊和鱼鹰。

这儿有堪察加半岛最原始的地区，还有令人惊叹的火山区。该火山区是太平洋火山带的典型，是太平洋大陆板块以每年10厘米的速度向亚欧板块下俯冲的地表显示。2001年增加的克鲁柴夫斯卡娅自然公园，体现了多种地质作用和丰富的地形，为该遗产地区的自然特色增色不少。

堪察加有300多座火山，其中29座目前仍为活火山，包括喷火山口、地层火山、外轮火山和混合型火山。该地区最大的火山是科洛诺兹卡娅·索普卡山（高3528米）。此外，这儿还有许多温泉、矿泉、间歇喷泉和其他活火山现象。

堪察加半岛周边环海，气候湿润温暖，植被覆盖繁茂，加之人类开发历史不长，这儿的植被大多保持了原始状态。该地区还有着特别丰富的古北界植物群（包括大量俄罗斯濒危的植物种类和至少16种当地特有植物）。堪察加半岛动物种类相对较少，呈现了一个岛屿特有的一些生物地理特征。

Vocabulary

1. spine *n.* 脊椎;脊柱;书脊;(动物身体上的)棘状突起;(植物上的)棘,刺,针

The disease had deformed his spine.

疾病导致他脊柱变形。

2. designation *n.* 名称;称号;标示;指定;命名;指派

The district is under consideration for designation as a conservation area. 正在考虑将这个地区指定为保护区。

3. pristine *adj.* 原始状态的;纯朴的,纯洁的;未受腐蚀的,新鲜的

Although the pristine forest around Ancient Olympia was burned, none of the ruins were damaged.

尽管古奥林匹亚周围的原始森林被烧毁了,古代遗迹一个都没有被破坏。

4. thermal *adj.* 热的;由热引起的;(小溪、浴水)天然温热的;(衣服)保暖的

Volcanic activity has created thermal springs and boiling mud pools.

火山活动产生了温泉和沸腾的泥浆池。

5. geyser *n.* 间歇泉

The geyser erupts periodically.

间歇泉周期性地喷发。

扩展阅读

The Ring of Fire

Kamchatka was born of fire, like the Earth itself. For most of the Earth, though, the violence of creation ended long ago. Kamchatka has never been quiet—its history is one of continuous, violent rebirth.

The native people of Kamchatka are intimately familiar with this history. They have always feared the peninsula's volcanoes, whose peaks they believed to be inhabited by mountain spirits known as gomuls. By night, the gomuls took to the sky and hunted whales, returning home with leviathans impaled on each finger. They would then roast the whales. This is why the volcanoes lit up at night. The natives believed that great heaps of whalebone lay on the mountaintops, but were too fearful to ascend the volcanoes and find out for themselves if this were true.

As someone who has experienced the awesome destructive power of volcanism, this fear is understandable to me. During my time on Kamchatka, I studied Karymsky Lake, an isolated body of water filling the caldera of what was thought to be an extinct volcano. On New Year's Eve 1996, however, a spectacular eruption burst from the lake floor. An ecological catastrophe ensued. The force of the eruption created tsunami waves 30 feet in height that leveled the forest surrounding the lake. The water in the lake became extremely acidic; all life in the lake, other than the simplest algae and bacteria, was destroyed in a matter of minutes.

For all their destructive power, volcanoes are vital to man's existence. Volcanic gases helped create earth's atmosphere, and continue to affect its composition today. On a more prosaic level, volcanic glass was used by ancient humans to make tools. Volcanic ash serves as a fertilizer, returning important nutrients and minerals to the soil. The city of Petropavlovsk, the main settlement on Kamchatka, is built of concrete made from cinder of the 1945 eruption of nearby Avachinsky Volcano, which watches over the city from its post 20km to the north.

Kamchatka's place in world volcanism

The Kamchatka Peninsula is the northern link in the 2,000 km Kuril-Kamchatka island arc. This region contains 68 active volcanoes, over 10 percent of the total found on land anywhere on Earth. This arc is part of the "Ring of Fire", a string of volcanoes that encircles the Pacific Ocean.

The existence of the Ring of Fire is explained by the theory of plate tectonics. According to this theory, Earth's surface is fractured into a number of rigid plates that move in slow motion. (The fastest plates move only a few inches per year, or about as fast as your fingernails grow.) The Ring of Fire is formed where the Pacific Plate collides with other tectonic plates.

The Pacific Plate slides beneath these other plates, plunging into the earth at a steep angle. As the Pacific Plate sinks into the hot interior of the earth, melting occurs. The resulting magma migrates to the surface, where it eventually bursts through the crust in the form of a volcano.

Volcanism's effect on Kamchatka's wildlife

The animals of Kamchatka have turned the harsh volcanic environment to their advantage. Birds build nests on the grooved rock formations that surround geysers. When the geysers erupt, boiling water lands and flows directly beneath the nest through channels carved into the rock. The bird is freed from having to sit on its nest all day; the geyser keeps the egg warm, and the mother needs only return periodically to turn the eggs over.

Kamchatka's most famous animal inhabitant, the brown bear, is often seen bathing in the peninsula's sulfurous hot springs. Bears, like humans, cherish the hot springs' curative properties—the sulfurous water drives off fleas, ticks and other infestations. Bears appear to be genuinely fearless of volcanoes. During the eruption of Karymsky Volcano in 1997, a volcanologist who ventured to the summit during a quiet period reported seeing fresh bear tracks near the edge of the crater; what a bear was doing at the summit of a volcano during an eruption is anyone's guess.

Life in a volcanic environment can nevertheless be treacherous for animals. Birds seem especially vulnerable, and they are frequently struck from the sky by falling volcanic bombs. During the massive eruption of Tolbachik Volcano in 1975—1976, volcanologists reported seeing birds flying at night into the flames of the volcano, like moths toward a candle. Larger animals are occasionally killed in the wintertime, when they plunge through the snow into boiling mud cauldrons or geysers. A region of Kamchatka called the Valley of Death has been especially lethal to animals. Numerous vents in the valley release a heavy, odorless, toxic gas. When the wind blows from a certain direction, the entire valley is filled with this gas, suffocating any animals (and humans) present. During one recent year six bears, four foxes and three hares perished, along with dozens of crows and assorted rodents.

In general, however, the number of animals (other than birds) killed by eruptions is quite low. This gives support to the idea that animals may be able to sense impending eruptions, and flee in time to save themselves. The 1996 eruption in Karymsky Lake that so surprised scientists did not, apparently, catch local wildlife off guard. Not a single dead animal was found near the lake, despite the 30 foot tsunamis that swept the shoreline, and the giant volcanic bombs that rained from the crater. Prior to the eruption, several million fish were known to live in Karymsky Lake. After the eruption the lake was devoid of life. Not a single dead fish was ever found, however, leading scientists to speculate that some change in water chemistry had tipped the fish off, causing them to flee through the lake's outlet into Karymsky River.

Karymsky Lake, its water turned to acid, is uninhabitable now. On its shores, life is slowly returning. Ash and mud from the eruption feed the soil, spurring the growth of plants, which in turn attract insects, birds, and larger wildlife. It will be somewhat longer before life recolonizes the lake, but in half a century all traces of this catastrophe will disappear. It is a process repeated countless times in this lake, on this peninsula called Kamchatka, where the earth is still young and unsure of itself, and where nature, like an unsatisfied artist, constantly destroys and remakes its canvas.

（资料来源：http://www.kamchatkapeninsula.com/ringoffire.html)

Questions

1. What is the "Ring of Fire"? How did it come into existence?
2. How do the volcanoes in Kamchatka influence the life of human beings and animals?

West Norwegian Fjords-Geirangerfjord and Nærøyfjord
挪威西峡湾-盖朗厄尔峡湾和纳柔依峡湾

简介

所属国家：挪威（Norway）

入选时间：2005

入选标准：（vii）（viii）

Situated in southwestern Norway, northeast of Bergen, Geirangerfjord and

Nærøyfjord, set 120 km from one another, are part of the west Norwegian fjord landscape, which stretches from Stavanger in the south to Andalsnes, 500 km to the northeast. The two fjords, among the world's longest and deepest, are considered as archetypical fjord landscapes and among the most scenically outstanding anywhere. Their exceptional natural beauty is derived from their narrow and steep-sided crystalline rock walls that rise up to 1,400 m from the Norwegian Sea and extend 500 m below sea level. The sheer walls of the fjords have numerous waterfalls while free-flowing rivers cross their deciduous and coniferous forests to glacial lakes, glaciers and rugged mountains. The landscape features a range of supporting natural phenomena, both terrestrial and marine, such as submarine moraines and marine mammals.

The West Norwegian Fjords are classic, superbly developed fjords, considered as the type locality for fjord landscapes in the world. These dramatic fjords are the grandest landscapes in a country of spectacular fjords, and the rivers which enter them have not been developed for hydroelectric power. Each is at the upper end of a major fjord system that developed along faults and fracture zones at right angles, giving them a characteristic zigzag form. Both fjords are submarine hanging valleys, which have floors between 300—500 m deep in ice-scoured basins.

Many carefully recorded relics are present in the area. Viking houses a thousand years old are present and over 350 registered old buildings. Remnants of old and now mostly abandoned transhumant farms add a cultural aspect to the dramatic natural landscape that complements and adds human interest to the area.

盖朗厄尔峡湾和纳柔依峡湾位于挪威西南部,卑尔根东北部,相互间隔距离120千米,是挪威西部峡湾自南部的斯塔万格市往东北方向绵延500千米至安道尔森尼斯风景的一部分。世界上最狭长的这两个峡湾拥有原始秀美的海湾景观,是风景最为秀丽的地区之一。挪威海上,耸立着1400米高的狭窄而陡峭的水晶岩壁,在海面以下绵延500米,造就了此处独特的自然美景。峡湾中,悬崖峭壁上是数不清的瀑布,自由欢畅的河水穿越落叶和松叶林流入冰湖、冰河和崎岖的山地。一系列的陆地和海洋景观,如海底冰碛和海洋哺乳动物,共同构成了这里突出的景致。

挪威西峡湾是典型的大型峡湾,也是最经典的峡湾地形研究地点。在挪威这个峡湾之国,这两个峡湾是最壮观的景点,流入峡湾的河水未曾用于水力发电。盖朗厄尔峡湾和纳柔依峡湾均沿着断层带和断裂带直角而形成,因此呈现出别具特色的锯齿形。这两个峡湾都是水下悬谷,悬谷的底部位于冰川冲刷而成的盆地以下300—500米。

该地区有许多历史遗迹,现存有1000年历史的维京时代房屋和350余处古建筑,还有一些古老游牧农场(现大多荒弃)遗址,为这一壮观的自然景观增添了一种文化氛围,为该地区增添了人文气息。

Vocabulary

1. archetypical *adj.* 典型的;有代表性的

Cricket is an archetypical English game.

板球是典型的英格兰运动。

2. deciduous *adj.*（树、灌木）每年落叶的

Deciduous trees shed their leaves in autumn.

落叶树在秋天落叶。

3. coniferous *adj.* 针叶树的

In Belarus side，88％ of the trees are coniferous and mixed forest.

在白俄罗斯一侧，树木 88％是针叶和针阔叶混交林。

4. terrestrial *adj.*（动植物）陆地的，陆生的，陆栖的；地球的；地球上的

The gills of fishes are analogous to the lungs in terrestrial animals.

鱼类的鳃与陆上动物的肺相似。

5. transhumant *adj.*（牲畜的）季节性迁移放牧的

This book brings together studies by national scientists on traditional transhumant grazing systems.

本书汇集了国内科学家关于传统游牧放牧系统的诸多研究。

▌ 扩展阅读

Dramatic Beauty in the Scandinavian Wilderness

With just a pinch of imagination—and perhaps a little early morning fog—it's easy to envision a fully laden Viking ship sailing up the Geirangerfjord and Nærøyfjord in western Norway. That's how pristine these landscapes are, seemingly untouched by modern times and preserved in a state that long-ago Norsemen would readily recognize if they could somehow voyage up these fjords today.

Set along the deeply indented coast between Bergen and Trondheim, the dramatic, seawater-filled inlets constitute the West Norwegian Fjords World Heritage site. Inscribed in 2005, the site sprawls across more than 120,000 hectares (or about 460 square miles) of Scandinavian wilderness where native flora and fauna have long coexisted with secluded rural farmsteads.

A branch of the larger Storfjord, the more northerly Geirangerfjord is flanked by sheer stone walls that one Norwegian writer called "the most preposterous mountains on the entire west coast". The more southerly Nærøyfjord lies almost 120 miles (193 kilometers) inland from the Norwegian Sea, near the town of Aurland.

"The main criteria for inscription is the geology," says the site coordinator, Katrin Blomvik, about these unique landscapes formed by water, ice and wind over millions of years. "It is almost overwhelming to travel in the fjords. Either you go paddling with kayaks or you travel on ferries or cruise ships in the fjords. It takes the breath out of you. And it does to me, all the time."

These are among the world's longest and deepest fjords. The S-shaped Geirangerfjord is more than nine miles in length; the Nærøyfjord meanders in a northsouth direction for around 11 miles. The height of the inlets' sides reaches an astounding 6,200 feet (1,890 meters)—nearly six times taller than the Eiffel Tower—about three-quarters of that above the surface and the rest below sea level.

The lofty plateaus above the fjord walls are covered in forests, meadows, glaciers, lakes and rivers that tumble over the walls as feathery cascades, like the Seven Sisters and Suitor waterfalls on opposite sides of the Geirangerfjord.

The highlands are home to a broad array of wildlife, including all four species of native deer, as well as lynxes, wolverines and otters. Virtually unpolluted, the fjord waters also swarm with wildlife that ranges from immense sperm whales and orcas to seals and salmon.

Fewer than 500 people currently live within the West Norwegian Fjords area, far fewer than in the 19th century, when the area was considered overpopulated. Migration to towns and abroad has left abandoned farms that cultural-heritage authorities and local groups are attempting to restore. Restoration managers work to educate local residents about why restoration is important and work with landowners to refurbish old buildings with traditional materials.

"The cultural dimension is also quite important to us, to the people who live there," says Blomvik, "We have quite remote, and unique, fjord farms that lie 300 meters above sea level. And you can only imagine how tough it must have been to live there on a daily basis—and agriculture, the land, keeping animals there, keeping children from falling into the fjords."

Each year, about 600,000 to 800,000 people visit the World Heritage site between May and September. Most arrive aboard the more than 300 cruise ships that ply the fjords each year, but the site is also accessible by car, train, ferry and foot. Having played host to visitors for more than 150 years, locals have a long history of balancing commercial activities and preserving their pristine landscape.

The struggle in the future will be keeping that balance. For that, Blomvik hopes to tap into the expertise of other marine World Heritage sites, in particular Glacier Bay in Alaska, which has already done a good amount of research on how to manage cruise tourism.

Without tourism, says Blomvik, the current inhabitants of Geirangerfjord and Nærøyfjord would not have the funds to maintain local schools and other public services year-round. "So it's the most important industry for us," she says, "But at the same time, we need to find solutions that are more environmental, that are more connected to the future, which I hope will be more green. My dream is to make the West Norwegian Fjords a more sustainable destination."

（资料来源：http://www. stranda-hamnevesen. no/files/PDF/16. 01. 12Tidesof TimeWestNorwegianFjords. pdf）

Questions

1. What are the attractions of the West Norwegian Fjords?

2. Do you have any suggestions for keeping the balance between commercial activities and the pristine landscape of the West Norwegian Fjords?

第三节 欧洲的世界文化和自然双重遗产

Ibiza, Biodiversity and Culture

伊维萨岛的生物多样性和特有文化

⇨ **简介**

所属国家：西班牙（Spain）

入选时间：1999

入选标准：(ii)(iii)(iv)(ix)(x)

Ibiza is an island in the Mediterranean Sea 79 km off the coast of the city of Valencia in Spain. It provides an excellent example of the interaction between the marine and coastal ecosystems. The dense prairies of oceanic Posidonia (seagrass), an important endemic species found only in the Mediterranean basin, contain and support a diversity of marine life. Ibiza preserves considerable evidence of its long history. The archaeological sites at Sa Caleta (settlement) and Puig des Molins (necropolis) testify to the important role played by the island in the Mediterranean economy in protohistory, particularly during the Phoenician-Carthaginian period. They are exceptional evidence of urbanization and social life in the Phoenician colonies of the western Mediterranean. The fortified Upper Town (Alta Vila) is an outstanding example of military architecture, engineering and the aesthetics of the Renaissance; it had a profound influence on the development of fortifications in the Spanish settlements of the New World. Its architecture and physiognomy have not been changed since the fortifications were built in the 16th century, based on the military precepts of the Renaissance. The defensive walls and bastions have incorporated those which existed before, thus making it possible to study the stratigraphy of all fortifications.

伊维萨岛位于地中海，距瓦伦西亚市海岸79千米。该岛的生物多样性和特有文化提供了一个海洋生态系统和沿海生态系统之间相互作用的极好范例。地中海盆地所特有的波西多尼亚海草生长茂盛，蕴含和支撑着海洋生物的多样性。另外，伊维萨岛的历史遗迹保存完好。萨·卡莱塔聚居地考古遗址和普伊格·德斯·墨林斯墓地遗址证实了一点：在史前，特别是腓尼基-迦太基时期，伊维萨岛对地中海经济的发展起到了非常重要的作用。这两处遗址充分体现了西地中海地区腓尼基殖民地的城市化及社会生活。坚固的高城要塞是文艺复兴时期军事建筑、土木工程及美学的杰出范例，对于西班牙殖民者在新大陆的防御性建筑的发展具有极其深远的影响。高城要塞建于16世纪，以文艺复兴时期军事规范为指导。至今该地的建筑和地貌仍保持原状。防卫墙和众多堡垒及原有建筑结合为一体,使人们得以研究该地所有要塞的地层情况。

Vocabulary

1. endemic *adj.* 某地特有的;(疾病)地方性的,流行的

In northwestern China, there is no evidence for endemic domestication of any animals.

在中国西北,没有任何当地动物驯化的迹象。

2. physiognomy *n.* 相貌,面相

His eyes were good, but otherwise there was nothing remarkable in his physiognomy.

他的眼睛长得好,其他方面倒也没有特别突出的地方。

3. precept *n.* 准则;规范;戒律

Example is better than precept.

言传不如身教。

4. bastion *n.* 堡垒

Like an iron bastion, the dam withstood the rushing floodwaters.

大坝好似铜墙铁壁,顶住了洪水的冲击。

5. stratigraphy *n.* 地层学;地层情况

Stratigraphy studies the sequence of the rocks in the earth's crust.

地层学研究地壳中岩石的层序。

扩展阅读

Would You Come to Ibiza?

Find refuge in a church

Ibiza's parish churches are quite different from ecclesiastical buildings elsewhere. They owe their unique architecture to the fact that they were once local strongholds in which local inhabitants took refuge when marauding pirates appeared on the scene. This combination of spirituality and protection is found in magical places like Santa Eulalia's Puig de Missa (Church Hill), where church and whitewashed houses crown a summit next to the sea—a beautiful ensemble that seems to have arrested time itself. Sant Miquel's Puig de Missa is another ancient church that in former times doubled as a rugged fortress. Such buildings continue to provide spiritual refuge, but these days are also in use for concerts and other leisure activities, above all during village fiestas. They all share their brilliant whiteness, but are really quite different from one another (Es Cubells, Sant Jordi, Sant Agustí or Sant Antoni, with canons in its tower), and a tour of them allows you to drift back to the days of Ibiza's legendary past, and understand the vigour and tenacity of its unconventional inhabitants. Don't be surprised during your circuit if you come across a couple of payesas in the porch, their faces a mass of wrinkles and smiles, or children playing hide-and-seek by the main door. These porches are a great place to meet up with friends, and also a handy nook for stealing away from the clamour of the world, sitting with a book, meditating, or simply enjoying a quiet chat.

Choose your sunset

Ibiza offers some of the most beautiful sunsets in the Mediterranean, a daily event which draws thousands to witness the unbeatable drama laid on by nature. Ses Variades in Sant Antoni was the first to pair chillout with this special moment, and the music of the seashore venue is now known across the world. Famous DJs try out new rhythms on a spellbound audience, reaching their climax as the sun makes a majestic exit by the western isles, a thousand hearts beating as one to a round of applause.

At Platges de Compte nature is unaccompanied, simply a horizon of crystal-clear waters sprinkled with islands and bathed by the setting sun in a mantle of gold. White sand, breaking waves, and slanting rays invite you to bid the day a lingering farewell, perhaps with a dip in the sea or sipping cocktails at the water's edge.

In front of mighty Es Vedrà the sight of the sinking sun is a very personal experience. The vertical cliff, the massive outline of the colossus, the sea's mysterious tranquility and the silence of the surrounding landscape turns dusk into something that remains in the memory long after the magical moment has come and gone.

At Benirràs the experience is accompanied by the beating of drums. Families, couples and friends witness the courtship between sun and Cap Bernat, until the glowing orb sinks beneath the waves and disappears from sight. Drummers mark out every stage of this entrancing natural spectacle.

There are countless sunsets to choose from on Ibiza: at Cala Vedella, the cliffs of Sant Joan, below Cap des Falcó, at Cala de Bou and Puig de Missa (Santa Eulalia's ancient church), etc. And with each setting orb, a dream begins to unfold.

Explore the ancient salt ponds

Sabina woods, coastal dunes and silence surround walkers in Ses Salines, the Natural Park whose ancient salt ponds provide a refuge for all kinds of protected wildlife. The chance to take a quiet stroll in this area, discovering the island's rich biodiversity at the same time, draws naturalists, photographers, environmental teachers and local historians.

The park offers some interesting optional activities, such as guided walks and bird nesting days, although islanders would probably recommend strolling at your own rhythm, past the saline ponds, the gleaming mounds of salt, the church of Sant Francesc, on through the pinewoods and sabina thickets, until you emerge at last on the beaches of Es Cavallet, Es Codolar or Ses Salines.

This protected area also harbours a good slice of Pityusan history. Back in Phoenician times it was here that Ibiza's first industry took shape, and from the steep coastal cliffs limestone was quarried for the magnificent city walls. History and nature blend here in a walk which is as much for families or enterprising solitary walkers as it is for romantic travellers.

（资料来源：http://www.ibiza.travel/en）

Questions

1. What is the difference between Ibiza's parish churches and ecclesiastical buildings elsewhere?

2. Among all the beautiful sunsets introduced in the passage, which one sounds the most appealing to you? Why?

3. Ibiza has been a popular tourist destination. How do you think the World Heritage site may be protected from the development and commercialization of the main cities?

Mount Athos
阿索斯山

⇨ **简介**

所属国家：希腊（Greece）

入选时间：1988

入选标准：(i)(ii)(iv)(v)(vi)(vii)

Mount Athos is a mountain and peninsula in Macedonia, Greece. The transformation of a mountain into a sacred place made Mount Athos a unique artistic creation combining the natural beauty of the site with the expanded forms of architectural creation. Moreover, the monasteries of Athos are a veritable conservatory of masterpieces, ranging from wall paintings to portable icons, gold objects, embroideries, or illuminated manuscripts which each monastery preserves. Mount Athos exerted a lasting influence on the Orthodox world, of which it has been the spiritual centre since 1054, and on the development of religious architecture and monumental painting.

Mount Athos has enjoyed an autonomous statute since Byzantine times. The "Holy Mountain", which is forbidden to women and children, is also a recognized artistic site. The monasteries of Athos display the typical layout of Orthodox monastic establishments, which had an influence as far afield as Russia, and its school of painting influenced the history of Orthodox art.

The monastic ideal has at Mount Athos preserved traditional human habitations, which are representative of the agrarian cultures of the Mediterranean world and have become vulnerable through the impact of change within contemporary society. Mount Athos is also a conservatory of vernacular architecture and agricultural and craft traditions. Today Athos includes 20 monasteries, 12 sketes, and about 700 houses, cells, or hermitages. Over 1,400 monks live there in communities or alone, as well as in the "desert" of Karoulia where cells cling to the cliff face rising steeply above the sea.

阿索斯山,是希腊马其顿的一座半岛山。半岛上建有众多的修道院,各种大型建筑与自然风光交相辉映,使阿索斯山成为独一无二的艺术杰作。这些修道院精心保存着大量艺术宝藏,包括壁画、圣像、金器、刺绣品和古抄本珍品等。阿索斯山自 1054 年以来就是东正教世界的精神中心,对东正教及其宗教建筑、绘画的发展都产生了持久的影响。

自拜占庭时期起,阿索斯山就享有自治权,圣山上禁止妇女、儿童进入。这儿也是公认的艺术胜地。山上修道院的规划设计有着典型的东正教修道院建筑特色,它的影响力远至俄罗斯。其绘画流派甚至影响了东正教艺术史。

阿索斯山的修道院较好地保存了人类传统的居住模式,代表着地中海地区的农业文化。这种模式在现代社会变化的冲击下已越发脆弱。阿索斯山也是民间建筑、农业及手工业传统的宝库。如今,山上有 20 座修道院、12 个僧侣团,还有大约 700 处小型修道院,住着约 1400 名修道士,他们有的过着集体生活,有的独居,还有的生活在海边陡峭而荒芜的卡罗莱娜岩壁上的静修院中。

Vocabulary

1. veritable *adj.* 真正的,十足的,不折不扣的(用于强调大小、数量或性质等)

Thank you for that lovely meal; it was a veritable feast!

谢谢你的款待,真是名副其实的盛宴!

2. conservatory *n.* 玻璃暖房;展览温室;音乐学院;音乐专科学校

The original conservatory has been rebuilt in replica.

温室已按原样重建。

3. embroidery *n.* 绣花;刺绣品;刺绣

This exquisite embroidery won people's great admiration.

这件精美的绣品使人惊叹不已。

4. illuminated *adj.* (手稿、书、正式文件等)带彩色插图的,彩色稿本的;被照亮的;发光的

In the library you may find some illuminated manuscripts from the 12th to 16th centuries.

图书馆有一些 12 世纪到 16 世纪的彩色稿本。

5. autonomous *adj.* 自治的;独立自主的;有主见的

Each of the U. S. states has an autonomous government.

美国的每个州都有一个自治政府。

6. vernacular *adj.* (建筑)民间风格的

The research and preservation of traditional housing and vernacular architecture is becoming a hot topic.

传统民居和地域性建筑的研究和保护正成为比较热门的课题。

扩展阅读

Mount Athos

A thickly forested, mountainous ridge thirty miles long and two to five miles wide,

Athos is the easternmost of the three promontories of the Halkidiki Peninsula in Northern Greece. Known as Agion Oros, or the "Holy Mountain" in modern Greek, Athos is a semiautonomous republic of the Greek Orthodox church. Many hundreds of monks inhabit twenty large monasteries, smaller monastic houses and remote mountain caves. The religious history of Athos goes back long before the birth of Christianity however. The great marble peak of Mount Athos (6670 feet, 2033 meters) was mentioned as early as Homer and Aiskhylos as being the first home of the Greek gods Zeus and Apollo before they moved to Mount Olympus. Pagan hermits have lived in the deep forests since prehistoric times for it was known then, as it has been forgotten now, that places where the ancient gods had lived still held great powers for humans.

According to legends told by the monks of the Athonite monasteries, the Christian history of Mount Athos begins with the Virgin Mary. In AD 49, Mary set sail for the Island of Cyprus to visit her friend Lazurus. During her journey a great storm arose and Mary's ship, blown far off course, was guided by divine signs to a protected bay on the eastern coast of Athos. Gazing upward at the towering mountain and its beautiful forests, Mary declared, "This mountain is holy ground. Let it now be my portion. Here let me remain." Mooring her boat near the site of the present day monastery of Iveron, Mary came upon an ancient temple and oracle dedicated to Apollo. As she stepped ashore a great crashing sound resounded across the peninsula and all the idols and pagan statues came crashing to the ground (it is interesting to note that a well-documented earthquake occurred in northern Greece in AD 49). The great stone statue of Apollo spoke out, declaring itself a false idol and calling the forest hermits of Athos to come and pay homage to the Panaghia, the true mother of God. So the legend goes, Mary baptized the hermits and thus began the glorious Christian history of Mount Athos.

According to historical sources however, Athos first became a refuge for Christian hermits and anchorites in the 6th and 7th centuries, and during the 8th and 9th centuries these hermits began to gather together into small monastic communities. The era of the great monastic establishments began with the founding in AD 963 of the first and most renowned of the monasteries, the Great Lavra, on the southeast coast of Athos. Under the protection of the Byzantine emperors, the building of monasteries flourished until, at its zenith in the 15th century, Mount Athos harbored 40 monasteries and some 20,000 monks. When the Turkish armies captured nearby Thessaloniki in 1430, the monastic community prudently surrendered, thus remaining unplundered and relatively autonomous. The long period of Turkish rule brought about a decline and impoverishment of the monasteries that was later somewhat alleviated by the patronage of the Russian tsars in the 19th century. In 1926, a decree by the Greek government made the Monks Republic an official part of Greece while allowing it to retain an autonomous theocratic government. Since the 1950s there has been a gradual reawakening of interest in the monastic life and currently more than 3,000 monks live amongst the monasteries and forest hermitages of Athos.

Most of the monasteries are along the coastal lands and consist of a quadrangle of buildings enclosing a church. The churches contain some of the finest examples of Byzantine art, icons and treasure, and the monastery libraries hold a vast number of classical and medieval manuscripts. There are 17 Greek monasteries, 1 Russian, 1 Bulgarian, and 1 Serbian. While a few of the Greek monasteries have basic electricity, most function very much as they did in Medieval times. The monks grow their own food, spend long hours each day in prayer, and rarely venture off the peninsula. The author has spent time in 17 of the 20 monasteries and finds Mount Athos to be one of the most wonderful sacred places he has visited in the world.

An edict of the Emperor Constantine Manomachos in the year 1060, enforced to this day, forbids women from setting foot on the peninsula. This stringent exclusion of females applies to domestic animals as well. While some readers may deem the original edict foolish and its continued enforcement to perpetuate anachronistic patriarchal attitudes, it is important to note that Athos is one of the very few remaining places on the entire planet that has resisted the relentless culture-destroying machines of "modernization" and "social liberty". Furthermore, it is interesting to note that the entire Peninsula of Athos has preserved a richness and luxuriance of vegetation unique in Greece and all of Europe. For nearly ten centuries the fields have lain ungrazed by cattle, the trees have escaped the ravages of goats, and the flowers have been unpicked. In a world so rapidly being destroyed and homogenized by the "culture of progress" it is, for this author at least, refreshing to know that at least a few ancient human ecosystems are left intact and relatively undisturbed. The so-called "enlightened" attitudes of science and democracy have neither promised nor provided this. Greek Orthodox monasticism, on the other hand, has done so and, in the process, has protected a place with a rare, enchanting and powerful presence of peace.

（资料来源：http://sacredsites.com/europe/greece/mount_athos.html）

Questions

1. Briefly describe the Christian history of Mount Athos.

2. What do you think of the exclusion of females from Mount Athos? What is the sensible relationship between religion and modernization?

Natural and Cultural Heritage of the Ohrid Region
奥赫里德地区文化历史遗迹及其自然景观

⇨ 简介

所属国家：马其顿共和国（Former Yugoslav Republic of Macedonia）

入选时间：1979

入选标准：(i)(iii)(iv)(vii)

Situated on the eastern shores of Lake Ohrid, the town of Ohrid, the seventh largest city in the Republic of Macedonia, is one of the oldest human settlements in Europe. With its numerous prehistoric sites and its traces of the material culture of more than 5,000 years ago, Ohrid is indeed an archaeological treasury. More than 250 archaeological sites with material remains dating from between the Neolithic period and the late Middle Ages have been excavated.

Built mainly between the 7th and 19th centuries, it has the oldest Slav monastery (St Pantelejmon) and more than 800 Byzantine-style icons dating from the 11th century to the end of the 14th century. After those of the Tretiakov Gallery in Moscow, this is considered to be the most important collection of icons in the world. Ohrid is notable for having once had 365 churches, one for each day of the year and has been referred to as a "Jerusalem (of the Balkans)". Writing, education and Slavonic culture—all spread out from Ohrid in the 7th to 19th centuries. It is a cultural centre of great importance for the history not only of this part of the Balkan Peninsula, but also for all nations of the Slavonic tongue and for world history and literature, with precious manuscripts and other rarities. This city and its historic-cultural region are located in a natural setting of exceptional beauty, while its architecture represents the best preserved and most complete ensemble of ancient urban architecture of the Slavic lands.

奥赫里德镇坐落在奥赫里德湖东岸，是马其顿共和国第七大城市。这儿是欧洲最古老的人类聚居地之一。众多的史前遗址和5000多年前的物质文明遗迹，使奥赫里德镇成为考古学的宝库。迄今为止，考古学家在此发掘出250余处新石器时代至中世纪后期的遗迹。

奥赫里德镇主要建于公元7世纪至19世纪，拥有最古老的古斯拉夫修道院——圣潘特莱捷门修道院，以及800多幅11世纪至14世纪末的拜占庭风格的画像。奥赫里德镇被誉为仅次于莫斯科托里托拉可夫画廊之后世界上最重要的收藏地。值得一提的是，这儿曾建有365座修道院，一年365天可以每天去一座不同的修道院，因此也被称为"巴尔干的耶路撒冷"。公元7—19世纪，奥赫里德镇的写作、教育和斯拉夫文化得到广泛传播。无数的珍贵手稿和其他珍品，使之不仅成为巴尔干半岛历史上重要的文化中心，更对所有斯拉夫语国家乃至世界历史和文学都产生了深远影响。奥赫里德镇及其历史文化地区自然风光优美，其建筑也是斯拉夫地区保存最好、最完整的古代城市建筑群。

Vocabulary

1. treasury *n.* （城堡、教堂等的）宝库，珍藏室

This book is a treasury of useful information.

这本书是有价值的信息宝库。

2. excavate *v.* 发掘，挖掘（古物等）；挖；开凿

It took a long time to excavate the ancient city of Troy.

挖掘古老的特洛伊城，花了很长时间。

3. Byzantine *adj.* 拜占庭的；拜占庭帝国的；（体制、程序）拜占庭式的，错综复杂的

The Byzantine Empire in theory represented the whole Christian world.

从理论上说，拜占庭帝国代表了整个基督教世界。

4. peninsula *n.* 半岛

It is difficult to imagine how the north and south could ever agree on a formula to unify the divided peninsula.

很难想象南北双方在统一半岛的方案上究竟怎样才能达成一致。

5. rarity *n.* 罕见的人（或物）；奇物；珍品；稀有；罕见

Women are still something of a rarity in senior positions in business.

在商界，位居高职的妇女仍然十分罕见。

扩展阅读

Ohrid—the City and the Lake

The city of the immortal Ohrid is the sublime lakeside point that for many represents the culmination of the Macedonian experience, a kingdom of light and water, a repository of ancient ruins from Macedonia's earlier kingdoms.

Ohrid's major attractions are all located within a remarkably concentrated and eminently walkable area, among and above the narrow streets of the old town lined with restaurants and cafés perfectly suited for relaxing in the cool summer evenings. Ohrid's many café bars and nightclubs also make for a vibrant nightlife.

As for the lake itself, it is so large and so deep that one might mistake it for a small sea. Full range of water sports, fishing and boating is available, and numerous churches alongside Ohrid's lake shores make for fascinating side trips and walks.

The wooded ridge above the lake's eastern shore is largely taken up by the National Park of Galichica, an unspoiled wilderness ideally suitable for nature enthusiasts.

The uniqueness of Lake Ohrid and the city's historical architecture has been attested by UNESCO, honoring it with an official designation as one of the few places on the cultural institution's list "World Inheritance".

Archaeological finds indicate that Ohrid is one of the oldest human settlements in all of Europe. The lake itself is over three million years old. Ohrid town is first mentioned in Greek documents from 353 BC, when it was known as Lychnidos or "the city of light". Only much later in AD 879, was it renamed Ohrid. The name probably derives from the Macedonian phrase "Vo Hrid"—roughly meaning "the town on the hill".

Apart from its ancient theater (which is still in use today), the ancient Lychnidos boasted a classical agora, gymnasium, civil basilicas and temples to the Gods of Greek Antiquity. When under Roman rule it developed more of the typical Roman architectural traits, and became an important transit point on the Via Egnatia trade route that bisected the Balkans.

The town as we know it today was built mostly between the 7th and 19th centuries. During the Byzantine period, Ohrid became a significant cultural and economic center serving as an Episcopal center of the Orthodox Church and as the site of the first Slavic university run by St Clement and St Naum at the end of the 9th century. At the beginning of the 11th century, Ohrid briefly became the capital of Macedonia's greatest medieval ruler, Samuel, whose fortress still presides over the city today.

During Ottoman times Ohrid remained the seat of the autocephalous Ohrid archiepiscopacy until 1726. During its Byzantine apogee, the town was renowned for its 365 churches and monasteries. These and a large number of sacral edifices have been preserved and make up a large part of Ohrid's rich Medieval past.

Today, one of the city's museums has a collection of more than 800 Byzantine and post-Byzantine icons, most of which were painted between the 11th and 14th centuries. Art historians consider this collection as one of the most important in the world, along with those of the Tretiakov Gallery in Moscow and Mount Athos in Greece.

（资料来源：http://www. exploringmacedonia. com/? ItemID＝D7B9801599F86 A45895CDBE20C3565BF&4ACF4279BF01504086095A7DE28FBBF4＝1）

Questions

1. If you were a tourist, how would you plan your stay in Ohrid?

2. It's said that if one is looking for fun, history, adventure and romance, the city of Ohrid is the place to see. Do you agree? Please explain.

第四节　欧洲的世界文化景观遗产

Jurisdiction of Saint-Emilion
圣艾米伦区

简介

所属国家：法国（France）

入选时间：1999

入选标准：（iii），（iv）

Saint-Emilion is a commune in the Gironde department in Aquitaine in southwestern France. It was granted the special status of a "jurisdiction" during the period of English rule in the 12th century. The Jurisdiction of Saint-Emilion is an outstanding example a historic vineyard landscape that has survived intact and in activity to the present day.

Viticulture was introduced to this fertile region of Aquitaine by the Roman Emperor Augustus, who created the province of Aquitania in 27 BC with the first vineyards by grafting new varieties of grape on the Vitis biturica that grew naturally in the region. The town was named after the monk Emilion, who settled in a hermitage there in the 8th century. It was the monks who followed him that started up the commercial wine production in the area. This industry intensified in the Middle Ages, when the Saint-Emilion area benefited from its location on the pilgrimage route to Santiago de Compostela and many churches, monasteries and hospices were built there from the 11th century onwards. It is an exceptional landscape devoted entirely to wine-growing, with many fine historic monuments in its towns and villages. In the 18th century, the quality of the Saint-Emilion wines was recognized as exceptional. Saint-Emilion has also been noteworthy for its innovations, such as the establishment of the first wine syndicate in 1884 and the first cooperative cellars in the Gironde in 1932. At the present time the Saint-Emilion vineyards produce an average of 230,00 hectolitres of wine (all red) annually, representing 10% of the AOC wines of the Gironde.

圣艾米伦区是法国西南部阿基坦地区吉伦特省的一个市镇。在 12 世纪英国统治期间,这里得到了"司法管辖区域"的特殊地位。圣艾米伦区是历史上得以完整保存且至今仍活跃的葡萄园的杰出典范。葡萄栽培技术最早由罗马皇帝奥古斯塔斯引入阿基坦地区这片肥沃的土地上:公元前 27 年,他创建了阿奎塔尼亚省,并通过移植该地天然生长的比图里吉新种葡萄而建立了第一批葡萄园。8 世纪,一位名叫艾米伦的修士隐居在当地的修道院,该地区因此得名。艾米伦修士的追随者们开始在当地从事葡萄酒的商业性酿造。中世纪时,圣艾米伦区的葡萄种植业得以长足发展,该地区位于圣地亚哥-德孔波斯特拉朝圣之路上,因其地理位置优越而受益匪浅,从 11 世纪开始,这里便修建了大量教堂、修道院和济贫院。大量的葡萄种植在这里形成了独特的景观,而且在乡镇和村庄里还有许多优美的历史古迹。18 世纪,该地区葡萄酒的优良品质得到公认。圣艾米伦区的葡萄酒酿造还以其创新著称,如 1884 年建立第一家葡萄酒辛迪加,1932 年在吉伦特建立了第一批合作酒窖。现在,圣艾米伦区的葡萄园平均年产红葡萄酒 230 万公升,占吉伦特省 AOC 等级(注:原产地命名控制)葡萄酒产量的 10%。

Vocabulary

1. jurisdiction *n.* 管辖区域;管辖范围;司法权;审判权;管辖权

It hardly falls within the area under the police station's jurisdiction.

它几乎不在该派出所的辖区之内。

2. viticulture *n.* 葡萄栽培;葡萄种植业

This is far from the only example of successful modern tropical viticulture.

这不是现代热带葡萄栽培的唯一成功例子。

3. pilgrimage *n.* 朝圣;朝觐;拜谒;重要旅程

Many people go on a pilgrimage to Mecca or Jerusalem.

许多人前往麦加或耶路撒冷朝圣。

4. hospice *n.* (宗教团体开办的)旅客招待所;(晚期病人的)安养院

They have started a hospice for terminal patients.

他们为身患绝症的病人开办了一个安养所。

5. syndicate *n.* 辛迪加；私人联合会；企业联合组织

A syndicate of local businessmen is bidding for the contract.

一个当地企业家的联合组织在向这一合同投标。

6. hectolitre *n.* 一百公升

Profits per hectolitre in China were US $30 last year compared with a global average of US $100.

中国每百升(啤酒)的酿造利润是 30 美元，而全球平均水平为 100 美元。

扩展阅读

Saint-Emilion Wine

Saint-Emilion is a key wine town in the Libournais district of Bordeaux, important in terms of both quality and quantity. It lies just a few miles north of the Dordogne river, in the final stages of its journey from the hills of the Massif Central to the Gironde Estuary. The town is renowned as much for its beautiful buildings and scenery as for its wine. Its steep, narrow, cobbled streets, overlooked by its Romanesque church and the iconic 13th-century Tour du Roy tower, are a reminder of the town's long history.

There have vineyards around Saint-Emilion since Roman times, and today the Saint-Emilion wine appellation is one of the most prolific in the Bordeaux region, generating more than 250,000 hL of wine each vintage. It is also responsible for some of the most prestigious, long-lived and expensive wines in the world; Chateaux Cheval Blanc, Ausone, Angelus, Figeac and Pavie, whose wines sell for hundreds of dollars per bottle, are all situated in and around Saint-Emilion.

Unlike the wines of the Medoc (which focus heavily on Cabernet Sauvignon), Saint-Emilion wines are predominately made from Merlot and Cabernet Franc. The other traditional Bordeaux varieties (Cabernet Sauvignon, Carmenere, Petit Verdot and Malbec) are permitted for use here, but are rarely used to any significant extent. This is not so much a question of taste and style as one of terroir; the clay and chalk-rich soils around Saint-Emilion are generally cooler than those on the Medoc Peninsula, so they are less capable of ripening Cabernet Sauvignon reliably. Merlot makes up the majority (about 65%) of vines planted around Saint-Emilion, and continues to increase in popularity because of the softer, more approachable wine styles it produces. There are two notable exceptions to this: Chateaux Cheval Blanc, where Cabernet Franc occupies 58% of the vineyard area, and Chateau Figeac, where Merlot, Cabernet Franc and (more usually) Cabernet Sauvignon enjoy equal representation in both vineyard and wine.

On the whole, the prevalence of Merlot in Saint-Emilion means that its wines are approachable at an earlier age than their more astringent, tannin-rich cousins from the Medoc. This is a key factor in their appeal and popularity in markets all around the world, and particularly in the United States.

Geologically speaking, Saint-Emilion can be divided into three main areas. The most significant is the limestone plateau on which Saint-Emilion town is located, and the slopes around it. Most of the very top vineyards and Chateaux are located here, within a mile of the town (Cheval Blanc and Figeac again provide two notable exceptions to the rule).

Immediately south of the limestone plateau is the alluvial, sandy plain which slopes gently down to the banks of the Dordogne. Few wines of any note are produced here, and none of the Grand Cru Classes properties are located here.

In the north western corner of the Saint-Emilion area is an ancient alluvial terrace, formed by glacial activity at the very beginning of the Quaternary period roughly 2 million years ago. This boasts the same free-draining "gunzian" gravels as are found in the best properties of the Graves and Medoc, which explains why the two most famous chateaux here (Cheval Blanc and Figeac) are able to grow and ripen both Cabernet Franc and Cabernet Sauvignon. This terrace—known as the Graves de Saint-Emilion—continues westwards into neighboring Pomerol, and underpins the vineyards of such revered estates as Le Pin and Petrus.

Saint-Emilion has four "satellites": Lussac-Saint-Emilion, Saint-Georges-Saint-Emilion, Puisseguin-Saint-Emilion and Montagne-Saint-Emilion. These cover distinct, slightly smaller areas immediately to the northeast of Saint-Emilion proper, and each has its own independent appellation title.

Saint-Emilion also has a Grand Cru appellation (Saint-Emilion Grand Cru), which imposes slightly tighter production restrictions. This has been the subject of much criticism since its introduction in 1954, as the restrictions are widely viewed as being too loose to warrant the use of Grand Cru—a title used in other regions only for the very finest wines or vineyard sites. Peculiarly, twice as much Saint-Emilion Grand Cru wine is made each year than regular Saint-Emilion. Fortunately, the Saint-Emilion Wine Classification system performs the task of marking out the area's top-tier wines. This works in much the same way as the classification of the Medoc, Graves and Sauternes, but with one significant difference: it is periodically reviewed to keep it up-to-date and relevant. It was first drawn up in 1955, and (after a controversial review in 2006) was most recently updated in 2012.

（资料来源：http://www.wine-searcher.com/regions-saint-emilion）

Questions

1. What can you learn about French wines, especially Saint-Emilion wines, from the above passage?

2. How does the geology of Saint-Emilion influence its wine industry?

Kalwaria Zebrzydowska: the Mannerist Architectural and Park Landscape Complex and Pilgrimage Park

卡瓦利-泽布日多夫斯津：别具一格的建筑园林景观群及朝圣公园

⇨ 简介

所属国家：波兰(Poland)

入选时间：1999

入选标准：(ii)，(iv)

Kalwaria Zebrzydowska, situated in southern Poland, is a breathtaking cultural landscape of great spiritual significance. Its natural setting—in which a series of symbolic places of worship relating to the Passion of Jesus Christ and the life of the Virgin Mary was laid out at the beginning of the 17th century—has remained virtually unchanged. The Counter Reformation in the late 16th century led to a flowering in the creation of Calvaries in Europe. Kalwaria Zebrzydowska is an outstanding example of this type of large-scale landscape design, which incorporates natural beauty with spiritual objectives and the principles of Baroque park design. Work on building the Calvary was begun in 1600 by Mikolaj Zebrzydowski. Later, he was persuaded to enlarge his original concept to cover an extensive landscape complex with many chapels, linked in form and theme to those in Jerusalem. It was conceived as being for the use not only of the local inhabitants but also of believers from elsewhere in Poland and in neighbouring countries. The layout was based on the landscape of Jerusalem at the time of Christ, using a system of measurement to enable the urban landscape of Jerusalem to be reproduced symbolically on the natural landscape. The result is a cultural landscape of great beauty and spiritual quality in which natural and man-made elements combine in a harmonious manner. It is still today a sacred place of pilgrimage.

卡瓦利-泽布日多夫斯津位于波兰南部，是一处将美丽风景和宗教内涵融于一身的文化景观。它的自然布景几乎完美地保留下来，其中包括一系列建于17世纪初的具有象征意义的宫殿，它们反映了耶稣受难及圣母玛丽亚的生平。16世纪末的反宗教改革运动使得修建耶稣礼拜堂在欧洲盛行起来。卡瓦利-泽布日多夫斯津正是这种大规模建筑景观设计的杰出典范，在这里，自然美景、宗教目的和巴洛克式园林设计完美地结合在一起。至今它仍然是人们朝圣礼拜的场所。1600年，米克莱·泽布日多夫斯基开始兴建新的耶稣礼拜堂。随后，在别人劝说下，他决定扩建其原设计规划，修建许多在形式及主题上都与耶路撒冷有关的小教堂，从而形成一个广阔的建筑景观群。这样的构思不仅方便当地居民朝拜耶稣，也使波兰其他地方甚至邻国的信徒可以来此朝拜。卡瓦利-泽布日多夫斯津的布局参照基督时期耶路撒冷的景观，设计者运用一种独特的测量方法,使耶路撒冷的城市特征象征性地再现于卡瓦利-泽布日多夫斯津的自然景观中,于是形成了该地自然风景和人造景观和谐共处、自然和宗教并重的文化景观。至今,这儿仍是朝圣圣地。

Vocabulary

1. virtually *adv.* 几乎;实际上;事实上;差不多

It would have been virtually impossible to research all the information.

要对所有的信息进行分析研究几乎是不可能的。

2. chapel *n.* 小教堂;(教堂里的)私人祈祷室

He built a chapel as a shrine to the memory of his dead wife.

他建了一座小教堂,作为悼念亡妻的圣地。

3. conceive *v.* 构思;设想;想出;认为;想象;相信

He conceived of the first truly portable computer in 1968.

1968 年,他构想出第一台真正的便携式计算机。

4. layout *n.* 布置;设计;布局

This boat has a good deck layout making everything easy to operate.

这艘船的甲板布局合理,使得所有操控都很方便。

扩展阅读

Sanctuary in Kalwaria Zebrzydowska

The Sanctuary in Kalwaria Zebrzydowska in Poland was one of Pope John Paul II's favourite places of pilgrimage. Situated in the foothills of the Carpathian Mountains 33km from Krakow, it was established in 1600 as Poland's first Calvary sanctuary to offer Christian pilgrims an alternative to Jerusalem that had been acquired by Muslim Turks.

It's humble origins began as quaint chapel dedicated to the Crucifixion of Christ, followed by a chalk model of the Chapel of the Holy Cross in Jerusalem. Over the next two centuries the sanctuary would become the largest pilgrimage site in Europe and today receives over a million visitors a year, making it one of the most visited places in Poland and is named among UNESCO's list of World Heritage sites.

Recognized as one of the most fascinating architectural projects in Europe, this vast complex features 42 churches and chapels including the domineering 17th century baroque Basilica dedicated to the Angelic Mother of God in the centre and the adjoining Franciscan monastery.

Pilgrimages to the Kalwaria sanctuary best exemplify Polish grassroots Catholicism. Pilgrims usually come in large groups to pray and contemplate together. The sanctuary complex gets very busy during Christian holidays and celebrations, particularly Good Friday and Assumption day on the 15th August. During the festivals visitors are treated to plays portraying the Passion of Christ and Our Lady's Life Mysteries.

The Kalwaria Zebrzydowska used to be the home of the Order of Friars Minor, a brotherhood of Franciscan monks. In the 20th century they were joined by High and Low Religious Seminary's, but they have since moved to Lodz. The current inhabitant of the sanctuary is an official Franciscan Publishing House called Calvarianum. Its books popularize the religious values and ideas of St Francis of Assisi together with books and albums connected with Pope John Paul II.

The Calvary sanctuary, immensely popular with pilgrims from the outset, soon gave rise to the town of Kalwaria Zebrzydowska that has also been famous for its cabinetmakers since the mid 18th century.

Nowadays some 1,500 artisans manufacture classy furniture, customized and largely hand-made, in the town of 4,500 or so. Every July they exhibit their skill at month-long furniture fairs.

（资料来源：http://www. krakow-poland. com/krakow-tourist-information/krakow-and-surrounding-areas/sanctuary-in-kalwaria-zebrzydowska, http://www. krakow-info. com/kalwaria. htm）

Questions

1. What was the purpose of building the Calvary sanctuary in Kalwaria Zebrzydowska?

2. What are some of the important festivals in Kalwaria Zebrzydowska? What do pilgrims usually do on these festivals?

Pyrénées—Mount Perdu
比利牛斯-珀杜山

🖙 **简介**

所属国家：法国、西班牙（France, Spain）

入选时间：1997

入选标准：(iii), (iv), (v), (vii), (viii)

This outstanding mountain landscape, which spans the contemporary national borders of France and Spain, is centred around the peak of Mount Perdu, a calcareous massif that rises to 3,352 m. The site, with a total area of 30,639 ha, includes two of Europe's largest and deepest canyons on the Spanish side and three major cirque walls on the more abrupt northern slopes with France, classic presentations of these geological landforms. With meadows, lakes, caves and forests on mountain slopes, the area is scenic and of high interest to science and conservation. There are also climatic differences between the northern and southern slopes. The French side is humid whereas the Spanish slopes are dryer. Climate also varies from the west (maritime influence) to the east (coastal Mediterranean climate). Located between two seas, their geological structure and the climatic asymmetries of the Pyrénées result in a rich mosaic of vegetation types, supporting many wildlife species typical of the Pyrénées. The site is also a pastoral landscape reflecting a socio-economic structure that has its roots in the past and illustrates a mountain way of life that has become rare in Europe. This agricultural way of life was once widespread in the upland regions of Europe but now survives only in this part of the Pyrénées. Thus it provides exceptional insights into past European society through its landscape of villages, farms, fields, upland pastures and mountain roads.

这处雄伟壮观的高山景观,横跨法国与西班牙当前的国界,以海拔 3352 米的石灰质山——珀杜山顶峰为中心,方圆 30639 公顷。在西班牙境内的是欧洲两个最大最深的峡谷,而在法国境内更加陡峭的北坡上则是三个大片环形屏障,充分代表了这里的地质地貌。山坡上的草地、湖泊、洞穴和森林构成了一派山地美景,在科学及环保方面都有极高的价值。山区各处气候不同:南坡(法国境内)较湿润,而北坡(西班牙境内)较干燥;东麓受海洋气候影响,西麓则是地中海气候。比利牛斯山位于地中海和大西洋之间,其地质结构和气候的不对称性使得该地有丰富的植被种类,为比利牛斯山特有的各种野生动物提供了充足的食物。这个地区还有着恬静的田园风光,反映了一种现已罕见的欧洲山区的古老社会经济结构:这种曾在欧洲高地非常普遍的农业生活方式,而今却仅存于比利牛斯地区。在这里,可以通过村庄、农场、原野、高地牧场和崎岖的山路等独特的景观,去回顾久远的欧洲社会。

Vocabulary

1. calcareous *adj.* 含碳酸钙的,钙质的;石灰质的

The soil is thin and calcareous, making agriculture very difficult.

这些岛的土壤很薄,而且是石灰质的,要发展农业非常困难。

2. massif *n.* 山峦;群山

But I find an easier route down, a route that takes me right under the limestone massif.

不过我挑了条好走一些的道路,直接下到这座石灰石山丘的下面。

3. cirque *n.* 环谷;冰斗;圆环,盆地

Others simply relax in the sun-washed glacial cirque and bask in the presence of the peak.

其他人则仅仅在沐浴着阳光的冰斗中放松,在峰峦面前晒晒太阳。

4. asymmetry *n.* 不对称;不匀称

In some cases the knowledge asymmetry is relatively transient.

在某些情况下,知识不对称是相对暂时的。

5. mosaic *n.* 马赛克;镶嵌图案;拼花图案

The sky this morning is a mosaic of blue and white.

今天早上的天空是一幅蓝白相间的画面。

6. pastoral *adj.* 田园式的;畜牧的;放牧的;牧师的

The ancient vase was painted with pastoral scenes.

这古老的花瓶上绘饰着田园景色。

扩展阅读

Midi-Pyrénées

The Midi-Pyrénées region covers a large portion of Southwest France, between the Atlantic and the Mediterranean. It is made up of 8 departments: Ariège, Aveyron, Haute-Garonne, Hautes-Pyrénées, Gers, Lot, Tarn and Tarn-et-Garonne. Toulouse, its capital city, with 437,000 inhabitants, is France's third-largest university town and the birthplace of Airbus, the world's leading aircraft manufacturer.

The Capitole building, Saint-Sernin basilica, musée des Augustins, musée des Abattoirs modern and contemporary art museum and the Cité de l'Espace are just a few of Toulouse's great attractions.

Great sites of Midi-Pyrénées

Midi-Pyrénées has gained international fame on account of its great sites such as the Millau viaduct, the Pic du Midi and its astronomy observatory, the cirque de Gavarnie, the Canal du Midi and Albi (and the Toulouse-Lautrec museum) which is a UNESCO World Heritage site, Lourdes and its Marian city, Cahors and Valentré bridge, as well as Conques, Rocamadour, Cordes-sur-Ciel, Moissac, Saint-Bertrand-de-Comminges, Marciac and this jazz festival, Figeac, Auch … Midi-Pyrénées features 24 emblematic great sites which are rich with historical, cultural or natural interest.

Landscape

The Midi-Pyrénées is a very spacious region with vast horizons, undulating countryside punctuated with hillsides and valleys and spectacular landscapes such as the gorges du Tarn, gorges de l'Aveyron, Lot valley and Dordogne valley. In the south, the region rests against the Pyrénées mountain range with its great peaks reaching 3,000m altitude, running along the border between France and Spain.

With an average 2,000 hours sunlight per year, Midi-Pyrénées is one of France's sunniest regions. Spring comes early, followed by summer which is often very hot and then a beautiful autumn season which continues until the first mountain snowfalls.

Heritage and nature: tours and activities

The Midi-Pyrénées safeguards an important heritage from the Middle Ages and Renaissance period, from the Templar and Hospitaller citadels in Larzac to the 16th century hotels particuliers in Toulouse. The region is crossed by the three main Saint-Jacques-de-Compostelle pilgrimage routes and is marked by the crusade against the Cathars, traces of which are to be found at emblematic sites such as the Montségur castle in Ariège. The castles, Medieval villages, bastide towns, and Roman cathedrals and churches are wonderful sites illustrating the rich diversity of a well-conserved heritage.

With its 26,000km of signposted trails, the Pyrenees National Park and four regional nature reserves, Midi-Pyrénées is a destination that revolves around nature and discovery, lending itself to a wide range of activities such as hiking, cyclotourism, horse trekking and white water sports.

Tourism activity is also developing along the region's waterways, with the rivers and canals of the Midi, including the Canal du Midi, forming one of southern Europe's largest river networks.

Skiing and board sports can also be enjoyed in Midi-Pyrénées, which is famous for its thermal bath resorts and well-being centres. Thermal bath resorts in the Midi-Pyrénées can be found in towns such as Luchon, Cauterets, Barèges, Bagnères-de-Bigorre, Ax-les-Thermes and Barbotan-les-Thermes.

Gastronomy and craftwork

Midi-Pyrénées is famous for a wide selection of fine produce such as Roquefort, foie gras, Quercy black truffles and saffron. Organic farming is becoming increasingly widespread in the region, which boasts around a hundred products with official quality labels such as AOC Chasselas grapes, Lautrec pink garlic and Quercy farm-reared lamb. Such products can be found at local markets which thrive in the majority of villages and towns across the region.

Midi-Pyrénées is a land of vineyards, producing high-quality wines such as AOC Cahors, Gaillac and Madiran and of course the well-renowned Armagnac produced in D'Artagnan's Gascony.

Midi-Pyrénées craftsmanship, inherited from time-honoured methods, has gained recognition both in France and internationally on account of creations such as Laguiole knives, Millau gloves and Revel furniture.

Festivals

Midi-Pyrénées has an active cultural and festive agenda, with around one hundred festivals organised each year dedicated to music, cinema, photography, astronomy, circus arts, etc. Such festivals include international events such as the jazz in Marciac festival, the country music festival in Mirande, Tempo Latino in Vic-Fezensac, the Sylvanès sacred music festival and the Rio Loco festival in Toulouse.

Accommodation

Midi-Pyrénées welcomes holiday makers in almost 1,300 hotels ranging from 2 to 4 stars, and in 600 campsites, many of which offer chalets and bungalows. There is also a wide selection of 1,000 guest houses and 13,000 gîtes for rent, the majority of which have been beautifully renovated in keeping with their rich rural heritage.

The inhabitants of Midi-Pyrénées can often be recognised by their southern accent and have a reputation for being spontaneous, friendly and sometimes brisk-natured, by and large bon viveurs, warmly hospitable and passionately enthusiastic about their trade or local environment.

（资料来源：http://cn. franceguide. com/partners/CRT-Midi-Pyrenees. html？ NodeID＝

Questions

1. If you were a tourist, what would you like to do in Midi-Pyrénées?
2. What kind of heritage can we find in Midi-Pyrénées?

Royal Botanic Gardens，Kew
伦敦基尤皇家植物园

➩ **简介**

所属国家：英国（The United Kingdom of Great Britain and Northern Ireland）

入选时间：2003

入选标准：(ii)，(iii)，(iv)

Set amongst a series of parks and estates along the River Thames' southwestern reaches, this historic landscape garden features elements that illustrate significant periods of the art of gardens from the 18th to 20th centuries. Since their creation in 1759, the Royal Botanic Gardens have made a significant and uninterrupted contribution to the study of plant diversity, plant systematics and economic botany. The gardens house extensive botanic collections (conserved plants, living plants and documents) that have been considerably enriched through the centuries. The first botanic garden at Kew was originally founded for medical plants. In the 18th century, internationally renowned architects, such as William Chambers and "Capability" Brown, not only created many edifices, but also remodelled the earlier Baroque gardens to make a pastoral landscape in the English style, establishing a fashion that then spread throughout the continent. The essential elements of the landscape garden designed by William Nesfield are one of the outstanding features of Kew. This garden is centred on an iron and glass structure, the Palm House (1844—1848), the first large-scale structural use of wrought iron. The temperate house, which is twice as large as the Palm House, followed later in the 19th century. It is now the largest Victorian glasshouse in existence. As the number of visitors increased, the scientific collections were enriched and glasshouses and spaces were altered to house living plant collections. Kew's exceptional and diverse living collections exemplify the active European cultural tradition of collecting and cultivating exotic plants for aesthetic, scientific and economic purpose.

伦敦基尤皇家植物园包括泰晤士河西南流域的一系列公园和庄园，是 18 到 20 世纪园林艺术发展最辉煌阶段的完美体现。自从 1759 年建立起，基尤皇家植物园就不断为植物多样性、植物分类学和经济植物学研究做出杰出贡献。经过了几个世纪的大量积累，现在植物园拥有极其丰富的有关植物学的收藏（包括植物标本、活的植物和文献）。1759 年建立的第一个植物园位于基尤，最初是药用植物园。18 世纪，一批享誉世界的建筑大师，如威廉·钱伯斯和"能人"布朗,不仅为植物园建造出许多新的建筑,还将早期的巴洛克式建筑重新塑造为带有英式田园风情的建筑,从而创建了一种风靡整个欧洲大陆的建筑风尚。由威廉·奈斯菲尔德设计的景观园林是基尤皇家植物园的标志性建筑,园林中间的玻璃和钢铁结构的棕榈室(建于 1844—1848 年),是第一次将锻铁用于大规模建筑构架。19 世纪建成的温带植物室,比棕榈室大一倍,是现存最大的维多利亚时代植物温室。随着植物园的游客日益增多,园内的科学收藏不断丰富,玻璃温室和空地也改建为活植物收集区。基尤皇家植物园收集了各种各样的植物,是欧洲人出于审美、科学和经济目的而收集、培养异域植物这一传统的典范。

Vocabulary

1. botanic *adj.* 植物学的,植物的

This picture shows how the botanic roots go deep into soil.

这张照片显示植物的根是如何深入土壤里去的。

2. systematics *n.* 分类学,分类法,系统学

Perhaps this subdivision does not meet completely the point of view of scientifically exact systematics.

这样的分类方法也许并不完全是科学上的严密的分类方法。

3. temperate *adj.* (气候)温和的;(地区)温带的;(行为)温和的,心平气和的

Perhaps a thousand of them live in one of the largest coastal temperate rain forest in the world.

其中大概有一千只生活在这个世界上最大的沿海温带雨林区域之一。

4. exemplify *v.* 作为……的例证;是……的典范

Nothing can exemplify this better than the problem of pollution.

没有什么比污染问题这个例子更能说明问题的了。

5. exotic *adj.* 具有异国情调的;外来的;奇异的

We saw pictures of exotic birds from the jungle of Brazil.

我们看到了来自于巴西热带雨林的各种奇异鸟类的照片。

扩展阅读

If We Save Our Trees, We Save Our Souls

Today, as over 1. 35 million people have done this year, I will take a stroll around Kew Gardens. Kew may be a global tourist magnet, but it started life as an idyllic escape, a hunting park from which Henry Ⅷ's court could escape the festering capital. George Ⅲ's parents, Prince Frederick and Princess Augusta, began a garden around Kew Palace. Under Queen Victoria's patronage, Kew became integral to the expanding empire, supplying seeds, crops, personnel and horticultural lessons to the globe.

Britain may no longer rule the world, but these Royal Botanic Gardens remain a powerhouse for botanical scientific research, plant conservation and cataloguing. There is barely a conservation project on the planet that does not depend upon its 253 years of investigation.

Still, for my money, one goes to Kew for the trees: over 14,000 across its 132 hectares. Some walkers favour the lavish excesses of summer, all dappled light on a sea of green. However, deep December holds its charms, not least for being able to see the shape of matters, the wood from the trees, ravelling in the beauties of bark and bud.

The American poet Joyce Kilmer's much-parodied 1913 lyric *Trees* ("I think that I shall never see/A poem as lovely as a tree") was a winter creation, inspired by hibernal boughs, "Upon whose bosom snow has lain; / Who intimately lives with rain." And there is a pleasing solidarity between the winter walker-ruddy-cheeked, bitten fingered— and these giants of landscape, stalwart where all other vegetation lays low.

Perhaps this is why we Brits identify so fundamentally with trees: witness the collective horror over Chalara fraxinea, which causes ash dieback, discovered in woods in East Anglia in October. In a form of arboreal anthropomorphism, trees remind us of ourselves—and our best selves at that: our robust, blitz-spirited, stoutly virtuous guise. We like to imagine ourselves as being solid as oak, that it takes much to fell us.

Britain's 80m-strong ash population has previously proved no less doughty. Ash is our third most commercial wood, a robust coppice species, the best furnace material, a straight, hardwood perfect for making tools, plough and plank. Ash supplied the arrows of Agincourt, the first furnaces of the industrial revolution. And it is beautiful, of course.

Long before hippies were deemed "tree-huggers", ashes bewitched us. Sick children were passed through its clefts, saints' staffs morphing miraculously into ash trees. As every schoolchild knows, the ash supports complex ecosystems. However, it no less supports humans, in spirit as much as oxygen emissions.

Today, as I admire the stately ashes of Kew's Princess Walk, I will do so while undertaking a series of resolutions. I am not merely going to wring my hands over dieback, I will campaign for commercial import bans as advocated by historical ecologist Professor Oliver Rackham. I will respect the fact that, in the same way that hunting created many of our forests, so it conserves them (my arboriculturalist brother, like many tree specialists, is also a qualified deer stalker—to save trees, one must manage deer).

I will engage charitably by joining the Woodland Trust, Royal Forestry Society, Trees for Cities and, of course, Kew. I will visit some of Britain's 5,500 woods, and the parklands of London, Birmingham and Sheffield (which boasts the highest number of trees per head in Europe). For the first time in 30 years, I will go about with a spotter's guide in my pocket. And I will hope that ash dieback will prove a spur for all of us to think more deeply about trees, because somewhere I maintain a lingering pagan intuition that, if we save our trees, we save our souls.

（资料来源：http://www.guardian.co.uk/commentisfree/2012/dec/26/save-trees-souls-british-identify-ash）

Questions

1. Briefly describe the significant roles of the Royal Botanic Gardens.

2. Why does the writer maintain that if we save our trees, we save our souls? How can we save our trees?

Cultural Landscape of Sintra
辛特拉文化景观

➯ 简介

所属国家：葡萄牙（Portugal）

入选时间：1995

入选标准：(ii)，(iv)，(v)

Sintra is a town in the Lisbon Region of Portugal. In the 19th century Sintra became the first center of European Romantic architecture. Ferdinand Ⅱ turned a ruined monastery into a castle where this new sensitivity was displayed in the use of Gothic, Egyptian, Moorish and Renaissance elements and in the creation of a park blending local and exotic species of trees. Other fine dwellings, built along the same lines in the surrounding serra, created a unique combination of parks and gardens. Although almost all the built heritage was destroyed in the 1755 earthquake, there are some outstanding court and military buildings, examples of religious architecture and archaeological sites, among which the Royal Palace, a fine example of this Mudejar technique on the Iberian Peninsula, is undoubtedly the dominant architectural feature. The cultural landscape of the Serra and the town of Sintra represents a pioneering approach to Romantic landscaping that had an outstanding influence on developments elsewhere in Europe. It is a unique example of the cultural occupation of a specific location that has maintained its essential integrity as the representation of diverse successive cultures. Its structures harmonize indigenous flora with a refined and cultivated landscape created by man as a result of literary and artistic influences.

辛特拉是葡萄牙里斯本大区的一个市镇。19 世纪，辛特拉成为第一块欧洲浪漫主义建筑云集的土地。费迪南德二世把一座被损毁的教堂改建成了一座城堡，这一建筑集中了哥特式、埃及式、摩尔式和文艺复兴时期的建筑特点，同时在城堡的公园里把许多国外树种与本地树木混合栽种。该地还有许多其他精美的建筑，全都倚着周围的山脉而建，这些公园和庭院景致交相辉映、美不胜收。尽管几乎所有的建筑遗产都在 1755 年地震中毁坏了，但还有一些杰出的宫殿、军事建筑、宗教建筑和考古遗址得以留存，其中的皇宫毫无疑问是辛特拉最重要的特色建筑，它被公认为伊比利亚半岛上穆德加技术的最佳范例。辛特拉山脉和辛特拉镇的文化景观是欧洲浪漫主义景观的先驱，对整个欧洲的景观建筑设计发展产生了重大影响。辛特拉历史上受过不同外来文化的影响，从而展现出丰富多彩的文化风貌。该地区的当地植物群与受到文学和艺术影响而出现的精美典雅的人文景观相得益彰。

Vocabulary

1. sensitivity *n.* 体恤；敏感；灵敏度

A good relationship involves concern and sensitivity for each other's feelings.

一段美满的恋情需要彼此关心并体恤对方的情感。

2. Gothic *adj.* (建筑等)哥特式的，哥特风格的；(小说)哥特派的

The tall Gothic windows glinted in the afternoon sun.

高大的哥特式窗户在夕阳的照耀下闪闪发光。

3. Moorish *adj.* 摩尔人的(公元 8—15 世纪在北非和西班牙具有伊斯兰教文明特点的)

Her life was like the past of this old Moorish city, full, deep, remote.

她的身世就像这座古老的摩尔城市的历史一样，丰富，深邃，辽远。

4. integrity *n.* 完整；完全；完善；正直；诚实

We all have an interest in maintaining the integrity of the ecosystem.

维持生态系统的完整是我们共同的利益。

5. indigenous *adj.* 当地的；本土的；土生土长的

Kangaroos are indigenous to Australia.

袋鼠为澳大利亚本地的动物。

扩展阅读

Sintra Tourism Guide

Sintra and its mystical hills dotted with fairytale palaces and extravagant villas have bewitched visitors for centuries.

The Romans made it a place of cult moon worshiping and named it "Cynthia" after the goddess of the moon. They were followed by the Moors who also fell in love with the lush vegetation and built a hilltop castle, a palace, and several fountains around the town. Later it became the summer residence of the Portuguese royal family and attracted a number of wealthy aristocrats who built huge mansions and villas.

Famous British poet and traveler Lord Byron stopped by in the 18th century, writing that the town is "perhaps in every respect the most delightful in Europe", and calling it a "glorious Eden" in his epic poem Childe Harold's Pilgrimage. His fellow countryman Robert Southey followed him and saw it as "the most blessed spot on the whole inhabitable globe". Others made it their own private retreat, such as William Beckford (one of 18th century England's wealthiest men), who lived in the splendid Monserrate Palace, later bought by Francis Cook.

It is indeed an extraordinary place with a surreal mixture of history and fantasy, a destination you should make the effort to see, especially if you visit Lisbon.

It is easy to reach from the capital, just a 30-minute drive on the IC19 highway, or a 40-minute train ride from Rossio Station in the center of Lisbon. In the main square is the National Palace, dating from the 14th century. Its two gigantic conical chimneys are the town's most recognizable landmarks, while the rest of the building is a combination of the Moorish, Gothic and Manueline styles. Inside it possesses what is said to be the most extensive collection of Mudejar Azulejos (colored glazed tiles) in the world, and several exceptional rooms. The "Coat-of-Arms Room" stands out for its domed ceiling decorated with stags holding the coats of arms of 74 Portuguese noble families and for its walls lined with 18th-century tiled panels. The former banquet hall, "Room of the Swans", also has a magnificent ceiling, divided into octagonal panels decorated with swans painted in the 17th century. Other highlights include the "Magpie Room" (named for the birds that decorate the ceiling), the Royal Chapter of King John I, the huge kitchen with a capacity for 1000 diners, and the interior courtyards where poet Camões read his verses to the king. But the most famous building in Sintra is Pena Palace. Built in the 1840s, it is one of Europe's most fantastic palaces, often compared to Neuschwanstein and the other mock-medieval castles of Ludwig of Bavaria in Germany, although it was actually built more than two decades before those. It includes a drawbridge, a conglomeration of turrets, ramparts, and domes, and a gargoyle above a Neo-Manueline arch, all washed in an array of pastel shades. The extravagant interior is decorated in late Victorian and Edwardian furnishings, rich ornaments, paintings, and priceless porcelain preserved just as the royal family left them. Other highlights include the spacious ballroom, the marvelous "Arab Room", and an impressive 16th-century chapel altarpiece. Surrounding the palace is the mystical Pena Park, filled with a variety of trees and exotic plants from the former colonies of the Portuguese empire, ponds, fountains, and black swans. There is also a charming lodge hidden among the trees that can be visited. At the highest point is a statue of King Ferdinand looking towards his palace, and a viewpoint called "Cruz Alta" overlooking Pena Palace and surroundings.

A number of luxurious old villas are scattered around the park. The most famous (for being part of the setting of Roman Polanski's "The Ninth Gate" starring Johnny Depp) is Challet Biester, with dark conic rooftops and Gothic windows.

Another remarkable building is the fantasy "Palace of the Millions", part of the Regaleira Estate. Built at the close of the 19th century in Gothic, Manueline and Renaissance styles, it sprouts turrets and towers. It is surrounded by a garden filled with mythological and esoteric symbols—statues of gods, mysterious wells, ponds, and grottoes. The highlight is an almost supernatural tunnel staircase that symbolizes death leading into a "Garden of Eden", symbolizing "rebirth" or the entrance to Heaven. You are free to look around unguided, although the option of a guided tour is worth taking to get the full flavor of the place.

Further down the road is the exotic Monserrate Palace and its romantic subtropical gardens. This palace was bought by Francis Cook and rented by William Beckford, and is now under renovation with plans to turn it into a museum. It combines the Gothic and Moorish styles with some Italian inspiration (the dome was modeled on the Duomo in Florence), and the gardens are a fabulous dreamscape of waterfalls and flora ranging from roses and conifers to tropical tree ferns, and at least 24 species of palms.

Contrasting with all of these fabulous palaces is the tiny but extraordinary Capuchos Convent. Visiting its labyrinth of narrow corridors, chapels, and child-sized cells cut out of rock, all lined with cork, is an Alice-in-Wonderland experience. The cork, used to keep out the humidity and to favor the acoustic isolation required for the meditation of the friars, has given it the nickname of "the cork convent".

Overlooking it all is the 8th century Moorish Castle, standing on top of Sintra's highest hill. Snaking along the mountain ridge, it offers breathtaking views of the area.

As you walk around Sintra you will encounter a number of natural fountains that have been given striking decorations. Two of the most eye-catching are the Moorish Fountain, so called for its Neo-Moorish decoration and geometrical tile patterns, and the Sabuga Fountain, where the water spouts from two breasts. Stop for a drink after all the sightseeing or to wash down a sweet Queijada de Sintra, a local specialty. It is a cheese tart spiced with cinnamon available at most cafes and pastry shops in town.

（资料来源：http://www.golisbon.com/portugal/cities/sintra.html）

Questions

1. What are some of the cultures that once influenced the landscape in Sintra?

2. Briefly describe the remarkable buildings in Sintra. Which one interests you most? Why?

世界遗产概论

第三章 亚洲的世界遗产

Introduction to the World Heritage

第一节　亚洲的世界文化遗产

Ancient City of Sigiriya
锡吉里亚古城

⇨ **简介**

所属国家：斯里兰卡(Sri Lanka)

入选时间：1982

入选标准：(ii)(iii)(iv)

Sigiriya, which can be loosely translated as the Lion's Rock, is a large stone and ancient rock fortress and palace ruin in Sri Lanka constructed by King Kashyapa at the end of the 5th century. It may have been inhabited through prehistoric times. And after the king's death, it was used as a Buddhist monastery until 14th century.

Sigiriya being a fortress, had been well designed for its defenses by having ramparts and moats built around it. From the summit of the rock, the land areas up to distances of tens of miles can be watched making it hard for the enemy to make a surprise attack to the kingdom.

King Kassapa had reverted his fortress to an ecological wonder by having Royal Pleasure Gardens, Water Gardens, Fountain Gardens and Boulder Gardens made inside the inner city as well as at the palace premises on the Rock summit.

The most renowned is the Sigiriya Rock Paintings on a Western Rock face cavity about 100 meters high from the rock base—"The Maidens of the Clouds", 21 non-identified female figures, comparable to the most beautiful creations of Ajanta.

Another interesting construction is the Mirror Wall. Made of porcelain, it was originally kept polished during Kasyapa's reign. After his death, it was no longer polished, and beginning in the 8th century visitors to the site began to leave messages written on the rock. Coming along the path of the mirror wall, one can find the Lion Paw Terrace or Platform. Only two huge Lion's paws are remaining now but earlier there had been an enormous Lion figure or statue at the entrance. Through the Lion's paw stairway, the summit can be reached.

锡吉里亚古城(可以粗略翻译为狮子岩)是公元 5 世纪末由斯里兰卡迦叶波一世建造的古老的岩石堡垒和宫殿的废墟。在史前时代可能已有人类居住在此。国王死后,它被用作佛教寺院,直到 14 世纪。

101

作为一个堡垒,锡吉里亚古城周围建有为其防御的城墙和护城河。从岩石山顶可以看到数百英里的区域,这让敌人很难对这个王国发起突袭。

迦叶波一世将他的堡垒还原成了一个由内城及山顶宫殿的御花园、水上花园、喷泉花园和圆石花园所构成的生态奇观。

最著名的是在离岩石底部约 100 米处西面一个洞穴里的锡吉里亚古宫岩画——《云中美女》,那是 21 幅未知身份的美女图,可与印度的阿占塔石窟中最美丽的作品相媲美。

另一个有趣的建筑是墙镜。镜子是瓷制的,在迦叶波一世时期,一直有专人进行打磨、保持光亮。迦叶波一世去世后,再也没人给它抛光了,从 8 世纪开始,访客开始在岩石上留下各种讯息。沿着墙镜走,人们可以发现狮爪台。现在这里只剩两个大狮爪,但过去在这个入口处是一个巨大的狮子雕像。通过这个狮爪台阶,就可以达到岩石的顶峰了。

Vocabulary

1. fortress *n.* 堡垒;要塞

The explosion burst the outer wall of the fortress.

爆炸摧毁了城堡的外墙。

2. inhabit *v.* 居住于;栖居在

Some tribes still inhabit the remote areas of the country.

某些部落仍然居住在这个国家的一些偏远地区。

3. revert *v.* 恢复;重提;回到……上

Shall we revert to the matter we mentioned yesterday?

我们回到昨天提到过的问题,好吗?

4. ecological *adj.* 生态(学)的

This kind of profit-oriented development can only bring about the ecological imbalance.

这种唯利是图的开发只会导致生态失衡。

5. premise *n.* 前提;〔复数〕房屋,房屋连地基

The persistent failures can always betraced back to the original false premise that all existence is controlled by an undefined and unassailable "god".

持续的失败总是能追溯到同一个错误的前提——一切都被没有定义、无懈可击的"上帝"所掌控着。

▌扩展阅读

History of Lion Rock

Nothing in Sri Lanka captures the imagination more than a 200 meter lump of granite that rises starkly above the flat central plains about three and a half hours' drive from Colombo.

Sigiriya (say see-gih-REE-yah) has it all—a blood-stained history full of intrigue, astonishing frescos of bare-breasted maidens painted 15 centuries ago, a wall covered in graffiti that is more than 1,000 years old and, to top it all, Asia's oldest surviving landscape garden.

Dark deeds led to the establishment of Sigiriya as the center of the ancient Sinhalese Kingdom for a period of 18 years in the late 5th century. The reign of King Dhatusena came to an abrupt end in AD 477 when his throne was seized by Kasyapa, his son by a wife of unequal birth. Kasyapa's action was prompted by the fear that his younger half-brother Mogallan, who was born of the anointed queen, would take over the throne. Kasyapa was convinced that his father was hiding a cache of treasure from him, and demanded that the King reveal where it was hidden. Dhatusena took the young usurper to the bund of the Kalawewa, the greatest of his irrigation works, below which lived a venerable monk who had been his teacher and companion for many years. There, the old King pointed, was the sum of all his wealth. In a fit of pique, Kasyapa ordered the old man to be walled up alive and naked in his own tomb. Meanwhile, Mogallan survived an assassination attempt by his brother and fled to India to raise an army. Paranoia, arrogance and delusions of divinity drove Kasyapa to leave the traditional Sinhalese capital of Anuradhapura and construct his palace on the peak of Sigiriya Rock, a perfect lookout which could be easily defended; a huge lion was carved out of the rock. Seven years after ascending the throne, he moved into his new home.

Visitors to the palace entered via a stone stairway that took them into the lion's mouth and through its throat—hence Sigiriya's alternative name, "Lion Rock". Only the lion's massive paws remain today, but they indicate how gigantic the rest of the carving must have been. A new stairway has been attached to the side of the rock to allow access to the summit, enabling visitors to stroll around the ruins of the palace and gasp at the panoramic views. Two water tanks, used for bathing and drinking, are still filled with rain water, but in Kasyapa's day a sophisticated pumping system was used to fill the tanks from a lake at the foot of the rock.

Sigiriya is approached from the west over a moat that encloses an elaborate water garden that runs up to the foot of the rock. A stone stairway takes visitors past caves and hollows, where early Buddhist monks lived and worshipped, to a gallery half way up the rock which is enclosed by a three-meter high wall. Large sections of the so-called Mirror Wall are still intact, and is here that graffiti artists have inscribed their neat messages, many of them more than ten centuries old and some, alas, partially obscured by the scrawled initials of modern egoists. Most of the ancient graffiti refers to the Sigiriya Maidens, who are to be found up a spiral staircase about 14 meters above the Mirror Wall gallery in a natural pocket in the rock which has been protected for centuries from the rain by an overhang. Nobody knows who painted these amazing frescos, but the Maidens testify to a highly advanced Sinhalese civilization at a time when Europe was in the Dark Ages.

It is not known whether Kasyapa knew of the existence of the beauties hidden just below his eyrie, but what is known is that the King came to a sticky end, perhaps deservedly. In 495, his brother Mogallan at last returned from India with an army of combined Chola and Sinhalese troops behind him and Kasyapa descended from his impregnable stronghold to meet him in battle. At a crucial stage in the battle, the King's elephant balked at a hidden swamp before him and momentarily turned aside, making his troops believe he was retreating. His army broke in confusion, leaving Kasyapa defenseless. Flamboyant to the last, he drew his dagger, slashed his own throat, raised the blade high in the air and sheathed it again before falling down dead.

（资料来源：http://www.holymtn.com/SriLanka/lionrock.htm）

Questions

1. Why was Sigiriya built?
2. Which part of the Lion Rock is remained to this day?

Ancient Villages in Southern Anhui—Xidi and Hongcun
皖南古村落——西递、宏村

▷ **简介**

所属国家：中国（China）

入选时间：2000

入选标准：(iii)，(iv)，(v)

The Ancient Villages in Southern Anhui—Xidi and Hongcun are two exceptionally well preserved traditional Chinese villages. Construction of Xidi Village began during the Northern Song Dynasty (960—1127), but the two villages are famed as being the "Ming and Qing Dynasty Local Residence Museum". They are graphic illustrations of a type of human settlement created during a feudal period and based on a prosperous trading economy. In their buildings and their street patterns, they reflect the socio-economic structure of a long-lived settled period of Chinese history. The streets area all paved with granite and the buildings, which are widely spaced, are timber-framed with brick walls and elegantly carved decoration. Their townscapes are developed in harmony with the natural environment, using the geomantic principles of Feng Shui.

The Huizhou style is the predominant architecture in the villages: white walls, dark tiles, horse-head gables, stone drums and open interior courtyards are common features. It was the style favoured by the local merchant class.

Xidi and Hongcun are similar in their historic importance. But they have their own characters. Xidi features more buildings and a nice lake with a mountain overlooking the small village. Hongcun has waterways, and buildings situated in a way that the map forms a cow. Hongcun is also prominently featured in Ang Lee's film *Crouching Tiger*,

Hidden Dragon.

位于安徽南部的西递和宏村是中国至今为止保存得特别完好的两座传统村落。西递最初在北宋年间开始建造,但两座村落都以"明清民居博物馆"著称。它们生动地体现了封建社会里依靠贸易繁荣兴建起来的人类聚居地。村里的房屋和街道反映出中国历史上很长一段时期内的社会经济结构。街道全部铺上岩石,宽敞的木制房屋外面砌着石墙,内部装饰精巧。村落景观的开发运用风水原则,注重与自然环境的和谐。

村落内大多数建筑都是徽州风格:以黛瓦、粉墙、马头墙、石雕、天井为共同特点,受到当地商人阶层的青睐。

西递和宏村的历史意义是相似的,但它们有自己的特点。西递拥有更多的建筑,依山傍水。宏村的水道和建筑的排列布置使得整个村子在地图上形成一头牛的形状。李安的电影《卧虎藏龙》有很多场景都是在宏村拍摄的。

Vocabulary

1. graphic *adj.* 生动形象的;图表的;绘画似的

When did you start graphic design?

你是什么时候开始从事平面设计的?

2. feudal *adj.* 封建制度的;领地的;世仇的

The May 4th Movement was anti-imperialist and anti-feudal.

五四运动既是反对帝国主义的运动,又是反对封建主义的运动。

3. granite *n.* 花岗岩;坚毅;冷酷无情

They are built of granite blocks.

它们由花岗岩石块建成。

4. timber *n.* 木材,原木

They export timber to China.

他们出口木材到中国。

5. predominant *adj.* 主要的,占主导地位的;占优势的,卓越的

Which is predominant—the advantage or the disadvantage?

哪个更占优势,是优点还是缺点呢?

扩展阅读

Hongcun Village

Hongcun is located in the southwestern foot of Mt. Huangshan and about 11 kilometers off the southwest of Yixian County. In ancient times, it's the only access to Beijing to do business from Yixian. The whole village covers an area of about 28 hectares. The place which is classed as old village spreads 19.11 hectares of land.

Hongcun was first founded in the Shaoxing period of the Southern Song Dynasty (about AD 1131—1162), with a history of about 900 years. Hongcun was first called "Hongcun (another Chinese word with the same pronunciation)". According to the record of "Pedigree of Wang Clan", because it was enlarged to the shape of the Taiyi elephant at that time, it was acclaimed as Hongcun. In the Qianlong period of the Qing Dynasty, its name was changed into Hongcun.

Hongcun is the main village where Wang families live together. Wang clan is a respectable family in Central Plains. Because of moving to the south at the end of the Han Dynasty, the descendants of Wang clan spread every part of the south of the lower reaches of the Changjiang River. The ancestral home of Wang clan is Jinling. In the Southern Song Dynasty, it moved to Huizhou. They are the earliest ancestors of Hongcun.

The allocation of the whole village looks like the shape of cow. The erect Leigang Mountain is regarded as the head of the cow; the old green and shadowy trees spreading all over the mountain are the horn of the cow; the long lines of buildings in the village are the body of the cow; the glittering lake is the belly of the cow; the crooked manmade canals which run through houses are the intestine of the cow, and four wood bridges near the village are the legs of the cow. Hongcun looks like a sleeping cow located among the hill which is surrounded by the green mountain and a large rambling rice fields.

Hongcun is 18 kilometers away from Xidi (introduced later). The climates are similar.

Among the folk residences, the Chengzhi Hall is touted as the Folk Summer Place, which is engraved carefully and covered with gold and painted with colors. The Dongxian Hall is vast and simple. The Moon Pond is as even as a mirror. The water of the Southern Lake dances and sparkles. The simple Guanyin Shop is in the deep of the alley and beside the cyan stone street. There are old lofty tree on the Thunder Hillock and peonies with a history of over 100 years. Green bines climb on the wall and enter the yard of domestic houses. The Xuren Hall and Shangyuan Hall, the ancestral temples, are strict. The Southern Lake Academy is given the words of "Yiwen Family School" on the stele by 93-year-old Liang Tongshu, Shijiang (a rank in the court) of the Imperial Academy. All these constructions constitute a perfect art whole with the Jingxiu Hall and Sanli Hall. One step is one view; one place is one picture. At the same time, these constructions reflect wide and deep cultural essence which is left by long history. Till the Qing Dynasty, Hongcun has become a big village with over 1000 families. Long lines of houses look like a big city. Until now, Hongcun is still the site of the People's Government of Hongcun Town. It starts to develop at the middle of the 1980s.

Hongcun has the system of streets and alleys which looks like a square net. The ground is covered by granite stones. The manmade water system through all families forms unique space of Water Street and Alley. The village centers on "the heart of the cow"—the Moon Pond which is a crescent-shaped pond. It's surrounded by houses and ancestral temples. It exhibits strong cohesion. There are 158 domestic houses in existence, which were built in the Ming or Qing Dynasty. 137 houses of them are in a good state of preservation. The buildings of the Qing Dynasty own not only beautiful surroundings, but also a proper layout.

The structure is elegant and blends closely with nature. It creates a suitable living environment, which is also full of affection. It's an outstanding representative of China's traditional domestic houses.

Most villagers divert water in canals into houses, and forms "House Garden" and "Water Yard" which exist only in village. This makes the construction of Hongcun inaugurate the special house pattern of water-side pavilion of Hui constructions. Hongcun is an outstanding representative of Huizhou traditional local culture, building techniques and landscape design. It is full of historical value, art and science. It indeed is the witness of Huizhou traditional architectural culture. Hongcun has been listed into the "Contents of World Cultural and Natural Heritage" by the United Nation's Educational, Scientific and Cultural Organization.

The people of Hongcun built six family schools at the north bank of the Southern Lake. They were called "Six Schools Leaning-on Lake". They were used to teach and learn for the scion of a family. In the 19th year of the Jiaqing period of the Qing Dynasty (AD 1814), six schools were combined together and rebuilt. It was given a name of "Yiwen Family School", or "Southern Lake Academy". The academy covers an area of over 6,000 square meters. The buildings are tall and majestic, grand and wide. It's an architectural representative of the ancient academies in Huizhou style.

（资料来源：http://www. chinahighlights. com/huangshan/attraction/hongcun-village. htm）

Questions

1. What is the exact location of Hongcun?
2. When was Hongcun first founded?

Angkor
吴哥窟

⇨ 简介

所属国家：柬埔寨（Cambodia）

入选时间：1992

入选标准：(i)，(ii)，(iii)，(iv)

Angkor, located amid forests and farmland near Siem Reap in Cambodia, is one of the largest archaeological sites in operation in the world. It contains the impressive remains of the different capitals of the Khmer Empire, which flourished from approximately the 9th to the 15th centuries. With magnificent temples, several different ancient urban plans and large water reservoirs, the intactness of the site very much reflects the splendor of the cities that once were. There are over one thousand temples in the Angkor area, ranging in scale from nondescript piles of brick rubble to the magnificent Angkor Wat, said to be the world's largest single religious monument. Many of the temples at Angkor have been restored, and together, they comprise the most significant site of Khmer architecture.

The structures one sees at Angkor today, are the surviving remains of a grand religious, social and administrative metropolis whose other buildings—palaces, public buildings, and houses—were built of wood and have long since decayed and disappeared. The architecture and layout of the successive capitals bear witness to a high level of social order and ranking within the Khmer Empire. Angkor is therefore a major site exemplifying cultural, religious and symbolic values, as well as containing high architectural, archaeological and artistic significance.

坐落在柬埔寨暹粒附近的森林和农田中的吴哥窟,是世界上现存最大的考古遗址之一。它包括高棉帝国兴盛于 9—15 世纪的几个首府的遗迹。吴哥拥有宏伟的寺庙、几个不同的古代城市规划和大型水库,其完整性很大程度上反映了这些城市曾经的辉煌。吴哥地区有超过一千个规模不等的寺庙,从难以辨认的砖头堆到据说是世界上最大的单体宗教纪念碑的壮丽的吴哥窟。吴哥的很多寺庙都已被重建,它们作为整体构成了高棉建筑最重要的遗址。

今天人们在吴哥所看到的构造,是一个由庞大的宗教、社会和管理综合体留下的遗迹。这个综合体的其他建筑,比如宫殿、公共建筑及房子都是用木头建造的,早已腐烂和消失。这些建筑和后来的几个首府的布局是高棉帝国的社会秩序和等级的极好见证。因此,吴哥是一个体现了文化、宗教和象征性价值的重大遗址,同时它也具有很高的建筑、考古和艺术意义。

Vocabulary

1. flourish *v.* 繁荣;兴盛;兴旺

Industry does not flourish if its financial roots are missing.

如果金融根基缺失,工业就不会繁荣。

2. nondescript *adj.* 无明显特征的,难以归类的,难以形容的

She is wearing nondescript clothes.

她穿着不太起眼的衣服。

3. metropolis *n.* 大都市,大都会;首府,首都;大主教区

Shanghai is an international metropolis full of vigor and variety.

上海是一座充满活力、多姿多彩的国际化大都市。

4. successive *adj.* 连续的,相继的;继承的

It rained for five successive days.

已经连续下了五天的雨了。

5. exemplify *v.* 是……的典型;例示,举例证明

To exemplify what I mean, let us look at their annual output.

为了举例说明我的意思,我们来看一下他们每年的产量。

扩展阅读

Drought Led to Demise of Ancient City of Angkor

The ancient city of Angkor—the most famous monument of which is the breathtaking ruined temple of Angkor Wat—might have collapsed due to valiant but ultimately failed efforts to battle drought, scientists find.

The great city of Angkor in Cambodia, first established in the ninth century, was the capital of the Khmer Empire, the major player in southeast Asia for nearly five centuries. It stretched over more than 385 square miles (1,000 square kilometers), making it the most extensive urban complex of the preindustrial world. In comparison, Philadelphia covers 135 square miles (350 sq. km), while Phoenix sprawls across more than 500 square miles (1,300 sq. km), not including the huge suburbs.

Suggested causes for the fall of the Khmer Empire in the late 14th to early 15th centuries have included war and land overexploitation. However, recent evidence suggests that prolonged droughts might have been linked to the decline of Angkor—for instance, tree rings from Vietnam suggest the region experienced long spans of drought interspersed with unusually heavy rainfall.

Angkor possessed a complex network of channels, moats, and embankments and reservoirs known as barays to collect and store water from the summer monsoons for use in rice paddy fields in case of drought. To learn more about how the Khmer managed their water, scientists analyzed a 6-foot (2-meter)-long core sample of sediment taken from the southwest corner of the largest Khmer reservoir, the West Baray, which could hold 1.87 billion cubic feet (53 million cubic meters) of water, more than 20 times the amount of stone making up the Great Pyramid at Giza.

Also, to collect samples from across the greater Angkor region, researcher Mary Beth Day, a paleolimnologist at the University of Cambridge in England, hired a "tuk-tuk" (motorized rickshaw) driver, and was able to convince him to drive her around the countryside, "often on tracks that tuk-tuks probably aren't designed to travel on," she recalled. "We nearly got stuck in the sand a couple of times, but my driver was remarkably accommodating given that he probably thought I was crazy."

The researchers deduced a 1,000-year-long climate history of Angkor from the baray. They found at around the time Angkor collapsed the rate at which sediment was deposited in the baray dropped to one-tenth of what it was before, suggesting that water levels fell dramatically as well. "The discovery really emphasizes how significant the events during this period must have been," Day said.

As both water levels and sediment deposits ebbed, the ecology of the baray changed as well, with more bottom-dwelling algae and floating plants coming into existence.

"The ecological shift primarily serves to underline how environmental conditions in the West Baray have been fundamentally different since the 17th century, post-collapse, as compared to what the baray was like during Angkorian times," Day said.

In the end, the water management systems of the Khmer might have been insufficient to cope with sudden and intense variations in climate.

"Angkor can be an example of how technology isn't always sufficient to prevent major collapse during times of severe instability," Day told LiveScience. "Angkor had a highly sophisticated water management infrastructure, but this technological advantage was not enough to prevent its collapse in the face of extreme environmental conditions."

"It's important to understand, however, that failure of the water management network was not the sole reason for the downfall of the Khmer Empire," Day added. "The collapse of Angkor was a complex process brought about by several different factors—social, political and environmental."

The scientists detailed their findings online Jan. 2 in the Proceedings of the National Academy of Sciences.

（资料来源：http://www. livescience. com/17702-drought-collapse-ancient-city-angkor. html）

Questions

1. What used to be the suggested causes of the the fall of the Khmer Empire?

2. How does the recent evidence explain the decline of Angkor?

Historic Monuments of Ancient Kyoto
(Kyoto, Uji and Otsu Cities)
京都遗址（京都、宇治和大津城）

⬡➡ **简介**

所属国家：日本（Japan）

入选时间：1994

入选标准：（ii）（iv）

Kyoto, the former capital of Japan, is located in central Honshu, north to Osaka. The UNESCO World Heritage site, Historic Monuments of Ancient Kyoto, consists of 17 constructions scattered over Kyoto, Uji and Otsu Cities. Of the designated buildings, 13 are Buddhist temples, three are Shinto shrines, and one a castle.

The 13 temples are Kyoogokoku-ji, Kiyomizu-dera, Enryaku-ji, Daigo-ji, Ninna-ji, Byodo-in, Kozan-ji, Saiho-ji, Tenryu-ji, Rokuon-ji (aka Kinkaku-ji), Jisho-ji (aka Ginkaku-ji), Ryoan-ji and Nishi Hongan-ji, and the three shrines are Kamowakeikazuchi Shrine, Kamomioya Shrine and Ujigami Shrine. The one castle is Nijo Castle.

Ever since Kyoto became the capital of Japan in 794, it has served as the center of religious and cultural life. The city—under the name of Heian-kyo at that time—was profoundly influenced by Chinese culture and modeled after the Chinese city of Chang'an. It remained Japan's capital until 1868 when the capital was transferred to Tokyo during the Meiji Restoration.

Among the historic properties representing the early Heian period, Kiyomizu-dera (Buddhist temple) has gained remarkable fame for its main hall's wooden platform. "Kiyomizu-no-butai," as the platform is called in Japanese, is supported by a total of 139 pillars on a mountain slope, and presents a distinct atmosphere.

The Buddhist temple of Byodo-in, built toward the end of the Heian era, reflects the period during which social unrest and religious fervor permeated the country. The main building in Byodo-in is the Phoenix Hall, which is depicted on the reverse side of the Japanese 10 yen coin.

京都,日本过去的首都,位于本州中部,大阪的北面。世界遗产——京都遗址,包括了17座分布在京都、宇治和大津城的建筑。其中13座是佛教寺院,3座是神社,还有1座是城堡。

这13座寺庙是东寺、清水寺、延历寺、醍醐寺、仁和寺、平等院、高山寺、西芳寺、天龙寺、鹿苑寺(又名金阁寺)、慈照寺(又名银阁寺)、龙安寺和西本愿寺。三座神社分别是贺茂别雷神社、贺茂御祖神社和宇治上神社。城堡名为二条城。

自从公元794年京都成为日本的首都后,它成了日本宗教和文化生活的中心。这座城市(当时称为平安京)深受中国文化影响并模仿中国唐朝都城长安来建造。直到公元1868年明治维新时期迁都东京之前,京都一直是日本的首都。

在代表平安时代早期的名胜古迹中,清水寺以其大殿的木制平台而著称。这个平台在日语里被称为"清水舞台",耸立于陡峭的悬崖上,由139根高大圆木支撑,气势雄伟。

建于平安时代末期的平等院,则反映了当时社会的动荡和弥漫全国的宗教热情。平等院的主体建筑是凤凰堂,是日币十元硬币背面的图案。

Vocabulary

1. designate *v.* 指明,指出;指派;表明,意味着;把……定名为

Mark offered to be the designated driver for the New Year Eve party.

马克主动提出愿意当除夕夜派对的指定司机。

2. profoundly *adv.* 深深地;深切地;深刻地;极度地

Major depression can profoundly alter social, family and occupational functioning.

重度抑郁症会极大地改变人的社会、家庭、职业机能。

3. fervor *n.* 热烈,热情

China's leaders are also using the space launch as a vehicle to boost patriotic fervor.

中国领导人还希望能通过航天飞船的发射来提高民众的爱国热情。

4. permeate *v.* 弥漫;遍布;渗入;渗透

A feeling of sadness permeates his music.

他的音乐中充斥着忧伤的情绪。

5. reverse *adj.* 反面的；颠倒的

Please read the names on the list in reverse order.

请以相反次序念名单上的名字。

▌扩展阅读

Historic Monuments of Ancient Kyoto

An approach covered with cherry-blossom petals, a garden colored with the tinted leaves of autumn and temples and shrines covered in clean white snow, Kyoto has something to offer in each of the four seasons while always preserving Japan's traditions and values.

Kyoto is a symbol of the origin of much of the Japanese culture and was the center of Japanese politics and culture for over 1000 years since first being established as capital in AD 794 Learning about the history of Kyoto today means learning about the development of Japan's traditions and culture.

Kyoto, "the thousand-year capital" contains many historical sites. Seventeen of them including shrines, temples and castles are inscribed on the World Heritage List and in 1994, the following remains were designated as "Historic Monuments of Ancient Kyoto": Kamowakeikazuchi Shrine (Kamigamo Shrine), Kamomioya Shrine (Shimogamo Shrine), Kyo-o-gokoku-ji Temple (To-ji Temple), Kiyomizu-dera Temple, Enryaku-ji Temple, Daigo-ji Temple, Ninna-ji Temple, Byodo-in Temple, Ujigami Shrine, Kozan-ji Temple, Saiho-ji Temple (Koke-dera Temple), Tenryu-ji Temple, Rokuon-ji Temple (Kinkaku-ji Temple), Jisho-ji Temple (Ginkaku-ji Temple), Ryoan-ji Temple, Hongan-ji Temple (Nishi-Hongan-ji Temple), and Nijo Castle. All are appreciated individually as precious properties whose structures produce the landscapes of the city that have fascinated visitors for so long.

During the Heian period Kamowakeikazuchi Shrine (Kamigamo Shrine), Kamomioya Shrine (Shimogamo Shrine), and Kyo-o-gokoku-ji Temple (To-ji Temple) were constructed as guardian shrines and temples for the city of Heiankyo, the new capital. At that time the authoritative Fujiwara family all but ruled Kyoto and helped in creating a rich and exquisite aristocratic culture based on the city. Byodo-in Temple and the images of Buddha, constructed by the Fujiwara family in late Heian period, embody the splendid style of this era. In 1192 power was transferred from the aristocracy to the samurai class and at the same time the center of politics shifted from Kyoto to Kamakura. It was not until 1338 when the Muromachi government was reestablished in Kyoto and the city regained the power it had lost 150 years earlier to once again become the nation's center of politics and culture.

Throughout the following decades and centuries the traditional aristocratic culture and the new culture of the emerging samurai class combined, all the while being heavily influenced by Zen Buddhism. This influence of Zen Buddhism led to the construction of Tenryu-ji Temple, Ryoan-ji Temple, Kinkaku-ji Temple, and Ginkaku-ji Temple with many Zen-style gardens called "Karesansui", featuring rocks and sand also constructed around the city. As this form of aristocratic culture spread the opposite aesthetics of "wabi and sabi" (austere beauty and elegant simplicity) became popular and much of the future foundation of Japanese culture was created in Kyoto in this era. In the 17th century, even after the Tokugawa government clawed its way to power, Kyoto remained the residential site of the emperor until he moved to Tokyo in 1868. During these centuries known as the Edo period, the Tokugawa family constructed Nijo Castle as their prime residence in the city and the castle today retains a great deal of its Momoyama-style design.

During World War II, many Japanese cities were hit by allied bombers but Kyoto and Nara were spared; believed by many to be the result of US Army studies showing the cities to contain many historical remains.

Why was modern day Kyoto selected as the site for the capital known as "Heiankyo"?

Kyoto was chosen as a new capital by Feng Shui (Chinese divination used in selecting safe ground). In this divination process Kyoto was selected as it is surrounded and protected by four guardian gods. The four gods are the blue dragon to the east, the white tiger to the west, the sacred bird to the south, and the water god to the north. These gods are translated to mean a river in the east, a road in the west, a lake in the south and a hill in the north; conditions that apply perfectly to Kyoto with the Kamogawa River in the east, the San-in do road in the west, Ogura pond in the south, and Mt. Funaoka in the north.

（资料来源：http://www. ar. jal. com/world/en/guidetojapan/world_heritage/kyoto/description/）

Questions

1. How long had Kyoto remained the center of Japanese politics and culture?

2. Why was modern day Kyoto selected as the site for the capital known as "Heiankyo"?

Kathmandu Valley

加德满都谷地

➪ 简介

所属国家：尼泊尔（Nepal）

入选时间：1979

入选标准：（iii）（iv）（vi）

Situated at an altitude of 1,336 m above sea level，Kathmandu is the cradle of Nepalese civilization and culture，and has at least 130 important monuments，including several places of pilgrimage for the Hindus and the Buddhists. It is a living museum of ancient temples，palaces，shrines，squares and courtyards.

The Kathmandu Valley World Heritage property is inscribed as seven Monument Zones：The centers of the three primary cities，Kathmandu Hanuman Dhoka，Patan and Bhaktapur，the two most important Buddhist stupas，Swayambhunath and Boudhanath and two famous Hindu shrines，Pashupatinath temple and Changu Narayan.

As Buddhism and Hinduism developed and changed over the centuries throughout Asia，both religions prospered in Nepal and produced a powerful artistic and architectural fusion beginning at least from the 5th century AD，but truly coming into its own in the three hundred year period between AD 1500 and 1800. These monuments were defined by the outstanding cultural traditions of the Newars，manifested in their unique urban settlements，buildings and structures with intricate ornamentation displaying outstanding craftsmanship in brick，stone，timber and bronze that are some of the most highly developed in the world.

加德满都位于海拔 1336 米处，是尼泊尔文明和文化的摇篮，拥有至少 130 个重要的古迹，包括多处印度教和佛教圣地。它是一个拥有各种古老的寺庙、宫殿、广场和庭院的活的博物馆。

加德满都谷地世界遗产被列为七个古迹区：三个主要城市的中心——加德满都、帕坦和巴德冈；最重要的两个佛塔——斯瓦扬布纳特佛塔和博大哈佛塔；两个著名的印度教圣地——帕斯帕提那寺和长古·纳拉扬神庙。

随着历代以来佛教和印度教在亚洲的传播，从公元 5 世纪开始，这两种宗教在尼泊尔兴盛起来，产生了艺术与建筑的融合，并在 15—18 世纪的这三百年里达到巅峰。这些古迹体现了尼瓦尔人非凡的文化传统，在这些独特的城市、装饰精美的建筑和结构中展现了他们精湛的砖砌、石刻、木雕、铜铸等工艺技术。

Vocabulary

1. altitude *n.* 高地；高度

As our car climbed higher in altitude，we passed through fewer villages.

我们的车驶向的海拔越高，从身边擦肩而过的村庄越少。

2. pilgrimage *n.* 朝圣

The Muslim delegation is shortly going on a pilgrimage to Mecca.

这个穆斯林代表团很快就要去麦加朝圣了。

3. shrine *n.* 圣地，圣陵，神龛

Wimbledon is a shrine for all lovers of tennis.

温布尔登是所有网球爱好者的圣地。

4. inscribe *vt.* 雕，刻；题写，题献

I told the jeweler to inscribe the ring with my name.

我叫珠宝商把我的名字刻在那只戒指上。

5. intricate *adj.* 错综复杂的；难理解的；曲折；盘错

Director Wang solved an intricate case soon after he took his post.

王局长刚上任不久就将一件无头案侦破了。

扩展阅读

Swayambhunath Stupa, Kathmandu

Perched atop a hill on the western edge of the Kathmandu Valley, the ancient Swayambhunath Stupa (known to tourists as the Monkey Temple) is Kathmandu's most important Buddhist shrine. The sleepy, all-seeing Buddha eyes that stare out from the top have become the quintessential symbol of Nepal.

History

When this temple was founded about 2,000 years ago, Kathmandu Valley was filled with a great lake. According to Buddhist legend, a single perfect lotus grew in the center of the lake. When the bodhisattva Manjusri drained the lake with a slash of his sword, the lotus flower settled on top of the hill and magically transformed into the stupa. Thus it is known as the "Self-Created (swayambhu) Stupa".

The earliest written record of the Swayambhunath Stupa's existence is a 5th-century stone inscription, but scholars believe there was probably a shrine here as early as the 1st century. Even before that, it is likely that animist rites took place on this hill. Swayambhunath is one of Nepal's oldest Buddhist temples and it has an ancient atmosphere, especially when one approaches on foot with the pilgrims.

Approach

The primary approach to the temple is from the eastern side, where 365 ancient steps lead up the steep forested hillside. The base is about a 20-minute walk from the center of Kathmandu. This staircase is the only route pilgrims would consider and is the most memorable way for any visitor to experience the stupa. However, an alternative is to drive or take a taxi to the west side, where there are only a few steps to climb to the top.

At the bottom of the eastern stairway is a brightly painted gate containing a huge Tibetan prayer wheel nearly 12 feet tall. It takes two people to turn it and a bell rings during each revolution. Around the gate are dozens more smaller wheels. Devotees spin prayer wheels to release prayers and mantras to heaven—visitors are welcome to do so as well.

The staircase is presided over by three painted Buddha statues from the 17th century near the base (women perform prostrations before them in the early morning); another group further up are from the early 20th century.

Strewn along the staircase are numerous mani stones, inscribed with the Tibetan mantra Om mani padme hum ("Hail to the jewel in the lotus"). Merchants sell smaller versions of the stones to tourists. The stairs run through a beautiful forest, which is populated with the hundreds of monkeys that give the temple its nickname.

Main Stupa

The central buildings and decorations of Swayambhunath are rich with Buddhist symbolism. The whitewashed dome of the main stupa represents the womb of creation, with a phallic complement in the square tower. Rising from the tower is a spire made of 13 golden disks, representing the steps to enlightenment. The umbrella on top symbolizing enlightenment itself; some say it contains a bowl of precious stones.

The famous Buddha eyes gazing out sleepily from each side of the tower (oriented to the four cardinal directions) are those of the all-seeing Primordial Buddha. Between each of the pairs of eyes is a symbol that looks like a question mark—this is the Nepali number "1" and represents the unity of all things. Gold plaques rising above the eyes like a crown depict the Five Dhyani Buddhas, celestial buddhas who are associated with the five senses, the four cardinal directions plus the center, and many other symbolic groups of five.

The Five Dhyani Buddhas are further honored with special shrines at the base of the stupa. They face the four cardinal directions, plus one slightly left of east to represent the center direction. Between them are shrines to four of the Buddhas' consorts. Linking all nine shrines together is a chain of prayer wheels and butter lamps. The five main shrines are enclosed in beautiful gilded copper repoussé work, for which the Kathmandu Valley is renowned.

Filling the platform around the main stupa are numerous other shrines and votive structures, most of which have been donated by kings and lamas in the last four centuries. Five of them are associated with the five elements: earth, air, fire, water and sky.

When to Go

The weather is most pleasant in Kathmandu in spring and fall. Swayambhunath is most atmospheric in the morning (before 9 a. m.), when it hosts more pilgrims than tourists. If possible, visit on a Saturday, the only day Nepalis have off from work. This is the primary day of activity around the Harati and other shrines.

Festivals and Events

The two main festivals celebrated at Swayambhunath are Buddha Jayanti (in April or May) and Losar (in February or March). During these times, many pilgrims visit the temple and the monks create a lotus pattern on the stupa with saffron-colored paint. Also important is the month-long Gunla celebration (August or September) marking the end of the rainy season.

（资料来源：http://www. sacred-destinations. com/nepal/kathmandu-swayambhunath-stupa）

Questions

1. When was Swayambhunath Stupa founded?

2. What is the best time to visit Swayambhunath?

Mausoleum of the First Qin Emperor
秦始皇陵及兵马俑坑

➪ **简介**

所属国家：中国（China）

入选时间：1987

入选标准：(i)(iii)(iv)(vi)

Situated at the northern foot of the Lishan Mountain 30 km east of Xi'an, the Mausoleum is the tomb of the first emperor of China's Qin Dynasty, Qin Shi Huang. Covering an area of 56.25 square km, the mausoleum was originally topped with a mound of 115 m and at present the height of the covering mound is 76 m. There are two city walls inside the cemetery—the inner city wall with a circumference of 3,840 m and the outer city wall 6,210 m. The height of the walls of both inner and outer cities ranges from 8 to 10 m. Today there are still relic sites of walls.

As the first imperial mausoleum in the history of China, the Mausoleum ranks first of all imperial mausoleums in terms of its massive scale and rich variety of burial objects. According to historical records, the mausoleum project had been initiated the next year after Emperor Qin Shi Huang ascending his throne. Completed in 208 BC, the construction lasted 39 years. A total of 720,000 laborers had been enlisted for its construction. At its peak period of construction, as many as 800,000 men had been recruited. The number of men involved was almost eight times as large as that mobilized for the construction of the Pyramid of Khufu.

The Qin Dynasty is a splendid page in the history of China. And the Mausoleum of the First Qin Emperor almost embodies the highest achievement of Qin civilization. The Terracotta Army unearthed in the Mausoleum has been acclaimed as the "Eighth Wonder of the World".

位于西安以北 30 千米骊山北麓的皇陵是中国历史上第一个皇帝秦始皇的陵墓。面积 56.25 平方千米，陵墓表面的土丘最初为 115 米高，现在大概为 76 米高。陵墓内部有两道城墙，内城墙周长 3840 米，外城墙周长 6210 米。内城墙和外城墙的高度为 8 到 10 米。今天仍有城墙遗址。

作为中国历史上第一个帝王陵墓，秦始皇陵以其庞大的规模及丰富的随葬品居于各皇陵之首。据史料记载，秦陵的工程在秦始皇登基后第二年就启动了。工程历时 39 年，于公元前 208 年完成。为了建设秦陵，登记在册的工人就有 720000 人。在施工高峰期，有多达 800000 人被招募。整个工程所涉及的人数几乎是建造胡夫金字塔所调动的人数的 8 倍。

秦朝是中国历史上的重要一页，秦始皇陵几乎体现了秦文明的最高成就。秦始皇陵出土的兵马俑，被誉为"世界第八奇迹"。

Vocabulary

1. mound *n.* 土堆，土丘

I've still got a mound of letters to answer.

我还有一大堆信要回复。

2. circumference *n.* 周围，圆周；周长

He went jogging around the circumference of the reservoir every morning.

他每天早晨绕着水库周围慢跑。

3. relic *n.* 遗物，遗迹；废墟

This ruined bridge is a relic of the Civil War.

这座毁坏的桥是南北战争时的遗迹。

4. embody *v.* 表现，象征；包含，收录

Laws embody the will of the people.

法律是人民意志的体现。

5. acclaim *v.* 欢呼，为……喝彩；称赞

The film received critical acclaim when it was released.

电影放映的时候获得了评论界的喝彩。

扩展阅读

Opening Secret Tomb of China's First Emperor Waits for Science

Buried deep under a hill in central China, surrounded by an underground moat of poisonous mercury, lies an entombed emperor who's been undisturbed for more than two millennia.

The tomb holds the secrets of China's first emperor, Qin Shi Huang, who died on Sept. 10, 210 BC, after conquering six warring states to create the first unified nation of China.

The answers to a number of historical mysteries may lie buried inside that tomb, but whether modern people will ever see inside this mausoleum depends not just on the Chinese government, but on science.

"The big hill, where the emperor is buried—nobody's been in there," said archaeologist Kristin Romey, curatorial consultant for the Terracotta Warrior exhibition at New York City's Discovery Times Square. "Partly it's out of respect for the elders, but they also realize that nobody in the world right now has the technology to properly go in and excavate it."

The warring states

Qin Shi Huang (pronounced "chin shuh hwang") was born in 259 BC, first son to the king of Qin, one of six independent kingdoms inside modern China. These kingdoms had been warring for more than 200 years, but through a combination of military strength, strategy and natural disasters, Qin Shi Huang conquered them all, proclaiming himself not just a king, but also an emperor—the first of China.

Scholars still debate the details of how this occurred, and what unique tactics allowed the Qin emperor to achieve what no one had managed before.

When he died, Qin Shi Huang was buried in the most opulent tomb complex ever constructed in China, a sprawling, city-size collection of underground caverns containing everything the emperor would need for the afterlife. The ancient Chinese, along with many cultures including ancient Egyptians, believed that items and even people buried with a person could be taken with him to the afterlife.

But instead of burying his armies, concubines, administrators and servants with him, the Qin emperor came up with an alternative: clay reproductions.

Shocking discovery

In 1974, a group of farmers digging wells near Xi'an, China stumbled upon one of the most shocking archaeological discoveries of all time. The life-size terracotta soldier they dug out of the ground turned out to be just one of an army of thousands, each utterly unique, with individual clothing, hair and facial features.

For almost four decades, archaeologists have been excavating the site. So far, they've uncovered about 2,000 clay soldiers, but experts estimate there are more than 8,000 in total.

"They're going to be digging there for centuries," Romey predicted.

Still, scientists have yet to touch the central tomb, which holds a palace containing the body of Qin Shi Huang.

"It's really smart what the Chinese government is doing," Romey told Live Science. "When we went into (Egyptian King) Tut's tomb, think about all the information we lost just based on the excavation techniques of the 1930s. There's so much additional that we could have learned, but the techniques back then weren't what we have now."

"Even though we may think we have great archaeological excavation techniques right now," she said, "who knows, a century down the road if we open this tomb, what they're going to say?"

To open the tomb?

The decision whether to explore the tomb anytime soon, or ever, is up to the government of China. That decision will likely be influenced by the pace of technological progress.

"In archaeological conservation, every year you have major new developments," Romey said, "When we began excavating (the soldiers) in the' 70s, the minute they were exposed to air and sunlight, the pigment just flaked off. Now they've figured out a new technique where they can actually preserve the paint as they excavate."

Perhaps, if science advances enough, that excavation wouldn't cause serious damage to the burial site, and the tomb will finally be opened.

"I wouldn't be surprised if you had some sort of robotic visual survey going in there at some point," Romey said.

And despite their desire to protect the treasures of antiquity, archaeologists are itching with curiosity to find out what's inside Qin Shi Huang's central tomb.

Rivers of mercury

Ancient writings say the emperor created an entire underground kingdom and palace, complete with a ceiling mimicking the night sky, set with pearls as stars. Pits full of terracotta concubines have never been discovered, though experts predict they exist somewhere in the complex.

And Qin Shi Huang's tomb is also thought to be encircled with rivers of liquid mercury, which the ancient Chinese believed could bestow immortality.

"It's kind of ironic," Romey said, "This is probably how he died, by ingesting mercury. He was taking all these mercury pills because he wanted to live forever and it killed him by the age of 39."

That moat of mercury also presents another reason why archaeologists are loath to explore the tomb just yet—doing so would likely be very dangerous, according to soil samples around the tomb, which indicate extremely high levels of mercury contamination.

In the end, scientists and historians must always weigh their desire to know more with the damage such inquiry would cause.

"Archaeology, ultimately, is a destructive science," Romey said, "You have to destroy stuff in order to learn about it."

（资料来源：http://www.nbcnews.com/id/48702868/ns/technology_and_science-science/t/opening-secret-tomb-chinas-first-emperor-waits-science/）

Questions

1. When were those terracotta soldiers in the Mausoleum of the first Qin emperor first dug out?

2. Why hasn't the central tomb been touched yet?

Samarkand—Crossroad of Cultures
处在文化十字路口的撒马尔罕城

▷ **简介**

所属国家：乌兹别克斯坦（Uzbekistan）

入选时间：2001

入选标准：(i)(ii)(iv)

Samarkand was founded at the same time as Babylon, Memphis, Athens and Rome,

Alexandria and vicinity—almost 2500 years ago.

Samarkand has been conquered by some of the most famous people of history—Alexander the Great, Genghis Khan, and Tamerlane. Tamerlane made it his capital and named it the "Center of the Universe". Culture was developed and mixed with those of Iran, India, Persia, and Mongolia, and being the central part of the Silk Road, was influenced by China, the Middle East, and Europe. Samarkand saw its glory at the height of trade on the Silk Road, beginning in the 2nd century and lasting until the 16th century.

At the time of its greatest splendor medieval Samarkand was a fabulous city of palaces and gardens, with paved and tree-lined streets and a water system that supplied most of the individual houses. It had great silk and iron industries and was the meeting point of merchants' caravans from India, Persia, and China.

The old quarter of Samarkand with its maze of narrow, winding streets occupies the eastern part of the city and centers on the Registan, a great square. It contains some of the most remarkable monuments of central Asia, built during the reign of Timur and his successors. The most famous of these is Timur's mausoleum, surmounted by a ribbed dome and faced with multicolored tiles; the conqueror's tomb was opened in 1941. Other buildings include the Bibi Khan Mosque, with its turquoise cupola, erected by Timur to the memory of his favorite wife; several other magnificent mosques; the mausoleums of the Timurid cemetery (Shah-i-Zinda); and the ruins of the observatory built by Ulugh-Beg, a grandson of Timur.

撒马尔罕城建立于大约 2500 年前, 与巴比伦、孟菲斯、雅典、罗马、亚历山大地区同属一个时期。

撒马尔罕曾被一些历史上的名人所征服, 比如亚力山大大帝、成吉思汗和帖木儿, 帖木儿把撒马尔罕定为自己的首都并将其命名为"宇宙的中心"。撒马尔罕的文化与伊朗、印度、波斯、蒙古文化融合在一起, 并且作为丝绸之路的中心, 又受到了中国、中东和欧洲的影响。公元 2—16 世纪, 丝绸之路的繁荣贸易见证了撒马尔罕城的辉煌。

在撒马尔罕城最辉煌的时代, 中世纪的撒马尔罕是一个拥有大量宫殿和花园的令人难以置信的城市。它的街道都经过铺设, 两边栽有道旁树, 并且拥有完善的供水系统, 能为绝大部分住宅提供用水。它的丝绸和钢铁业非常发达, 是印度、波斯和中国商队的交汇点。

撒马尔罕老城区在城市东部、雷吉斯坦广场的中心, 街道像迷宫般狭窄和蜿蜒。它拥有不少在帖木儿和他的继任者们统治时期修建的、中亚地区最引人注目的古迹, 其中最著名的是帖木儿的陵墓。陵墓带有肋拱圆顶, 表面饰有五彩瓷砖。这座陵墓在 1941 年被打开了。其他建筑物还有绿松石色穹顶的撒马尔罕大清真寺, 是帖木儿为了纪念他最爱的妻子所建造的, 另外还有几座宏伟的清真寺、帖木儿王族陵墓, 以及由帖木儿的孙子兀鲁伯建造的古观象台遗址。

Vocabulary

1. vicinity *n.* 附近, 邻近; 附近地区

Don't store any combustibles in the vicinity of this appliance.

不要在家电附近存放任何易燃物品。

2. caravan *n.* 车队；商队；大篷车

One day a caravan of 500 carts came by the village.

一天，有一支由 500 辆大篷车组成的商队经过村子。

3. reign *n.* 君主的统治；君主统治时期；任期；当政期

The streets ran with blood during the tyrant's reign of power.

在这个独裁者统治时期，到处都充满了血腥味。

4. surmount *vt.* 战胜，克服；登上，攀登；居于……之上；顶上覆盖着

Ann was able to surmount her fear of heights by learning to rock climb.

学会攀岩后，安妮终于克服了恐高症。

5. erect *vt.* 使直立，使竖起；建立，创立；安装

They plan to erect an apartment house on that property.

他们计划在那片地产上建造一座公寓楼。

扩展阅读

History of Samarkand

There are cities whose centuries-old history embodies the history of whole nation and countries, reflecting the way passed by many generations. Samarkand is one of the most ancient cities in the world. As other first centers of human civilization—Babylon and Memphis, Athens and Rome, Alexandria and Byzantium—Samarkand was intended to go through many events and shakes.

History of Samarkand goes back in remote days. Archeological findings and chronicle records of eyewitnesses and ancient historians allowed to establish with full reliability that a man lived on the territory of modern city many centuries before the Common Era.

Advantageous geographical location, rather favorable climate, abundance of natural springs with fine water, nearness of mountains with large wild fowl, flowing Zaravshan river—all these factors always provided favorable conditions for human settlings in that area, where strong walls, castles, majestic buildings and temples of Samarkand raised some centuries before the Common Era.

In historical events of ancient times the earliest mention about Samarkand (also known as Marakand) dates to 329th year BC, in descriptions of eyewitnesses and participants of conquering army of Alexander the Great. By that time Samarkand was a big city with crowded population, developed crafts, trade, and culture. It had unassailable citadel and outside defensive wall with length of 10.5 kilometers.

According to new archeological excavations scientists concluded that Samarkand was founded much earlier than the Greek-Macedonian Conquer and already during the epoch of the Akhemenids State (6—4th centuries BC) it was quite a developed city. Hence the "age" of Samarkand is over 2500 years, starting from the origin on the forest hill of Afrosiab, though it is far older.

Over the history the city saw half-savage tribes of Sacs and Massagets, iron flanks of Greek-Macedonin army, hordes of cruel Kara-Kidani. The city resisted the destructive invasion of fanatic Arabic commanders—followers of Islam religion. Bloody hordes of Ghengis-Khan attacked its peaceful houses with fire and sword. Samarkand became the capital of Great Empire of Tamerlane, ranged from Ind River to Bosfor.

After Timur's death all his empire came to the power of his children and grandchildren. Samarkand and surroundings devolved to Ulugbek, Timur's grandson. Ulugbek ruled Samarkand during 40 years. For the whole history Ulugbek was the most peace-loving ruler. He almost did not participate in aggressive campaigns over ruling his state. He visited other countries many times but only to study traditions, culture, and customs of those countries. He was a great scientist, astronomer, and mathematician; therefore he brought many scientists from different countries for science development in his county.

14—15th centuries is the period of the Golden Age of the city. City construction is at its zenith: the city is surrounded by strong fortified wall and new streets; pavements of stone are laid through the city; blue domes of magnificent ensembles tower above the city. Most of these objects survived our days and are the main symbols of the city.

Today, Samarkand, like most cities of Central Asia, is divided into two parts: old and new city. New part is an administrative part of the city, including industrial and cultural centers, high educational institutions. Old part of the city includes historical monuments, shops, workshops, old private houses. Generally, an excursion is held in the old part of the city. Samarkand numbers 500 thousand people. This is a multinational city. More than 100 nations live in Samarkand. Samarkand takes second place in Uzbekistan by number of population and territory.

（资料来源：http://www.advantour.com/uzbekistan/samarkand/history.htm）

Questions

1. When was Samarkand first mentioned in historical event?
2. What period was the Golden Age of the city?

Taj Mahal
泰姬陵

▷ 简介

所属国家：印度(India)

入选时间：1983

入选标准：(i)

The Taj Mahal is a white marble mausoleum in Agra, India. It is widely considered to be a premier example of Mughal architecture, which combines elements of Indian, Persian, and Islamic styles, and is one of India's top tourist attractions. It is commonly referred to as the Jewel of India. It is also inarguably the world's greatest monument of love.

The Taj Mahal was built by Mughal Emperor Shah Jahan in memory of his wife Mumtaz Mahal with construction started in AD 1632 and completed in AD 1648. Though the 145-foot-tall domed marble mausoleum is the most iconic element of the Taj Mahal, the site is actually a complex of structures located on the right bank of the Yamuna River. The complex covers nearly 42 acres, incorporating gardens and a red sandstone guesthouse, mosque, and gates. The red sandstone on the lesser buildings and white marble on mausoleum corresponds with the traditional Indian caste system, in which Brahmins had white buildings and the warrior caste had red.

The Taj Mahal is an aesthetic wonder of symmetry and balance created from solids and voids, lights and darks, domes and arches. The domed mausoleum features uniform shapes that are perfectly symmetrical, including twin domes astride the primary onion dome, arches and four minarets from which calls to prayer can be heard.

泰姬陵是一座位于印度阿格拉的白色大理石陵墓。它被广泛认为是莫卧儿建筑的表率。它结合了印度、波斯的元素和伊斯兰风格，是印度最受欢迎的景点之一，通常被称为印度的宝石，也可以说是世界上最伟大的爱的纪念碑。

泰姬陵是由莫卧儿皇帝沙贾汗为了纪念爱妻蒙泰姬·马哈尔而建造的，工程始建于公元 1632 年，完成于 1648 年。泰姬陵实际上是一个位于亚穆纳河右岸的综合体，145 英尺高的大理石圆顶陵墓是其最具标志性的元素。它占地面积近 42 亩，包括花园、红砂石翼殿、清真寺和大门。陵墓的白色大理石和翼殿的红砂石，与传统的印度种姓制度中婆罗门的白色建筑物和战士种姓阶层的红色相对应。

泰姬陵是个由虚实、明暗、圆直构成的对称与平衡的美学奇迹。陵墓的建筑包括主穹顶两侧的小穹顶、拱门和四个尖塔，都是完全对称的造型，在这里能听见召唤信徒祈祷的声音。

Vocabulary

1. premier *adj.* 第一的，首位的；首要的；最先的；最早的

There was a full house at the film premier.

这部影片首映的时候，电影院里座无虚席。

2. iconic *adj.* 符号的；图标的；图符的；偶像的

After all, the iconic singer only recorded 52 songs under his own name.

这位偶像歌手本人只录了 52 首歌曲。

3. align *v.* (使)成一线，(使)结盟；排整齐

Could you align this table with those?

你能把这张桌子同那些桌子排成一行吗？

4. aesthetic *adj.* 美的，美学的；有关美的；审美的；具有审美趣味的

These exotic settings greatly add to the aesthetic appeal of the movie.

这些充满异国情调的场景大大增加了影片的美感。

5. symmetry *n.* 对称；对称美；整齐，匀称

Symmetry has been a source of fascination since ancient times.

自古以来，对称就是魅力之源。

扩展阅读

Tips for Visiting the Taj Mahal

Ever wonder what a building that took 22 years to build with the help of 20,000 workers looks like in person? If so, you may want to stop by one of the "new" seven wonders of the world on your next visit to India.

The Taj Mahal is an incredible landmark with rich cultural significance. It's a must-see if you have an opportunity to reach that corner of the world.

Background of the Taj Mahal

The Taj Mahal was built in 1630 by Mughal emperor Shah Jahan and is the final resting place of his wife, Mumtaz Mahal. It is considered to be one of the most grandiose burial sites ever created.

No expense was spared to bring this monument of his love for her to life. It consists of marble and many other precious materials as well as very formal and complex gardens and water features. It's a sight to behold, indeed.

How to get to the Taj Mahal

The Taj Mahal is located in Agra, which is about 210 kilometers outside of Delhi. It is included in what is known as India's Golden Triangle tourist circuit of sites. Two ideal ways to get there are by high speed rail service from Delhi, or by joining a tour from Delhi, which will provide transport for you.

When to visit the Taj Mahal

If you get a chance to pick the time of year to visit, you might want to consider coming during the Taj Mahotsav, which takes place from February 18 to the 27th each year near the Taj Mahal. This gives you the opportunity to enjoy a cultural festival that includes arts, crafts, and entertainment from the Mughal time period. Included are drummers, elephant rides, and games for children.

Best time of day to visit the Taj Mahal

Whenever you do decide to come, be aware of the Taj Mahal's open hours, which are typically from 6 a.m. to 7 p.m. every day except on Friday because this is a day of prayer. Be sure to check out the moonlight viewing, from 8.30 p.m. until 12.30 a.m., which is two days before and after each full moon.

And, speaking of an ideal time to go, the color of the building changes as the light hits it throughout the day, so you may want to try sunrise or sunset to get a varying effect.

Tourist Attractions Near the Taj Mahal

If you want to avoid admission and the beggars, consider getting a view from across the river bank. You can see it in all of its glory while also taking in Mehtab Bagh, a 25-acre garden, which has a lower admission fee.

While there are not many tourist attractions in the city of Agra proper, you might want to check out the city of Fatehpur Sikri, the Bharatpur Bird Sanctuary at the Keoladeo Ghana National Park, or Akbar's Mausoleum.

Admission Fees for Visiting the Taj Mahal

While pricing is subject to change, the current entrance fee for foreigners is a 250 rupees Entry Tax and a 500 rupees Toll Tax. Indian nationals pay 20 rupees. Children under 15 years of age are free.

Night time tickets cost the same 750 rupees for foreigners and 500 rupees for Indian nationals, but are good for only a half hour's admission. Tickets must be purchased 24 hours in advance—you can get from the Archaeological Survey of India office on Mall Road.

（资料来源：http://video. about. com/goindia/Tips-for-Visiting-the-Taj-Mahal. htm）

Questions

1. What would be the ideal ways to get to the Taj Mahal?
2. What is the best time to visit the Taj Mahal?

第二节　亚洲的世界自然遗产

Jiuzhaigou Valley Scenic and Historic Interest Area
九寨沟风景名胜区

⇨ **简介**

所属国家：中国（China）

入选时间：1992

入选标准：（vii）

The Jiuzhaigou Valley gets its name from the fact that there are nine Tibetan villages in the valley. Stretching over 720 km² in the northern part of Sichuan Province, the jagged Jiuzhaigou valley reaches a height of more than 4,800 m, and comprises a series of diverse forest ecosystems. Its superb landscapes are particularly interesting for their series of narrow conic karst landforms and spectacular waterfalls.

The best-known features in the area are its lakes. Many of these, lying at the base of glacially formed valleys, are classic ribbon lakes which have been dammed naturally, for example behind rock falls from avalanches. The waterfalls flow down from different heights; the lakes of various sizes reflect the red leaves, green trees, snow-capped peaks and blue sky. Water flows around tree roots and the trees grow in water. The views vary from one place to another.

Some 140 bird species inhabit the valley, as well as a number of endangered plant and animal species, including the giant panda, golden monkeys and the Sichuan takin. The languages, costumes and customs of the people of the Qiang and Tibetan minority peoples are also unique and attractive.

九寨沟以其所在的山谷里有九个藏族村寨而得名。错落有致的九寨沟位于四川省的北部,跨越720平方千米,高达4800多米,构成了多样化的森林生态系统。由于其窄圆锥形的岩溶地形和壮观的瀑布,其无与伦比的景色引人入胜。

该地区最著名的特征是拥有众多湖泊。许多湖泊位于冰河时期形成峡谷的地方,是自然造就的典型带状湖,如由雪崩引起的岩崩而形成的湖。瀑布高低不同,错落有致;大大小小的湖水中倒映着红叶、绿树、雪山和蓝天。树水相依,移步易景,千姿百态。

栖息在该峡谷的有约140种鸟以及大量的濒危动植物,包括大熊猫、金丝猴和四川羚羊。当地的少数民族羌族和藏族的语言、服饰和风俗也是一道引人注目的独特风景。

Vocabulary

1. stretch v. 伸展,张开,伸展

She stretched out on the grass in the sun.

她伸展四肢躺在阳光下的草地上。

2. superb adj. 极好的;华丽的;丰盛的,豪华的;杰出的

My cooking skills are neither superb nor too bad.

我的厨艺算不上一流,但也不算太坏。

3. dam vt. 用水坝阻止;阻塞,抑制

Whatever happens, you have to dam up your feelings.

无论发生什么,你必须控制住感情。

4. avalanche n. 雪崩

He was dug out from under the avalanche.

他被人从坍崩的雪堆中挖出来。

5. endanger v. 危及;使遭到危险

The expansion of the city has endangered the wildlife animals.

市区的扩展危及野生动物。

扩展阅读

Go Native-Tibetan Style——in Jiuzhaigou

When traveling to Nanjing earlier this year, I met a young man from Sichuan province who told me that if I ever found my way to central China, I should visit the most beautiful place in the country, Jiuzhaigou.

When trekking plans to Tibet fell through, Jiuzhaigou, home of a pristine national park chock full of alpine lakes and waterfalls located in northwest Sichuan province, seemed like a worthy alternative.

Many tours equipped with flag bearing guides depart from Chengdu by bus (11 hours) or plane (one hour) and after the trip, return to the originating city. I wasn't interested in the flag, the tour guide or returning to a city that I had already visited, so I began searching for an alternative route.

A Tibetan experience minus the permit

While in Chengdu, I was tipped off by a local magazine about a home stay with a Tibetan family in Jiuzhaigou. The contact was an Irish man who relocated to the UNESCO world heritage site to promote tourism while preserving the local Tibetan culture.

He told me about two brothers, Zhuo Ma and Ke Zhu, who recently opened their home to guests and provided dinner and breakfast.

As the only family offering home stays in this area, both brothers speak their native Tibetan language as well as fluent Mandarin. Since my Chinese vocabulary had recently surpassed survival level, he said that communicating with the guys wouldn't be a problem.

The trek

A few days later, I found myself on an airplane maneuvering around mountain peaks and slicing through thick fog before landing at the small Jiuzhai Huanglong Airport.

Jiuzhaigou, which means Nine Village Valley in English, is a two-hour drive from the airport. I found the most affordable option when traveling solo is the airport shuttle bus (RMB 45 one-way). The only drawback to this form of transportation is that you have to wait until at least five passengers board the shuttle. In the 45-minute lapse before the others arrived, with the help of my electronic translator, I chatted with the driver of my shuttle and two other drivers taking a break.

When we set off from the airport, the vehicle spiraled its way up and down the tree-covered mountains draped with waterfalls. Prayer flags sporadically wound up the side of hills and fields of grazing yaks dominated the terrain. The landscape in Jiuzhaigou is made for the perfect romantic weekend getaway. I now understood why everyone else in the car was coupled off.

My Tibetan home (stay)

After passing hotels and facades of resorts, the main road came to a cross where a smiling Zhou Ma waited for me in his small grey car. We turned off the main juncture and onto a small rocky road lined with Tibetan style homes and high standing prayer flags. Ten minutes of small talk passed then I arrived at Zhou Ma's home.

His mother emerged in full Tibetan garb including a fluffy red and white hat, a long sleeved white blouse that necklaces and small braids cascaded over, and a long black skirt trimmed with a wide band of red and green at the bottom fastened by a bright colored belt. This is when I realized the home stay was the right decision.

I found myself in a dimly lit space acting as living room, dining room and kitchen. The light source came from a wood-burning stove, a neon bulb dangling from an extension cord and the glow from a small TV in the corner of the room.

Zhou Ma offered me "milk tea" (nai cha). The soup-like beverage was the first of many things I would consume in Jiuzhaigou containing some part of yak.

No showers. No toilet. No sink. A large bowl of warm water heated by the wood-burning stove was brought outside to use for freshening up before getting to bed. I was shown a toilet that consisted of a rectangle hole with a 4-foot drop off to the ground cut in the center of a small boarded up area adjacent to the house. Not what I'm used to.

Far from a deal breaker but after two days of no shower, myself, and probably those around me, began to feel the wrath.

Yak as a food group

After a day at the Jiuzhai Valley National Park, Zhou Ma drove us to Abuluzi, the Tibetan restaurant of his younger brother, Ke Zhu. There we were served local specialties such as buttered tea made from tea leaves and yak butter, sauteed pepper, onion and yak meat served on a skillet, mashed potatoes in a tasty red sauce, and cold yak meat with a side of dry red pepper and salt for dipping. Sensing a trend here?

The food was authentic and delicious.

The rest

In a room with a cord strung around all four walls, the family's clothes hung as if in a closet. Two queen-sized beds lay low to the ground and a pull at a string near the door turned the room's single light on and off. I cleared a path before turning the room into darkness, carefully stepped toward the bed, tucked myself in, took a deep breath and lay back on the hay filled pillow. I was in Jiuzhaigou, exactly where I wanted to be.

（资料来源：http://travel.cnn.com/shanghai/play/tibetan-home-stay-jiuzhaigou-167132）

Questions

1. Where did the author stay overnight when he traveled Jiuzhaigou?

2. How's the food there?

Kinabalu Park
基纳巴卢山公园

➡️ 简介

所属国家：马来西亚（Malaysia）

入选时间：2000

入选标准：(ix)(x)

The area around Mount Kinabalu, spanning 754 square kilometers, was converted into a National Park in 1964 because of its geographical and geological importance and the abundance of diverse flora, 4,500 species of plants, 1,200 types of orchids, 290 known species of butterflies and 326 types of birds.

At 4,095.2 m, Mount Kinabalu is Malaysia's highest mountain. In December 2000, UNESCO recognised Mount Kinabalu as Malaysia's first World Heritage site for its "outstanding universal values" and its role as one of the most important biological sites in the world.

Located at 1,585 metres above sea level, Kinabalu Park showcases a complete and interesting ecological system unrivalled anywhere else in the world. It also carries lowland, mountain and alpine vegetation that are not seen anywhere else between the Himalayas and the snow-capped peaks of New Guinea.

The Park boasts more than 5,000 vascular plant species, an estimated 1,000 orchid species, 621 fern species, nine Nepenthes species, 29 Rhododendron species and two Rafflesia species. The Park has no shortage of fauna as well, being home to some 90 lowland mammal species, 22 montane mammal species, 21 bat species, 326 bird species, 62 toad and frog species and a large population of the 850 butterfly species that occur in Sabah. Out of the 29 bird species that are endemic to Borneo, at least 17 are confined to the mountains, notably Mount Kinabalu. Such diversity is truly the makings of a naturalists' paradise.

基纳巴卢山周边地区的面积为 754 平方千米,1964 年因其重要的地理和地质意义以及植物的多样性改建成国家公园。这个公园拥有 4500 种植物、1200 种兰花、290 种已知种类的蝴蝶和 326 种鸟类。

基纳巴卢山高 4095.2 米,是马来西亚最高的山。2000 年 12 月,基纳巴卢山由于其"卓越的全球价值"被联合国教科文组织认定为马来西亚的第一个世界遗产,并被认可为世界上最重要的生物基地之一。

基纳巴卢山公园的海拔高达 1585 米以上,展示了一个世界上无与伦比的既完整又精彩的生态系统。它还有喜马拉雅山和冰雪覆盖的新几内亚山峰一带等其他地方都没有的低地、山地和高山植被。

这个公园里有超过 5000 种维管束植物,约 1000 种兰科植物,621 种蕨类植物,9 种忘忧草,29 种杜鹃花和两种大王花。公园里动物的种类繁多,共有 90 种低地哺乳动物,22 种山地哺乳动物,21 种蝙蝠,326 种鸟类,62 种蟾蜍和青蛙,850 种蝴蝶。在婆罗洲特有的 29 种鸟类中,至少有 17 种只存在于山间,尤其是基纳巴卢山。这种多样性构成了博物学家的天堂。

Vocabulary

1. flora *n.* 植物区系；植物群

There was a restaurant in Garden Road where one could be served like in a tropic array of screening flora.

花园路上有一家餐馆,在那里用餐几乎像是置身于一排热带遮护植物中一样。

2. convert *vt.* (使)转变;使皈依;兑换,换算

Solar cell can absorb sunlight and convert it into electricity.

太阳能电池能吸收阳光并把它变成电。

3. showcase *vt.* 使展现;在玻璃橱窗陈列

They are set to showcase the fine food that China has to offer.

他们计划向世人展示中国的美食。

4. fauna *n.* 动物群;[动] 动物区系

The unique fauna in Africa fascinated me.

非洲特有的动物群令我着迷。

5. endemic *adj.* 地方性的;风土的

There are quite a few interesting endemic species on the island.

这个岛上有不少有趣的地方性物种。

▌扩展阅读

Scenic Kinabalu Park under Threat

Unplanned development is destroying the beauty of the highlands of Sabah and threatening the existence of the Kinabalu National Park which is a gazetted World Heritage site.

The scenic, meandering stretch of highway from the farming town of Tamparuli at the foothills of the Crocker Range is rapidly being defaced, according to the Sabah Environment Protection Association (Sepa).

"We can see rampant hill-cutting and tree-felling activities taking place right outside the World Heritage site of Mount Kinabalu.

"So much degradation is occurring that it feels like our icon is being treated like a garbage dump," Sepa president Wong Tack said.

He criticised the state government for failing to protect the fragile environment of the area surrounding the park and the park itself.

"The hill slopes are being cut and cleared of all vegetation, and structures are being put up indiscriminately," he said.

Wong claimed that huge areas of land are also being cleared near Mesilau following the sub-division of the land near the foot of the mountain.

He said large stretches of land were being cleared for illegal farming even on steep slopes.

"The consequences of allowing people to do just as they please will be disastrous to the environment.

"They are destroying the charm of the place, which is what lures people and tourists there. They are not considerate towards the environment.

"Worse still, no restoration work is being done on exposed areas near the park," he said.

Proper planning needed

Wong said the authorities appeared unconcerned about encroachment on state land.

"Farmers have begun cutting down trees and are said to be eager to move there to re-settle. They have been at it for the last two to three weeks and the relevant authorities have been informed.

"But the farmers are still carrying on with their activity and no one is doing anything to stop them," he said.

"The government should look for an appropriate site to re-settle the farmers and not allow them to do anything they like.

"It is unfair they do not have a proper site for re-settlement.

"Allowing them to simply do anything is another example of unplanned development near the heritage site," he said.

He added that Sepa wanted the state government to conduct a comprehensive environmental study of the area from Tamparuli town to Poring Hot Springs, near Ranau town.

Wong said the study would help control development in the huge swath of land that business interests have been eyeing for a long time.

Corrective measures

Sepa has suggested that licensing authorities, tour operators, local authorities, Land and Survey Department as well as the tourism, culture and environment ministry be included in the planning of the area.

Wong said Sepa would continue to highlight the issue until the government takes corrective measures to protect the heritage site and its surroundings.

"We have had enough lip service from the authorities. We want to see action," he said, adding that Sepa will be forming a stakeholder committee to get the local community involved in caring for the area.

According to real estate sources as well as residents, most businesses that have moved into the area and set up resort-style establishments or eateries, have brought little benefit to the locals.

"The locals sell their land to businessmen to get some money and end up being even poorer after a few years as they have lost their land.

"They then move to a new area and start opening up the land to do some farming to sustain themselves so it's like a vicious cycle," said a businessman familiar with the property market in the area.

He said that in some cases, those who have established resorts and restaurants in the area sometimes paid the villagers in the surrounding areas to illegally clear the land for them.

（资料来源：http://www. freemalaysiatoday. com/category/nation/2011/04/21/scenic-kinabalu-park-under-threat/）

Questions

1. What is threatening the existence of the Kinabalu National Park?
2. What should be done to improve the situation?

Socotra Archipelago
索科特拉群岛

简介

所属国家：也门（Yemen）

入选时间：2008

入选标准：（x）

Socotra Archipelago，in the northwest Indian Ocean near the Gulf of Aden，is 250 km long and comprises four islands and two rocky islets which appear as a prolongation of the Horn of Africa. Some 250 million years or more ago，when all the planet's major landmasses were joined and most major life-forms roamed freely from one region to another，Socotra already stood as an island apart. Ever since Socotra has been a breeding ground of birds，plants and animals. The isolation from other landmasses meant whatever evolutionary process the flora and fauna underwent never spread to the mainland.

Socotra is globally important for biodiversity conservation because of its exceptionally rich and distinct flora and fauna; 37 per cent of its plant species，90 per cent of its reptile species and 95 per cent of its land snail species do not occur anywhere else in the world. The site also supports globally significant populations of land and sea birds (192 bird species，44 of which breed on the islands while 85 are regular migrants)，including a number of threatened species. The marine life of Socotra is also very diverse，with 253 species of reef-building corals，730 species of coastal fish and 300 species of crab，lobster and shrimp. Socotra，one of the most biodiverse and distinct islands in the world，has been termed the "Galapagos of the Indian Ocean".

索科特拉群岛位于印度洋西北面的亚丁湾附近，有 250 千米长，由 4 个岛屿和 2 个岩石小洲构成，看上去像是"非洲之角"的延伸部分。2.5 亿年或更久以前，当地球上所有主要的陆地都还连成一片，大部分的生物还在各个区域之间自由漫步时，索科特拉岛已经是一个独立的岛屿了。从那时候开始索科特拉群岛就已经是鸟类、植物和动物的繁殖地。这种与世隔绝意味着岛上的任何动植物进化过程都从未传播到大陆。

由于索科特拉群岛拥有极其丰富独特的动植物群，因此对于保护全球生物的多样性具有重要意义。该岛上 37% 的植物、90% 的爬虫类动物和 95% 的蜗牛都是世界上独一无二的。这里还拥有大量的鸟类,其中包括一些濒危物种(192 种鸟类,其中 44 种生长在岛上,85 种是候鸟)。索科特拉岛的海洋生物也很丰富,有 253 种人造礁珊瑚,730 种沿海鱼类和 300 种蟹、龙虾和虾。索科特拉是世界上生物种类最丰富、最独特的岛屿之一,被称为"印度洋上的处女岛"。

Vocabulary

1. archipelago *n.* 群岛,列岛;多岛的海区

Indonesia is the largest archipelago in the world.

印尼是世界上最大的群岛。

2. roam *v.* 漫游;漫步

I used to roam around the building after dark.

我过去常常在天黑后在建筑物周围闲逛。

3. reptile *adj.* 爬虫类的

You should not be surprised to see someone keep a reptile as a pet.

你不必惊奇有人养了一只爬行动物作为宠物。

4. terrestrial *adj.* 地球的;陆地的

Asia is one of the main terrestrial lands of the earth.

亚洲是地球的主要陆地之一。

5. marine *adj.* 船舶的;海生的;海产的;航海的,海运的

John specializes in marine law.

约翰专门研究海事法。

扩展阅读

New Reptile Discovered in World's Strangest Archipelago

Few people have ever heard of the Socotra Archipelago even though, biologically-speaking, it is among the world's most wondrous set of islands. Over one third of Socotra's plants are found no-where else on Earth, i. e. endemic, while 90 percent of its reptiles are also endemic. Adding to its list of unique life-forms, researchers have recently uncovered a new skink species that is found only on the island of Abd al Kuri, which is slightly smaller than New York City's Staten Island. Dubbed the "the other Galapagos", the four Socotra islands are under the jurisdiction of Yemen, although geographically speaking the islands are actually closer to Somalia.

"While in Socotra in 2010, we eventually had the chance to organize a short trip to the smaller islands of the archipelago, which are hardly reachable due to heavy seas for most of the year, and pirate activity in the area facing Somalia," team member Fabio Pupin, herpetologist and photographer, told mongabay. com. "(We were) able to spend at least one day and one night in each of the three islands (Samha, Darsa and Abd al Kuri). While in Abd al Kuri, Cristina Grieco, one of the team members, found a quite huge skink under a bush. We captured it for identification and measurements and we instantly realized that the skink was clearly different from all the others we met before on the islands. However, we had to hold down excitement until we properly compared its morphological features with other species and molecular results definitively confirmed our suspicions. "

Describing the new species in a paper in *Zoological Scripta*, the team of researchers named it Christine's mabuya (*Trachylepis cristinae*), after its discoverer. With the discovery of the new skink, the small island of Abd al Kuri is now home to five reptiles found no-where else on Earth.

"As probably happened quite often in other parts of the world, skinks may have reached the archipelago by rafting on logs or other floating vegetation. Reptiles such as skinks and geckos have proved to be incredibly good dispersers, and they are even known to have crossed the Atlantic ocean," Pupin says.

The paper hypothesis that skinks in the Trachylepis genus arrived in the Socotra Archipelago twice this way. The first immigrant arrived around 10 million years ago and colonized three islands (Socotra, Darsa and Samha), eventually evolving into the species known today as the Socotra mabuya (*Trachylepis socotrana*). A second immigrant arrived seven million years later on Abd al Kuri Island and has now taken its rightful place as Christine's mabuya.

The other worldly archipelago

The landscape of the Socotra islands resembles a Hollywood film set on another planet: rocky and dry, but hauntingly beautiful, with strange umbrella-shaped trees—evocatively named the dragon blood tree (*Dracaena cinnabari*), because the species' resin is the color of blood.

"These are some of the oldest islands in the world. Millions of years of isolation from nearby continents provided the flora and fauna of the islands with the textbook situation of surviving and evolving in their own ways. That's why the islands are inhabited by such an impressive number of endemics. It's quite a general rule to find peculiarities on islands, but what makes Socotra Archipelago so amazing is its amount of endemics: just considering reptiles, they are almost all endemic (except those which are believed to have reached the islands thanks to us) with ancient lineages and genera, including multiple species clearly adapted to different habitats," explains Pupin.

In addition to reptiles, the Socotra Archipelago is also home to around 145 bird species, 10 of which are only found on the islands; and around 100 land snail species, 95 of which are endemic. The only native mammals are bats. Given this rich biodiversity, it's not surprising that the islands were designated a UNESCO World Heritage Natural site in 2008.

Perhaps, however, the most surprising thing about the Socotra Archipelago is that it has not been swept by extinctions like many other islands. To date, scientists believe the islands have lost none of their endemic birds, reptiles, or mollusks in the last century; compare that to the Hawaiian Islands which has lost nearly one-third of its endemic birds. Still, even though the Socotra Archipelago is largely protected and are not unused to humans (a population of around 50,000 has lived on the archipelago, mostly Socotra Island, for thousands of years), researchers fear that the Socotra Archipelago could soon begin to see its biodiversity vanish if the region is mismanaged.

Alien world in peril?

Socotra's biodiversity face a number of common island threats, including habitat loss, overpopulation, invasive species, climate change, and more recently a sudden rise in tourism. Although benefiting the local economy, poorly-regulated tourism can put a hefty toll on the very ecosystems that visitors long to see. In 2010, over 3,000 tourists visited Socotra Island.

In addition, recent upheavals in Yemen have made the island's future tenuous. Like many Middle Eastern nations, Yemen felt the impacts of the Arab Spring. After widespread protests, including violent crackdowns on protesters, power in the country was transferred to the then vice president, Abd Rabbuh Mansur Al-Hadi, in a vote where Al-Hadi was the only candidate. The vote, however, ended the 33-year reign of Ali Abdullah Saleh.

"Currently the conservationist's main concern is the political instability in Yemen and the results it will have on the biodiversity conservation of the islands in the incoming years. By now, almost any project in the islands involving westerner personnel has been stopped and no one knows how the situation will evolve," Pupin says, "What we hope is that the endless finding of new species—our skink is just one of the many new discoveries of the islands' fauna and flora—will hold the attention of the general public and decision-makers on this biodiversity paradise."

In the meantime, researchers will just have to wait to see how much the new government in Yemen values its alien islands.

（资料来源：http://news.mongabay.com/2012/0425-hance_socotra.html）

Questions

1. How many reptiles are endemic in Socotra Archipelago?
2. What is the conservationist's main concern about the island right now?

Tubbataha Reefs Natural Park
图巴塔哈群礁自然公园

⇨ 简介

所属国家：菲律宾（Philippines）

入选时间：2009

入选标准：（vii）（ix）（x）

Tubbataha Reefs Natural Park covers a pristine atoll reef ecosystem with a very high diversity of marine life. It comprises the only two atolls in the Philippine archipelago, North and South Reef, separated by an 8 km wide channel. North Reef is a large, oblong, continuous reef platform some 16 km long and 4.5 km wide, completely enclosing a sandy lagoon some 24 m deep. The reef flat is shallow and emergent in some places at extreme low tide. The most prominent subarea feature is the North Islet which is a coralline sand cay, which serves as a nesting site for birds and marine turtles. Steep and often perpendicular walls extending to a depth of 40—50 m characterize the seaward face of the reef.

South Reef, a small, triangular-shaped reef about 1—2 km wide, consists, like the North Reef, of a shallow platform enclosing a sandy lagoon. South Islet, a coralline-sand cay of approximately 800 square meters (m²), is located on the southern tip of the reef, and is also used as a nesting site.

The Tubbataha Reefs are the largest concentration of coral reefs in the Philippines. Hundreds of different species of vivid corals cover more than two-thirds of the area. This intact and remote ecosystem rivals the Great Barrier Reef—having 300 coral species and 400 fish species. Animal species that inhabit the reefs include whales, manta rays, lionfish, turtle, clownfish, spotted dolphin and sharks.

图巴塔哈群礁自然公园是个原始的环状珊瑚礁生态系统，具有很高的海洋生物多样性。它由菲律宾群岛仅有的两座环礁组成——北礁和南礁，两者之间相隔一道 8 千米宽的海峡。北礁是一个巨大的、连绵不断的椭圆形平台，长 16 千米，宽 4.5 千米，看上去就像是将一个 24 米深的含沙礁湖装入袋子里。礁石平台所处位置很浅，只有涨低潮时才能浮现出来。北礁属沙质珊瑚礁，是鸟类和海龟的主要栖息地；朝海的一边则是高达四五十米的峭壁。

南礁宽约 1—2 千米，呈较小的三角状。与北礁类似，南礁也是动物的栖息地，也像是把一个含沙礁湖装入袋子里。位于礁石南端的南礁是一片面积约为 800 平方米的沙质珊瑚礁。（跟北礁一样，）南礁也为鸟类和海龟提供了栖息地。

图巴塔哈群礁是菲律宾最大的珊瑚礁集中地。不同种类的珊瑚覆盖了整个区域的三分之二。这里有 300 多种珊瑚与 400 多种鱼类，其生态环境的完整性和多样性可以媲美澳大利亚的大堡礁。栖息在珊瑚礁的动物物种包括鲸鱼、蝠鲼、狮子鱼、龟、小丑鱼、斑海豚和鲨鱼。

Vocabulary

1. pristine *adj.* 太古的，原始状态的；纯朴的，纯洁的；未受腐蚀的，新鲜的

The jungle was pristine—it looked like no person had ever been there.

这个丛林是原始的，看起来像没有人到过那里。

2. atoll *n.* 环状珊瑚岛

Bomb tests resulted in the annihilation of the atoll.

原子弹试爆毁灭了那个珊瑚岛。

3. enclose *vt.*（用墙、篱笆等）把……围起来；把……装入信封；附入

Please enter the number of your ID Card and enclose a photocopy.

请输入身份证号并附上复印件。

4. intact *adj.* 完整无缺的，未受损伤的，完好无损的

The cellphone remained intact after being dropped down the stairs.

这部手机掉下台阶后仍然完好无损。

5. prominent *adj.* 突出的，杰出的；显著的；著名的

Another very prominent symbol of Christmas is the Christmas tree.

圣诞节另一个显著的象征是圣诞树。

扩展阅读

72 US Sailors Leave Ship Stuck in Tubbataha Reef

The US Navy minesweeper that ran aground on a coral reef remained stuck at the Tubbataha Reefs Natural Park for the second day on Friday but most of the US sailors had left the ship for safety reasons after initial efforts to free the vessel failed, the US Navy's 7th Fleet said in a statement on Friday.

It said 72 of the 79 crew of the USS Guardian were transferred to a military support vessel by small boat. A small team, including the commanding and executive officers, would remain on board to try to extricate the ship with as little damage to environment as possible, the statement said.

How the US warship managed to enter the marine sanctuary puzzles the Philippine Navy.

Commodore Joseph Peña of the Naval Forces West said there are designated sea-lanes where ships could sail, which was outside and "far" from the Tubbataha Reef.

The US Navy also said that initial efforts to free the Guardian during high tide were not successful. Philippine officials said the weather yesterday was choppy with strong winds and rough seas.

The ship ran aground Thursday while in transit through the marine park, a coral sanctuary in the Sulu Sea, 640 kilometers southwest of Manila. There were no injuries or oil leaks, and Philippine authorities were trying to evaluate damage to the protected coral reef, designated by UNESCO as a World Heritage site in 1992.

The USS Guardian, a 68-meter long minesweeper, reportedly hit the upper side of the South Atoll, one of the two main atolls comprising the Tubbataha Reefs, at dawn of Thursday.

Park rangers ignored

The World Wide Fund (WWF) for Nature Philippines said that according to an initial visual inspection, the 68-meter-long, 1,300-ton Guardian damaged at least 10 meters of the reef. Aerial photographs provided by the Philippine military showed the ship's bow sitting atop corals in shallow turquoise waters. The stern was floating in the deep blue waters.

The US Navy said the cause of the grounding, which took place around 2 a. m. Thursday, was under investigation.

The US 7th Fleet claimed it had formally notified the Philippine government of the accident but has apparently bypassed the small detachment of park rangers guarding the marine park.

"They (US authorities) have not communicated with us so far," said Angelique Songco, head of the government's Protected Area Management Board that supervises the marine park.

Tubbataha to file protest

Songco said the marine park's management would file a formal protest with the US government over the behavior of the Guardian's commander who prevented park rangers from approaching the vessel.

She said that park rangers were not allowed to board the ship for inspection and were told to contact the US Embassy in Manila. Their radio calls to the ship were ignored, she said.

She said it was unclear how much of the reef was damaged. She said the government imposes a fine of about $300 per square meter (yard) of damaged coral.

In 2005, the environmental group Greenpeace was fined almost $7,000 after its flagship struck a reef in the same area.

Maj. Oliver Banaria, spokesperson for the Armed Forces of the Philippines, said the US Navy did not request assistance from the Philippines.

The Philippine Navy has deployed a ship to the area to "provide assistance" to the stricken vessel but it said it would be mainly the US Navy that would pull the Guardian out of the reef.

A second US vessel, identified by park authorities as the USS Champion, arrived early Friday, apparently to help get the USS Guardian off the reef.

"Our (Navy) would be on standby because these are still our territorial waters and we would be providing information to our higher headquarters. We would be there for monitoring and to provide any help or assistance if they (US) ask for it," Banaria said. US Navy ships have stepped up visits to Philippine ports for refueling, rest and recreation, plus joint military exercises as a result of a redeployment of US forces in the Asia-Pacific region.

The Philippines, a US defense treaty ally, has been entangled in a territorial dispute with China in the West Philippine Sea (South China Sea).

Palace weighs words

Malacañang on Friday confirmed that the US minesweeper had come from Subic Bay for a "regular port call", but declined to be drawn into a discussion this early on the subject of seeking damages from Washington.

"We don't want to make any speculations yet at this point. We want to proceed where everything has been thoroughly established before we make any further comment on this matter," said the deputy presidential spokesperson Abigail Valte.

Valte stressed that the government was concerned about the possible damage to the reef by the US ship.

She also tried to discourage the media from treating the incident as an offshoot of the increased US presence in the country following the new US "pivot policy" to the Asian region.

Peña said the Navy had patrolled the area of the Tubbataha Reef last week to make sure that no ship would be crossing the waters of the marine sanctuary.

But just as the Philippine ship returned to shore to replenish its supplies, the USS Guardian had struck the coral reef.

Explanation demanded

Sen. Francis Pangilinan, a member of President Aquino's Liberal Party, called on the DFA to demand a satisfactory explanation from the US government over the reported incursions into Philippine territory of US military forces over the past couple of weeks.

"First, it was a US drone. Now, it's a minesweeper," Pangilinan said in a statement.

"Friends and allies must exercise good faith by coming clean," he added.

Pangilinan finds the US government "sketchy in providing answers in both incidents".

Sen. Loren Legarda, chair of the Senate committee on foreign relations, expressed "extreme concern" over the damage to the Tubbataha Reef.

She said those who caused the incident should be made accountable.

（资料来源：http://newsinfo. inquirer. net/342997/72-us-sailors-leave-ship-stuck-in-tubbataha-reef）

Questions

1. How did the US warship manage to enter the marine sanctuary?

2. How much was the environmental group Greenpeace fined after its flagship struck a reef in the same area in 2005?

第三节　亚洲的世界文化和自然双重遗产

Mount Emei Scenic Area, Including Leshan Giant Buddha Scenic Area
峨眉山-乐山大佛

▢⇨ **简介**

所属国家：中国（China）

入选时间：1996

入选标准：(iv)，(vi)，(x)

Mount Emei, a sacred mountain for Buddhists in China, stands towering the southwestern part of the Sichuan Basin. Its summit the Wanfo (Tens of Thousands of Buddhas) Peak rises up to 3,099 m in altitude and the whole mountainous area covers more than 4 square kilometers. Seen from afar, the undulating mountain silhouette looks like the face and long eyebrows of a demure young lady; hence the name Emei (long eyebrows).

The first Buddhist temple in China was built here in the first century AD in very beautiful surroundings atop Mount Emei. The addition of other temples turned the site into one of Buddhism's main holy places. Over the centuries, the cultural treasures grew in number. The most remarkable was the Giant Buddha of Leshan, carved out of a hillside in the eighth century and looking down on the confluence of three rivers. At 71 m high, it is the largest Buddha in the world.

As one of the four holy lands of Chinese Buddhism, this site is of great historical importance. It's also a vital sanctuary for a many internationally threatened animal species, including lesser panda, Asiatic black bear, and Asiatic golden cat.

Mount Emei is also notable for its very diverse vegetation, ranging from subtropical to sub-alpine pine forests. Some of the trees are more than 1,000 years old.

峨眉山是一座中国佛教名山，屹立在四川盆地西南部。其最高峰万佛峰海拔高达3099米，整座山覆盖了多达4平方千米的面积。从远处看，绵延起伏的山脉的轮廓看起来像一位淑女的脸和她修长的眉毛，故名峨眉（长眉）。

中国的第一座佛寺于公元1世纪建于峨眉山顶的美丽环境中。后来陆续建成的其他寺庙遗址变成了佛教的主要圣地之一。几个世纪以来，这里出现了大量的文化宝藏。最引人注目的当数乐山大佛。乐山大佛于8世纪雕刻于一座山边，俯瞰着3条河的汇流处。

大佛高 71 米,是世界上最大的佛像。

作为中国佛教的四大圣地之一,该遗址具有非常重要的历史意义。它还是国际上许多濒危动物的重要保护区,包括小熊猫、亚洲黑熊和亚洲金猫。

峨眉山还以其非常多样化的植被而著称于世,山上分布着从亚热带到亚高山带的松林。有些树的树龄长达 1000 多年。

Vocabulary

1. undulate *v.* 起伏;波动;(使)呈波浪形;震动

The field of wheat was undulating in the breeze.

麦田在微风中麦浪滚滚。

2. silhouette *n.* 轮廓,剪影;(人的)体形;(事物的)形状

The leather-silhouette show originates in China and then goes round the world.

皮影戏起源于中国,在世界范围内流传。

3. confluence *n.* (河流的)汇合、汇流点;(人或物的)聚集

We are facing the most dangerous part of the river, the confluence.

我们来到河上最危险的一段,这是两条河交汇的地方。

4. sanctuary *n.* 避难所;至圣所;耶路撒冷的神殿

The outlaw found a sanctuary in the nearby church.

这名犯法者在附近的教堂里避难。

5. sub-alpine *n.* 亚高山

sub-alpine meadow 亚高山草甸

扩展阅读

Four Great Spectacles of Mt. Emei

Sunrise

In Golden Summit, the sky before dawn is amazing. The ground and the sky are in the same dark purple. Then gradually wisps of rosy clouds appear above the horizon, indicating the coming of a pleasant day. Under the pink clouds on the royal purple velarium, all of a sudden, a small mauve point comes out and rises slowly, and then little by little it becomes an arc and then a semicircle. The color turns from mauve to jacinth and then golden red. At last the semicircle makes an elegant jump thus the sun appears in the east sky.

Due to the different weather conditions and seasons, the sunrise is varied. On a fine day you can enjoy the whole process of sunrise. If there is cloudy haze in the east sky, it is already a red sun far above the horizon when you see the sunrise; if the sky is covered with cloud, you can only see the sunglow and clouds sea sometimes.

After the sunrise, millions of sun rays shoot onto the ground. At this time the Mt. Emei is gold in color, from the head to the feet, showing all her glamour to the visitors.

Clouds sea

When the sky is clearly blue, white clouds rise slowly among the mountains. Just in a moment, vast clouds sea appears above the horizon like a snowy white woolen blanket, smooth, clean and thick. Sometimes there are clouds either above the horizon or in the sky, so people stand between two cloud layers, which makes you feel like a supernatural being. When wind comes, the cloud sea is wafted to all the directions and then mountains become small islands floating in an ocean; when the cloud sea gathers together, peaks are invisible again; when wind gets strong, the cloud sea sometimes moves at a full gallop like a horse; sometimes makes a welter like a big wave of the sea; sometimes becomes elegant and stretching like a fair lady. The most sublime scene is that once in a while you have the chance to enjoy countless cloud columns in the shape of mushroom. They fly up to the sky, sprinkle gradually and then turn into filmy flowing clouds.

Buddha rays

In the afternoon, at the foot of the Sheshen Rock, every place is full of pure white clouds. Then an aura the color of red, orange, yellow, green, black blue, blue and purple extends within a radius of around one to two meters (about 3 to 7 feet). It looms and shines in the center like a mirror. Back against the sunlight from the west, sometimes you can find your own shadow in the aura. And your every action is followed by the figure in the aura, as if you were facing a bright mirror. To your most surprise, even if millions of people were viewing at it or two persons hugging each other were enjoying it, they could only see themselves. And this is the magic Buddha rays, which are rare in other places but appear in Mt. Emei frequently.

Saint lamps

In the dark nights of Golden Summit, occasionally, you can see a point of fluorescence flowing between the valleys, then changing into several and step by step into numerous. This is the famous scenery saint lamps in Mt. Emei.

The saint lamps can be seen under four conditions: firstly, the weather must be fine right after the rain; secondly, there is no moon in the sky; thirdly, there are no clouds layers at the foot of the mountain; fourthly, there are no heavy wind and rain on top of the mountain. As for the conditions, it is clear that the saint lamps are really hard to be observed.

（资料来源：http://scenery. cultural-china. com/en/109S128S11134. html）

Questions

1. What are the four great spectacles of Mt. Emei?
2. How does the Buddha rays look like?

Mount Huangshan
黄　山

⇨ **简介**

所属国家：中国（China）

入选时间：1990

入选标准：（ii）（vii）（x）

Located in southern Anhui Province, Mount Huangshan covers an area of 250 square kilometers, of which 154 square kilometers are scenic attractions. Its landscape features "four wonders" of hot spring, spectacular rocks, odd-shaped pines, and a sea of clouds.

Mount Huangshan boasts 72 peaks, more than 1,000 meters above sea level, with three main peaks rising majestically. They are both fascinating and dangerously steep. Cliffs, stone forests, stone pillars, stone blocks and egg-shaped stones form the unique granite geomorphological scenery. When it is cloudy the pinnacles loom in mists as if they were illusionary, while the sun is shining they unfold in all their majesty and splendour.

The pines on the mountain are tall and have fascinating shapes. The famous Welcoming Guests (Yingke) Pine (1,500 years old) and See-Guest-Off Pine have become a symbol of being faithful, unyielding and hospitable. More than 200 days each year on Mount Huangshan are misty and cloudy. The vapors coagulate to form a sea of clouds. As the clouds cloak the mountain, they give a feeling of being in fairyland.

Mount Huangshan also provides the natural habitat for a wide variety of fauna. The vertebrate fauna comprises 300 species and includes mammals, birds, reptiles, amphibians and fishes. Large mammals include rhesus and stump-tailed macaques, Asiatic black bear, wild dog, civet, Chinese ferret-badger, clouded leopard, wild boar, sika deer, mainland serow, red-bellied and spotted squirrels, and pangolin.

黄山位于安徽省南部，占地 250 平方千米，其中 154 平方千米为景区。其美景以温泉、怪石、奇松和云海"四绝"著称。

黄山有七十二峰，三大主峰海拔 1000 米以上，山体峻峭秀丽。悬崖、石林、石柱、石块、蛋形岩石形成了黄山独特的花岗岩地貌景观。阴天的时候，山峰在云雾里若隐若现，仿佛是虚幻的，而当阳光普照，山峰便尽展其威严壮丽。

黄山松通常较高并且千姿百态。著名的迎客松（1500 年）和送客松成了忠诚、不屈不挠和好客的象征。黄山一年之中有云雾的天气达 200 多天。水汽升腾或雨后雾气未消，就会形成云海。云雾遮盖着山峰，宛若仙境。

黄山还是种类繁多的动物的自然栖息地，包括三百多种脊椎动物，如哺乳动物、鸟类、爬行动物、两栖动物和鱼类,其中大型哺乳动物有恒河猴、树桩尾猴、亚洲黑熊、野狗、麝猫、鼬獾、云豹、野猪、梅花鹿、鬣羚、赤腹斑点松鼠和穿山甲等。

Vocabulary

1. impose $v.$ 强加;征税;利用;欺骗;施加影响

The government has imposed a 15 % tax on petrol.

政府已征15%的汽油税。

2. loom $v.$ 隐约地出现;赫然耸现;迫在眉睫

The issue of pay will loom large at this Easter's teacher's conference.

在今年复活节举行的教师会议上,工资问题将显得很突出。

3. unyielding $adj.$ 坚硬的,不能弯曲的,不屈的;刚强;不屈服;倔强

The self-confidence bought with unyielding efforts is of endless benefit to one's whole life.

通过不懈努力换来的自信心可以使人受益终生。

4. coagulate $v.$ 凝固;使结块,使变稠

Build up the partnership between teaching and administration in order to coagulate the group strength

通过建立教学与行政互相支援的关系来凝聚团队力量

5. vertebrate $n.$ 脊椎动物

The American Museum of Natural History has the largest collection of vertebrate fossils in the world.

美国自然历史博物馆搜集了全世界最多的脊椎动物化石。

扩展阅读

Mount Huangshan

"After a trip to Huangshan, China's Five Sacred mountains pale in comparison…" so goes the old Chinese saying. Hundreds, thousands and hundreds of thousands of people have journeyed to Huangshan every year for centuries to see for themselves if the Yellow Mountain is, as rhapsodized by ancient poets, indeed the most beautiful in China.

Yellow Mountain, also known as Mount Huangshan, is located in the southern part of Anhui Province. It is undoubtedly China's most celebrated mountain for all its grandeur and beauty.

In the Qin Dynasty (221—206 BC) Huangshan was collectively known as Yishan—Black Mountains—because of its dark peaks. It was in June of the year 747 that Tang Dynasty (618—907 BC) Emperor Xuan Zong, a follower of Taoism, commanded that its name be changed to Huangshan. His decree was based on Taoist writings on Huang Di—the Yellow Emperor and ancestor to the Chinese nation—and how he created his elixir of immortality on Huangshan. As set out in this Taoist volume, after working on a secret elixir for 480 years Huang Di took seven pills, achieved immortality and flew to Heaven.

So what is it about Huangshan that makes people come again and again? Because, perhaps, the best features of China's other famous mountains are here. Huangshan's peaks are as lofty as Taishan's and as steep as Huashan's. They are shrouded in a sea of clouds like Hengshan, have waterfalls as majestic as those on Lushan, Emei mountain's tranquil coolness and the picturesque rock formations of the Yandang Mountains. Aside from all these similarities, Huangshan has its own grotesquely shaped pines, imposing cliffs, and hot springs.

Within an area of 154 square kilometers, the mountain offers a crowd of peaks. 72 of them have names indicating the shapes they resemble. Lotus, Brightness Apex and Celestial Capital are the three major ones, all rising above 1,800 meters. The mountains are a body of granite, often with vertical joints. When it is cloudy the pinnacles loom in mists as if they were illusionary. When the sun shines, they unfold in all their majesty and splendor.

From ancient times Mt. Huangshan has been frequented by tourists seeking their mystery and admiring their scenery. They come to the conclusion that the fantastic pines, the grotesque rocks, the sea of clouds and the hot springs are the four major attractions of the Yellow Mountains. As a matter of fact there are marvels almost everywhere, especially in scenic areas such as Wenquan (Hot Spring), Yupinglou (Jade Screen Tower), Xihai (West Sea), Beihai (North Sea), Yungusi (Cloud Valley Temple) and Songgu'an (Pine Valley Nunnery).

Because of its peculiar terrain, the Yellow Mountain's climate is marked by a vertical change, and the vertical distribution of vegetation is also distinctive: plants on the summit, on the middle levels and at the foot belong to the frigid, temperate and subtropical zones respectively. There are more than 1500 species of plants, of which trees comprise one third. So the Yellow Mountain occupy an important place in China's botanical research. Here you will find century-old pines, firs, ginkgoes, Chinese torreyas, Chinese sweet gums, nanmus, camphor woods and the precious Magua trees, remnants of the glacial era.

The Yellow Mountains abound in flowering plants; many of them are rare ones, such as Goddess Flower, the Yellow Mountains Azalea as well as camellia, plum, lily, crape myrtle, orchid, Spring Heralding Flower and so on. It has a rich store of medicinal herbs; more than 300 kinds are found here; the notable ones being glossy ganoderma ginseng, Chinese gold thread rhizome and Chinese cinnamon. Maofeng tea of the Yellow Mountains is well known at home and abroad.

Though looking fresh and young, Yellow Mountains have a long history to which ancient books, poems and paintings as well as carved inscriptions all bear witness. Poetic phrases in handsome calligraphy can be found in many spots on the mountain.

They have become part of the fascinating scene themselves.

Tourists should not miss a visit to North Sea (Beihai), West Sea (Xihai), Celestial Capital (Tiandu) Peak, Jade Screen (Yuping) Tower, and Cloud Valley (Yungu) Temple, which are among the prettiest sights on Mount Huangshan. Cool (Qingliang) Terrace is the best place for watching the sunrise and the clouds.

Huangshan's deep green pine trees that have adapted to local conditions are one of the biggest local wonders. Growing from crannies in stones, many have existed for hundreds of years, and are regarded as symbols of stability and longevity. Most of Huangshan's pines are more than 100 years old and 10 truly symbolize longevity, having stood for an incredible 1,000 years. The weird shapes into which these famous trees have grown are intimated by their names "Pine Greeting a Guest", "Pine Parting with Friends" and "Lovers." There is also a pine called "Unity," named for its 56 branches that match exactly the number of China's ethnic minorities.

Huangshan is a popular spot for honeymooning newly-weds, and also has special significance for couples in general. This is evident in the hundreds of padlocks that can be seen hanging in the most remote spots. It is popularly believed that lovers or married couples can secure their union by hanging a padlock from some point on a mountain summit and throwing the key down to the valley below. If a couple decides to part they can do so only after coming back to Huangshan, searching the relevant valley for the key to their padlock and unlocking it.

（资料来源：http://www.chinadiscover.net/china-tour/anhuiguide/mount-huangshan.htm）

Questions

1. What is it about Huangshan that makes people come again and again?
2. What are the four major attractions of the Yellow Mountains?

Mount Taishan
泰　山

简介

所属国家：中国（China）

入选时间：1987

入选标准：(i)(ii)(iii)(iv)(v)(vi)(vii)

Mount Taishan locates in the middle part of Shandong province spanning two cities (Tai'an city and Jinan city) with total area of 426 square kilometers in China.

Mount Taishan is well known for its spectacular, grandness, elevation, width, steadiness and massiness. The typical character of natural scenery of Mount Taishan is imposing, steepy, surprising, serene, secluded, profound, and spacious. The picturesque of the Mount Taishan has various sceneries like cragged cliff, deep canyon and gorge, grotesque peak and strange rocks, luxuriant vegetation and the flowing springs and twittering birds… The mountain also has the unique marvelous wonders: the rising sun at dawn, the jade plate of sea of clouds, the aura appearing around Bixia Temple, rosy clouds at sunset etc.

The reputation of Huangshan comes mostly from its cultural position. Since ancient time, Mount Taishan is recognized as holy and sacred Mountain and held the accolade as "Most Revered of the Five Sacred Mountains". Furthermore, Mount Taishan symbolized the peaceful life and unified country. For thousands of years, more than dozens of emperors paid their homage to the mountain. Vast quantities of poetry and stone inscriptions were left by emperors, poets and scholars of every era. Confucians and Taoists coexist harmoniously on the mountain. And civilians worshiped the mountain with sincere esteem. In other words, the Mount Taishan has become the symbol of Chinese spirit.

泰山位于中国山东省中部,横跨两个城市(泰安市、济南市),总面积为 426 平方千米。

泰山以其巍峨、雄奇、沉浑、俊秀著称,其主要特点为雄、奇、险、秀、幽、奥。泰山具有极其美丽壮观的自然风景,峰峦竞秀,谷深峪长,怪石嶙峋,植被繁茂,溪水潺潺,鸟语啾啾,并有旭日东升、云海玉盘、碧霞佛光、晚霞夕照等独特的自然奇观。

黄山的名声主要来自它的文化地位。自古以来,泰山便是公认的圣山,被誉为"五岳之首"。此外,泰山象征着天下太平和国家统一。几千年以来,历代帝王接踵到泰山封禅致祭,刻石纪功。历代文人雅士纷至泰山进行诗文著述,留下了数以千计的诗文刻石。儒家和道家的文化在泰山上和谐共存。百姓们也诚心地祭拜泰山。换句话说,泰山已经成为中国精神的象征。

扩展阅读

Mount Taishan: Close to Perfect

One of the five sacred Chinese Taoist peaks, Mount Taishan is a bit crowded at the top. Favored by monks and emperors since Qin Shihuang (259—210 BC), the mountain seems incredibly peopled—especially at the Jade Emperor's Summit, 1,545 meters above sea level.

Tourist traffic has multiplied over the years, from 1.7 million in 2004 to 3.4 million in 2011. As footfalls increase, the task of protecting this national treasure becomes more demanding.

Protecting Paleolithic rocks is no mean task. And neither is preserving the ecological balance and the spiritual ambience of a mountain that seems like a homage to more than 2,000 years of Chinese culture, which the historian Sima Qian (135—86 BC) saluted and Tang Dynasty poet Du Fu (712—770) marveled at.

To find out if Mount Taishan was suffocating under heavy tourist traffic, we recently visited the site.

Indeed, the summit was rather noisy. The courtyard of the Goddess Bixia buzzed with pilgrims offering prayers and fastening newer locks to an ever-expanding brass pile of these, in the hope of bringing luck and blessings to their families.

A bevy of people eagerly awaited their turns to be photographed in front of the Sea-exploring Stone, which bore the inscription, "Mount Taishan—Mountain of Mountains".

A group broke into a synchronized drill and a song about the greatness of the mountain and Shandong province, where the peak is located.

All this was a bit at odds with the somber ambience one would have expected at a mountain that, traditionally, has served as a place of retreat for Buddhist, Taoist and Confucian pilgrims.

The Mount Taishan Scenic Spots Management Committee, which works with the local Tai'an government to protect the mountain and develop its potential as a tourist destination, is doing its bit.

As Wan Qinghai, the vice-director, told us, "We do take some measures trying to maintain quietness at the peak. The kiosks and tour guides on the mountain are not allowed to use high-decibel loudspeakers. Tourists are asked to lower their voices when they step inside the temples at the peak. Actually, most tourists are very devout and lower their voices on their own."

One of the 1,600-odd regular people employed by the management committee is garbage collector Sun Jiyu, who says his task is getting lighter with time. He picks up about 200 bottles a day in winter and more than double that in summer.

"Nowadays, tourists use the bins rather than littering," he says.

The more than 100 volunteers who serve as tour guides and environmental watchdogs during peak seasons have had a role in sensitizing tourists.

The Tai'an City Community Volunteers' Association sends a huge number of these people—students, workers, retirees and officials—to work alongside the staff.

As Hua Liangping, the Association, says: "The idea is to lead by example, rather than trying to impose. We ask volunteers to pick up the garbage that a visitor might have, carelessly, dropped on the ground. But if they find a visitor smoking, they ask him to stop, as smoking is strictly prohibited on the mountain."

Checking the trees for pests is a major thrust of protecting the expansive green cover on Mount Taishan. It was quite bare until 1999, when a forestation drive was launched.

"Today, 82.4 percent of the total 12,000-hectare area is covered by forests while 94 percent is covered by foliage," Wan says.

Sun Xugen, professor of Plant Protection College of Shandong Agriculture University in Tai'an, says there is a potential threat from pests, such as the fall webworm moth and pinewood nematode, which, although not yet found on Taishan, have been located in the mountains of Zibo, only 200 km away.

A provincial pest control and research center has been established at Shandong Agriculture University to study treatments of the damage caused by pinewood nematodes.

Sometimes, the research center conducts experiments on Mount Taishan with the staff of the Pest Control and Quarantine Station at the mountain.

The man in charge of the arduous task of managing a team of 200 staff members who run checks—working both day and night shifts—on Taishan's trees is Shen Weixing, director of the Pest Control and Quarantine Station.

Shen, who often scrutinizes the trees at night, has introduced other measures to keep the pests at bay that seem to be working.

"There are checkpoints at every gateway to prevent people from carrying wooden furniture on the mountain, as these are potential carriers of pests. Only environmentally friendly pesticides are used, rather than chemical-based products. We often use one pest to kill another," Shen says.

Bird species like the magpie and the swallow have been brought in to help kill pests. And trees like oaks, pines and firs that better suit the mountainous terrain were planted in recent years to ensure a greater ecological balance, Shen says.

"The fact that Taishan is being reforested is very impressive," says John Wallace from the Asia Pacific Journalism Center in Melbourne, who has run several international conferences on climate concerns.

He also lauded the fact that only electronically powered vehicles were allowed to go up—and in limited numbers.

Some of the amazingly colorful stones at Taishan—some formed 2.8 billion years ago—around Peach Blossom Valley gateway (see sidebar) were under layers of scum for years. These were cleaned up, at the cost of 50 million yuan ($7.9 million), according to Wan, revealing the mystifying patterns created on them were made through tectonic shifts.

"We have also built 23 dams to channel more water into the streams," Wan says.

Since the clean-up, visitors have stopped throwing trash into the stream.

"Earlier, the streams would get clogged up because rubbish thrown in them accumulated in the riverbed. Now, as you can see, the streams are absolutely crystal clear," Hua says.

"Generally speaking, the ecological balance around Mount Taishan is changing for the better," Professor Sun, of Shandong Agriculture University, says.

It's not perfect yet, but there seems to be a concerted effort to get there.

（资料来源：http://news. xinhuanet. com/english/travel/2012-06/01/c_131624858. htm）

Questions

1. How many volunteers serve as tour guides and environmental watchdogs during peak seasons on Mount Taishan?

2. What measures have been introduced to keep the pests at bay on Mount Taishan?

Mount Wuyi
武夷山

➱ **简介**

所属国家：中国（China）

入选时间：1999

入选标准：（iii），（iv），（vii），（x）

The Mount Wuyi Scenic Area lies to the south of Wuyishan City, Fujian Province, China. Its tranquil beauty and intact environment offer a refuge to the primitive forest, so it is called the "Natural Arboretum".

Mount Wuyi is the most outstanding area for biodiversity conservation in southeast China. It contains what is probably the largest and best preserved areas of humid subtropical forest in the world, and is a refuge for a large number of ancient, relict species, many of them endemic to China. The riverine landscape of the Nine Bend River (lower gorge) is also of exceptional scenic quality in its juxtaposition of smooth rock cliffs with clear, deep water. Its serene beauty is complemented by numerous temples and monasteries, many now in ruins. These provided the setting for the development and spread of neo-Confucianism, a doctrine that played a dominant role in the countries of eastern and southeastern Asia for many centuries and influenced philosophy and government over much of the world.

Another important historical sites is the ruins of an ancient Han city built during the 1st century BC as an administrative center. Its massive walls enclose an archaeological site of great significance.

Mount Wuyi has received international recognition for its high diversity and large numbers of rare and unusual fauna. Endangered species include Chinese tiger, clouded leopard, black muntjac and Chinese giant salamander.

武夷山风景区位于中国福建省武夷山市南部，它那宁静美丽、保存完好的生态环境为原始森林提供了一个避难所，因此被称为"天然植物园"。

武夷山是中国东南部最著名的生物多样性保护区，它的亚热带雨林区可能是世界上最大的、保护最好的亚热带雨林区。它还是大量古代残遗物种的避难所，其中很多是中国特有的物种。九曲溪（低峡）河景毗邻光滑的岩石峭壁和深深的清澈河水，也具有特别的景观价值。其静谧的美景与许多现在已经废弃的寺庙和修道院相得益彰。这一切为朱子理学(几个世纪以来在东亚和东南亚国家起支配性作用并在哲学和政治方面影响了世界上很大一部分地区的学说)的发展和传播提供了背景。

武夷山的另一个重要历史遗迹是一座汉代古城遗址。公元1世纪时,汉朝统治者在此建立了一处较大的行政首府。厚重坚实的围墙环绕四周,极具考古价值。

武夷山因其各种各样大量的稀有和不寻常的动物群而在国际上享有盛誉。其中濒危物种包括华南虎、云豹、黑麂和大鲵。

Vocabulary

1. tranquil *adj.* 安静的;平静的;宁静的

Everything here is so peaceful and tranquil.

这儿的一切都是如此安宁、恬静。

2. primitive *adj.* 原始的;发展水平低的;落后的;[生物学]原生的

The black art is still practised among the primitive tribes in Africa.

在非洲原始部族中,巫术仍然在用。

3. subtropical *adj.* [地理]亚热带的

Lying in the subtropical zone, Hangzhou enjoys a mild climate and plenty of water.

杭州地处亚热带,气候温和,雨量充沛。

4. refuge *n.* 避难;避难所;庇护

He took refuge in a cave last time.

他上次是在一个洞里避难的。

5. complement *v.* 补足,补助

Our local bus and metro system complement each other very well.

我们这里市内公共汽车与地铁互相补充,交通极为便利。

扩展阅读

A Tourist's Divine Time on Heavenly Peak of Wuyi Mountain in Fujian

The path to the top of Tianyou Peak—which means traveling in heaven—on Wuyi Mountain has a total of 800 steps. I should know; I counted every one of the narrow slabs as I took the zigzagging path up the peak. And to make the ascent a little more challenging, early morning dew gave them a slippery sheen.

Don't stop. Do it in one stretch, my tour guide Liu told me.

Liu is a good guide. Most of the time, he spouted funny stories and historic anecdotes about the mountain to take my mind off the slog, but occasionally came up with some terse, light-hearted words of advice. "If you take a break half way, you probably won't make it to the end."

Wuyi Mountain boasts more than 500 historical inscriptions on its rock faces and a centuries-old tea garden hidden in its depths that once only made tea for emperors.

The range has been described as a piece of green jade inlaid in the northwest of Fujian Province.

The mountain is a masterpiece of nature, created through its forces over millions of years. A typical dan xia landform, it is characterized by steep red sandstone sides, deep, narrow valleys and almost vertical ridges. The geology has created numerous shallow and isolated caves of various sizes and shapes that captured the imagination of ancient Chinese.

But what makes Wuyi Mountain unique is its large number of rock inscriptions carved by a host of great ancient writers, calligraphers, painters and political leaders, who flocked to the mountain to meditate, attain enlightenment and communicate with the gods.

Tianyou Peak, the highest point of Wuyi Mountain, has become something of a must-do climb for tourists, rewarding them with a magnificent bird's-eye view of the area.

Though it's an energy-sapping journey to the top for me, it's also an inspiring and eye-opening one, because the road is studded with historic sites and cultural relics all the way. I was never bored.

We started at the foot of the mountain in early morning, the peak veiled in mist.

Among the early views is the remains of Wuyi Vihara, once the learning center of Zhu Xi, a Confucian scholar and the most influential rationalist Neo-Confucian in China during the Song Dynasty (960—1279).

Today only a dilapidated wall is left and it's hard to imagine Zhu giving lectures and promoting Confucian theories for more than 10 years in the once grand, imposing building that was a spiritual home to emperors and other important figures of the age.

History is like the ebb and flow of the tide. This was once at the center of a high civilization, but then the tides of time receded, leaving only ruins, like shells on a beach.

On I climbed. A few hundred meters from the Wuyi Vihara are caves of different sizes and shapes. At dawn and dusk in winter and spring, thin mists waft out of the caves, flowing gently between the rocks and ridges; gathering, scattering, then gathering again.

"We call it the Nest of Clouds," Liu said. Out of the mist, past a stone bridge spanning a meandering creek, we reached Shui Yue Pavilion—Water and Moon Pavilion.

It's said on a clear night, ancient scholars would hold banquets in the pavilion. They would eat, drink and admire the moons—yes moons; four actually.

Seen from the distance, the Cloud Nest shrouds a huge black rock, which looks like a crouching elephant. The rock is split in the middle, creating a gap big enough only for one ray of sunshine and one person.

In ancient times, the rock was a quiet and secluded place for Taoism masters to meditate and attain enlightenment. Then, in 1538, vice military minister Chen Sheng built more than 10 pavilions, kiosks and halls near the elephant rock.

Today they are all abandoned, with only inscriptions on the rocks to remind people of past glories.

To its left, a giant rock caught my eye. Its smooth surface is marked with long sunken hollows that look exactly like a handprint.

These were shaped by waterfalls eroding away the rock, but local legend goes that it is the handprint accidentally left by a god who stopped by and was enchanted by the beautiful scenery. He held on to the rock as he stopped for a closer view of Wuyi Mountain, leaving his handprint.

Continuing further to the south, we reached a stone gate, carved with the name "Liu Yun House". This is where scholar Dong Maoxun finished the "Wuyi Mountain Record" 200 years ago, which helps people have a detailed knowledge about this mountain.

We passed the Jixiong and Longjuan rocks, narrow and dangerous spots, to get to Xianfan Rock. Two large characters Xian (the Immortal) and Fan (the Mortal) inscribed on the rock told us that we were at the dividing line between the heaven and the human world. Crossing the line, we were entering the kingdom of gods.

Some 400 years ago, great explorer and travel writer Xu Xiake, who traveled around China for 34 years and documented the country's geography, climbed the same path I took.

When he reached the top of Tianyou, he described it in his "Travel Diaries of Xu Xiake" as "the most breathtaking peak".

It was indeed. When we got to the summit, it was as if the world had suddenly opened up into brightness.

From my vantage point I looked down at the Jiuqu River, twisting, turning and traversing the mountainous area like an emerald green dragon snaking away into the distance, carrying an occasional bamboo raft.

Then I turned around to survey the scene around me. The peak was still blanketed in thick cloud, along with the nearby Dawang Peak and Sanjiao Peak. Looking at these majestic surroundings, you felt that you were indeed traveling in heaven.

(资料来源：http://www. whatsonxiamen. com/news28603. html)

Questions

1. How many historical inscriptions are on Wuyi Mountain's rock faces?

2. How many years had Zhuxi been giving lectures here?

第四节　亚洲的世界文化景观遗产

Cultural Landscape and Archaeological Remains of the Bamiyan Valley

巴米扬山谷的文化景观和考古遗址

🔎 **简介**

所属国家：阿富汗（Afghanistan）

入选时间：2003

入选标准：(i)，(ii)，(iii)，(iv)，(vi)

The kingdom of Bamiyan was a Buddhist state positioned at a strategic location along the trade routes that for centuries linked China and Central Asia with India and the West. Many statues of Buddha were carved into the sides of cliffs facing Bamiyan city. The two most prominent of these statues were standing Buddhas, measuring 55 and 37 meters high respectively, that were the largest examples of standing Buddha carvings in the world. They were probably erected in the 4th or 5th century.

The cultural landscape and archaeological remains of the Bamiyan valley represent the artistic and religious developments which, from the first to the thirteenth centuries, characterized ancient Bakhtria, integrating various cultural influences into the Gandhara school of Buddhist art. The area contains numerous Buddhist monastic ensembles and sanctuaries, as well as fortified edifices from the Islamic period. The site is also testimony to the tragic destruction by the Taliban of the two standing Buddha statues in March 2001.

The Bamiyan Valley is a high pass (2,500 m) that formed one of the branches of the Silk Road. Its beautiful landscapes is associated with legendary figures which contributed to its development as a major religious and cultural centre.

古巴米扬王国是一个佛教国家，位于几个世纪以来将中国、中亚和印度及西方国家相连的丝绸之路沿线的战略位置。许多佛像被刻在面向巴米扬市区的悬崖峭壁上。其中最著名的是两座立佛，分别高达 55 米和 37 米，是世界上最大的立佛。他们大约建于公元 4 世纪或 5 世纪。

巴米扬山谷的历史遗址向世人展示了从公元 1 到 13 世纪期间以古代巴克蒂阿里族的文化为特征的艺术和宗教的发展。从其发展过程中，我们可以见证佛教艺术中的干达拉流派如何在各种文化的相互影响及融合过程中逐渐形成。这片保护区汇集了大量佛教寺院、庙宇,也保存了伊斯兰时期的防御建筑。它同时也见证了 2001 年 3 月塔利班组织犯下的暴行——两尊立佛遭到了他们的无情摧残。

巴米扬山谷是一个高达 2500 米的山口,并形成了丝绸之路的其中一个分支。巴米扬山谷遗址风景秀丽,充满传奇色彩,传说中的传奇人物对巴米扬山谷发展成为主要的宗教和文化中心做出了重大贡献。

Vocabulary

1. respectively *adv.* 各自地;各个地;分别地

Both pure market regulation and government regulation have defects respectively.

纯粹的市场调节和政府调节方式各有其缺陷。

2. archaeological *adj.*[古] 考古学的;[古] 考古学上的

The storm stopped us from visiting the archaeological site.

由于风暴的来临,我们没能参观考古现场。

3. ensemble *n.* 全体;总效果;全套服装;全套家具;合奏组

Over the last five years, the ensemble has performed in 15 countries.

过去 5 年来,这个合奏团已在 15 个国家演出过。

4. fortify *v.* 加强;增强;设防于

We will fortify the coastal areas.

我们将加强沿海地区的防御。

5. edifice *n.* 大厦;大建筑物

There is a huge Gothic edifice nearby.

这附近有一幢哥特式的庞大建筑物。

扩展阅读

Stone Carvers Defy Taliban to Return to the Bamiyan Valley

Under perfectly carved niches that once held dozens of small buddha statues, the purposeful tap of chisel on stone echoed over the Bamiyan valley for the first time in centuries.

Twelve young Afghans had gathered to take the first tentative steps back towards a stone-working tradition that once made their home famous, at a workshop in a cave gouged out as a monastery assembly hall more than 1,000 years ago.

The cave-hall was part of a complex built around two giant buddhas that loomed serenely over Bamiyan for about 15 centuries—until the Taliban government condemned them as un-Islamic in early 2001 and blew them up.

"I was interested in this course because I want to restore our culture," said Ismael Wahidi, a 22-year-old student of archeology at Bamiyan University, who set aside more conventional studies for a week to learn how to turn a lump of stone into a sculpture. "If you want to destroy a people, you first destroy their heritage and history."

The workshop, held just a few metres from where the larger buddha's face was once carved from the cliff face, aimed to reintroduce stone-carving to the valley by showing that creating basic pieces is easy, even if mastery takes years.

Under the guidance of Afghan, American and German artists, the group picked the stone they would shape from some of the rich seams of marble, quartzite and travertine (a form of limestone) that thread through the local mountains, foothills of the Himalayas. Then they set to work, with chisels forged by local blacksmiths from the suspension springs of old cars. "We wanted to give young people the idea that it is possible to do stone carving with what you have here," said Bert Praxenthaler, a sculptor and conservationist who has been working on the valley's monuments for several years, including stabilising the niches that once held the buddhas.

The Bamiyan valley is pockmarked with hundreds of caves that were once part of sumptuous monasteries, packed with statues and lavishly painted with frescoes. This rich artistic heritage was funded by centuries of taxes on caravans passing through what is now an isolated backwater, but was once a wealthy and important stop on the silk road.

"There must have been at least 2,000 years of sculptural tradition," said Praxenthaler, "Even excavating the caves is a kind of architectural sculpture. It was not just hacking holes into the cliff but also shaping the rooms, and they are quite extraordinary."

That tradition was probably killed off around 1,000 years ago, Praxenthaler said, when the valley was conquered by Mahmoud of Ghazni, a leader whose epithet suggested little interest in figurative art. "Anyone who calls themselves the 'destroyer of idols' probably wouldn't support further stone carving," Praxenthaler said.

Sculpture has remained largely off limits in Afghanistan because of strict Islamic prohibitions on idolatry. Depictions of any human or animal are strongly discouraged in art, and calligraphy, floral and geometric patterns dominate the country's more recent cultural heritage, from the majestic minaret of Jam, to mosques and monuments in cities such as Kabul and Kandahar.

"As you know, extremists often make propaganda about idols. But this is our heritage, not something religious," said 20-year-old Abdur Rahman Rosta, one of the student sculptors. He added that that in Bamiyan itself the sculptors were feted. The valley's people suffered badly under the Taliban, and have little sympathy for their hardline views, and Bamiyan has remained one of the most peaceful places in Afghanistan as insurgent violence spreads elsewhere.

The provincial governor came to a small ceremony unveiling the sculptures, and picked up a chisel herself as musicians played in a niche that once held the cave's largest statue—and might perhaps one day hold another.

"During this course we realised we had much more ability for working with stone than we could have imagined, and we understood we can do so much more," said Jawed

Mohammadi，a 20-year-old history student at the university，who used the week to chisel out a human face，"The buddhas were destroyed，but maybe we can build them again. "

（资料来源：http://www. guardian. co. uk/world/2012/may/16/stone-carvers-taliban-bamiyan）

Questions

1. What is the workshop established for?
2. How long was the history of sculptural tradition in the Bamiyan valley?

Bam and Its Cultural Landscape
巴姆城及其文化景观

▭➪ **简介**

所属国家：伊朗（Iran）

入选时间：2004

入选标准：(ii)，(iii)，(iv)，(v)

Bam is situated in a desert environment on the southern edge of the Iranian high plateau. The origins of Bam can be traced back to the Achaemenid period，sixth to fourth centuries BC. Its heyday was from the seventh to eleventh centuries，being at the crossroads of important trade routes and known for the production of silk and cotton garments. For centuries，Bam had a strategic location on the Silk Roads connecting it to Central Asia in the east，the Persian Gulf in the south，as well as Egypt in the west and it is an example of the interaction of the various influences.

Bam and its Cultural Landscape is an exceptional testimony to the development of a trading settlement in the desert environment of the Central Asian region. The existence of life in the oasis was based on the underground irrigation canals，the qanats，of which Bam has preserved some of the earliest evidence in Iran. Arg-e-Bam，the Citadel of Bam is the most representative example of a fortified medieval town built in vernacular technique using mud layers combined with mud bricks.

Bam is an outstanding expression of the interaction of man and nature in a desert environment. The civilization depended on a strict social system with precise tasks and responsibilities，which have been maintained in use until the present.

巴姆城位于伊朗高原南端的沙漠地区,其历史可以追溯至公元前6世纪至公元前4世纪的阿契美尼德王朝时期。其全盛时期为16—18世纪,曾是丝绸和棉质服装生产贸易商道的交汇地。几个世纪以来,巴姆在丝绸之路上拥有显著的战略位置,它东接中亚,南连波斯湾,西壤埃及,是各种影响相互作用的一个例子。

巴姆城及其文化景观是中亚地区沙漠环境中贸易定居地的一个特殊见证。巴姆城堡沙漠中人的生存痕迹有如下证据：地下灌溉渠坎儿井，且坎儿井还保存了早期的痕迹。巴姆古城是应用本国技术，用泥砖和泥层建造的一个最有代表性的中世纪要塞的典范。

巴姆是人类与沙漠环境进行斗争的突出范例。巴姆文明依赖于一个严格的社会体系，这里分工明确，人们各司其职，这种社会制度时至今日仍在沿用。

Vocabulary

1. plateau *n.* 高原；稳定水平；托盘

Our efforts to ban drilling on the plateau seemed to have failed.

我们希望禁止高原开采的努力看起来已经失败了。

2. heyday *n.* 全盛期

She was a great badminton player in her heyday.

她在鼎盛时期是个了不起的羽毛球手。

3. oasis *n.* 绿洲；舒适的地方；令人宽慰的事物

This park is an oasis in the center of the city.

这个公园是城市中心的绿洲。

4. irrigation *n.* 灌溉；［临床］冲洗；冲洗法

Irrigation by electric power has been used in this area.

这个地区已经开始施行电灌农田了。

5. vernacular *adj.* 本国的；地方的；白话的，通俗话的

Lu Xun is one of the pioneers in vernacular writing.

鲁迅是白话文写作的先驱之一。

扩展阅读

Bam: Five Years after

Arash Arjmand and his family made the day's drive from Shiraz to wonder what this room with no roof and no door might have been. The family sidestepped mound after mound of ruined terracotta as they toured the ghost fortress of Bam Citadel, just five years ago a 25-century-old monument but now merely ruins.

At the UNESCO World Heritage site in the ancient Silk Road city of Bam, Iran, engineers from around the world are attempting to piece together what used to stand as the world's largest adobe structure and best example of a fortified medieval walled city.

On December 26, 2003, an earthquake killed 32,000 people, flattened 70% of Bam's buildings and equally devastated the nearby town of Baravat and 260 area villages. Bam Citadel (or Arg-e-Bam) was reduced from a stunning byzantine garrison, visited by more than 100,000 people yearly, to a canyon of pulverized rubble not much different than the other treeless, rock-strewn mountains that delineate the central Iranian plateau from the southern desert.

"I don't know what it was, but it must have been something," said Mr. Arjmand, whose face beamed with patriotic pride as he began talking not of this exemplar of Iran's storied past, but of the public school across the street remarkably constructed of glossy yellow granite and regal marble.

Iran seems to be taking advantage of Mother Nature's demolition by replacing an antiquated Bam with a contemporary one that can resist the inevitable next earthquake. The metropolitan area is further along than the Citadel in a vast, government-led reconstruction effort that has significantly restored the luster to a city formerly known as "The Emerald of the Desert."

"Bam is 80% what it used to be," gauges Mr. Mohammad Saeedi-Kia, Iran's Minister of Housing and Urban Development. This seems to be a fair assessment: Startling signs of progress routinely emerge amid half-completed homes and countless piles of debris.

But 80% of a modern city may prove to be better than 100% of the rickety town that fell. Bam's picturesque but archaic mud-brick buildings were the primary instrument of the quake's carnage. When these buildings collapsed they didn't leave the voids and air pockets that emerge when modern concrete buildings crumble, claiming more than a quarter of Bam's population.

Foreign governments immediately promised more than $800 million in humanitarian assistance—slightly more than $50 million was ever delivered, according to reports published by the Iranian government. The reconstruction was left to the federal government and supported by committed humanitarian organizations such as The International Red Cross and Red Crescent, the United Nations and countless Iranian charities and aid workers.

Billions for Bam

In 2004 the World Bank anticipated that rebuilding Bam would cost $1 billion. According to reports published by the Ministry of Housing and Urban Development, nearly $1.5 billion has been spent in combined public and private funds, with the Iranian government shouldering about 85% of the total. Many Iranians warned me that the money for Bam has been embezzled—that seems to be the ongoing assumption here— but touring Bam leaves no doubt that a great deal of money has been expended and value was realized.

The reconstruction statistics are impressive: The number of schools more than doubled from 90 to 183. 50 new mosques have replaced the 100 that fell. 11 cultural centers have been built, along with six libraries and three universities—two public and one private. An enormous government worker complex, replete with fountain, wrought-iron gate and covered in Iran's famed tile, is set to open this spring. Five new fire stations, new police headquarters, new courthouse, amusement park—in short, almost everything a city needs to function is present and brand-new. Everything the federal government constructed has been officially turned over to the city and the state of Kerman, according to Mr. Keshavarzmehr.

It's a New Bam

In another five years, at the current rate, Bam will no longer be in recovery but an entirely new place. "This will be a very nice city to live in and much better than before," opined Mr. Keshavarzmehr. "There won't be any comparison."

In a remark typical of the perfectionist and idealistic nature of Iranians, Mr. Keshavarzmehr concluded, "I expected better results in Bam," which might have floored a visitor from New Orleans. "We should have gotten more support from the local people and local government in the beginning," he said, "We could have used more government coordination."

Back in Tehran, Iranians have had difficulty accepting that the government-led reconstruction is a budding success. Their knee-jerk reaction was, to a person, "It must have all been done by the charity organizations." But the facts don't bear that out.

"This mistrust of the government goes back 2,500 years," said Minister Saeedi-Kia, "It's ingrained in the culture: They expect more than can be delivered."

Everyone has their own opinions on the ideals of the Islamic government of Iran, but to properly judge the specific actions of a government requires an objective suspension of personal ideology.

Everyone may also have different standards of what constitutes a "good reconstruction", but a reasonable yardstick may be the most appropriate gauge, such as: "Have the essential components of every society been re-established, such as adequate housing, education, health care, employment opportunities, infrastructure, etc.?" By that measure, in a few years Bam may qualify as a success.

（资料来源：http://payvand.com/news/09/may/1227.html）

Questions

1. What has destroyed Bam recently?
2. How's the reconstruction going on right now in Bam?

Ancient Villages of Northern Syria
叙利亚北部古村落群

⇨ 简介

所属国家：叙利亚（Syria）

入选时间：2011

入选标准：（iii）（iv）（v）

The Ancient villages of Northern Syria are the remains of rural societies from late Antiquity and Byzantine period. Basilicas, pagan temples, bathhouses, residential areas, pilgrim dwellings, inns, Roman tombs and temples are found among the ruins.

These ruins are among the greatest treasuries of Byzantine architecture to be found anywhere in the ancient world.

Deserted and desolate today, the region once supported an immense and prosperous population, for it was rich in olive groves and was the hinterland of the great Christian city of Antioch.

After the Islamic conquest of the Byzantine world, the political and demographical center moved from Antioch to Damascus and this region, which depended on Antioch for its prosperity, went into decline. Its inhabitants moved away, leaving behind ghost towns. As it has been abandoned for nearly one thousand years since its occupation in ancient times, it has been called the region of "dead cities". In the absence of invasions or natural disasters, these towns and villages remained remarkably well-preserved over the centuries.

叙利亚北部古村落群是古代晚期和拜占庭时期乡村生活的遗迹。圣殿、异教庙宇、澡堂、住宅区、朝圣者的居所、旅舍、罗马古墓和寺庙等建筑遗存依然可见。这些遗迹属于现存的最伟大的拜占庭式建筑。

这个地区今天看起来荒凉而冷清，但过去却曾经人丁兴旺，因为它拥有大量的橄榄树，并且是伟大的基督教城安提阿城的腹地。

在伊斯兰教征服拜占庭世界后，政治和人口的中心开始从安提阿转移到大马士革，而这个依赖于安提阿而繁荣的地区也开始走向衰落。它的居民搬走了，留下的是一座座鬼城。这个地区至今已被废弃了近千年，因此被称为"死亡之城"。由于没有遭受过侵略和自然灾害，这些城镇和村庄数百年来仍然保存完好。

Vocabulary

1. dwelling *n.* 住处，处所；寓所；居住

He changed his dwelling recently.

他最近搬了家。

2. desolate *adj.* 无人的；荒凉的；孤独的，凄凉的；荒废的

Her house stood at the end of a desolate street.

她的房子位于冷清的街尾。

3. prosperous *adj.* 繁荣的，兴旺的；富裕的

The city at one time must have been prosperous.

这座古城肯定一度很繁荣。

4. hinterland *n.* 内陆地区，内地；穷乡僻壤；腹地

There is the enormous underdeveloped hinterland with excess rural population in China.

中国广大的内陆地区农村人口过多，不发达。

5. demographical *adj.* 人口统计的

Demographical features of tourist flows are the basic content in the research of tourism geography.

旅游客流是旅游目的地与旅游客源地之间空间相互作用的结果。

US-led Sanctions Contribute to the Destruction of Syria's Millenary History

What "civil war"? What "crisis"? One is tempted to ask himself even though there continues to be intermittent "thuds" and a jet streaking overhead now and then en route apparently to one of the suburbs where clashes erupt intermittently.

There is plenty of anger here among the Syrian public, the NGO's, and increasingly the international legal community among others—not toward the American people but toward the US government—over the effects of its sanctions which are severely and illegally targeting the civilian population. At the same time they are directly contributing to prospects of irreparably damaging many of this millenary country's historic sites.

According to archeological experts here, Syria, with its six UNESCO world heritage sites testifying to its deserved reputation as being one of the most archeologically well-preserved cradles of civilization, may soon to be the most wantonly destroyed in modern times (Iraq being the other). This frequently-predicted catastrophe is a result, not only of war in the usual sense, but war in it's more subtle form of US-led sanctions aimed at political regime change.

Of particular concern to UNESCO, whose UN mandate includes registering and protecting World historical sites, is the preservation of the Ancient Cities of Damascus, Bosra, Palmyra, Aleppo, Crac des Chevaliers and Qal' at Salah El-Din, as well as the ancient villages of Northern Syria.

This week, the Syrian Directorate of Antiquities and Museums has released its detailed report of acts of vandalism and illegal excavations by armed groups and foreign thieves across Syria. The Directorate has documented violations against archeological sites and Syrian museums, as well as the emerging phenomenon of artifact forgery. In Aleppo, the Antiquities division reported that al-Diriya caves in Samaan Mountain suffered from acts of sabotage, adding that "terrorists have looted the equipment of excavations, wooden columns and timbers".

Also, this week, Human Rights Watch issued a report that Saudi-Qatar-US backed militants destroyed religious locations following a four-day investigation in the provinces of Latakia and Idlib. According to HRW, a Husseiniyah (a congregation hall for Shia commemoration ceremonies) was destroyed by the militants in Idlib, while two Christian churches were looted in Latakia. The Middle East director at the Human Rights Watch, Sarah Leah Whitson claimed that Syria "will lose its rich cultural and religious diversity if armed groups do not respect places of worship".

Against this backdrop, it is not totally surprising that my UNESCO hostess, less than half a minute after I entered her office, literally threw at me a statement in French from Director Irina Bokova of the UNESCO HQ in Paris. It read:

I am deeply distressed by the daily news about the escalation of damage to cultural heritage throughout Syria. We saw damage to the Citadel in July and the souks ten days ago, and the Umayyad Mosque, heart of the religious life of the city, one of the most beautiful mosques in the Muslim world, is being severely endangered. In Northern Syria, the region of the Ancient Villages inscribed on the World Heritage List in 2011 is heavily struck and it seems that the invaluable Saint-Simeon Byzantine complex might have been torched.

Before I could finish reading, the lady exclaimed, "These testimonials from the past! …" raising her voice and glaring at me while pointing to the posters of Syrian historical sites on her wall, "the destruction of this heritage for which your sanctions are partly responsible. Your government is responsible today and will be tomorrow, for the whole of humanity." When I was eventually able to get a word in sideways, I explained that I had come to her office precisely because I have been studying the immoral, illegal and "un-American" sanctions and that I was spending my time in Syria learning first-hand about the sanctions' utter disregard for the humanitarian concerns of the Syrian people—in contravention to what one hears repeatedly from US officials.

"Let me tell you something!" she exclaimed and launched into describing the dire effects of the current US-led sanctions on UNESCO's work in preserving and protecting historical sites. In her view, the American assault on UNESCO and its work began when UNESCO committed a sin in March of 2011 by admitting Palestine as a full member.

She explained, "For months our offices had been warned by Israeli officials and then Americans, that there would be a big price-tag were we to admit Palestine." And there was. In October 2011, the U. S. cut off funding to UNESCO as payback for admitting Palestine as a member and in November 2012, the United States was one of nine member states out of 193 in the General Assembly who, on behalf of the Zionist occupiers of Palestine, tried to unsuccessfully bar Palestine from gaining non-member observer state status at the UN.

UNESCO and some other NGO staff here claim that much of the damage here could have been prevented if there was a lifting of the US 2011 cut-off of UNESCO's budget. As a direct result, UNESCO cannot even replace more than 400 staffers who left from normal attrition or even hire "neighborhood watch", local volunteer personnel, to coordinate the guarding by of many archeological sites around Syria.

I left the UNESCO office sort of crestfallen. Not because of the lady's roughness with me, but rather because of the realization, yet once again, that our species quite simply does not learn much from history and apparently will repeat it until the end of times. May God protect the people, everywhere, from the politicians.

（资料来源：http：//www. counterpunch. org/2013/01/25/us-led-sanctions-contribute-to-the-destruction-of-syrias-millenary-history/）

Questions

1. What is damaging many of Syria's historic sites?
2. What does the author think about the situation?

Rice Terraces of the Philippine Cordilleras
菲律宾科迪勒拉山的水稻梯田

⊡⇨ **简介**

所属国家：菲律宾（Philippines）

入选时间：1995

入选标准：(iii)(iv)(v)

The Rice Terraces of the Cordilleras (on the island of Luzon) are a cultural landscape developed 2000 years ago by the Ifugao people. These terraces are still in use, and are under continuous maintenance by the current Ifugao farmers.

The Ifugao Rice Terraces, which follow the natural contours of the mountains, only enhance the region's rugged natural beauty. They also epitomize a harmonic, sustainable relationship between humans and their environment. These fields, and the knowledge to farm and sustain them, have been passed down from generation to generation for centuries.

There are many more rice terraces in Asia, f. e. on Bali, but these in the Philippine Cordilleras are outstanding because of their altitude (up to 1500 meters) and steep slopes (maximum of 70 degrees).

The structures' original builders used stone and mud walls to carefully carve and construct terraces that could hold flooded pond fields for the cultivation of rice. They also established a system to water these plots by harvesting water from mountaintop forests. A complex system of dams, sluices, channels and bamboo pipes keeps whole groups of terraces adequately flooded. These incredible engineering feats were done by hand as was (and is) the farming itself.

The rice terraces have long been central to the survival of the Ifugao peoples but they also occupy a central importance within their culture. Entire communities cooperate on cyclical, seasonal systems of planting, pest control, and harvest, which are tied to lunar cycles and sometimes accompanied with religious rituals.

科迪勒拉山水稻梯田（吕宋岛）是伊富高人民在两千年前开发的一个文化景观。这些梯田至今仍然在使用，并由现代伊富高农民维护着。

伊富高水稻梯田依山而建，更增加了山地高低起伏的自然美景，同时也集中体现了人类及其环境之间可持续的和谐关系。这些田地及耕种和维护田地的常识多年来一直世代相传。

亚洲还有其他许多处的梯田,比如巴厘岛就有,但菲律宾科迪勒拉的梯田由于它们的高度(可达 1500 米)和陡峭的山坡(最大 70 度)而显得尤为突出。

最初的建造者用石制和泥制的围墙细心雕琢、建造了梯田。这些梯田能容纳种植水稻所需的水田。他们还建立了一个系统,从山顶的森林集水来浇灌这些地块。大坝、水闸、水渠、竹管构成一个复杂的系统,保证所有梯田得到充分灌溉。这些令人难以置信的工程壮举完全靠人工完成。

梯田历来是伊富高民族生存的核心,在他们的文化中也占据了核心的地位。当地人民根据阴历,有时伴随着宗教仪式以循环、季节性的周期来合作耕种,防治病虫害和进行收割。

Vocabulary

1. contour *n.* 外形,轮廓

The smooth contour of the sculpture is wonderful.

雕塑物平滑的轮廓线简直太美了。

2. epitomize *vt.* 作……的摘要;成为……的缩影;概括;集中体现

Though clumsy on land, Cape fur seals epitomize grace underwater.

虽然南非海狗在陆地上行动笨拙,但是在水底下是优美的。

3. plot *n.* 一块地;(戏剧、小说等的)情节

Peasants can only plough the land plot by plot.

农民犁田只能一块一块地犁。

4. feat *n.* 功绩,伟业;技艺表演;卓绝的手艺,技术

Only the most talented young filmmakers will even attempt such a feat.

只有最富才气的青年电影制作人才会尝试完成这个壮举。

5. Lunar *adj.* 月的,月球的;阴历的

The most exciting time is the Eve of the Lunar New Year.

大年三十的晚上最让人激动。

扩展阅读

Philippine Rice Terraces No Longer in Danger

Manila, Philippines—The World Heritage Committee on Tuesday 06/26/2012 removed the Philippine Rice Terraces in Ifugao from its List of World Heritage in Danger.

The Philippines has successfully restored the terraces in a desired state of conservation, the 36th Session of the World Heritage Committee said.

Aside from restoring the terraces, local authorities have also undertaken their protection, planning, and proper management.

The international body said the Philippines has restored at least 50 percent of the collapsed terraces.

The required documentation and rehabilitation of major irrigation systems at the site has also been completed, it added.

The World Heritage Committee also said policies and laws preserving the site are now in place.

Community-based land use and zoning plans are being developed, and measures ensuring the site's proper management and its protection from natural disasters had been implemented, according to a United Nations Educational, Scientific and Cultural Organization (UNESCO) official.

"This decision is a historic moment for the Philippines," said Ambassador Christina Ortega, Philippine Permanent Delegate to UNESCO.

"To have the international community recognize our commitment and effort in reinstating the Rice Terraces of the Philippine Cordilleras in the World Heritage List is, for us, a great honor and accomplishment. Its removal from the List of World Heritage in Danger reinforces anew its grandeur and relevance as a globally important cultural landscape," she added.

The centuries-old rice terraces, which are found in the Cordilleras, are considered as a global cultural treasure.

The UNESCO said the rice terraces represent the "fruit of knowledge handed down from one generation to the next, and the expression of sacred traditions and a delicate social balance."

UNESCO said the rice terraces show a "landscape of great beauty that expresses the harmony between humankind and the environment".

They became the first-ever property in 1995 to be included in the cultural landscape category of the World Heritage List.

However, 6 years later, the rice terraces were placed in the endangered list.

Neglected systems and migration

During its 25th session held in December 2001 in Helsinki, Finland, the World Heritage Committee said the rice terraces were threatened by neglected irrigation systems and migration.

It also warned against unregulated developments in the site, lack of focus on tourism requirements, and a weak management system.

Photo by Rem Zamora for ABS-CBNNews.com

The International Committee on Monument and Sites (ICOMOS) warned that "a worrying percentage of (the) rice terraces had deteriorated; springs had dried up and deforestation within the watershed had occurred; subsistence farming and limited alternative economic opportunities had forced many Ifugaos to seek work elsewhere; and traditions and rituals associated with the cultivation of rice had been disappearing."

The Philippines established the Ifugao Cultural Heritage Office (ICHO) to save the terraces. It closely worked with various groups, such as the provincial government of Ifugao and the non-profit Save the Ifugao Terraces Movement.

The groups managed to help restore the rice terraces and their watersheds, while promoting or re-introducing the site's ancestral traditions that are crucial to its sustained development.

The UNESCO National Commission of the Philippines (UNACOM), meanwhile, joined forces with Department of Environment and Natural Resources (DENR), Department of Agriculture (DAR), National Mapping and Resource Information Authority (NAMRIA), and National Commission for Culture and the Arts (NCCA) to map out programs to protect the terraces.

UNACOM secretary-general Dr. Virginia Miralao thanked various organizations and individuals such as Governor Eugene Balitang, rep. Teddy Baguilat, Jr., the past and present members of the UNESCO NatCom Cultural Committee, various international UNESCO units, IUCN, and academic institutions such as UP, UST and Ifugao State University for helping restore and protect the terraces.

（资料来源：http://www. abs-cbnnews. com/-depth/06/26/12/philippine-rice-terraces-no-longer-danger）

Questions

1. When were the Philippine Rice Terraces included in the cultural landscape category of the World Heritage List?

2. Why and when were the rice terraces placed in the endangered list?

世界遗产概论

第四章　非洲的世界遗产

Introduction to the World Heritage

第一节　非洲的世界文化遗产

Archaeological Site of Carthage
迦太基遗址

⇨ **简介**

所属国家：突尼斯（Tunisia）

入选时间：1979

入选标准：（ii）（iii）（vi）

Carthage was founded by the Phoenicians in the 9th century BC on the Gulf of Tunis. From the 6th century onwards, it developed into a great trading empire covering much of the Mediterranean and was home to a brilliant civilization. Metropolis of Punic civilization in Africa and capital of the province of Africa in Roman times, Carthage has played a central role in Antiquity as a great commercial empire. In the course of the long Punic wars, Carthage occupied territories belonging to Rome, which finally destroyed its rival in 146 BC A second-Roman-Carthage was then established on the ruins of the first. The site of Carthage bears exceptional testimony to the Phoenico-Punic civilization being at the time the central hub in the western basin of the Mediterranean. It was also one of the most brilliant centres of Afro-Roman civilization.

Exceptional place of mixing, diffusion and blossoming of several cultures that succeeded one another (Phoenico-Punic, Roman, Paleochristian and Arab), Carthage has exercised considerable influence on the development of the arts, architecture and town planning in the Mediterranean, and has always nourished universal imagination through its historic and literary renown. Its antique ports bear witness to commercial and cultural exchanges over more than ten centuries.

迦太基毗邻突尼斯湾，由腓尼基人始建于公元前 9 世纪。自公元 6 世纪起，迦太基逐步发展成为一个强大的贸易帝国，也创造了一段辉煌的文明。其领土曾扩展到地中海大部分地区。古罗马时期，迦太基是非洲布匿文明的大都市，也是罗马的阿非利加省首府，作为强大的贸易帝国，它享有重要地位。在漫长的布匿战争中，迦太基占领了罗马的领土，但最终于公元前 146 年被罗马打败。第二个迦太基城建立在古迦太基的废墟之上。迦太基遗址是位于地中海地区西部盆地中心的腓尼基-布匿文明的充分证明，也是非洲-罗马文明最辉煌的中心之一。

迦太基及其众多港口先后经历了腓尼基-布匿文明、罗马文明、早期基督教文明和阿拉伯文明,不同的文化在这里混合、传播并兴盛,对地中海地区的艺术、建筑及城市规划有着重要影响,其重要的历史地位和文学盛名也一直滋养着全世界人们的想象力。迦太基的诸多古港口见证了 1000 多年来的文化交流和商品贸易盛况。

Vocabulary

1. territory *n.* 领土;版图;范围

They penetrated into territory where no man had ever gone before.

他们已进入先前没人去过的地区。

2. hub *n.* 轮轴;中心;电线插孔

Chicago is a hub of airline traffic.

芝加哥是航运中心。

3. diffusion *n.* 扩散;传播

The invention of printing helped the diffusion of learning.

印刷术的发明有助于知识的传播。

4. renown *n.* 名望;声望

Seldom has a city gained such world renown.

很少有城市能在世界上享有这样的盛名。

扩展阅读

Carthage

According to legend, Carthage was founded by the Phoenician Queen Elissa (better known as Dido) sometime around 813 BC. The city (in modern-day Tunisia, North Africa) was originally known as Kart-hadasht (new city) to distinguish it from the older Phoenician city of Utica nearby. The Greeks called the city Karchedon and the Romans turned this name into Carthage. Originally a small port on the coast, established only as a stop for Phoenician traders to re-supply or repair their ships, Carthage grew to become the most powerful city in the Mediterranean before the rise of Rome.

After the fall of the great Phoenician city of Tyre to Alexander the Great in 332 BC, those Tyrians who were able to escape fled to Carthage with whatever wealth they had. Since many whom Alexander spared were those rich enough to buy their lives, these refugees landed in the city with considerable means and established Carthage as the new centre of Phoenician trade. The Carthaginians then drove the native Africans from the area, enslaved many of them, and exacted tribute from the rest. From a small town on the coast, the city grew in size and grandeur with enormous estates covering miles of acreage. Not even one hundred years passed before Carthage was the richest city in the Mediterranean. The aristocrats lived in palaces, the less affluent in modest but attractive homes, while tribute and tariffs regularly increased the city's wealth on top of the lucrative business in trade. The harbour was immense, with 220 docks, gleaming columns which rose around it in a half-circle, and was ornamented with Greek sculpture.

The Carthaginian trading ships sailed daily to ports all around the Mediterranean Sea while their navy, supreme in the region, kept them safe and, also, opened new territories for trade and resources through conquest.

It was this expansion which first brought Carthage into conflict with Rome. When Rome was weaker than Carthage, she posed no threat. The Carthaginian navy had long been able to enforce the treaty which kept Rome from trading in the western Mediterranean. When Carthage took Sicily, however, Rome responded. Though they had no navy and knew nothing of fighting on the sea, Rome built 330 ships which they equipped with clever ramps and gangways (the corvus) which could be lowered onto an enemy ship and secured; thus turning a sea battle into a land battle. The First Punic War (264—241 BC) had begun. After an initial struggle with military tactics, Rome won a series of victories and finally defeated Carthage in 241 BC. Carthage was forced to cede Sicily to Rome and pay a heavy war indemnity.

Following this war, Carthage became embroiled in what is known as The Mercenary War (241—237 BC) which started when the Carthaginian army of mercenaries demanded the payment Carthage owed them. This war was finally won by Carthage through the efforts of the general Hamilcar Barca. Carthage suffered greatly from both these conflicts and, when Rome occupied the Carthaginian colonies of Sardinia and Corsica, there was nothing the Carthaginians could do about it. They tried to make the best of their situation by conquering and expanding holdings in Spain but again went to war with Rome when the Carthaginian general Hannibal attacked the city of Saguntum, an ally of Rome. The Second Punic War (218—201 BC) was fought largely in northern Italy as Hannibal invaded Italy from Spain by marching his forces over the Alps. Hannibal won every engagement against the Romans in Italy. In 216 BC he won his greatest victory at the Battle of Cannae but, lacking sufficient troops and supplies, could not build on his successes. He was defeated by the Roman general Scipio Africanus at the Battle of Zama, in North Africa, in 202 BC and Carthage again sued for peace.

Placed, again, under a heavy war indemnity by Rome, Carthage struggled to pay their debt while also trying to fend off incursions from neighbouring Numidia. Carthage went to war against Numidia and lost. Having only recently paid off their debt to Rome, they now owed a new war debt to Numidia. Rome was not concerned with what Carthage and Numidia were involved with but did care for the sudden revitalization of the Carthaginian army. Carthage believed that their treaty with Rome was ended when their war debt was paid; Rome disagreed. The Romans felt that Carthage was still obliged to bend to Roman will; so much so that the Roman Senator Cato the Elder ended all of his speeches, no matter what the subject, with the phrase, "Further, I think that Carthage should be destroyed." In 149 BC, Rome suggested just that course of action.

A Roman embassy to Carthage made demands to the senate which included the stipulation that Carthage be dismantled and then re-built further inland. The

Carthaginians, understandably, refused to do so and the Third Punic War (149—146 BC) began. The Roman general Scipio Aemilianus besieged Carthage for three years until it fell. After sacking the city, the Romans burned it to the ground, leaving not one stone on top of another. A modern myth has grown up that the Romans forces then sowed the ruins with salt but this story has no basis in fact. It is said that Scipio Aemilianus wept when he ordered the destruction of the city and behaved virtuously toward the survivors.

Utica now became the capital of Rome's African provinces and Carthage lay in ruin until 122 BC when Gaius Sepronius Gracchus, the Roman tribune, founded a small colony there. Memory of the Punic wars still being too fresh, however, the colony failed. Julius Caesar proposed and planned the re-building of Carthage and, five years after his death, Carthage rose again. Power now shifted from Utica back to Carthage and it remained an important Roman colony until the fall of the empire.

Carthage rose in prominence as Christianity grew and Augustine of Hippo lived there before coming to Rome. The city continued under Roman influence through the Byzantine Empire (formerly the Eastern Roman Empire) who held it against repeated attacks by the Vandals. In 698 BC, the Muslims defeated the Byzantine forces at the Battle of Carthage, destroyed the city completely, and drove the Byzantines from Africa. They then fortified and developed the neighbouring city of Tunis and established it as the new centre for trade and governorship of the region. Carthage still lies in ruin in modern day Tunisia and remains an important tourist attraction and archaeological site. The outline of the great harbor can still be seen as well as the ruins of the homes and palaces from the time when the city of Carthage ruled the Mediterranean.

（资料来源：http://www. ancient. eu. com/carthage/）

Questions

1. Could you make a timeline of the development of Carthage?
2. If you were to visit Carthage, what would you be most interested in?

Kairouan

凯鲁万

⬛▷ 简介

所属国家：突尼斯（Tunisia）

入选时间：1988

入选标准：(i)(ii)(iii)(v)(vi)

Founded in 670, Kairouan flourished under the Aghlabid Dynasty in the 9th century. Despite the transfer of the political capital to Tunis in the 12th century,

Kairouan remained the Maghreb's principal holy city, and a place of outstanding diffusion of Arabo-Muslim civilisation. Kairouan bears unique witness to the first centuries of this civilisation and its architectural and urban development. Its rich architectural heritage includes the Great Mosque, with its marble and porphyry columns, and the 9th-century Mosque of the Three Gates. The Great Mosque, rebuilt in the 9th century, is not only one of the major monuments of Islam but also a universal architectural masterpiece. The Great Mosque served as a model for several Maghreban mosques, particularly for its decorative motifs, which are unique. Moreover, the Mosque of the Three Doors, built in 866, is the oldest known Islamic mosque with a sculpted facade. Kairouan is one of the holy cities and spiritual capitals of Islam. Next to the Great Mosque, the first place of worship founded in the Maghreb only 38 years after the death of the Prophet, is the Zawiya of Sidi Sahâb where the remains of Abu Djama, one of Mahomet's companions, are kept.

Protected by its walls and three gates, the Medina of Kairouan, whose skyline is punctuated by the minarets and the cupolas of its mosques and zawiyas, has preserved its network of winding streets and courtyard houses. Very few small windows or arched doorways are cut in the exterior walls, but inner walls have larger openings that give onto the central courtyard. This traditional architecture, having become vulnerable through the impact of socio-economic changes, constitutes a valuable heritage which must be protected in its entirety.

　　凯鲁万始建于公元670年,公元9世纪曾在阿夫拉比德王朝统治下繁盛一时。尽管到了12世纪时其政治首都的地位被突尼斯市取代,凯鲁万仍是马格里布地区首屈一指的圣城,阿拉伯—穆斯林文明在此地得以广泛流传,该城是这一文明的最初几百年及其城市发展和建筑演变的独特见证。这里有着丰富的建筑遗产,例如由大理石和斑岩制成柱子的大清真寺,以及修建于公元9世纪的三门清真寺。重建于9世纪的大清真寺,不仅是伊斯兰世界的主要丰碑之一,在全世界也堪称建筑杰作。大清真寺,尤其是它独一无二的装饰图案,成为马格里布地区其他一些清真寺仿效的范例。建于866年的三门清真寺,是已知最古老的拥有雕刻正面的伊斯兰清真寺。凯鲁万是伊斯兰教的圣城和精神首都之一。位于大清真寺一侧的西迪萨哈布修道院,是先知穆罕默德圆寂38年后,人们在马格里布地区修建的第一个伊斯兰朝拜地,阿布贾马(穆罕默德的随从之一)的遗体就保存在这里。

　　凯鲁万的麦地那市被城墙环绕,城墙上有3个城门。清真寺和修道院的尖塔和穹顶勾勒出美丽的城市弧线。麦地那还保留了其蜿蜒的街巷和院落式房屋纵横交织的布局。该地房屋的外墙鲜有小窗口或拱形门廊,内墙则都有通往中庭的较大通口。在社会经济变化的冲击下,这种传统建筑风格极为脆弱,成为亟须整体保护的宝贵遗产。

Vocabulary

1. motif *n.* 主题;图案

The jacket has a rose motif on the collar.

这件夹克衫的领子上有一朵玫瑰花的图案。

2. medina *n.* 麦地那;老城;(北非城市中的)阿拉伯人聚居区

Mohammed died in Medina soon after this victory，in 632.

此次胜利后不久,穆罕默德于 632 年在麦地那去世。

3. punctuate *v.* 不时打断;使用标点符号;加强,强调

The silence of the night was punctuated by the distant rumble of traffic.

夜晚的宁静不时被远处车辆的隆隆声打断。

4. minaret *n.* (清真寺的)宣礼塔;尖塔

Around the minaret are other cultural assets，including ruins of three watchtowers，a castle，a Jewish cemetery and a bazaar.

围绕该塔还有其他文化遗产,包括三座瞭望塔、一处城堡、一处犹太墓地和一处集市的遗址。

5. cupola *n.* 圆屋顶;穹顶;炮塔

A cupola in the distance caught their attention.

远处的一个穹顶状物引起了他们的注意。

扩展阅读

Kairouan

The holy city

Kairouan is defined as the holiest city of Tunisia，being the oldest Islamic settlement，having the oldest mosque in North Africa and the world's oldest minaret.

But there is more to the story：In 670，the general of the invading Arab forces，Oqba bin Nafi，found a golden cup in the sands here，a golden cup that he had lost in the holy well of Zamzam in Mecca a few years earlier. When picking the cup up，water sprang from the ground. This is said to be source of the Bi'r Barouta，Kairouan's most popular attraction among Muslim.

Among the very first projects of the conquering Arabs was to built a great mosque. A city grew quickly up，and around 800，Kairouan became the capital of the Aghlabid dynasty. This would last a little bit more than a century，before the Fatimids made Mahdia their capital.

The city was for a long time characterized by not being much touched by the French，who wanted to respect the sentiment of the Tunisians. For a long time the whole city was kept inside the city walls，and no Ville Nouvelle was ever constructed.

Judging by its name，many visitors to Kairouan wonder if the place is named after Cairo of Egypt. The answer is no. When Kairouan was founded，there was no place called Cairo. Moreover，"Cairo" is a bad transliteration from the Arabic name "Qahira"，while Kairouan is a fairly correct transliteration of the Arabic "Qayrawan".

Kairouan is a great tourist destination，being the best place in Tunisia to learn about the country's Islamic history. In addition to the Great Mosque there are a number of smaller, still very interesting and attractive, religious institutions open to non-Muslims too.

The famous great mosque

The Great Mosque of Kairouan dates back to 670 BC and was built by the command of Arab Muslim general Oqba bin Nafi. Although it has been destroyed a couple of times, then rebuilt, today's structure rests much upon the original mosque.

The most extensive destruction came few years after the original construction, in 688 when it was destroyed in a rebellion. The present layout was created in the 9th century, but it is hard to establish which parts date back to this date. The base of the minaret is thought to be some 100 years older than this.

Still, the columns of the prayer hall are even older, having been taken from Roman and Byzantine structures in Carthage and Hadrumetum (Sousse).

Standing inside the mosque's courtyard you will probably not be able to see that everything tilts, none of the corners are 90 degrees and the minaret does not stand on the axis running from the mihrab through the entrance to the prayer hall, rather about 8 metres to the right.

The colonnade along the 3 other sides but the minaret one, is impressive. Simple and beautiful.

World's oldest minaret

The first mosques erected in early Muslim time did not have minarets—the believers were called to prayer by the muezzin standing on the mosque roof.

But it is believed that with the expansion of Islam, the many churches with their towers paved the ground for adding towers to minarets as well. Most seem to agree that the lowest storey of the minaret in Kairouan are the remains of the first real minaret in the world, dating back to 730, more than 100 years after the death of the Prophet Muhammad.

It is quite impressive even today, but note how much thicker it is than more recent minarets. It is 31.5 metres high with a base of 10.7 metres square. It consists of 3 sections, where the first is 19 metres, the second 5 metres and the third 7.5 metres including the dome.

The minaret appears first as very simple, but a closer look will reveal some interesting details.

The two top photos show how it at first was built with bits and pieces from older structures. The decorations around the door do not even fit, intriguing.

The second photo shows one of two Roman bricks with inscriptions. The other brick is placed upside down.

Looking further up the minaret can usually only be done with your camera zoom or with binoculars. Most of the time it is closed for entry, but if you're lucky you may be able to climb its 128 steps to the top. Note here the Roman columns used as the only form of decoration.

Beginning from below, note how the window niches get larger the further you get to the top.

Prayer hall

One of the legends on the prayer hall of the Great Mosque says that anyone trying to count its columns will become blind.

The columns were of Roman and Byzantine origin, and brought here from as far away as Carthage and Hadrumetum (Sousse). None two are said to have the same shape and size.

It must have been with great awe that the Muslims of the early centuries of North African Islam entered this vast hall, some 70 times 40 metres. Unfortunately, the hall is closed for non-Muslim visitors, but usually, some of the doors are open. The impressive 19th century allows limited views, but you will be able to see the mihrab, which is noted for being framed by 130 faience tiles imported from Baghdad in the 9th century.

By the way, the number of columns is 414.

（资料来源：http://looklex.com/tunisia/kairouan.htm）

Questions

1. Why is Kairouan defined as the the holiest city of Tunisia?

2. Which part of the Great Mosque interests you the most?

Lamu Old Town
拉穆古镇

⏎ 简介

所属国家：肯尼亚（Kenya）

入选时间：2001

入选标准：（ii）（iv）（vi）

Lamu Old Town is the oldest and best-preserved Swahili settlement in East Africa, retaining its traditional functions. Built in coral stone and mangrove timber, the town is characterized by the simplicity of structural forms enriched by such features as inner courtyards, verandas, and elaborately carved wooden doors. The architecture and urban structure of Lamu graphically demonstrate the cultural influences that have come together over 700 hundred years from Europe, Arabia, and India, utilizing traditional Swahili techniques that produced a distinct culture.

Unlike other Swahili settlements which have been abandoned along the East African coast, Lamu has continuously been inhabited for over 700 years. The growth and decline of the seaports on the East African coast and interaction between the Bantu, Arabs,

Persians，Indians，and Europeans represents a significant cultural and economic phase in the history of the region which finds its most outstanding expression in Lamu Old Town，its architecture and town planning.

Lamu has maintained its social and cultural integrity，as well as retaining its authentic building fabric up to the present day. Once the most important trade centre in East Africa，Lamu has exercised an important influence in the entire region in religious，cultural as well as in technological expertise.

Its paramount trading role and its attraction for scholars and teachers gave Lamu an important religious function in East and Central Africa. A conservative and close-knit society，Lamu has retained its important status as a significant centre for education in Islamic and Swahili culture，and hosted major Muslim religious festivals since the 19th century.

拉穆古镇是东非最古老、保存最完整的斯瓦希里人聚居地，并仍然保持着它的传统功能。这个镇以珊瑚石和红树林木材建造而成，以结构简朴为特色，同时，庭院、阳台走廊、精心雕刻的木门为其增添了很多特有风貌。拉穆古镇的建筑和城市结构生动地体现出700 多年以来欧洲、阿拉伯地区和印度文化对当地的深刻影响。这些文化色彩和斯瓦希里传统的建筑艺术一同造就了拉穆古镇的独特风貌。

和其他东非沿海地区被荒弃的斯瓦希里人聚居地不同，拉穆古镇 700 多年来一直有人居住。东非沿海港口城镇的兴衰及班图人、阿拉伯人、波斯人、印度人和欧洲人的相互交流，反映了该地历史上一个重要的文化、经济发展时期。拉穆古镇及其建筑风格和城镇规划正是这一时期最突出的体现。

拉穆古镇至今仍保持着其建筑结构、社会和文化的完整性。这儿曾是东非最重要的贸易中心，拉穆古镇对整个地区的宗教、文化和技术发展都有着重要的影响。

拉穆重要的贸易角色及其对学者和教师的吸引力使它在东非、中非具有重要的宗教功能。作为一个保守且团结的社会，拉穆一直是伊斯兰和斯瓦希里文化中重要的教育中心。从 19 世纪开始，主要的穆斯林宗教节日活动都在这里举行。

Vocabulary

1. retain *v.* 保留；保持；保存

The interior of the shop still retains a nineteenth-century atmosphere.

这家商店的内部装修仍然保留着 19 世纪的风格。

2. timber *n.* 木材；原木；树木；林木

These trees need more time to grow into useful timber.

这些树不够年头，还没成材呢。

3. veranda *n.* （房屋外带屋顶的）走廊，游廊，阳台

They had their coffee and tea on the veranda.

他们在阳台上喝咖啡和茶。

4. elaborately *adv.* 苦心经营地；精巧地

The room was elaborately decorated.

这个房间摆设得很考究。

5. utilize *v.* 利用；使用

The Romans were the first to utilize concrete as a building material.

罗马人首先使用混凝土作建筑材料。

6. paramount *adj.* 最重要的；首要的；卓越的

Nitrogen is of paramount importance to life on earth.

氮对地球上的生命至关重要。

扩展阅读

Lamu Cultural Festival, History and the Experience of a Medieval Old Town

Along the Kenyan coastline is Lamu Town, one of the oldest towns along the East African coastline and only rivaled by Zanzibar in Tanzania. Lamu is an island region in Kenya and is the origin of Swahili people and Swahili culture.

The history of Lamu Town started in 1415 when a Chinese ship sunk near the coastline while on its exploration adventures of Africa along the East African coastline.

The survivors from the ship settled at a place now called Lamu and married the locals. In 1506 the Portuguese invaded and took control of the island. The Portuguese invasion was prompted by the island's success in controlling the trade along the Indian Ocean.

For many years, Lamu Island was under the control of Portuguese who had a complete monopoly of trade, shipping and taxes on trade activities. The Oman Empire was a regional power by then. The empire controlled most of the Middle East, East African and South East African regions.

In early years, Lamu's economy was based on slave trade until when this trade was abolished in 1907. Other trade exports included mangrove, turtle shells, ivory, and rhinoceros horns. These exports were shipped to the Middle East and India through the Indian Ocean.

On numerous occasions, Lamu Island would try to rebel against the Portuguese but it wasn't successful until 1652 when the Oman Arabs assisted Lamu to resist the Portuguese control.

This marked the beginning of the Lamu Island town as it is known today, an island with diverse culture and preserved poetry, politics, cultural practices, festivals, arts and crafts as well as trade.

Lamu Island is a place whose history is as mysterious and fascinating as the winding streets of it's medieval stone town.

The island itself is a serene place of rolling sand dunes and endless sandy beaches, where tiny coral made villages nestle among coconut and mango plantations and lateen sailed dhows ply the blue waters.

The island can be accessed through daily flights from Nairobi, Mombasa and

Malindi or dhows, yachts and ferries arriving to Lamu Town or Shela.

One thing that will fascinate you about Lamu is the fact that there are no vehicles in Lamu Town. The winding streets of Lamu are best explored on foot. Alternatively you can use the dhows that regularly carry passengers back and forth from Lamu Town to Shela.

To access the surrounding islands of Manda, Pate or Siyu, either you can take an organized dhow safari or for the adventurous traveler you can just hitch a ride on a passing dhow and explore. It is also possible to hire donkeys to ride around the island. You will be surprised that donkeys here are an added asset and so there is even a special sanctuary clinic for them.

Petley's Inn is Lamu's oldest hotel mostly preferred by tourists due to its waterfront location. Other high class hotels and resorts in Lamu Town include the 20-room Bahari Hotel, Lamu Palace Hotel, the American-restored Amu House, Doda Villas, Swedish-owned Jannat House and Stone House Hotel. Tourism contributes heavily to the local economy with many locals providing dhows trips to tourists.

One of the biggest cultural festivals in Lamu Island is the Lamu Cultural Festival that is held every year. The festival is held to celebrate the distinctive Swahili heritage and culture of the Lamu archipelago, honoring both the past and the future values and customs of the Swahili community.

The festival has been held faithfully for years but it become more popular when the UNESCO declared Lamu Old Town a World Heritage site in 2001. Other festivals that are held in Lamu includes Maulidi Festival, which is held every year during the last week of the month of Prophet Muhammand birth, Lamu Annual Painters Festival, Lamu Artistic Hat Competition and the New Year's Eve in Shela.

Lamu Cultural Festival

Lamu Cultural Festival is a collection of cultural activities that takes place for a whole week, day and night. It showcases traditional Swahili poetry, traditional dances, musical performances, Swahili bridal ceremony, handicrafts, Henna painting, dhow sailing, door carving and the biggest highlight of the festival is the famous donkey race. The festival is held during the last week of November and it draws sponsorship from various international embassies and private sponsors.

Reading and performances by the various storytellers is one of the activities to enjoy at this festival. You will be amazed by the richness of Swahili poetry presented using old Swahili poetry skills.

The main performance takes place at the main town square where all the islands of the archipelago converge to present traditional dances (ngoma) in a single venue that warms the streets of this medieval old town.

The whole festival is a thriller where different activities takes place to the entertainment of everyone including non Swahili speakers, tourists and visitors to

Lamu. Traditional displays that comprises of dhow building，henna painting，door carvings，palm weaving，Swahili bao games and fish trap making are presented. The donkey races along the Lamu seafront and the dhow races are thrilling to watch.

Other presentations that are a must to watch include the display of various types of dhows. You will be amazed at how the Swahili people are capable of building big dhows called Jahazi in Swahili and even small portable ones called Mashua. The Sultan elegant Mozambique dhow is certainly one of the biggest attractions in dhows display. Throughout the festival there is a lot to sample in terms of Swahili culinary.

The Lamu Cultural festival is a wonderful event to experience the mystery of a medieval old town with magnificent architectural art and unspoiled beaches of an enchanted island where culture was born and continues to live.

（资料来源：http：//www. infobarrel. com/Lamu_Cultural_Festival_history_and_the _experience_of_a_medieval_old_town）

Questions

1. What are the options for tourists to explore the Lamu Island?
2. What are some of the major festivals held in Lamu?

Memphis and Its Necropolis—the Pyramid Fields from Giza to Dahshur

孟菲斯及其墓地金字塔
——从吉萨到代赫舒尔的金字塔区域

▷ 简介

所属国家：埃及（Egypt）

入选时间：1979

入选标准：（i）（iii）（vi）

Egypt is one of the four main cradles of civilization. The site—"Memphis and its Necropolis—the Pyramid Fields from Giza to Dahshur"—recognizes the universal admiration for the Pyramids，their antiquity and the exceptional civilization they represent. In ancient times, the site was considered one of the Seven Wonders of the World. The area contains approximately eighty pyramids，including the three great pyramids of pharaohs Khufu，Khafre，and Mankaure. The Great Pyramid of Khufu is one of the world's largest pyramids；it is 230 meters at the base，approximately 138 meters tall (it was 146 meters tall at the time of completion)，and is supposedly made of approximately 2. 8 million stones，each of them weighing an average of 2. 5 tons.

Memphis was the capital of the Old Kingdom of Egypt from its foundation (3100 BC) until 2200 BC，and served as the center of ancient Egypt for 3，000 years. The ruins of Memphis are 19 km south of Cairo，on the west bank of the Nile. There are some extraordinary funerary monuments, including rock tombs, ornate mastabas, temples and pyramids.

Giza, located ca. 25 km southwest of Cairo center, is a complex of ancient monuments including the three pyramid complexes known as the Great Pyramids, the massive sculpture known as the Great Sphinx, several cemeteries, a workers' village and so on.

Dahshur is a royal necropolis located in the desert on the west bank of the Nile approximately 40 km south of Cairo. It is known chiefly for several pyramids, two of which are among the oldest, largest and best preserved in Egypt: the Bent Pyramid and the Red Pyramid.

埃及是四大古文明摇篮之一。"孟菲斯及其墓地金字塔——从古萨到代赫舒尔的金字塔区域"这一世界遗产体现了全世界对古老的金字塔及其代表的辉煌文明的赞誉。该遗址曾是"古代世界七大奇观"之一。这里大约有80座金字塔,包括3座最大的法老金字塔:胡夫金字塔、卡夫拉金字塔和孟卡拉金字塔。胡夫金字塔是世界上最大的金字塔之一:底边长230米,高约138米(建成时原高146米),用了约280万块石灰岩建造,每块岩石平均重达2.5吨。

自公元前3100年建成到公元前2200年,孟菲斯是古埃及史上古王国时期的首都,3000年中,孟菲斯一直是古埃及的中心。它的遗址位于开罗以南19千米的尼罗河西岸一带,仍留存了许多著名的墓葬遗迹,如石墓、华丽的石墓室、寺庙和金字塔等。

吉萨位于开罗中心西南约25千米处,其陵墓群包括被称为大金字塔的三个金字塔群、狮身人面像、几处公墓、一个工人村庄等。

代赫舒尔是位于开罗以南40千米、尼罗河西岸的沙漠之上的埃及王室大型墓地,该处坐落着数座金字塔,其中弯曲金字塔和红色金字塔是埃及最大、最古老、保存最完好的金字塔。

Vocabulary

1. necropolis *n.* 墓地;坟地

It is both national park and necropolis, a city of the dead dating back to the first century.

这里既是国家公园,也是公墓,是可以追溯至公元一世纪的逝者之城。

2. pharaoh *n.* 法老(古埃及国王)

So Moses and Aaron went to pharaoh and did just as the Lord commanded.

摩西、亚伦进去见法老,就照耶和华所吩咐的做。

3. ornate *adj.* 装饰华丽的;修饰繁复的

They entered the big dining-room with its massive fireplace and ornate ceiling.

他们走进带有巨大壁炉和华美天花板的宽敞餐厅。

4. mastaba *n.* 石室坟墓

The Egyptian pyramids developed from the mastaba.

埃及金字塔是从古埃及墓室发展而来的。

扩展阅读

Steeped in History

Hardly a bucket list exists in the world that does not include a trip to the Great Pyramids of Giza in Egypt. Since the year 140 BC when Antipater of Sidon updated the list of the Ancient Seven Wonders of the World to include the Great Pyramid of Giza, this colossal tomb and the smaller, though no less impressive, pyramids surrounding it have captured and held the world's collective imagination.

The enormous complex of the Giza Necropolis is located 25km southwest of Cairo and 9km from the town of Giza, on the western bank of the Nile River. It comprises the three pyramid complexes known collectively as the Great Pyramids, the mammoth sculpture of the Great Sphinx, a workers' village, industrial complex and several cemeteries. In 1979 it achieved UNESCO World Heritage site status, under the name "Memphis and Its Necropolis—the Pyramid Fields from Giza to Dahshur".

Breath taking in its scope, awe inspiring in its sheer audacity, no Egyptian pyramid is larger and certainly no visit to Egypt is complete without a trip to the Great Pyramid of Giza.

The Great Pyramid of Giza

While the facts will remain forever lost in the passage of the millennia since its construction, most historians believe the Great Pyramid was constructed in approximately 2560 BC, during the fourth Egyptian Dynasty. What is certain is that it was built for and under the orders of Pharaoh Khufu.

The Great Pyramid of Khufu, which is located in the Giza Necropolis on the Giza Plateau, just outside of Cairo, has an estimated mass of a staggering 5.9 million tons, a volume of 2.6 million cubic metres and stands 146.5 metres high. By modern estimates it would have taken some 300,000 workers at least 20 years to build.

For reasons of both symmetry and aesthetics, the exterior of the Great Pyramid and the other pyramids at Giza, were originally encased in smooth blocks of highly polished white limestone. In 1300 an earthquake loosened many of these stones however and in 1356 Bahri Sultan An-Nasir Nasir-ad-Din al-Hasan ordered them to be taken away to Cairo and used in the building of mosques and fortresses. The sad effect of this was to leave the less visually appealing, stepped core of the pyramids exposed to the harsh elements and erosion.

The extraordinary precision with which these casing stones were made can, however, still be seen today in the few stones that remain at the base of the Great Pyramid.

How did they do it?

For centuries, scholars, philosophers, historians, archaeologists, architects, builders and laypersons have discussed, debated and argued how such a colossal structure could have been constructed by so ancient a civilisation, without the benefit of modern cranes and equipment.

One popular theory is that external ramps were built to lift the blocks, each weighing between two and 15 tons, ever higher and were later deconstructed. Another proposes that wooden cranes were employed for the task. Some fringe groups even suggest that the pyramids were the work of extra-terrestrials. All that these theories have in common are the holes in them. An external ramp with the maximum possible 8% slope would have been more than one and half kilometres long, which is longer than the Giza Plateau allows for. As for cranes, the maximum standing room near the top of the pyramid is at times 45cm—not nearly enough room to support a crane.

One of the newer and perhaps more plausible theories, proposed by French architect Jean-Pierre Houdin, is that an internal ramp was constructed for this purpose and later sealed. This theory appears to be supported by the images from a microgravimetry survey conducted in the 80s, which shows less dense areas in the pyramid's walls that correspond to a corkscrew-like internal ramp.

Still, the debate continues and one has to wonder if solving this mystery would be nearly as satisfying as simply leaving it unresolved and open to debate for scholars in the centuries yet to come?

...

The Sphinx

Thought by some to have been built somewhere between 2558—2532 BC, during the reign of Pharaoh Khafre, and by others to have been built in 10,000 BC, the Great Sphinx is to this day the world's largest monolithic statue. It stands 73.5 metres long, six metres wide and 20.22 metres high.

Although the name "Sphinx" was first attributed to the statue in classical antiquity, some two millennia after its supposed construction, it is almost certainly a misnomer. The statue bears only a passing resemblance to the sphinx of Greek mythology—a creature with a lion's body, woman's head and eagle's wings. The Great Sphinx has no wings and the head is clearly that of a man.

Of all the monuments of the Giza Necropolis, the Sphinx is perhaps the one that has given up the least of its secrets. Little is known about the precise date of its construction or of its purpose. Certainly it predates Egypt's New Kingdom period, which is the time during which the first recorded references to it were made.

Whatever the secrets it so closely guards, like the Great Pyramids, the sheer size and antiquity of the Sphinx is awe inspiring, as this extract from John L. Stoddard's Lectures (1911), Volume 2, p.333 attests to:

"It is the antiquity of the Sphinx which thrills us as we look upon it, for in itself it has no charms. The desert's waves have risen to its breast, as if to wrap the monster in a winding-sheet of gold. The face and head have been mutilated by Moslem fanatics.

The mouth, the beauty of whose lips was once admired, is now expressionless. Yet grand in its loneliness—veiled in the mystery of unnamed ages—the relic of Egyptian antiquity stands solemn and silent in the presence of the awful desert—symbol of eternity. Here it disputes with Time the empire of the past; forever gazing on and on into a future which will still be distant when we, like all who have preceded us and looked upon its face, have lived our little lives and disappeared. "

（资料来源：http://www. legacyinspires. com/news. cfm? articleid ＝ 138 & Nextstart＝4）

Questions

1. From the passage, what can be learned about the Great Pyramid?
2. What do we know about the Sphinx? What remains unknown?

Nubian Monuments from Abu Simbel to Philae
阿布辛拜勒至菲莱的努比亚遗址

简介

所属国家：埃及（Egypt）

入选时间：1979

入选标准：(i)(iii)(vi)

The Nubian Monuments from Abu Simbel to Philae, located on the shores of Lake Nasser in the far south of Egypt, include temples from 11 separate sites between the Sanctuary of Isis at Philae and the Great Temple of Ramses Ⅱ at Abu Simbel, 280 km to the south. The open-air Museum of Nubia and Aswan brings together cultural properties closely associated with the unfolding of a long sequence of Egyptian Pharaonic history.

Abu Simbel is an archaeological site comprising two massive rock temples in southern Egypt on the western bank of Lake Nasser about 290 km southwest of Aswan. Abu Simbel is a temple built by Ramses Ⅱ in ancient Nubia in the 13th century BC; he chose to build the temple dedicated to himself on the site where there were two grottoes consecrated to the cult of the local divinities. The sovereign in this way reaffirmed the fact that Nubia belonged to the Egyptian Empire. It was dedicated to the gods Amun, Ra-Horakhty, and Ptah, as well as to the deified Ramses himself. It is generally considered the grandest and most beautiful of the temples commissioned during the reign of Ramses Ⅱ, and one of the most beautiful in Egypt. However, the complex was relocated in its entirety in the 1960s, on an artificial hill made from a domed structure, high above the Aswan dam reservoir. Nine other temples were moved in a similar way.

阿布辛拜勒至菲莱的努比亚遗址位于埃及最南端的纳赛尔湖畔，包括从菲莱岛上的伊西丝女神神庙到 280 千米以南的阿布辛拜勒神庙及其之间 11 个不同遗址的神庙。努比亚和阿斯旺地区正如一个露天博物馆,汇集了埃及法老统治时期历史长卷中的诸多文化特点。

阿布辛拜勒神庙遗址位于埃及南部的阿斯旺西南 290 千米处,坐落于纳赛尔湖西岸,由两个用岩石雕刻而成的巨型神庙组成。这座神庙是公元前 13 世纪的埃及法老拉美西斯二世修建的。开凿神庙的峭壁上原有两个奉给当地神灵的洞穴,拉美西斯二世把这座献给自己的神庙选址于此,重申了埃及帝国对努比亚的统治权。这座神庙是献给阿蒙、拉·哈拉凯佩和普塔神的,并且还纪念神圣的拉美西斯二世本人,被公认是拉美西斯二世统治时期下令修建的神庙中最宏伟、最精美的,也是全埃及最美的神庙。20 世纪 60 年代,由于兴建阿斯旺水库,阿布辛拜勒神庙被整体搬迁到高于阿斯旺大坝水库的后山上。以同样方式迁移的还有 9 座其他的神庙。

Vocabulary

1. sanctuary *n.* 圣所,圣堂;神殿

Many of the ruins incorporate ceremonial features, so it could possibly have been a religious sanctuary.

许多废墟上仍残留某些仪式特征,因此它可能是一所宗教圣殿。

2. sequence *n.* 顺序;连续;一系列

She made a sequence of dance movements.

她做了一个连续的舞蹈动作。

3. grotto *n.* 岩洞,洞穴

The sound of dripping water is always heard in this grotto.

这个洞穴经常能听到水滴声。

4. cult *n.* 狂热崇拜;膜拜

This was the mysterious nature-worship cults of these ancient peoples.

这是古人向神秘的大自然顶礼膜拜的仪式。

5. divinity *n.* 神,上帝;神学

Lauren Winner is an assistant professor at Duke Divinity School.

劳伦·温纳是杜克大学神学院的助理教授。

6. sovereign *n.* 君主;最高统治者

In March 1889, she became the first British sovereign to set foot on Spanish soil.

1889 年 3 月,她成为第一位踏上西班牙领土的英国君主。

7. deified *adj.* 神化的

No moral dogma must be taken for granted—no standard of measurement deified.

道德教条不必承认,衡量标准不得神化。

扩展阅读

Sun to Illuminate Inner Sanctuary of Pharaoh's Temple

For most of the year, the inner sanctum of the main temple at Abu Simbel is shrouded in darkness.

On two days, traditionally the anniversary of the birthday and coronation of pharaoh Ramses Ⅱ, a shaft of sunlight pierces the gloom, illuminating statues of gods and the king in the temple's inner sanctum.

On February 22, a day celebrating the king's birthday and again on October 22, a day celebrating his coronation, sunlight illuminates seated statues of the sun gods Re-Horakhte and Amon-Re, as well as a statue of king Ramses II. The statues sit in the company of the Theban god of darkness, Ptah (who remains in the shadows all year).

The spectacle—which has endured more than 3,200 years of Egyptian history—draws thousands of tourists to Abu Simbel to watch this ancient tribute to a pharaoh whose name is still known up and down the Nile Valley for his military exploits and monumental building projects.

Temple of a God-King

Ramses, who ruled Egypt for 66 years from 1270 to 1213 BC (about 50 years after the death of Tutankhamen, better known as King Tut) made a name for himself by battling the Hittites and the Syrians, Egypt's enemies to the north.

To celebrate his victories, Ramses erected monuments up and down the Nile with records of his achievements. He completed the hypostyle hall at Karnak (Thebes), and completed the funerary temple of his father, Seti Ⅰ, at Luxor on the West Bank of the Nile.

The main temple at Abu Simbel, which Ramses ordered built near the border of Nubia and Upper Egypt, was dedicated to two sun gods, Amen-Re and Re-Horakhte. Standing 100 feet (33 meters) tall, the temple was carved into an already-standing sandstone mountain on the banks of the Nile.

Four colossal statues of Ramses, each 66 feet (22 meters) high, guard the entrance to the temple. Rising to the pharaoh's knees are smaller statues of family members: his mother; favorite wife, Nefertari; and son, Prince Amonherkhepshef.

Inside the temple, three connected halls extend 185 feet (56 meters) into the mountain. Images of the king's life and many achievements adorn the walls. A second temple at Abu Simbel is dedicated to Nefartari, who appears to have been Ramses' favorite wife.

"Abu Simbel was one of, if not the largest, rock-cut temples in Egypt," says Bruce Williams of the Oriental Institute of Chicago, "The rock was sacred because the Egyptians believed the deity was living inside the mountain."

Rock-cut temples may have been especially significant in ancient Egypt because the bulge in the otherwise flat land may have signified the location where the gods emerged from the Earth, says Williams.

Monumental Move

The Abu Simbel temples do not sit in their original location. Egypt's growing need for electricity prompted the controversial construction of the Aswan High Dam in the

1960s. The dam created Lake Nasser, and rising waters flooded a number of important archaeological sites along the banks of the Nile and displaced thousands of people who lived in the area.

The rising waters threatened the temples at Abu Simbel. Members of the United Nations Educational, Scientific and Cultural Organization (UNESCO) orchestrated a massive construction project that moved the temple back 690 feet to its present site.

Piece by piece, craftsmen cut the temple, and the nearby temple of Nefertari into massive blocks of sandstone up to thirty tons. Both temples were carefully reassembled on a new steel and cement "mountain," safe from the water's edge.

The only result of the move is that the days of illumination have shifted by one—the illumination used to occur on February and October 21.

Festival of the Sun

That the days of illumination correspond to actual days in the life of Ramses is highly unlikely, says Leo Depuydt, an egyptologist at Brown University.

"The Egyptian calendar was based on 365 days and while it was precise, the solar calendar is minutely different from year to year," says Depuydt, who adds that it is also difficult to know the precise date of the birth or coronation of Ramses Ⅱ.

"Regardless of the alignment, if the temple faces East, the sun is going to shine in it twice a year," says Depuydt, who adds that "excitement is the key here—people are going to come to see the sun in the temple. But science is a different matter".

（资料来源：http://news. nationalgeographic. com/news/2001/02/0221_abusimbel. html）

Questions

1. What are the amazing features of Abu Simbel?

2. Why did the Abu Simbel temples have to be relocated? What was the role of UNESCO in the huge project?

Saint Catherine Area
圣卡特琳娜地区

⇨ 简介

所属国家：埃及（Egypt）

入选时间：2002

入选标准：(i)(iii)(iv)(vi)

The Orthodox Monastery of St. Catherine stands at the foot of Mount Horeb where, the Old Testament records, Moses received the *Tablets of the Law*. The mountain is known and revered by Muslims as Jebel Musa. The entire area is sacred to three world religions: Christianity, Islam, and Judaism. The Monastery, founded in the 6th century, is the oldest Christian monastery still in use for its initial function. Its walls and buildings of great significance to studies of Byzantine architecture and the Monastery houses outstanding collections of early Christian manuscripts and icons. The rugged mountainous landscape, containing numerous archaeological and religious sites and monuments, forms a perfect backdrop to the Monastery.

Ascetic monasticism in remote areas prevailed in the early Christian church and resulted in the establishment of monastic communities in remote places. St. Catherine's Monastery is one of the earliest of these and the oldest to have survived intact, being used for its initial function without interruption since the 6th century. It demonstrates an intimate relationship between natural grandeur and spiritual commitment.

The holiest part of the Monastery is the Chapel of the Burning Bush, which incorporates the 4th-century chapel built by the pious Empress Helena, mother of Constantine the Great, and dedicated to the Blessed Virgin Mary. The neoclassical bell tower is the work of the monk Gregorius and was built in 1871. The rectangular Old Refectory has 16th-century murals on the walls. The most ancient library in the Christian world is considered to be second only to that of the Vatican, in terms of both number and value of its collection.

The architecture of St. Catherine's Monastery, the artistic treasures that it houses, and its domestic integration into a rugged landscape combine to make it an outstanding example of human creative genius.

圣卡特琳娜东正教修道院坐落在何烈山脚下,就是基督教《旧约全书》记载摩西接受"律法石板"的地方。这座山以"杰别尔·穆萨"之名在穆斯林中广受尊敬。这个地区是包括基督教、伊斯兰教和犹太教在内的世界三大宗教共同的圣地。修道院始建于公元6世纪,是世界上仍在使用的最古老的修道院。修道院的墙体和房屋对拜占庭式建筑风格的研究具有很重要的意义。修道院内有大量杰出的收藏,包括早期基督教手稿和圣像。修道院所在的地区山峦高峻,蕴藏着无数的考古遗迹和宗教古迹,给修道院提供了完美的环境。

基督教早期盛行苦行修道,因此在偏远地区产生了许多修道院。圣卡特琳娜修道院就是最早的此类修道院之一,也是世界上现存完整的最古老的修道院,自6世纪以来一直为基督徒提供服务。这座修道院体现了壮观的自然环境与人类精神信仰之间的密切关系。

圣卡特琳娜修道院最神圣之处是燃烧荆棘礼拜堂,其中包括4世纪由君士坦丁大帝的母亲(虔诚的海伦娜皇太后)下令修建的、献给圣母玛丽亚的礼拜堂。修道院中新古典主义的钟楼是格雷戈里修道士于1871年建成的。长方形的修道院旧食堂,墙上绘有16世纪的壁画。修道院的图书馆是基督教世界最古老的,其藏书的数量和价值仅次于梵蒂冈图书馆。

圣卡特琳娜修道院的雄伟建筑、其收藏的艺术珍品及其与险峻环境的融合,无一不使之成为人类创造力的卓越典范。

Vocabulary

1. icon *n.* [宗]圣像；肖像

There is an icon of Confucius hanging in the main living room of the academy.

书院的正厅里悬挂着一幅孔夫子圣像。

2. backdrop *n.* 背景

The mountains provided a dramatic backdrop for our picnic.

群山如画，给我们的野餐平添景色。

3. ascetic *adj.* 禁欲的；禁欲主义的；苦行的

He left the luxuries of the court for the life of an ascetic.

他放弃宫廷的奢华，过起了清贫的生活。

4. grandeur *n.* 壮观；宏伟；富丽堂皇

These ruins sufficiently attest the former grandeur of the place.

这些遗迹充分证明了其昔日的恢宏气势。

5. pious *adj.* 虔诚的；信神的

Mrs. Prodie is an excellent lady，kind-hearted，charitable，pious.

普劳迪夫人是一位极出色的女人，宽厚仁慈，虔诚善良。

6. mural *n.* 壁画；墙的；墙壁的

One of the walls enclosing the park is decorated with a huge mural showing Hollywood stars.

公园一处围墙上装饰着好莱坞明星的巨幅壁画。

7. rugged *adj.* 崎岖的；险峻的

The Rocky Mountains have rugged mountains and roads.

落基山脉有崇山峻岭和崎岖不平的道路。

扩展阅读

Monks in Egypt's Lawless Sinai Hope to Preserve an Ancient Library

Just as they have done for 17 centuries，the Greek Orthodox monks of St. Catherine's Monastery in Egypt's Sinai desert and the local Jabaliya Bedouins worked together to protect the monastery when the 2011 revolution thrust Egypt into a period of uncertainty. "There was a period in the early days of the Arab Spring when we had no idea what was going to happen，" says Father Justin，a monk who has lived at St. Catherine's since 1996. Afraid they could be attacked by Islamic extremists or bandits in the relatively lawless expanse of desert，the 25 monks put the monastery's most valuable manuscripts in the building's storage room. Their Bedouin friends，who live at the base of St. Catherine's in a town of the same name，allegedly took up their weapons and guarded the perimeter.

The community's fears of an attack were not realized，but the monks decided they needed a new way to protect their treasured library from any future threats. Last year， they accelerated a program of digitally copying biblical scripts with the help of multispectral imaging specialists from around the world, while simultaneously renovating and modernizing the library itself. The Sinai library houses 1.8 million pages of script, including essential texts that document the early church. St. Catherine's ranks high among the world's preeminent Christian text collections: their Greek manuscripts are second in number only to the Vatican's, and their hallmark Arabic and Turkish scrolls document the interaction between the monastery and the surrounding world of Islam over the centuries. The monastery's project will create a digital library for scholars around the world. "The technology, the conservation—they are our protection. Many people are concerned about the safety of what we have here, so we have to make them sure that we are protecting our materials and appreciating our responsibility," says Father Justin, the monastery's librarian.

Security concerns are once again at the forefront after the July 3 military ouster of former President Mohamed Morsi and the violence that came in the wake of the change in the country's leadership. Two days after Morsi's ouster, the Egyptian army declared a state of emergency in Sinai after Islamist gunmen opened fire on the region's el-Arish airport and several military checkpoints, killing several police officers and a soldier. St. Catherine's is geographically vulnerable at the best of times, positioned as it is on a peninsula plagued by a security vacuum. Crimes like human trafficking and kidnappings along the Egypt-Israel border make Sinai one of Egypt's most dangerous regions.

Father Justin acknowledges that the conservation efforts have been inspired by neighborhood insecurity. "Libraries are precious places where you can store the past in the present, and we are treating what happened to Cairo—the riots, looting and violence that surrounded the revolution—as a reminder that libraries are vulnerable, and right now they are more vulnerable than ever," he says, sitting in his no-frills office in front of a MacBook Pro. He politely steps out to a dark room every few minutes to turn the page of an ancient manuscript so that an imaging crew from Greece can scan the palimpsest.

The two-plus years since the toppling of former President Hosni Mubarak have been unsettling for Egypt's Christians, the majority of whom belong to the Coptic Church and account for a significant minority (up to 10%) of the country's population. There have been violent clashes between Christians and Muslims, with deaths on both sides. St. Catherine's has nevertheless maintained its track record of friendly relationships with its Muslim neighbors. The Greek Orthodox monks and the Jabaliya Bedouin tribe, who are the area's majority residents, have shared land, food and friendly relations since the monastery was built centuries ago. The Jabaliya are believed to be descendants of the Byzantine soldiers who built the monastery in the 6th century, and many of them continue to guard the monastery as their own. "The monastery is a very special place for me and all Bedouins. It is a holy place for all religions. Our ancestors built St.

Catherine's," explains Ramadan, 26, who has been a tour guide at the monastery since he was 15.

Another Bedouin resident, Faraj, just out of Friday morning prayers at a nearby mosque, adds:"(The Jabaliya and the monks) have been here for so long that we have grown together. We've been through times when we had to share our food and gardens. We share everything, we always have. There is even a mosque on the monastery. We don't use it often anymore because our population is too big now, but it is a still a symbol of our friendly relationship."

Eager to maintain similarly peaceful relations with all Egyptians, the monks hope their ongoing project will act as a reminder of the monastery's historical bond with Egypt. "We have to present ourselves in a way to convince the Arabic-speaking world that we are a part of Egypt's ancient history," Father Justin says. In preserving their manuscripts, the monks of St. Catherine's may also be preserving their way of life.

(资料来源：http://world.time.com/2013/07/21/monks-in-egypts-lawless-sinai-hope-to-preserve-an-ancient-library/)

Questions

1. What posed security threats to St. Catherine's Monastery?
2. What did the monks of St. Catherine's Monastery do to preserve their precious library?

第二节　非洲的世界自然遗产

Air and Ténéré Natural Reserves

阿德尔和泰内雷自然保护区

简介

所属国家：尼日尔(Niger)

入选时间：1991

入选标准：(vii)(ix)(x)

This is one of the largest protected area in Africa, covering some 7.7 million ha, though the area considered a protected sanctuary constitutes only one-sixth of the total area. It comprises two main zones: the mountain massifs of Aïr rising up to 2,000 m in altitude and the vast plain of the Ténéré desert. It includes the volcanic rock mass of the Aïr, a small Sahelian pocket, isolated as regards its climate and flora and fauna, and situated in the Saharan desert of Ténéré. The reserves boast an outstanding variety of landscapes, plant species and wild animals.

The Aïr constitutes a Sahelian enclave surrounded by a Saharian desert, thus forming a remarkable assemblage of relict ecosystems combined with mountain and plain landscapes of outstanding esthetic value and interest.

The Reserve of Aïr and Ténéré is the last bastion of Saharo-Sahlien wildlife in Niger. The isolation of the Aïr and the very minor human presence are the reasons for the survival in this region of numerous wildlife species that have been eliminated from other regions of the Sahara and the Sahel. The property contains a wide variety of habitats necessary for the conservation of the Saharo Sahelian biological diversity. The property contains important natural habitats for the survival of the three antelopes of the Sahara Desert on IUCN's Red List of threatened species. In total, 40 species of mammals, 165 species of birds, 18 species of reptiles and one amphibian species have been identified in the Reserve.

The property was inscribed on the List of World Heritage in Danger in 1992 due to political instability and dissention among the peoples.

阿德尔和泰内雷自然保护区是非洲最大的自然保护区之一,占地约770万公顷,但整个区域只有约六分之一面积的地区被认为真正具有保护意义。该保护区由两大部分组成:海拔2000多米的阿德尔山和广袤的泰内雷沙漠。该地区包括阿德尔火山断层和小萨赫勒地区,虽然位于泰内雷的撒哈拉沙漠,但是那里的气候、动物和植物却与周围地区明显不同。阿德尔和泰内雷自然保护区以拥有各异的环境、多样化的植物和野生动物而著称。

在该保护区,萨赫勒地带的一段为撒哈拉沙漠环绕,形成了各种各样的孑遗生态系统,其中的高山、平原具有极高的审美价值。

阿德尔和泰内雷自然保护区是尼日尔境内撒哈拉—萨赫勒地带野生动植物最后的一片天地。阿德尔山与世隔绝、人迹罕至,使得许多在撒哈拉、萨赫勒地区灭绝的野生动植物品种在此得以存活。该保护区内多种多样的动物栖息地环境使撒哈拉—萨赫勒地区的生物多样性得以保护。该保护区为世界自然保护大会所列濒危物种红色名录中的3种羚羊提供了重要的自然栖息地,区内已验明共有40种哺乳动物、165个鸟类品种、18种爬行动物和一种两栖类动物。

因政局动荡、民族纷争,该保护区于1992年被列入濒危世界遗产名录。

Vocabulary

1. comprise v. 包括;由……组成;构成
The exhibition comprises 50 oils and watercolours.
展览陈列了50幅油画和水彩画。
2. enclave n. (国家或城市中隶属另一民族或文化的)飞地,孤立地区
Nagorno-Karabakh is an Armenian enclave inside Azerbaijan.
纳戈尔诺—卡拉巴赫是阿塞拜疆境内亚美尼亚人聚居的一块飞地。
3. assemblage n. (人或物的)组合,集合,聚集
Tropical rainforests have the most varied assemblage of plants in the world.

热带雨林集聚了世界上种类最繁多的植物。

4. relict *n.* 遗物,残遗物

Ginkgo biloba is the oldest existing plant seeds of the relict plant.

银杏是现存种子植物中最古老的孑遗植物。

5. antelope *n.* 羚羊

The lion buried its teeth in the antelope's neck.

狮子咬住羚羊的脖子。

6. reptile *n.* 爬行动物

The sea turtle is the largest reptile in the aquarium.

海龟是现今海洋世界中躯体最大的爬行动物。

7. amphibian *adj.* 两栖动物

Both the toad and frog are amphibian.

蟾蜍和青蛙都是两栖动物。

扩展阅读

Aïr and Ténéré Natural Reserves, Niger

Threats to the Site

The region suffered from military and civil disturbance in the 1990s: six members of the Reserve staff were held hostage in 1992. In compliance with the request from Niger's Permanent Delegation to UNESCO, the World Heritage Committee inscribed the site on the List of World Heritage in Danger in 1992.

A peace agreement with rebels was signed in April 1995 and the impact of rebel activities on the integrity of the site has been found to be less severe than expected. An IUCN/WWF project has since helped to re-establish a management regime. Missions to the site in 1998 and 2001 found that the numbers of most wildlife species were recovering and the flora to be mostly intact except in some valleys over-used by the local people. Some species continue to be seriously threatened by poaching and the international trade in live animals, animal by-products and ostriches are now almost extinct on site. However, the State Party has submitted an emergency program for rehabilitation of the site and it may be considered for removal from the List of World Heritage in Danger.

Conservation Management

Since 1981 the area has been administered by foresters of the government's Service Faune. A reserve rather than a national park was mandated to allow people to continue living on their land. It was created and has been run since 1988 with the help of an IUCN/WWF project initiated in 1982. The 1988 legislation recapitulates existing national laws which prohibit hunting of wild animals and exploitation of certain tree species, all commercial collection of firewood, abusive cutting or pruning of any tree or bush for fodder, artifacts or fuel, and organized motor sports (the Paris-Dakar Rally used to pass through the area). The legislation defined 16% of the center of the reserve as a sanctuary to protect the small population of addax from tourist and other disturbance. Access to it is now banned without express permission from the Minister in charge of wildlife. This has not greatly affected the local Twareg, who rarely entered the area since there is very little pasture there and it does not lie across any of their traditional caravan routes.

Training has been an important objective of the IUCN/WWF project. By 1990, locals had been trained as masons, construction workers, tree nurserymen, first aid helpers, midwives, mechanics, guides, and drivers. A large number of unskilled short-term laborers had been employed to build dry-stone barrages and to plant trees. Several Nigerien foresters had been sent abroad on study scholarships funded by the project. The nomads are told about the authorities' intentions and changes in reserve legislation during periodic visits from forester patrols and from four camel-mounted extension workers who visit areas inaccessible by vehicle. To integrate the people into the reserve's management, a network of 47 headmen and clan chief representatives was appointed to report infractions of the law in their areas. A reunion of these men and the reserve authorities is held once a year when discussions are two-way and last three to four days.

A subsidiary IUCN project funds a magazine called Alam which highlights conservation issues and environmental problems. This is distributed free to school children in the departments of Agadez and Tahoua and in the reserve. IUCN Niger is now also working on a conservation project based on co-operation between local stakeholders and institutions. This aims to increase the economic value of the reserves to the local people by developing decentralized and sustainable ecotourism, agriculture and animal husbandry. Some specific projects are: tree planting, methods of construction without wood, better market farming and plant nurseries, producers' cooperatives, check dams, maintaining wells and more efficient wood-burning ovens.

A peace accord with the Twareg was signed in 1995: there were no longer serious security problems in the area, but some wildlife populations had declined. Realising its benefits, the local people restarted the development project after the civil unrest had declined. Peace encouraged a plan for rehabilitating the reserves for submission to prospective donors such as the Global Environment Facility (GEF), Band Aid and the Swiss and Danish governments. The plan included restoring sites used as rebel bases, improved surveillance, rapid evaluation of the impacts of disturbances on wildlife, establishing a committee for development and management of the reserves and training for reserve staff, police and customs officers about threats to wildlife. By 2001 a WHF funded Rapid Wildlife Assessment Report concluded that the main large mammal populations had recovered but were not yet assured and ostriches were locally extinct. However, addax were rare and reliable survey techniques were needed, as was also a wildlife census including the participation of local people. Reintroduction of the ostrich from Chad and the breeding of ostriches and large mammals for reintroduction was to be encouraged and had local support. The Fonds Francais de l'Environment Mondiale with the Direction Nationale de la Faune had initiated a 5-year support program for equipment and reintroductions and for monitoring, in cooperation with IUCN, GEF and UNDP.

Management Constraints

In 1992, the site was placed on the list of World Heritage in Danger as a result of conflict between the government and the Twareg. The Twareg traditionally hunted gazelle, aoudad, addax and occasionally ostrich, using snare traps and dog packs, but as wildlife has declined so has hunting. The decline was caused by uncontrolled illegal hunting with firearms and motor vehicles by military and mining personnel both foreign and Nigerien. Tourists also frequently chased addax and gazelles until they died of heat exhaustion. Harassment has decreased, due to improved surveillance and greater environmental awareness amongst Europeans, but unpunished poaching of gazelle and ostrich by the Nigerien military continues. Successive droughts have also caused competition for grazing land with livestock.

Other main management problems have been livestock predation by golden jackals and cheetah which the locals countered by indiscriminate poisoning; and destruction of trees for fodder, fuel and wood-working which has been reduced by replacing local wooden artifacts by imported ones. Both problems were solved in consultation with the local representatives at the annual reunions. The local tourist agencies initially opposed a reserve as a restriction on their independence, but they have gradually realized that the reserve protects the landscape and wildlife that tourists come to see. But pillaging archaeological sites for souvenirs can only be overcome with the cooperation of the tourists and agencies themselves, since it is too difficult to police the sites. However, by 2001, management of the reserve have been seen to have deteriorated and UNESCO supplies haven't reached it from the capital.

（资料来源：http://www.eoearth.org/view/article/150351/）

Questions

1. Why was the site placed on the list of World Heritage in Danger?
2. What measures have been taken to protect the reserve?

Aldabra Atoll
阿尔达布拉环礁

▷ 简介

所属国家：塞舌尔（Seychelles）

入选时间：1982

入选标准：（vii）（ix）（x）

Located in the Indian Ocean, the Aldabra Atoll is an outstanding example of a raised coral atoll. The atoll is comprised of four large coral islands which enclose a shallow lagoon; the group of islands is itself surrounded by a coral reef, providing a superlative spectacle of natural phenomena. Due to difficulties of access and the atoll's isolation, Aldabra has been protected from human influence and thus retains some 152, 000 giant tortoises, the world's largest population of this reptile. The least-disturbed large island in the Indian Ocean, Aldabra is of outstanding scientific interest. It is the only place in the world where a reptile is the dominant herbivore. Aldabra is one of the largest atolls in the world, and contains one of the most important natural habitats for studying evolutionary and ecological processes. The richness and diversity of the ocean and landscapes result in an array of colours and formations that contribute to the atoll's scenic and aesthetic appeal.

Aldabra provides an outstanding natural laboratory for scientific research and discovery. The atoll constitutes a refuge for over 400 endemic species and subspecies. The property is an outstanding example of an oceanic island ecosystem in which evolutionary processes are active within a rich biota.

阿尔达布拉环礁位于印度洋，是典型的上升珊瑚环礁，它由 4 个大的珊瑚岛组成，岛群内怀抱一片浅浅的礁湖，同时岛群本身又被一座珊瑚礁所包围，形成了绝佳的自然景观。因其地理上与外界隔绝，常人难以到达，阿尔达布拉未受到人类的破坏，成为约 15.2 万只巨型龟的栖息地，也是世界上此类爬行动物最为密集的地方。阿尔达布拉环礁是印度洋中最与世隔绝的珊瑚环礁，是世界上唯一的以爬行动物为主要食草动物的地方。作为世界最大的环礁之一，这儿是研究进化和生态进程最重要的自然栖息地之一。海洋和地形的丰富多样使得这里五光十色、层次多元、美不胜收。

阿尔达布拉为科学研究、科学发现提供了极好的自然实验室。这里的环礁是 400 余种当地特有物种和亚物种的天堂，也是丰富的生物区中进化过程活跃的海洋岛屿生态系统的杰出典范。

Vocabulary

1. atoll *n.* 环状珊瑚岛；环礁

An atoll is a circular reef surrounding a lagoon.

环礁是环绕着一个潟湖的环形礁石。

2. superlative *adj.* 极佳的；最优秀的；卓越的

The Regent Hotel has a superlative view of Hong Kong Island.

在丽晶酒店看香港岛的美景，视野绝佳。

3. herbivore *n.* 食草动物

This shy African herbivore kept the world guessing until 1901, when it was identified as a new genus of giraffes.

这种害羞的非洲草食动物让全世界迷惑了许久，直到 1901 年，它被确认为长颈鹿的一个新种。

　　4. array *n.* 一大批；一大群；陈列；布置

One is dazzled by the endless array of beautiful exhibits.

展品琳琅满目，美不胜收。

　　5. biota *n.* 一个地区的动植物；生物群

They have had serious effects upon the biota of stream.

它们对河流中的生物群体产生了严重影响。

扩展阅读

Paradise Found at Aldabra Atoll

Declared a protected UNESCO site, Aldabra Atoll is comprised of four main islands—Picard, Polymnie, Malabar, and Grande Terre—that encircle an immense lagoon. Lying 715 miles southwest of the capital city of Victoria and 261 miles north of Madagascar, Aldabra's remote setting has largely protected its islands from intense pressure from fishing or human habitation. Open solely to researchers plus a small number of visitors via permit, Aldabra supports a largely unspoiled tropical ecosystem with healthy populations of land and sea life as well as pristine coral reefs. Other than for a small cluster of research settlement buildings on Picard Island, development is forbidden. Extremely remote, one must arrive by boat after sailing 24-hours from more far flung islands of the Seychelles island group. Consequently, this natural isolation has engendered unique populations of wildlife.

...

Restricted to visiting a small area of the entire atoll, what the visitor encounters nevertheless is jaw-dropping. Entering the lagoon on a zodiac by way of one main channel, another world awaits. One is struck by limestone pinnacles that have been eroded into jagged shapes within the tranquil lagoon, their mushroom-shaped coral heads dotting the surface of the water. Tiny mollusks attached to these coral heads cling to life, dependent upon the daily ebb and flow of tides. Razor-sharp mollusk shells stand ready to shred any boat or flesh unfortunate to come into contact with their sharp edges. For those keen on birds, avian life abounds, with large colonies of red-footed boobies, frigate birds, brown noddies and other seabirds roosting or nesting on mangrove trees. It's a place that is full of life, the cries and croaks of the seabirds punctuating the stillness.

...

Green and hawksbill turtles are abundant. Attracted to lush undersea grasses, Aldabra Atoll offers refuge to these beleagured dwellers of the deep. With no fishing nets to entangle and drown them, plentiful sea grass for food and no hunting pressure from humans, Aldabra Atoll is a safe haven for sea turtles. Some turtles are enormous, at least 4.5 feet in length. Parrot fish well over two feet in size keep out of the way of barracuda the length of adult human beings. The very size and quantity of these animals is heartening, indicative of the healthy nature of this atoll's waters. Aldabra's reefs are thriving. Unlike most of the Seychelles' islands, there is no run off from development to smother the reefs nor is there pressure from fishing.

Largely due to the practice of taking their fins for use in Asian cooking, shark populations are under siege around the world. At Aldabra, with no human predation sharks are plentiful as well as inquisitive. During one snorkel session, harmless black-tipped reef sharks repeatedly trailed me mere feet from my dive fins. When I wheeled on them quickly, they'd abruptly turn away, reminding me—forgive my anthropomorphizing—of guilty teenagers caught in the act of doing something forbidden. Trailing other snorkelers, the sharks were equally curious about these strange creatures in their midst, going so far as to nibble some dive fins. While the majority of sharks I encountered were harmless black-tipped reef sharks, I noted a few lemon and tiger sharks cruising nearby. We reached a respectful mutual agreement to ignore each other. This magnificent predator is so well-represented that I lost count after seeing 20 sharks, surely indicative of a healthy predator population in balance with Nature.

...

Giant Aldabra tortoise, Seychelles.

Indigenous to the Seychelles, many different species of giant tortoises once inhabited other islands, the majority of them now extinct in the wild with the remainder under severe pressure from habitat destruction as well as predation by cats, rats, and other introduced predators. In long-gone days of sailing ships, tortoises were hunted by passing sailors for food. Not requiring great amounts of water or food to survive over long periods of time, giant tortoises were perfect sources of fresh meat on interminable ocean voyages. Aldabra tortoises faced extinction before being protected by international agreement. On Aldabra, the good news is that the tortoises are hanging on, an estimated 150,000 documented on the atoll's four islands. Despite this, the Aldabra giant tortoise is listed by the IUCN (International Union for Conservation of Nature) as "Threatened" or, in the estimation of other organizations, "Endangered". Today no predators threaten the tortoises yet their range is restricted to such a small habitat that their continuing existence is considered to hang in the balance. More mundane threats include falling into a limestone pothole and not being able to extricate themselves or simply tumbling over on uneven ground, unable to right themselves.

Most tortoises are timid, retracting their heads into their shells if humans approach. Yet some tortoises that have been living in close proximity to the research station have become very used to human company, offering their soft, wrinkly, leathery necks to be scratched. I found their necks to be cool to the touch despite the intense, humid tropical heat. Friendly tortoises also enjoy fruit that is proffered to them. One had to be cautious around the tortoises for one reason—highly sensitive to locating water in this dry landscape, tortoise are attracted to moisture on human skin. Able to wring moisture out my shirt in the searing, humid island climate, I was warned to be alert to any tortoise that might nip my legs in search of a quick drink. Capable of crushing a finger with a single bite, this experience was to be avoided at all costs.

Tortoises' primary diet consists of "tortoise turf", grasses that they closely crop from the top down. These plants have developed an interesting evolutionary adaptation that demonstrates yet another fascinating facet of Mother Nature—contrary to most plants we recognize, these grasses grow seeds toward the bottom of the plants to thwart being eaten by tortoises, thus enhancing the chances of propagating their species.

（资料来源：http://www. redbubble. com/people/whalegeek/writing/3086266-paradise-found-at-aldabra-atoll）

Questions

1. What has kept Aldabra's ecosystem unspoiled?
2. Of all the wild species in Aldabra, what amazes you the most?

Dja Faunal Reserve
德贾动物保护区

⇨ 简介

所属国家：喀麦隆（Cameroon）

入选时间：1987

入选标准：（ix）（x）

Founded in 1950, the Dja Faunal Reserve is an integral part of the dense rain forests that form the Congo Basin. This is one of the largest and best-protected rainforests in Africa, with 90% of its area left undisturbed. Almost completely surrounded by the Dja River, which forms a natural boundary, the reserve is located in a transition zone between the forests of southern Nigeria, south-west Cameroon and the forests of the Congo Basin. Except in the south-east of the reserve, the relief is fairly flat and consists of a succession of round-topped hills. A major fault line on the southern edge of the reserve, which is followed by the Dja River, has lead to the formation of rather deeper cut valleys on the south-eastern edge of the plateau. Cliffs run along the course of the river in the south for some 60 km, and are associated with a section of the river broken up by rapids and waterfalls.

The Dja Reserve is especially noted for its biodiversity and a wide variety of primates. One of Africa's most species-rich rainforests, it includes the habitat of numerous remarkable animal and plant species. It contains 107 mammal species, five of which are threatened.

The primary forest of the Dja Reserve is interesting for its diversity of species and its unique pristine condition. With its topographical diversity and its three biogeographical and geological influences, it has a rich and varied ecosystem that reflects the ecological evolution in progress in this type of environment.

A population of pygmies lives within the reserve, in small sporadic encampments, maintaining an essentially traditional lifestyle.

德贾动物保护区成立于 1950 年,是构成刚果盆地的茂密雨林的重要部分,同时也是非洲最大、保存最为完好的热带雨林之一,保护区内 90％的区域尚未受到人类活动干扰。德贾河几乎把保护区团团围住,构成了保护区的天然边界。保护区位于南尼日利亚林区、喀麦隆西南地区和刚果盆地的交界处。除东南部以外,保护区的其他地域地势平坦,仅有一些隆起的小山丘;南部边界处有一大型断层,在德贾河的共同作用下形成许多深谷;南部德贾河沿岸蜿蜒着约 60 千米长的峭壁,有的山崖在河流上形成急流和瀑布。

保护区特别因其物种的多样性和众多的灵长类动物而著名。作为非洲物种最繁多的雨林之一,这儿为众多动植物品种提供了栖息地。保护区内生存着 107 种哺乳动物,其中有 5 种濒临灭绝。

德贾保护区的雨林因其多元的物种、独特的原始状态而闻名。保护区地形多样,三种不同的生物地理和地理因素使这儿的生态系统丰富多彩,反映了此类环境中的生态演进。

该保护区中居住着一些俾格米人,他们住在零星的小型营地里,依然保留着原始的生活方式。

Vocabulary

1. integral *adj.* 基本的；完整的；构成整体所必需的

Rituals and festivals form an integral part of every human society.

仪式与节日构成了任何人类社会不可或缺的一部分。

2. transition *n.* 过渡,转变,变迁

We hope there will be a peaceful transition to the new system.

我们希望能够和平过渡到新的制度。

3. fault *n.* [地质] 断层

The scientists positioned the seismic activity as being along the San Andreas fault.

科学家们确定了圣安德烈亚斯断层周围地震活动的位置。

4. primate *n.* 灵长类的动物

With our present data, we don't know what precisely the interactions were between a primate and a big carnivore.

根据现有的数据,我们无法确切了解灵长目动物与大型食肉动物之间的相互影响。

5. topographical *adj.* 地志的;地形学的

Switzerland comprises three basic topographical areas: the Swiss Alps, the Swiss plateau, and the Jura Mountain.

瑞士的主要地形有三种：瑞士阿尔卑斯山、瑞士高原和汝拉山。

6. sporadic *adj.* 零星的，分散的

The work will be seasonal，sporadic and informal，but it will be work，and it will be welcome.

这份工作是季节性的、分散的和非正式的，但它会成为一份工作，也会受到欢迎。

7. encampment *n.* 宿营，营地

Our vigilance was stimulated by our finding traces of a large encampment.

我们发现了一次大规模的驻营痕迹，这促使我们提高警觉。

▌ 扩展阅读

Dja Faunal Reserve, Cameroon

Date and History of Establishment

Protected as a "réserve de faune et de chasse" by Law No. 319 of 25 April 1950，and then as a "réserve de faune" under the National Forestry Act Ordinance No. 73/18 of 22 May 1973. Reported to have received some protection as early as 1932，protection for certain species within Dja was stipulated by Decree No. 2254 of 18 November 1947，which regulated hunting in the French African territories. Internationally recognized as a Biosphere Reserve under UNESCO's Man and the Biosphere Programme in 1981 and inscribed on the World Heritage List in 1984. Proposed as a national park.

Climate

Equatorial type climate，with two rainfall peaks (May and September)，and temperatures similar throughout the year. Mean annual temperature is 23.3°C (recorded at 640 m) and the mean annual rainfall around 1570 millimeters (mm). August is the coolest month，with a mean monthly minimum of 18°C and maximum of 27°C，and April is the hottest with mean minimum temperature of 19°C and maximum of 30°C. There is less than 100 mm rainfall during 3 months of the year.

Cultural Heritage

A population of pygmies lives within the reserve，in small sporadic encampments，maintaining an essentially traditional lifestyle (although there would appear to be an increasing use of more modern methods).

Local Human Population

The pygmies are free to hunt within the reserve using traditional methods. Although population density in the region is low，there are some villages close to the reserve. Inhabitants near Somalomo fish in the Dja and tributaries on its left bank，and cultivate mainly coffee，cocoa and cucumbers (for their seeds，which fetch high prices).

Conservation Management

Agriculture and hunting are prohibited within the reserve，and access is restricted. No commercial logging has taken place within the reserve itself，and few people have lived there since villages were relocated in the 1940s prior to establishment. Traditional hunting rights are allowed and hunting is heavily practiced, but the use of non-traditional hunting methods needs to be controlled. The Dja River forms a natural boundary round much of the reserve, and there are currently three guard posts to the east and north-west. Two new posts are in the process of being established to the north and north-west but surveillance and management is inadequate. Since establishment of the reserve in 1950, management has been restricted to protection of the resources, and in particular anti-poaching activities; however, there is little infrastructure and few staff, which means that there is currently little effective management. This is not at present a problem because of the relatively low level of threat, but may well become so. A provisional management plan for the proposed national park has been prepared at L'Éole de Faune at Garoua which discusses further this and other problems and outlines possible solutions. Dja is one of the sites identified by IUCN/WWF Project 1613 (which aims to further the conservation of primates and tropical rain forest) as important for primate and rain forest conservation in West Africa.

Management Constraints

Cocoa, coffee and subsistence plots encroach onto the reserve, particularly on the northern and western borders, and poaching occurs. According to Gartlan and Agland the traditional hunting methods of the pygmies are being superseded, and the pygmies are tending towards a more sedentary life. This may cause problems in the future, and will need to be closely monitored. However, Bedel et al. (1987) stress the importance of hunting to the livelihood of the local population and of establishing local associations to monitor hunting pressure. The reserve has been subject to mineral exploitation in the past but no exploitable deposits were located within its boundaries. However, further investigation is being made on calcareous bodies on the south-east border of the reserve and this may lead to open-cast mining for cement production. Perhaps of more current concern is the possible routing of the Trans-African highway close to the southern boundary of the reserve.

The greatest threats to biodiversity in Cameroon come from deforestation and poaching. Larege—scale commercial logging has been encouraged by the government and low prices for cocoa and coffee have made sales of bushmeat more important to local people. New logging roads and and concessions are resulting in forest clearance right up to the boundary. Logging is mainly by international companies, provides few benefits to local people, and currently is practiced in an ecologically unsustainable manner. The logging roads are facilitating access to Dja by poachers and there are increasing reports of heavy poaching inside the park. Employees of one logging company threatened park guards with violence when they were apprehended taking poached wildlife.

（资料来源：http://www.eoearth.org/view/article/151758/）

Questions

1. What are the greatest threats to biodiversity in Cameroon?

2. Why are agriculture and hunting prohibited within the reserve, and why is access restricted?

ISimangaliso Wetland Park
伊西曼格利索湿地公园

🔖 **简介**

所属国家：南非(South Africa)

入选时间：1999

入选标准：(vii)(ix)(x)

ISimangaliso Wetland Park (previously known as the Greater St. Lucia Wetland Park), spanning 280 km of coastline, is South Africa's third-largest protected area. The ongoing fluvial, marine and aeolian processes in the site have produced a variety of landforms, including coral reefs, long sandy beaches, coastal dunes, lake systems, swamps, and extensive reed and papyrus wetlands. The interplay of the park's environmental heterogeneity with major floods and coastal storms and a transitional geographic location between subtropical and tropical Africa has resulted in exceptional species diversity and ongoing speciation. The mosaic of landforms and habitat types creates breathtaking scenic vistas. Three natural phenomena are judged outstanding. One is the shifting salinity states within Lake St. Lucia which are linked to wet and dry climatic cycles, with the lake responding accordingly with shifts from low to hyper-saline states. A second is the spectacle of large numbers of nesting turtles on the beaches and the abundance of dolphins and migration of whales and whale sharks off-shore. Finally, the huge numbers of waterfowls and large breeding colonies of pelicans, storks, herons and terns are impressive and add life to the wild natural landscape of the area.

The five interlinked ecosystems found in iSimangaliso provide critical habitats for a range of species from Africa's marine, wetland and savannah environments. Of the over 6,500 plants and animals (including 521 birds) species recorded from the Park, populations of species of conservation importance include 11 species endemic to the park, 108 species endemic to South Africa, while 467 species are listed as threatened in South Africa.

伊西曼格利索湿地公园(旧称大圣卢西亚湿地公园)是南非第三大保护区,跨越海岸线约 280 千米。河流、海洋和风的不断侵蚀使得该地呈现多样地貌,包括珊瑚礁、漫长的沙滩、海岸沙丘、湖泊、沼泽、大片的芦苇丛和纸莎草沼泽。公园内环境的异质性、洪水和海洋风暴以及热带和亚热带的非洲地理状况相互作用,使这里拥有异常多的物种,并有新的物种不断形成。多样的地貌和生物种类使这里景色不凡。以下三种自然现象举世闻名:圣卢西亚湖的盐度随雨季、旱季转换而变化(雨季盐度低,旱季反之);沙滩上大量海龟筑巢,近海里海豚众多,还能观察到鲸鱼和鲸鲨;大量的水鸟和大型的鹈鹕、鹳、苍鹭、燕鸥繁殖群令人印象深刻,使这儿的自然美景充满生机。

该公园汇集了 5 个独立而又相互连接的生态系统,为从非洲海洋、沼泽地到大草原的各种物种提供了栖息地。公园中有记录的 6500 余种动植物(包括 521 种鸟类)中,具有保护价值的包括 11 种公园特有物种、108 个南非特有物种,还有 467 种被列为南非濒危动物物种。

Vocabulary

1. fluvial *adj.* 河的;河流的

The main sedimentary system includes fluvial, delta, alluvial fan and lake facies.

主要沉积体系包括河流、三角洲、冲积扇及滨浅湖相。

2. aeolian *adj.* 风的

All these characters suggest aeolian dunes.

这是风成沙丘的特征。

3. papyrus *n.* 纸莎草纸

Woollen cloth and timber were sent to Egypt in exchange for linen or papyrus.

羊毛料和木材送到埃及以换取亚麻布或纸莎草纸。

4. heterogeneity *n.* 异质性;不纯一性

In tropical areas, larger plots have proved more useful due to greater heterogeneity of the forest.

在热带地区,由于森林的异质性较大,已证实大一些的样地更有效。

5. vista *n.* 远景

I, however, was fascinated by the vista over the sea.

我却被此时此刻海上的景色吸引住了。

6. salinity *n.* 盐度

By 1999 the average salinity of the river in South Australia had fallen by over 20%.

到 1999 年时,南澳大利亚州的平均河水含盐度降低了 20% 多。

7. waterfowl *n.* 水鸟,水禽

Thousands of waterfowls breed round the lake and live off the fish.

数以千计的水鸟在湖边繁殖,以鱼为食。

扩展阅读

ISimangaliso: South Africa's Coastal Jewel

The iSimangaliso Wetland Park is one of the jewels of South Africa's coastline, with a unique mosaic of ecosystems—swamps, lakes, beaches, coral reefs, wetlands, woodlands, coastal forests and grasslands—supporting an astounding diversity of animal, bird and marine life.

Formerly known as the Greater St. Lucia Wetland Park, the Park was renamed in 2007 to better reflect its unique African identity—and to avoid confusion with the

Caribbean island country St. Lucia.

Located on the north-eastern coast of KwaZulu-Natal, stretching from Kozi Bay in the north to Cape St. Lucia in the south, the iSimangaliso Wetland Park was the first site in South Africa to be inscribed on the World Heritage List by the United Nations Educational, Scientific and Cultural Organisation (UNESCO).

Remarkable diversity

ISimangaliso's uniqueness lies in its remarkable diversity, particularly its combination of a subtropical coastline and a classic African game park.

It is South Africa's third-largest park, spanning 280 kilometres of coastline, from the Mozambican border in the north to Mapelane south of the St. Lucia estuary, and made up of around 328,000 hectares of pristine natural ecosystems—including swamps, lake systems, beaches, coral reefs, wetlands, woodlands and coastal forests.

The park takes in a 60-kilometre river mouth that creates a huge estuary, Lake St. Lucia, running parallel to the coast and separated from the sea by the world's highest forested sand dunes. The lake is part of the St. Lucia estuarine system, the largest estuarine system in Africa.

The park incorporates the whole of Lake St. Lucia, the St. Lucia and Maputaland Marine Reserves, the Coastal Forest Reserve and the Kosi Bay Natural Reserve. The 40,000 hectare Mkuzi Game Reserve is also in the process of being incorporated into the park.

Variety of ecosystems

ISimangaliso's wide variety of ecosystems and natural habitats provide an astounding diversity of species for the area. With its lakes, lagoons, freshwater swamps and grasslands, iSimangaliso supports more species of animal than the better-known and much larger Kruger National Park and Okavango Delta—from the country's largest population of hippos and crocodiles to Giant Leatherback turtles, black rhino, leopards, and a vast array of bird and marine life.

According to Living Lakes, more than 530 species of birds use the wetland and other areas of the Lake St. Lucia region. "These waters also are graced by 20,000 greater flamingos, 40,000 lesser flamingoes, as well as thousands of ducks. With 36 species, this area has the highest diversity of amphibians in South Africa.

"... Here, and nowhere else in the world, can one find hippopotamuses, crocodiles and sharks sharing the same waters."

In proclaiming the iSimangaliso Wetland Park a World Heritage site in 1999, UNESCO said: "The interplay of the park's environmental heterogeneity with major floods and coastal storms, and a transitional geographic location between sub-tropical and tropical Africa, has resulted in exceptional species diversity and ongoing speciation."

"The mosaic of landforms and habitat types creates superlative scenic vistas. The site contains critical habitat for a range of species from Africa's marine, wetland and savannah environments. "

In 1989, a mining company seeking titanium and other metals sought to bulldoze the dunes along the eastern shore of Lake St. Lucia.

In 1996, the South African government followed the recommendations of an environmental assessment in barring the mining proposals—and began work on an integrated development and land-use planning strategy for the entire region.

Under the Lubombo Spatial Development Initiative, the governments of South Africa, Swaziland and Mozambique aim to foster sustainable investment and job creation in the area, using the iSimangaliso Wetland Park as the core.

Tourist attraction

The variety of natural settings, the abundance of wildlife, and the sheer beauty of the place draw tourists to the area in increasing numbers. There is plenty to do—from fishing, boating and scuba diving to hiking, horseriding, game viewing, whale and bird watching.

The park is also one of South Africa's most popular fishing destinations, lending itself to rock and surf fishing, kite fishing, spear fishing, fly fishing, estuary fishing and deep sea fishing.

There are plenty of hiking trails through the park—ranging from a few hours' to a few days' worth—offering the opportunity to see a huge variety of animal and bird life. Accommodation options are extensive, ranging from camping to private game lodges, and including hotels, flats and chalets in the nearby town of St. Lucia.

Wonders and miracles

Announcing the park's new name in May 2007, Tourism Minister Marthinus van Schalkwyk said the change followed two years of extensive consultations.

Van Schalkwyk said the isiZulu word iSimangaliso—meaning "miracle"—had a rich historical context. "Ujeqe was King Shaka's insila (aide who keeps all the king's secrets and gets buried with the king when the king dies). He fled after uShaka's death to avoid the customary burial with his master. "

"He wandered into Thongaland, present-day Maputaland, and came back, saying: I saw wonders and miracles in the flat land and lakes of Thonga. From that follows an isiZulu saying that if you have seen miracles, you have seen what uJeqe saw: Ubone isimanga esabonwa uJeqe kwelama Thonga. "

"Ujeqe might just have been one of the first tourists to visit what is now the iSimangaliso Wetland Park. "

(资料来源: http://www.southafrica.info/about/animals/stlucia.htm#.UzObwVPAicQ)

Questions

1. For what reasons was the Greater St. Lucia Wetland Park renamed in 2007?

2. What is so unique about iSimangaliso?

第三节　非洲的世界文化和自然双重遗产

Cliff of Bandiagara（Land of the Dogons）
邦贾加拉悬崖（多贡斯土地）

⇨ **简介**

所属国家：马里（Mali）

入选时间：1989

入选标准：（v）（vii）

The Bandiagara site, Land of the Dogons, is a vast cultural landscape covering 400, 000 ha and includes 289 villages. It is an outstanding landscape of cliffs and sandy plateaux with some beautiful architecture（houses, granaries, altars, sanctuaries and Togu Na, or communal meeting-places）. The communities at the site are essentially the Dogon, and have a very close relationship with their environment expressed in their sacred rituals and traditions. This hostile milieu and difficult access has been, since the 15th century, a natural refuge that corresponded to the need for defence of the Dogons in the face of formidable invaders. The Dogon were able to conserve their centuries-old culture and traditions（masks, feasts, rituals, and ceremonies involving ancestor worship）, thanks to this defensive shelter. The architecture of the Dogon land has been adapted to benefit from the physical constraints of the place. Whether on the high plateau, the cliff-faces, or on the plain, the Dogon have exploited all the elements available to build their villages that reflect their ingenuity and their philosophy of life and death. The Land of the Dogon is the outstanding manifestation of a system of thinking linked to traditional religion that has integrated harmoniously with architectural heritage, very remarkably in a natural landscape of rocky scree and impressive geological features. The geological, archaeological and ethnological interest, together with the landscape, make the Bandiagara plateau one of West Africa's most impressive sites.

邦贾加拉悬崖（多贡斯土地）占地 40 万公顷，包括 289 个村庄。这里的突出地形是悬崖和沙土高原，悬崖和高原上有一些精美的建筑（房屋、粮仓、圣坛、神殿和集会厅）。居住在此的大多是多贡人，其宗教仪式和宗教传统体现了人与环境的密切联系。这一地区环境恶劣、人迹罕至，自 15 世纪以来，一直为多贡人提供天然的避难所，以抵御强敌。在这一天然防御工事屏障下，多贡人得以保留其有几百年历史的文化传统（面纱、集会、宗教仪式、祭祀祖先等）。多贡斯土地的建筑也依据当地的自然限制而有所变化。不论在高原、悬崖壁还是平原上，多贡人充分利用各种条件，建造的村庄反映出他们的创造力和人生哲学。在这片满是碎石、有着惊人地理特征的自然景观中，传统宗教与建筑传统完美结合，构成独特的思想体系。正是这些地质学、考古学和民俗学的价值，以及优美的风景，使邦贾加拉高地成为最具西非地质地貌特征的地方之一。

Vocabulary

1. communal *adj.* 群体的；社区的；团体的；公共的；公用的

We each have a separate bedroom but share a communal kitchen.

我们各有一间独立的卧室，但共用一个厨房。

2. milieu *n.* 周围环境；社会背景

Foods usually provide a good milieu for the persistence of viruses.

食品通常为病毒存续提供了一个良好的栖身所。

3. formidable *adj.* 可怕的；令人惊叹的；艰巨的

There's no formidable obstacles in the world.

世上没有无法逾越的障碍。

4. constraint *n.* 限制；束缚；约束

Water shortages in the area will be the main constraint on development.

水资源匮乏将是制约该地区发展的一个主要因素。

5. scree *n.* 山麓碎石；岩屑堆

Occasionally scree fell in a shower of dust and noise.

偶尔会有碎石滚下，扬起大团尘土，噼啪作响。

6. ethnological *adj.* 民族的，人种学的

Their researches are conducted from the folklore and ethnological perspectives.

他们的研究集中在民俗学、民族学方面。

扩展阅读

Africa：The Cliffs Of Bandiagara

We arrived in Bandiagara, at the edge of the region, before dawn in the dusty lot of the bus station. We had been on the bus from Bamako, Mali's capital, for twelve hours. Around us, men were dispersing and the families with children were settling down to rest in the dusty terrain of the bus depot until morning. We looked around us, more than a little clueless. The night was pitch black.

A motorcycle came roaring up out of the dark. Its light was blinding, but it honed in on us and approached swiftly. A man descended from it and approached us. Mamadou Traore would be our guide in Dogon Country.

Dogon Country denotes a region of roughly 400,000 hectares, following the Bandiagara Escarpment, an astonishing line of cliffs which climbs up to 500 m at its highest points in 150 km. The stunning views from the top went for miles. Savannah went all the way to the horizon, or sand, or rock. The area felt at times impossibly remote, but it was one of Mali's first tourist groups. Mamadou was one of a few dozen guides who led American and German and French tourists along the Dogon cliffs each year.

Mamadou had been leading groups through Dogon Country for 15 years. Two years ago, he led at Italian on a hike who was so grateful that after he returned home he made Mamadou a website to help other tourists find him. Mamadou checks it every time he comes back to Bandiagara. A town of more than 10,000 people, it has one Internet cafe a mile from the bus station where we arrived.

Mamadou would lead us across the expanses of desert and rock and take us up and down the traditional Dogon stairways, cascades of stone down crevices in the cliff face. Dogon women climbed right past us with buckets of water on their heads. One woman had a basket on her head and a baby on her breast. Mamadou did all the climbing in a pair of blue flip-flops.

The region's inhabitants mostly belong to the Dogon and Peul ethnic groups, but is identified exclusively with the Dogon, who began arriving from elsewhere in the 15th century. Before the Dogon, the Tellem lived in the Bandiagara cliffs from the 11th century, constructing the top line of shelters bored into the cliffs. In Dogon stories, Tellem may figure in, sneaking back to the Bandiagara escarpment, though no one sees them. A thorough archaeological exploration from 1964 to 1971 definitively found evidence of the presence of this Dogon myth.

The Tellem were agriculturalists, traditionally believed to be unusually small, who stored their food and buried the dead in caves high up the face of the cliffs. Caves have been discovered with the remains of up to 3000 people. One theory, ascribed to by our guide, suggests the Tellem ascend the cliffs on vines back when the valley was greener.

Today, Dogon Country is dry. The average in 1994 was only 600mm of rain, and droughts generally lasted 8 months of the year. Desertification has only worsened with scrub clearance. The temperature nears 120 in the summer, when Mamadou takes a few months off. It's too hot for the hike.

The Tellem disappeared gradually from the valley after the 15th century, forced out by raids, and perhaps by a change in climate. The Dogon are believed to have migrated from the east to this extreme region to escape the spread of Islam, which threatened animist traditions. The Dogon were agriculturalists from the start and arrived and settled in small groups, often isolated from each other. They often constructed their original villages some ways up the cliff walls. The buildings they erected on the sides of the Bandiagara cliffs were built of stones and mortar. The Dogon constructed mainly houses, but also granaries.

The Dogon cultivate rice, millet and sorghum. We would come upon fields of green onions for export to Bamako, a startlingly brilliant green in all that desert. The villages halfway up the cliffs had been gradually abandoned for more accessible terrain below closer to the crops and to available water supplies.

Today the Dogon villages are arrayed along the tops and bottoms of the cliffs. The villages are small and often long distances from each other. There are at least 15 dialects of Dogon today, some of which defy the comprehension of other Dogon speakers beyond the basic, rhythmic greetings.

Above certain villages on the cliff tops, Mamadou showed us crevices in the rocks where masks are stored. The Dogon would fascinate colonial anthropologists and archaeologists, the first European travelers to write accounts of Dogon Country, most of all intrigued by Dogon ritual and exquisitely carved masks. The Sigui ceremony, held every sixty years, is best-known of these rituals and occasion for some of the most elaborate masks. Researchers suggest Dogon culture is fluid and accumulative and these festivals could have changed over the many years of their continuation.

Mamadou told us the first tourists to Dogon Country arrived in the 1970s. The interest in Malian antiques began during the same period and the leakage of the country's national heritage to foreign parts worsened. The head of Mali's national museum, Samuel Sidibe, has decried the systematic looting of the Bandiagara caves for tellem artifacts for resale to foreign antiquities dealers. Efforts have been made to organize and educate local population and outlaw the export of Malian artifacts, but the fight is a difficult one in a very poor region in one of the world's poorest countries.

We were told that the Dogon guides had been put in place to control the influence of the tourists on the Dogon villages. What's mentioned most often is that the tourists gave the children things, candy and toys, and that their elders fear what will happen to the children's work ethic.

Granting the validity of their parents' concerns, Dogon Country was also one of the most visibly suffering regions I saw in West Africa: villages where there were more children than not had distended bellies, others where there was only well water, and one village where the well water was such a dark, muddy yellow color that not even the bravest of our group would try to drink it with only our chlorine tablets.

The Cliffs of Bandiagara were named a UNESCO World Heritage site in 1989, but the most obvious benefit this seems to bring is more tourists. Our guide helped us climb up to the lowest level of Dogon homes embedded in the cliffs. Walking through the abandoned villages, the structures date back centuries, but still appear virtually untouched. We passed through certain of the doorways and stood inside. At one point, our guide pointed us to a burial site, where a hole had been punctured through the walls. There were bones inside. Bowls and shards of pottery lay abandoned in the rooms of the homes.

Mamadou mentioned with pride the restorations of the cliff dwellings taking place with funding from UNESCO. Some of the buildings on the cliffs have undergone retouching. A man with a clipboard would approach us back in Bandiagara at the end of the week with a survey on sustainable tourism. Mamadou seemed unimpressed. "Tourists have been coming to this region for thirty years," he told us, "The region didn't need that study."

When the World Heritage program made its case for the significance of the Cliffs of Bandiagara back in the late 1980s, its report cited the cliff cemeteries and Dogon stairways, but the writer of the essay go on to cite the living Dogon cultural history embedded in this region. You can feel it just beneath the surface, an accumulation of many years of tradition and change.

（资料来源：http://www. travelthruhistory. com/html/memoirs14）

Questions

1. Describe the natural environment and local life of Dogon Country.
2. Which part of Dogon culture impresses you the most? Why?

Ngorongoro Conservation Area
恩戈罗恩戈罗自然保护区

⇨ 简介

所属国家：坦桑尼亚（The United Republic of Tanzania）

入选时间：1979

入选标准：(iv)(vii)(viii)(ix)(x)

The Ngorongoro Conservation Area spans vast expanses of highland plains, savanna, savanna woodlands and forests. Established in 1959 as a multiple land use area, with wildlife coexisting with semi-nomadic Maasai pastoralists practicing traditional livestock grazing, it includes the spectacular Ngorongoro Crater, the world's largest unbroken caldera, and Olduvai Gorge, a 14 km long deep ravine. The stunning landscape of Ngorongoro Crater combined with its spectacular concentration of wildlife is one of the greatest natural wonders of the planet. The variations in climate, landforms and altitude have resulted in several overlapping ecosystems and distinct habitats. The property is part of the Serengeti ecosystem, one of the last intact ecosystems in the world which harbours large and spectacular animal migrations. The property has global importance for biodiversity conservation due to the presence of globally threatened species, the density of wildlife inhabiting the area, and the annual migration of wildebeest, zebra, gazelles and other animals into the northern plains, which is one of the largest animal migration on earth.

Extensive archaeological research has also yielded a long sequence of evidence of human evolution and human-environment dynamics, collectively extending over a span of almost four million years to the early modern era. The evidence include early hominid footprints dating back 3. 6 million years.

恩戈罗恩戈罗自然保护区幅员辽阔,横跨大片高地平原、热带草原、热带稀树草原林地和森林。该保护区建立于 1959 年,各种野生动植物和仍保持传统放牧方式的半游牧牧民马赛人共同生活在这个区域。区内有世界上最大的完整火山口——恩戈罗恩戈罗火山口,和 14 千米长的奥杜瓦伊峡谷。恩戈罗恩戈罗火山口景色壮观,野生动植物种类繁多,构成了世界上最伟大的自然奇观之一。这里气候、地形及海拔高度的多元性形成了数个互有交叠的生态系统和不同的动物栖息地,是塞伦盖蒂生态系统的一部分。塞伦盖蒂生态系统是世界上最后一个尚有大型壮观的动物迁徙的完整生态系统。该保护区内有多种濒危动植物,野生动物非常集中,角马、斑马、瞪羚等动物每年会迁徙到北部平原,形成世界上最庞大的动物迁徙活动,这一切使该保护区在全球生物多样性保护上具有重要地位。

在该保护区进行的长期考古研究提供了一系列证据,证据显示了从约 400 万年前至今该地的人类进化史和人类与自然相互作用的情况,其中包括距今 360 万年前的原人足迹。

Vocabulary

1. crater *n.* 火山口;(撞击或爆炸形成的)坑,弹坑

With a telescope you can see the huge crater of Vesuvius.

用望远镜你能看到巨大的维苏威火山口。

2. caldera *n.* 破火山口;喷火山口

Much of Yellowstone National Park is a giant collapsed volcano,or a caldera.

黄石国家公园的大部分地方是一座坍塌的大火山,或是一个喷火山口。

3. ravine *n.* 沟壑;深谷;峡谷;山涧

The river had worn a ravine between the hills.

那条河已在两山之间造成一个深谷。

4. dynamics *n.* 相互作用;动态

Sibling dynamics and friendships can also change a child's eating habits.

兄弟姊妹的动力和友谊也可以改变孩子的饮食习惯。

5. hominid *n.* 原人,类人动物

Excavations here from 1936 to 1941 led to the discovery of the first hominid fossil at this site.

这处遗址从 1936 年至 1941 年进行挖掘,发现了早期原始人类化石。

扩展阅读

Tanzania:Ngorongoro—Conservation Area Is for Wildlife, Not Farming

Ngorongoro—TANZANIA has eight out of more than 980 coveted "World Heritage sites" dotting the globe; these are officially endorsed by the United Nations Educational,Scientific and Cultural Organisation (UNESCO).

While there are efforts to add the Udzungwa Mountains National Park of Iringa to the list,so far the official World Heritage sites mapped in the country include the

Zanzibar Stone Town, ruins of Kilwa Kisiwani, ruins of Songo Mnara, Kondoa Old Rock paintings, Mount Kilimanjaro, Selous Game Reserve, Serengeti National Park and the Ngorongoro Conservation Area Authority (NCAA).

The NCAA which is an autonomous authority, is home to the legendary crater, abundant wildlife species and due to its outstanding position as multiple use vicinity, native Maasai people, who are nomadic livestock grazers are allowed to live alongside the beasts.

The Maasai were allowed to co-exist with wildlife in the Ngorongoro because they don't eat any other meat other than that slaughtered from their menagerie, which means wild animals (the fauna) are safe with them. The other thing is, since their main survival activity is just keeping cattle, animals that only eat low-cut grass, even the flora (natural growth) will be preserved in their presence.

When the NCAA was being established in 1959 it had a population of just 10,000 Maasai residents and 50 years later in 2009 the number had risen to over 66,000 and during this year's specialised census in the division, the figure has clocked at 87,000.

Available statistics indicate that the 8,292 square kilometres NCAA in addition to nearly 90,000 human beings, also supports more than 130,000 livestock, mostly cattle with some 20,000 goats and sheep thrown in. Deputy Minister for Natural Resources and Tourism, Mr Lazaro Nyalandu had warned that the carrying capacity of the conservation area is about to tip its scale when it comes to ecological stability.

Five years ago, in 2009 UNESCO raised a "red flag" against Ngorongoro Conservation Area, threatening to remove it from the list of the World Heritage sites, due to what was described as "ecological deterioration" in the territory.

Increased human activities in Ngorongoro were cited as the factors threatening the world heritage site, because at that time people within the NCAA were practising serious cultivation; maize and beans farms dotted the landscape defeating the whole purpose of conservation.

It all started in 1992 when serious drought and famine wreaked havoc in the country decimating much of the Maasai livestock, something which made the then Prime Minister Mr Samuel Malecela permit subsistence farming to rescue them from hunger.

After that, they never stopped and in fact, even people from other districts moved into the NCAA and opened up farms much to the alarm of UNESCO, prompting the United Nations body to raise warning.

The Environment and Natural Resources committee from the National Assembly, then led by Mr Job Ndugai went round the NCAA and admitted that it was time agriculture ceased from the conservation area. Also, as per UNESCO guidance, cattle were restricted from going down the crate floor where they previously used to graze.

This caused uproar because nothing tastes better to cows than the salty, alkaline grass found in the caldera. The Ngorongoro conservation reconstruction move also called for the population reduction a problem which was solved by repatriating "immigrants" who had taken up residence in the conservation area.

The exercise saw some 538 people being shifted to a newly formed village called 'Jema' located in Oldonyo-Sambu area. But recently, the farming agenda reared up its ugly head again; this time it was brought before a public meeting held at Endulen Village and which was being addressed by Prime Minister, Mr Mizengo Pinda who made the first tour in the NCAA this week.

Ngorongoro residents tried to persuade the prime minister to once more let them carry out subsistence farming in the conservation area so as to sustain themselves with own grown food. But the premier pointed out that if the issue was just food then his office pledges to provide each household with free grains, enough to see them fill their dinner tables with food.

"There are about 20,000 households in the Ngorongoro Conservation Area, my office offers to give each household ten sacks of grain (one ton of maize) every year, free of charge to supplement food requirements as we work to find other means of sustaining the population here," said Mr Pinda.

The premier calculated that the 200,000 sacks of maize to be supplied for the 85,000 residents of NCAA in two six-months instalments, add up to 20 tonnes of grain valued at 11.2 bil—which his office can easily take care of, thus there should be no more need for most Maasai people there to contemplate farming.

（资料来源：http://allafrica.com/stories/201309231618.html）

Questions

1. Why did UNESCO raise a "red flag" against Ngorongoro Conservation Area in 2009?

2. How did NCAA settle the conflict between increased human activities and wildlife conservation? Do you have any suggestions?

Maloti-Drakensberg Park

马洛蒂-德拉根斯堡公园（马洛蒂山公园）

⤷ 简介

所属国家：莱索托（Lesotho）、南非（South Africa）

入选时间：2000

入选标准：（i）（iii）（vii）（x）

The Maloti-Drakensberg Park is a transboundary site composed of the uKhahlamba Drakensberg National Park in South Africa and the Sehlathebe National Park in Lesotho. The uKhahlamba Drakensberg Park is renowned for its spectacular natural landscape, importance as a haven for many threatened and endemic species, and for its wealth of rock paintings made by the San people over a period of 4,000 years. The Park, located in the Drakensberg Mountains, covers an area of 242,813 ha, making it the largest protected area along the Great Escarpment of southern Africa.

The property has numerous caves and rock shelters containing an estimated 600 rock art sites, and the number of individual images in those sites probably exceeds 35,000. The images depict animals and human beings, and represent the spiritual life of this people, now no longer living in their original homeland. This art represents an exceptionally coherent tradition that embodies the beliefs and cosmology of the San people over several millennia. There are also paintings done during the nineteenth and twentieth centuries, attributable to Bantu speaking people. The rock art of the Drakensberg is the largest and most concentrated group of rock paintings in Africa south of the Sahara and is outstanding both in quality and diversity of subject.

The property contains significant natural habitats for in situ conservation of biological diversity. It has outstanding species richness, particularly of plants. It is recognised as a Global Centre of Plant Diversity and endemism, and occurs within its own floristic region—the Drakensberg Alpine Region of South Africa. It is also within a globally important endemic bird area and is notable for the occurrence of a number of globally threatened species.

马洛蒂-德拉根斯堡公园由南非的乌坎兰巴-德拉根斯堡公园和莱索托的塞赫拉巴泰贝国家公园组成。乌坎兰巴-德拉根斯堡公园自然景色壮观；为众多濒危物种和当地特有物种提供避风港；它还拥有大量由非洲原住民桑人所创作的岩画，画作的时间跨度长达4000年。这些特色景观使得乌坎兰巴-德拉根斯堡公园扬名世界。该公园坐落于德拉根斯堡山脉，占地242813公顷，是南非大陡崖沿线最大的保护区。

该公园的众多洞穴和岩窟中有约600处岩画遗址，所描绘的形象有动物也有人类，其数量超过35000种，反映了桑人（现已移居他处）的精神生活。这些岩画体现了桑人几千年来的信仰和坚持宇宙哲学的传统。岩画中有的是以班图语为母语的人们在19、20世纪创作的。德拉根斯堡的岩画是撒哈拉以南非洲地区最大、最集中的，其艺术品质和主题丰富性均非常突出。

该景观有着重要的自然栖息地，可供生物多样性的就地保护。该地物种丰富，尤其植物种类众多。人们公认这里是植物多样性的全球中心，当地（德拉根斯堡山脉的高山地区）植物区生物物种的特有分布也值得一提。这儿是全球重要的特有鸟类保护区，一些全球濒危的物种也生活在此处。

Vocabulary

1. haven *n.* 避风港

So is China establishing itself as a haven?

那么，中国是否正在成为投资避风港？

2. endemic *n* (动，植物)某些特产的

Over 300 bird species are found; 32 of which are endemic to southern Africa.

这里有 300 多种禽鸟,其中 32 种是南非特有的品种。

3. cosmology *n.* [天] 宇宙学

One of the key scientific questions in cosmology today is: what is the average density of matter in our universe?

今天宇宙学的一个关键问题就是:宇宙中物质的平均密度是多少?

4. millennia *n.* 几千年

For two millennia, exogamy was a major transgression for Jews.

两千年来,异族通婚一直是犹太人的一大禁忌。

5. in-situ *adv.* 在原处;在原位置

Ming Yongle decade and in-situ rock rebuild the temple.

明永乐十年又在原址上重建岩庙。

扩展阅读

The Special Place that Is the uKhahlamba Drakensberg Park

"*The uKhahlamba Drakensberg Park, situated in KwaZulu-Natal and bordering the mountain kingdom of Lesotho, is renowned for its spectacular landscape, as a haven for many threatened and endemic species, and its wealth of rock paintings done by the San people over a period of 4,000 years. It covers an area of 242,813 hectares, making it the largest protected area along the Great Escarpment of southern Africa.*"

In recognition of Heritage Day tomorrow, NIKKI TILLEY takes us on a journey along the Maloti Drakensberg Route, where two World Heritage sites can be found.

The Maloti Drakensberg Route is the longest designated tourism route in southern Africa, embracing northern Lesotho and eastern Free State, the Lesotho eastern highlands and KwaZulu-Natal, west and central Lesotho, southern Lesotho and the Eastern Cape highlands.

It encompasses some of the most awe-inspiring high altitude scenery in Africa and not surprisingly, within its region is found two World Heritage sites.

The uKhahlamba Drakensberg Park, situated in KwaZulu-Natal and bordering Lesotho, is renowned for its spectacular landscape, as a haven for many threatened and endemic species, and its wealth of rock paintings done by the San people over a period of 4,000 years.

It covers an area of 242,813 hectares, making it the largest protected area along the Great Escarpment of southern Africa. Within its pristine steep-sided river valleys and rocky gorges are numerous caves and rock shelters, containing an estimated 600 rock-art sites and in excess of 35,000 individual images depicting animals and human beings, and the spiritual life of the long-gone San people. It contains almost all of the remaining subalpine and alpine vegetation in KwaZulu-Natal, and it has been identified as an important bird area, forming part of the Lesotho Highlands Endemic Bird Area.

Listed in 2000 as a World Heritage site, the park qualifies in several distinct categories required for this status: its wealth of rock art (the largest and most concentrated group of paintings south of the Sahara), the cultural history of the once-resident San people found in this art form, its exceptional natural beauty, and its diversity of habitats that support a variety of endemic bird and floral species.

Of great interest, too, is the unique relationship between the San and the eland. This, over the years, has been heightened by rock-art research in Lesotho, with many of the paintings and images being of the eland. Although the eland was hunted by the San, it was also of major spiritual importance to them. In interpreting therianthropic figures in ancient San rock art (e. g. humans with antelope ears or hooves), David Lewis-Williams suggests that they represent healers in trance. Accordingly, the San healer, possessing eland medicine may feel him or herself take on the form of that antelope, and retain that form throughout the journey into the spirit world. Taking on the form of an animal involves a radical shift in self-image, which includes brain chemistry, energy structures in the body and consciousness itself, which are transformed through dance, and the San encapsulate their inner understanding of these shifts by linking them to their observation of the animals that sustain them. And so the bonds between the San and the eland are brought to life through intricate natural symbolism. This alone is a beckoning call to visit the ancient sites.

The conservation management of the uKhahlamba Drakensberg Park is entrusted to Ezemvelo KZN Wildlife, which also provides a range of accommodation types and tourist attractions within its boundaries. Accessibility is via a number of national roads, with towns such as Winterton, Bergville and Underberg along the way. Domestic and international tourism brings economic benefits that are enjoyed by the neighbouring communities, as well as by the stakeholders.

Situated on the southeastern border of Lesotho, Sehlabathebe National Park was proclaimed as a World Heritage site in 2013. It is recognised as an extension to the uKhahlamba Drakensberg Park, which is now to be named the Maloti Drakensberg Transboundary World Heritage site. Members of UNESCO praise the "spectacularly beautiful watershed area" that hosts flora and fauna of scientific importance.

It is home to three endangered species, the Maloti Minnow, a species of fish found only in the park, and the Cape and Bearded vultures.

Home to striking biological diversity as well as important cultural heritage, the park comprises 6,500 hectares at an average elevation of 2,400 metres, and is the only designated park, established in 1969, in Lesotho.

The landscape is dominated by grassland of various types and the larger ecosystem as a whole performs invaluable functions, including providing fresh water to Lesotho, South Africa and Namibia.

The many small lakes, dams and rivers are a fisher's paradise and the park may owe its existence to the fact that the prime minister of Lesotho at the time, Leabua Jonathan, was keen on trout fishing. The park lodge where the prime minister used to stay is called Jonathan's Lodge.

The remoteness of the park accounts for the difficulty in accessing it, but from the Bushman's Nek Pass near Underberg, a commercial tour operator provides this service on horseback.

（资料来源：http://www.malotidrakensbergroute.com/news/special-place-ukhahlamba-drakensberg-park/）

Questions

1. What are the findings of the rock-art research in the uKhahlamba Drakensberg Park?

2. Could you describe the biological diversity in Sehlabathebe National Park?

第四节　非洲的世界文化景观遗产

Ecosystem and Relict Cultural Landscape of Lopé-Okanda
洛佩-奥坎德生态系统与文化遗迹景观

⤷ 简介

所属国家：加蓬（Gabon）

入选时间：2007

入选标准：（iii）（iv）（ix）（x）

The Ecosystem and Relict Cultural Landscape of Lopé-Okanda represents an unusual interface between dense and well-conserved tropical rainforest and relict savannah environments with a great diversity of species, including endangered large mammals, and habitats. The site illustrates ecological and biological processes in terms of species and habitat adaptation to post-glacial climatic changes. Over 1,550 plant species have been recorded, including 40 never recorded before in Gabon, and it is anticipated that once all the floristic surveys and research are completed the number of plant species could reach over 3,000, making it one of the most outstanding areas in relation to floristic diversity and complexity in the Congo Rainforest Biogeographical Province.

It contains evidence of the successive passages of different peoples who have left extensive and comparatively well-preserved remains of habitation around hilltops, caves and shelters, evidence of iron-working and a remarkable collection of some 1,800 petroglyphs (rock carvings). The property's collection of Neolithic and Iron Age sites, together with the rock art found there, reflects a major migration route of Bantu and other peoples from West Africa along the River Ogooué Valley to the north of the dense evergreen Congo forests and to central east and southern Africa, that has shaped the development of the whole of sub-Saharan Africa. The rich archaeological ensembles of the middle stretches of the River Ogooué Valley demonstrate 400,000 years of almost continuous history. The archaeological sites have revealed detailed evidence for the early use of forest produce, cultivation of crops and the domestication of animals.

洛佩—奥坎德生态系统与文化遗迹景观展示了保护完好的茂密热带雨林与残存的热带草原环境之间的奇妙接合,这里的物种丰富,是包括濒危大型哺乳动物在内多种生物的栖息地。该遗址展现了生物及其栖息地适应冰川后期气候变化的生态和生物进程。该景观目前共有1550多个植物品种,其中40种在加蓬是新发现品种。据估计,待所有植被调查和研究结束后,该地植物品种可多达3000余种,使得洛佩—奥坎德成为刚果热带雨林生态区植物种类最丰富的地区之一。

这里有不同民族生活的证据,他们在山岭、岩洞和庇护所周围留下了大量保存比较完好的居住遗迹,包括炼铁的遗迹,以及约1800幅杰出的岩石雕刻。该遗产包括新石器时代和铁器时代的遗址,和岩刻艺术一起共同反映了班图人和西非其他民族沿奥果韦河谷向茂密的常绿刚果森林北部,再到中东部和南部非洲的主要移徙路线,这一移徙书写了撒哈拉以南非洲的发展。奥果韦河谷中段的丰富考古发现向我们展现了长达40万年的历史画卷,这些考古遗迹提供了先人使用林产品、种植农作物、驯化动物的详尽证据。

Vocabulary

1. savannah *n.*(热带和亚热带)无树大草原

The southern African python occurs in open savannah, riverine scrub and rocky areas.

辽阔的非洲稀树草原,溪流边的灌木丛,以及多岩石地带,这些都是南非蟒经常出没的地方。

2. floristic *adj.* 花的,植物的,植物种类的

The term association has been used throughout by British workers for their floristic units.

群丛一词始终被英国工作者用作他们的植物区系单位。

3. petroglyph *n.*(尤指史前的)岩画

A petroglyph can be found on cave walls, depicting spirals in the sky.

可在洞穴的墙上找到描绘天空中螺旋的岩石雕刻画。

4. domestication *n.* 驯养;驯化

Sheep are particularly well suited for domestication.

绵羊特别适合驯养。

扩展阅读

Welcome to Gabon—the World's Last Eden

An oasis of peace in Africa

Did you know that the young Republic of Gabon, the size of Colorado, can apply for a Guinness World Record in this century? Here you will find a country with endless ecological wonders and pristine environment. 83 percent of its national territory is covered by tropical forests. But there is more due to his wise environmental policy, perhaps one of the world's best environmental projects, Gabon—the only French-speaking countries who had no civil wars in the world—has a range of wildlife, including waterfowl, lowland gorillas, forest elephants, hippos, whales and dolphins. Curiously, Gabon is one of the few countries in the world where you can see hippos "go to the beach". Today, the African nation, a mosaic of ethnic groups, has a World Heritage site: The Lopé-Okanda National Park (also known as the Ecosystem and Relic Cultural Landscape of Lopé-Okanda). The property contains a wide variety of species, including wild animals endangered. All these treasures of the country are the ideal site to practice eco-tourism and, of course, in contact with nature. In recent years, Gabon, a resource-rich republic, was recognized by nature lovers as one of the wildlife sanctuaries of the most beautiful in the world. This nation's rainforest—ninety-third of Earth's largest country—lies in West Africa and the borders of Congo, Cameroon and Equatorial Guinea. Despite being one of the least populous, Gabon brings together more than 40 ethnic groups: Fang (representing some 23% of the population), Eshira, Bapounou, Bateke, Bantu Mbede, Okande, Bauta and other groups. Gabon today was one of the four dependencies of French Equatorial Africa in the first half of the 20th century. On August 17, 1960, it declared its independence from Paris. From there, the country became one of the most modern nations and brought peace to the region. Gabon has largely escaped the civil war in many African blacks. As such, it is a place of peace and beauty, a country that has not been a conflict for four decades. The country has vast natural resources: petroleum, manganese, uranium and wood. Due to the offshore oil—a major producer of sub-Saharan Africa's oil—it is among the most prosperous states on the continent. Libreville, the capital, surrounded by desert, is one of the most modern cities in sub-Saharan Africa, and the largest city in the country. In this French-speaking city, therefore, there are international class hotels, skyscrapers, shopping malls, historic buildings (palaces were incredibly preserved!), modern museums and, of course, traditional restaurants. Apart from that, here you can buy the famous African masks—it is known for its handicrafts and excellent music as well—and other things, pottery and fresh tropical fruits to regional natural medicines and clothing.

A Paradise Lost

This oil-rich country, not a very large republic, is the size of the UK, but it has a much smaller population, only 1.5 million euros by the wild animals exceeds the number of people. Indeed, it is one of the last unspoiled areas of Africa awaiting you. The Gabonese Republic is one of the world's most unknown republics, yet it is home to the third / fourth largest African rainforest belt(after wilderness of Congo and the jungles of Botswana). Similarly, this region has a number of beaches and lagoons, where there are surprises galore.

Since then, the land size of Colorado is proud of its ecological wealth. Nature reserves in Gabon have a record number of species documented in mammals, exotic birds, fish, reptiles, amphibians, snails, crustaceans, insects, arachnids and butterflies (virtually impossible to quantify!). But there are more "world records": these park lands are home to 80,000 African elephants, and more than 35,000 gorillas, chimpanzees and 64,000 other mammals. As such, Gabon is an "ideal living laboratory" for studying the biodiversity of wildlife and forest in Africa. For a small nation, it includes several National Parks! The country's best known tropical park is the Loango National Park. With an area of 32,000 km², Loango is four times the size of Connecticut or Northern Ireland. Unlike most parks, this nature reserve has more than 100 km² of coastline with many beautiful beaches, where there are a lot of "special guests": elephants, monkeys, buffalo, leopard and mandrills. Most of them to walk or even find tropical fruits. Even so, this site offers another fabulous show: Here you can watch whales and dolphins. Gabon has other attractions such as the Lopé-Okanda National Park, where there are over 4,000 lowland gorillas. This amazing property, a World Heritage site since 2007, is located in the heart of the country. Undoubtedly, Gabon is the world's last Eden. Let's go to Africa!

（资料来源：http://android. digestbit. com/Welcome-to-Gabon-the-world-Last-Eden/）

Questions

1. What are some of the ecological wonders you may find in Gabon?

2. Apart from its amazing ecological wealth, what else do you think is special about Gabon?

Konso Cultural Landscape
孔索文化景观

➡️ 简介

所属国家：埃塞俄比亚(Ethiopia)

入选时间：2011

入选标准：（iii）（v）

Konso Cultural Landscape is a 55 km^2 arid property of stone walled terraces and fortified settlements in the Konso highlands of Ethiopia. It constitutes a spectacular example of a living cultural tradition stretching back 21 generations (more than 400 years) adapted to its dry hostile environment. The landscape demonstrates the shared values, social cohesion and engineering knowledge of its communities. The site also features anthropomorphic wooden statues—grouped to represent respected members of their communities and particularly heroic events—which are an exceptional living testimony to funerary traditions that are on the verge of disappearing. The Konso erect stone steles to commemorate and mark the transfer of responsibility from the older generation to the younger. Stone steles in the towns express a complex system of marking the passing of generations of leaders. This tradition makes the Konso one of the last megalithic people.

The Konso Cultural Landscape integrates spectacularly executed dry stone terrace works, which are still actively used by the Konso people, who created them. The terraces retain the soil from erosion, collect a maximum of water, discharge the excess, and create terraced fields that are used for agriculture. The terraces are the main features of the Konso landscape and the hills are contoured with the dry stone walls, which at places reach up to 5 meters in height.

The walled towns and settlements of the Konso Cultural Landscape are located on high plains or hill summits selected for their strategic and defensive advantage. These towns are circled by between one and six rounds of dry stone defensive walls. The relation of the stone terraces and the fortified towns of Konso Cultural Landscape, and its highly organized social system, illustrates an outstanding example of a traditional human settlement and land-use, based on common values that have resulted in the creation of the Konso cultural and socio-economic fabric.

孔索文化景观占地面积55平方千米，位于干旱的埃塞俄比亚孔索高地。在这片高地上，除了石墙梯田构成的景观外，还分布着人类的定居点。作为人类克服干燥、恶劣的自然环境，顽强生存下来的杰出范例，孔索文化景观代表着一个已传承了21代（即400多年）并依然具有活力的文化传统，展现出各社区的共同价值观、社会凝聚力及其所拥有的工程知识。这里还保存着具有人格化特征的木雕，这些木雕相互组合在一起，代表着受到尊敬的各社区成员，特别是英雄事件。对正处消失边缘的丧葬传统而言，它们是特殊的活生生的见证。孔索文化中有竖立石碑以示纪念、标志责任转移到下一代人肩上的传统，矗立在城镇中的石碑则共同构成了一种纪念一代代逝去的领导人的复杂体系。这使孔索人成为最后的巨石文化民族之一。

孔索文化景观包括壮观的石墙梯田，其创造者——孔索人至今仍在大量使用。这些梯田能防止水土流失，能尽可能多地储水并排出余水，从而形成可供种植之用的农田。石墙梯田是孔索文化景观的主要特点，石墙环绕山丘，有的地方高达5米。

出于战略和防御考虑,孔索文化景观中石墙环绕的村镇和定居点都位于平原地势较高处或山丘之顶。村镇外围的石头防卫墙从一圈到六圈不等。该景观中石墙梯田和防卫严密的村镇之间的关系,及其高度有组织的社会体系,构成了以创造了孔索文化、社会经济基本结构的共同价值观为基础的传统人类定居和土地利用的杰出典范。

Vocabulary

1. arid *adj*. 干旱的;不毛的;枯燥无味的;乏善可陈的

The Sahara Desert is arid.

撒哈拉沙漠非常干燥。

2. fortified *adj*. 加强的

He remains barricaded inside his heavily-fortified mansion.

他躲在防卫森严的宅院里把自己与外界隔绝开来。

3. anthropomorphic *adj*. 被赋予人形(或人性)的;拟人的

The world of the gods is anthropomorphic, an imitative projection of ours.

神界是拟人化的,是模仿我们人类世界的一个投影。

4. stele *n*. 石碑,石柱

In addition, the stele is providing invaluable information about the social dimension at the site.

另外,在当时的社会规模方面,石碑为我们提供了非常宝贵的信息。

5. commemorate *v*. 纪念

Some galleries commemorate donors by inscribing their names on the walls.

一些美术馆把捐赠者的姓名镌刻在墙上以示纪念。

6. erosion *n*. (气候等的)侵蚀,腐蚀;逐渐丧失,削弱

Soil conservation is intended to curb erosion.

土壤保持旨在控制水土流失。

扩展阅读

Ethiopia: Konso People Celebrate UNESCO World Heritage Support

On a recent sunny day in southwestern Ethiopia, the Konso people danced through the streets and sang enthusiastically to the music of a marching band.

Their colorful clothing, traditional masks and shields, and decorative feathers hinted at what a special occasion they were marking: the announcement by the United Nations Educational, Scientific and Cultural Organization (UNESCO) that Konso has been added to the official list of World Heritage sites.

The Konso Cultural Landscape has found a place on this prestigious list in recognition of the unique biocultural resources that thrive there. The landscape consists of productive and unique terraced settlements spread over 21 square miles in the semi-arid Konso highlands, 375 miles southwest of Addis Ababa. Deputy Prime Minister Hailemariam Desalegn travelled to Konso to mark the occasion.

Distinctive Traditions and Practices

The Konso, a Cushitic-speaking people of southwest Ethiopia, are well known for their distinctive religious and cultural traditions including their unique funerary rituals involving elaborate music and dance. Konso culture is also famous for its carved wood statues called wagas, which memorialize important people in the community. The wagas are often arranged in groups and erected on graves or at the entrances of the maze-like paths that lead to Konso villages. UNESCO describes these statues as "exceptional living testimony to funerary traditions that are on the verge of disappearing."

The Konso's resilient agricultural techniques, centered on extensive terracing and productive methods that nurture a web of agrobiodiversity, have also gained them attention. Farmers in Konso practice a highly sophisticated brand of terrace, agroforestry and manure agriculture that consistently provides bountiful harvests. When there are food shortages in the surrounding area, the web of relations that exists throughout the biocultural landscape responds and provides for all. For centuries, the Konso have succeeded in sustainably growing millet, sorghum, corn, cotton and coffee, khat, beans, moringa, and many varieties of trees in their fields. They also raise cattle, sheep and goats that serve as important currency to exchange with other communities.

A Cultural and Sacred Landscape

Konso is the first place in Ethiopia to be recognized as a "cultural landscape", a nod to its importance as a repository for biocultural diversity evolved over many centuries. Ethiopia's other UNESCO Heritage sites include the rock churches of Lalibela and the obelisks of Axum.

Konso "constitutes a spectacular example of a living cultural tradition stretching back 21 generations (more than 400 years) adapted to its dry … environment," UNESCO's description of the site reads. "The landscape demonstrates the shared values, social cohesion and engineering knowledge of its communities."

The Konso Cultural Landscape distinction hints at the role of Konso as a sacred site for its people. Sacred sites are ecologically and spiritually powerful natural places that human societies conserve as essential to the wellbeing of their cultures and natural environments. These places may be, among other things, water sources, forests, ancestral burial grounds or mythical mountains that are known to be homes to the gods or centers of creation.

Those who protect sacred sites are essential to the preservation of biodiversity around the globe. Acknowledging and protecting sacred sites taps into the knowledge and spirituality of indigenous and local communities to enable conservation of both nature and culture. Such recognition validates indigenous beliefs and strengthens the rights of indigenous people everywhere.

Powerful Recognition

UNESCO's announcement on the importance of Konso sends a powerful message, especially to those in Ethiopia who may be losing touch with their heritage. For the stewards of Konso's sacred sites, the international recognition brings legitimacy to their efforts and their methods, which are often at odds with efforts to introduce new values and development. Ethiopia is extremely rich with cultural and linguistic diversity, and Southern Ethiopia is important historically for forging regional and national identity that is based on unity in diversity.

In the case of the Konso, as with many Indigenous groups, the younger generation can particularly benefit from the clear message that their cultural traditions are worth holding onto.

"Most of the young people are forgetting their culture," Dinote Kusia Shankere, a cultural officer in Konso, told the Agence France-Presse, "I'm happy because this inauguration can change the young generation's mind so they will be devoted to (preserve) the culture."

The World Heritage site designation may also provide a boost for biocultural tourism in Ethiopia, which is important in securing sustainable economic growth.

All of this gives the Konso much to celebrate—not only the UNESCO designation itself, but the continued flourishing of their own special culture that is now recognized around the world.

（资料来源：http://www. christensenfund. org/2012/08/01/ethiopia-konso-people-celebrate-unesco-world-heritage-support/）

Questions

1. What is the significance of the World Heritage site designation for the Konso?

2. What challenges may Konso face in the modern society? What can be done to ensure its conservation?

Le Morne Cultural Landscape
莫纳山文化景观

🗂 简介

所属国家：毛里求斯（Mauritius）

入选时间：2011

入选标准：(iii)(vi)

Le Morne Cultural Landscape, a rugged mountain that juts into the Indian Ocean in the southwest of Mauritius was used as a shelter by runaway slaves, maroons, through the 18th and early years of the 19th centuries. It is an exceptional testimony to maroonage or resistance to slavery in terms of the mountain being used as a fortress to shelter escaped slaves. Protected by the mountain's isolated, wooded and almost inaccessible cliffs, the escaped slaves formed small settlements in the caves and on the summit of Le Morne. Le Morne represents maroonage and its impact, which existed in many places around the world, but which was demonstrated so effectively on Le Morne mountain. It is a symbol of slaves' fight for freedom, their suffering, and their sacrifice, all of which have relevance beyond its geographical location, to the countries from which the slaves came—in particular the African mainland, Madagascar, India, and South-east Asia. Indeed, Mauritius, an important stopover in the eastern slave trade, also came to be known as the "Maroon republic" because of the large number of escaped slaves who lived on Le Morne Mountain.

莫纳山文化景观位于毛里求斯西南部，山势险峻，直伸入海。18世纪到19世纪初期，莫纳山是逃亡黑奴的避难地。这里的崇山峻岭成为黑奴的防御要塞，为他们提供庇护，这使得莫纳山成为黑奴反抗奴隶制并逃亡的独特证明。这里的险峻山崖地处偏僻、森林茂密、人迹罕至，许多逃奴在山洞里或山顶建立起小型的定居点。逃奴现象及其影响在世界其他地方也有所体现，但在莫纳山得到了有力的证实。莫纳山象征着逃奴们的苦难生活，以及他们为争取自由而进行的努力、所做出的牺牲，这不仅与其地理位置有关，也与奴隶们的来源国有关——他们大多来自非洲大陆、马达加斯加、印度和东南亚。事实上，毛里求斯作为重要的东部奴隶贸易中转站，又被称为"逃奴共和国"，因为有大量的逃奴在莫纳山生活。

Vocabulary

1. jut *v.* 凸出；伸出；(使身体部位)凸出；(尤指)翘起(下巴)

The northern end of the island juts out like a long, thin finger into the sea.

岛屿的北端像一根细长的手指一样伸入海中。

2. maroon *n.* 逃亡黑奴；孤立的人

No maroon community could survive completely cut off from the outside world.

逃奴群体无法完全脱离外面的世界而生存下去。

3. stopover *n.* 中途停留

We had a two-day stopover in Fiji on the way to Australia.

我们去澳大利亚时中途在斐济停留了两天。

扩展阅读

Le Morne, Mauritius···
Once upon a Numinous Sanctuary

Le Morne—a breathtaking and buzzing panorama; that's the least we can say about this gorgeous peninsula located at the south-west of the island.

We cannot talk about the Mauritius' colonisation without paying homage to the sweat, blood and tears of slaves and indentured labourers.

Le Morne is not only a gorgeous landscape and top tourist attraction of the island, but was a revered numinous sanctuary for marooned slaves where they could find solace from the atrocities inflicted upon them by their masters.

Following the abolition of slavery many indentured labourers transited through the Aapravasi Ghat to shape the kismet of the Mauritian Society alongside all those people who came here earlier, whether through Fate, coercion or on their own free will.

Without a smidgeon of doubt the wild scenery alone is mesmerizing, but the most striking feature is the majestic monolithic mountain—an enormous basaltic rock dominating the surrounding landscape by its splendor and which rises 560 metres above sea level. On its summit lush vegetation, unseen from the bottom, flourish on a fertile plateau.

Le Morne transcends its natural lofty beauty in a profound spiritual and cultural symbolism. The mountain is considered a national holy monument bearing testimony to the slaves' quest and fights for freedom.

The early history of Mauritius is indissociably linked to slavery. During the Dutch and French periods many slaves were brought in, mainly from the African mainland and Madagascar, to transform this faraway uninhabited island into a thriving economy. They endured many hardships and corporal punishments while toiling the fields and building infrastructures. Unable to bear the physical and emotional atrocities inflicted upon them by their masters, many fled to the forests.

The mountain with its many steep slopes and cliffs, intersected by deep ravine and countless fissures, soon became associated with maroonage or fugitive slaves. By its topography the mountain easily lent itself as a natural inaccessible fortress where maroons find a perfect hideaway.

At their perils many runaway slaves confronted frightening heights and negotiated hazardous passes to find refuge in the many caves on the summit. Gradually a small community started to evolve around.

According to oral accounts and traditions passed through the generations we gather that the place was a sanctuary where the fugitives could find solace and peace. Through traditional African healing practices they were healed from fear, anger, guilt and other negative thought patterns. Concoctions and baths from natural herbs cured their bodies from ailments.

After the local British administration abolished slavery on February 1, 1835, British soldiers made their way to that part of the island to announce the good news to the fugitives. Seeing them approaching from the top of the mountain, the escaped slaves—women, children, elderly and men alike—not realizing that the soldiers were sent to tell them about the abolition of slavery, threw themselves off the cliffs to their death below. They preferred death over the chains of captivity.

For some this is just a folkloric tale, but many believe that the tragedy really happened. The story has inspired many poets, singers, writers, historical travelers and painters to unleash their creative potentials.

Le Morne, like the Aapravasi Ghat, has been inscribed on the World Heritage List of UNESCO on July 10, 2008 and is considered as Mauritius' Cultural Landscape.

Besides its historical and cultural value, the countryside is a renowned upmarket tourist destination with a crystal clear turquoise lagoon and white sandy beaches. Here you can enjoy water sports or golf. The most luxurious hotels in this part of the island are situated along the coast.

Nowadays all nearby inhabitants have settled a few kilometers away at L'embrasure Village. Walking around the village's lanes, all named after exotic flowers like Dahlia, Coquelicot, Hortensia, Lila and Saponere, is a pure bliss. In addition to the gorgeous landscape and inviting sea waters, the warmth of the villagers is simply fabulous. Always in a strikingly laid-back mood, the folks will welcome you by waving a friendly "hello".

http://www.mauritius-holidays-discovery.com/tourist-attractions-in-mauritius.html

（资料来源：http://www.mauritius-holidays-discovery.com/le-morne.html）

Questions

1. Why is Le Morne considered a national holy monument?
2. Describe the life of maroons in Le Morne.

Mapungubwe Cultural Landscape
马蓬古布韦文化景观

➡ 简介

所属国家：南非（South Africa）

入选时间：2003

入选标准：(ii)(iii)(iv)(v)

Mapungubwe is set hard against the northern border of South Africa, joining Zimbabwe and Botswana. It is an open, expansive savannah landscape at the confluence of the Limpopo and Shashe rivers. Mapungubwe developed into the largest kingdom in the sub-continent before it was abandoned in the 14th century. What survives are the almost untouched remains of the palace sites and also the entire settlement area dependent upon them, as well as two earlier capital sites, the whole presenting an unrivalled picture of the development of social and political structures over some 400 years.

The Mapungubwe Cultural Landscape demonstrates the rise and fall of the first indigenous kingdom in Southern Africa between AD 900 and 1300. Mapungubwe's position at the crossing of the north/south and east/west routes in southern Africa also enabled it to control trade, through the East African ports to India and China, and throughout southern Africa. From its hinterland it harvested gold and ivory—commodities in scarce supply elsewhere—and this brought it great wealth. This international trade also created a society that was closely linked to ideological adjustments, and changes in architecture and settlement planning. Until its demise at the end of the 13th century AD, Mapungubwe was the most important inland settlement in the African sub-continent and the cultural landscape contains a wealth of information in archaeological sites that records its development. Mapungubwe's demise was brought about by climatic change. During its final two millennia, periods of warmer and wetter conditions suitable for agriculture in the Limpopo/Shashe valley were interspersed with cooler and drier pulses. When rainfall decreased after 1300 AD, the land could no longer sustain a high population using traditional farming methods, and the inhabitants were obliged to disperse.

马蓬古布韦坐落于南非的北部边境,连接着津巴布韦与博茨瓦纳。它是位于林波波河和沙希河汇流处的一处开放广阔的热带大草原。它曾是非洲次大陆最大的王国,直到14世纪之后被人逐渐遗忘。现在幸存的是几乎完整无损的宫殿遗址和依此而建的居留地以及两处早期的首都遗址。而这一切都为我们提供了约400年中那里的社会与政治结构发展的一幅无与伦比的图画。

马蓬古布韦文化景观展现了9—13世纪南非首个王国的兴衰史。马蓬古布韦王国处于南非的南北、东西交通枢纽之地,控制了南非和从东非港口到印度、中国的贸易;非洲内陆出产的黄金、象牙也给王国创造了巨大财富;国际贸易的发展转变了马蓬古布韦社会的意识形态,也改变了其建筑及定居点规划。在13世纪末该王国消亡以前,它一直是非洲次大陆最重要的内陆定居点。马蓬古布韦文化景观诸多考古遗址记录了这个古王国的成长和衰落。气候变化导致了该王国的消亡。两千年来,林波波河和沙希河河谷的气候时而温暖潮湿、适合农耕,时而凉爽干燥。13世纪时,此地少雨,传统的农耕方式无法满足众多人口的需要,人们只好移居别处。

Vocabulary

1. confluence *n*. (河流的)汇合处,交汇处;汇集;汇合

The 160-metre falls mark the dramatic confluence of the rivers Nera and Velino.

内拉河和韦利诺河的汇合处是落差达160米的瀑布,景象十分壮观。

2. indigenous *adj*. 当地的;本土的;土生土长的

Kangaroos are indigenous to Australia.

袋鼠为澳大利亚本土的动物。

3. hinterland *n*. (海岸或大江、大河的)后方地区,腹地,内地

A century ago, eastern Germany was an agricultural hinterland.

一个世纪前,德国东部是个农业的内陆地区。

4. demise *n*. 终止;消亡;死亡

The war brought about the industry's sudden demise.

战争导致这个行业就这么突然垮了。

5. intersperse *v*. 散布;散置;点缀

Originally the intention was to intersperse the historical scenes with modern ones.
最初是想用现代景观点缀历史景观。

扩展阅读

Mapungubwe: SA's Lost City of Gold

One thousand years ago, Mapungubwe in Limpopo province was the centre of the largest kingdom in the sub-continent, where a highly sophisticated people traded gold and ivory with China, India and Egypt.

The Iron Age site, discovered in 1932 but hidden from public attention until only recently, was declared a World Heritage site by the United Nations Educational, Scientific and Cultural Organisation (UNESCO) in July 2003.

Mapungubwe is an area of open savannah at the confluence of the Limpopo and Shashe Rivers and abutting the northern border of South Africa and the borders of Zimbabwe and Botswana. It thrived as a sophisticated trading centre from around 1220 to 1300.

In its statement on the listing, UNESCO describes Mapungubwe as the centre of the largest kingdom in the sub-continent before it was abandoned in the 14th century.

"What survives are the almost untouched remains of the palace sites and also the entire settlement area dependent upon them, as well as two earlier capital sites, the whole presenting an unrivalled picture of the development of social and political structures over some 400 years," UNESCO said.

Mapungubwe was home to an advanced culture of people for the time—the ancestors of the Shona people of Zimbabwe. They traded with China and India, had a flourishing agricultural industry, and grew to a population of around 5,000.

Mapungubwe is probably the earliest known site in southern Africa where evidence of a class-based society existed (Mapungubwe's leaders were separated from the rest of the inhabitants).

Gold, copper, exotic beads…

The site was discovered in 1932 and has been excavated by the University of Pretoria ever since. The findings were kept quiet at the time since they provided contrary evidence to the racist ideology of black inferiority underpinning apartheid.

Nevertheless, the university now has a rich collection of artefacts made of gold and other materials, as well as human remains, discovered there. According to the University of Pretoria's Mapungubwe website, "Subsequent excavations revealed a court sheltered in a natural amphitheatre at the bottom of the hill, and an elite graveyard at the top—with a spectacular view of the region."

"Twenty-three graves have been excavated from this hilltop site," the website continues, "The bodies in three of these graves were buried in the upright seated position associated with royalty, with a variety of gold and copper items, exotic glass beads, and other prestigious objects. ""These finds provide evidence not only of the early smithing of gold in southern Africa, but of the extensive wealth and social differentiation of the people of Mapungubwe."

The most spectacular of the gold discoveries is a little gold rhinoceros, made of gold foil and tacked with minute pins around a wooden core. The rhino, featured in one of South Africa's new national orders—the Order of Mapungubwe—has come to symbolise the high culture of Mapungubwe. The rhino is also a symbol of leadership among the Shona people of Zimbabwe.

Other artefacts made in similar fashion include the Golden Sceptre and the Golden Bowl, found in the same grave on Mapungubwe Hill.

Evidence of complex social formations

What is so fascinating about Mapungubwe is that it is testimony to the existence of an African civilisation that flourished before colonisation. According to Professor Thomas Huffman of the archaeology department at the University of the Witwatersrand, Mapungubwe represents "the most complex society in southern Africa and is the root of the origins of Zimbabwean culture".

Between AD 1200 and 1300, the Mapungubwe region was the centre of trade in southern Africa. Wealth came to the region from ivory and later from gold deposits that were found in Zimbabwe. The area was also agriculturally rich because of large-scale flooding in the area. The wealth in the area led to differences between rich and poor.

In the village neighbouring Mapungubwe, called K2, an ancient refuse site has provided archaeologists with plenty of information about the lifestyles of the people of Mapungubwe.

According to the University of Pretoria website: "People were prosperous, and kept domesticated cattle, sheep, goats and dogs. The charred remains of storage huts have also been found, showing that millet, sorghum and cotton were cultivated."

"Findings in the area are typical of the Iron Age. Smiths created objects of iron, copper and gold for practical and decorative purposes? both for local use and for trade. Pottery, wood, ivory, bone, ostrich eggshells, and the shells of snails and freshwater mussels, indicate that many other materials were used and traded with cultures as far away as East Africa, Persia, Egypt, India and China."

Mapungubwe's fortune only lasted until about 1300, after which time climate changes, resulting in the area becoming colder and drier, led to migrations further north to Great Zimbabwe.

Mapungubwe National Park

In 2004, South African National Parks (SAN Parks) opened Mapungubwe National Park, incorporating the UNESCO-designated Mapungubwe Cultural Landscape in an area covering well over 28,000 hectares.

The park forms part of an ambitious project to develop a major transfrontier conservation area, the Limpopo/Shashe Transfrontier Park, which will cross the borders of Botswana, South Africa and Zimbabwe, linking Mapungubwe National Park with Botswana's Tuli Block and Zimbabwe's Tuli Safari area.

Besides the rich cultural heritage of Mapungubwe National Park, most of the continent's big games roam here. There is also a tremendous diversity of plant and animal life.

Sandstone formations, mopane woodlands and unique riverine forest and baobab trees form an astounding scenic backdrop for a rich variety of animal life.

Elephant, giraffe, white rhino, eland, gemsbok and numerous other antelope species occur naturally in the area, while visitors can spot predators like lions, leopards and hyenas, and birders can tick off 400 species, including kori bustard, tropical boubou and pel's fishing owl.

（资料来源：http://www. southafrica. info/about/history/mapungubwe. htm）

Questions

1. What was Mapungubwe like a thousand years ago? Could you describe its economic features and social structure?

2. Please explain the significance of the Mapungubwe Cultural Landscape?

Osun-Osogbo Sacred Grove
奥孙-奥索博神树林

⇨ 简介

所属国家：尼日利亚（Nigeria）

入选时间：2005

入选标准：(ii)(iii)(vi)

The dense forest of the Osun Sacred Grove, on the outskirts of the City of Osogbo, is one of the last remnants of primary high forest in southern Nigeria. Regarded as the abode of the goddess of fertility Osun, one of the pantheon of Yoruba gods, the landscape of the grove and its meandering river is dotted with sanctuaries and shrines, sculptures and art works in honour of Osun and other deities. The sacred grove, which is now seen as a symbol of identity for all Yoruba people, is probably the last in Yoruba culture. It testifies to the once widespread practice of establishing sacred groves outside all settlements.

Sacred groves used to be found near every Yoruba settlement, but their disappearance over time has made Osun-Osogbo an important reference point for Yoruba identity and the Yoruba diaspora. The grove remains a place of worship, and it is now the site of an annual festival，but it also faces a number of modern challenges．The rapid growth of the city of Osogbo is causing pressure on land use that is already affecting the area around the site．Meanwhile，the Osun River is becoming increasingly polluted，and bush fires that grow out of control pose a continuing threat to the sacred area.

奥孙神树林密集的林地位于奥索博市郊外,是尼日利亚南部主要乔木树种的最后残留地之一。这里被视为约鲁巴神的万神殿之一,即生育女神奥孙的住所,大量的神祠、雕塑品和艺术作品星罗棋布地分布在树林中蜿蜒的小河边,以纪念奥孙和其他约鲁巴神灵。目前看到的作为所有约鲁巴人身份象征的神树林,可能是约鲁巴文化中最后一片神圣的树林。奥孙-奥索博神树林是曾经在所有定居点之外广泛种植神圣树林做法的见证。

所有的约鲁巴定居点都曾经在外围种植神圣树林,可随着时间流逝,这些树林大多不复存在,这使得仅存的奥孙-奥索博神树林成为约鲁巴民族特性和流散在外的约鲁巴人的重要标志。这片神树林至今仍是人们敬拜之处,每年人们在此举行奥孙-奥索博节。然而该遗址也面临着许多问题,如:奥索博城的迅速发展带来土地使用上的压力,已经影响到该遗址周边区域;奥孙河污染日益严重;难以控制的森林火灾也时时威胁着神树林。

Vocabulary

1. remnant *n.* 剩余部分;残余部分;残迹;残存物

Beneath the present church were remnants of Roman flooring.

在现在的教堂下面是古罗马时期地面的遗存。

2. pantheon *n.* 万神庙;众神;诸神;要人;名流

Marie Curie's remains were exhumed and interred in the Pantheon.

玛丽·居里的遗体被移出葬在先贤祠中。

3. meander *v.* (河流、道路)蜿蜒而行,迂回曲折;漫步;闲荡;信步

The small river meandered in lazy curves down the centre.

小河缓缓地绕着中心地区迤逦流过。

4. deity *n.* 神;女神

Many animals were seen as the manifestation of a deity.

许多动物被看作神的化身。

5. diaspora *n.* 移民社群

People from every country of the Diaspora now live in Israel.

当年流落他乡的犹太人现在生活在以色列。

扩展阅读

Osun-Osogbo：Carnival of Culture in a Sacred Forest

Culture，religion and language are universal concepts．To some degree，the universality of the three concepts is underscored by the origins of some major religions and their spread across the countries making up the earth's six continents.

The Osun-Osogbo Festival to a large extent continues to unify the culture，art and identity of the Yoruba race 400 years on.

The Osun-Osogbo grove is a sacred forest along the banks of the Osun River, which is located on the outskirt of Osogbo. It is part of the wider Yoruba community, divided into 16 kingdoms, which legend says were ruled by the children of Oduduwa, the mythical progenitor of the Yoruba, who descended via a rope from heaven to earth in Ile-Ife, the ancestral home of Yoruba.

The universality of tradition could be seen in the origin of the Osun River, which has its source in Igede-Ekiti, Ekiti State. The Onigede of Igede-Ekiti, Oba James Aladesuru, who spoke to our correspondent through the Olumose of Igede, Pa Felix Ojo, on Friday, explained that the source of Osun River in Igede-Ekiti is called Odo-Uri.

Aladesuru said, "The Osun River has its source in Igede-Ekiti. The river is known as Odo-Uri in Igede. Its votary in Igede is called Yeye L'Osun. A few days to the hosting of Osun-Osogbo Festival in Osogbo, worshippers visit its source in Igede to perform some rites. Igede is a progressive, accommodating and peaceful community, where love and unity reign."

The early history of Osogbo is essentially the legendary account of a spirit world; it is the history of the early people referred to as spirits and fairies. This is in line with Yoruba traditions, which use mythical stories to explain the origins of Yoruba's ruling families.

Oso-Igbo, the Goddess of Osun River, was the Queen and original founder of Osogbo. She lived in a beautiful surrounding and possessed magical powers which inspired her people and frightened their enemies. She is ascribed with the powers of fertility, healing and protection. She is also credited with the ability to bless her adherents with the good things of life.

Human beings came to populate Osogbo and moved the emerging geographical landmass away from the predominance of spirits and fairies when Oba Larooye came from Ipole-Omu to settle along the bank of River Osun in the 17th Century.

In 1840s, after the fall of the old Oyo Empire, Osogbo became a refugee town for people fleeing Fulani forces. As a result, Osogbo increased in population largely due to migration from other Yoruba towns. For want of more open place than the bank of the river, which is also a grove, Larooye and his people abandoned their settlement, including the already flourishing market and moved to Ode-Osogbo. At Ode-Osogbo, he built his new palace at the present day Idi-Osun while Timehin built the Ogun shrine now known as Idi-Ogun. The Fulani attacks on Osogbo were repelled and, as a result, Osogbo has become a symbol of pride for all the Yoruba.

In 1914, British colonial rule begun. As it was delivered under a system of indirect rule through traditional rulers, the authority of the Oba and priests were sustained. For a while, all three religions co-existed but as time went on it became less fashionable to be identified with Osun traditional worship.

By the 1950s, the combined political and religious changes were having a marked detrimental effect on the Osun grove: customary responsibilities and sanctions were weakening, shrines were becoming neglected and traditional priests began to disappear. All this was exacerbated by a rise in the looting of statues and movable sculptures to feed a global antiquity market. Trees were felled; sculptures were reportedly stolen and hunting and fishing begun to be recorded—previously forbidden in the sacred Osun grove.

An Austrian woman, Suzanne Wenger, came and stopped the abuse going on in the grove. She, along with her German-Jew husband, Ulli Beier, and Nigerian consummate dramatist, the late Duro Ladipo, co-founded an arts movement called Mbari Mbayo, which sought to promote all forms of arts. According to Wikipedia, "It was at this crucial point in the history of the grove that Austrian-born Wenger moved to Osogbo and, with the encouragement of the Oba and the support from local people, formed the New Sacred Art movement to challenge land speculators, repel poachers, protect shrines and begin the long process of bringing the sacred place back to life by establishing it, again, at the sacred heart of Osogbo."

"The artists deliberately created large, heavy and fixed sculptures in iron cement and mud, as opposed to the smaller traditional wooden ones, in order that their intimidating architectural forms would help to protect the grove and stop thefts. All the sculptures have been done in full respect for the spirit of the place, with inspiration from Yoruba mythology and in consultations with the gods in a traditional context. The new work has made the grove a symbol of identity for the Yoruba people."

Many Africans in the Diaspora now undertake a pilgrimage to the annual festival. In 1965, part of the Osun grove was declared a national monument. This was extended in 1992 so that now the whole 75 hectares are protected. The grove was recognised by UNESCO as world heritage site in 2005. Osun-Osogbo Festival has grown to become a brand sought after by several companies willing to position their goods and services.

As the Ataoja of Osogbo, Oba Jimoh Olanipekun, begins the "Iwopopo" ceremony with the 16-face torch, on Monday, Osogbo appears set for the two-week socio-cultural rejuvenation expected to climax on Friday, 23 August, 2013.

The Commissioner for Information and Strategy, Osun State, Mr Sunday Akere, said, "Osun State Government has done some reconstructions in the groove without altering its natural state. This is aimed at improving tourists' movement and visibility during the festival."

（资料来源：http://www.punchng.com/feature/people-places/osun-osogbo-preserving-culture-arts/）

Questions

1. Why does the author say that the Osun-Osogbo Festival continue to unify the culture, art and identity of the Yoruba race?

2. What did Suzanne Wenger do to stop the abuse going on in the grove and bring the sacred place back to life?

世界遗产概论

第五章　北美洲的世界遗产

Introduction to the World Heritage

第一节　北美洲的世界文化遗产

Cahokia Mounds State Historic Site
卡俄基亚土丘历史遗址

⇨ **简介**

所属国家：美国（America）

入选时间：1982

入选标准：（iii）（iv）

Cahokia Mounds State Historic Site, located in southern Illinois directly across the Mississippi River from modern St. Louis, Missouri, is the largest and earliest pre-Columbian settlement and most complex archaeological site north of Mexico. The main features of the site are the remaining man-made 69 mounds out of the original 120 earthen ones. The largest mound is Monks Mound, the largest prehistoric earthwork in the Americas, covering over 5 ha and standing 30 m high. It is a typical sample of a complex chiefdom society, with many satellite mound centres and numerous outlying hamlets and villages. This agricultural society may have had a population of 10,000—20,000 at its peak between 1050 and 1150.

The site is now preserved as the pre-eminent example of a cultural, religious, and economic centre of the Mississippian cultural tradition, as well as an exceptional example of pre-urban structuring, which demonstrates the existence of a pre-urban society and provides an opportunity to study a type of social organization, on which written sources are silent. It is most comprehensive affirmation of the pre-Columbian civilizations in the Mississippi region.

Other physical features include a reconstructed stockade wall and "woodhenge", a circle of posts around a large central post from which the sunrise can be aligned to the season and time of year. The Cahokia Mounds State Historic Site was designated a National Historic Landmark in 1964 and a site for state protection.

卡俄基亚土丘历史遗址位于美国伊利诺伊州南部境内，与密苏里州密西西比河隔河相望，这是哥伦布发现美洲前墨西哥以北地区最大、最早的人类聚居地，亦是最复杂的考古遗址。原有的 120 座人工土丘，现仍保有 69 座，是遗址上重要的古建筑特征。其中最大的是"寺庙土丘"，这是美洲大陆上最大的史前土木工程，占地超过 5 公顷，高约 30 米。这是古代部落社会的典型例证，以众多土丘卫星城为中心，外围布满了星罗棋布、大大小小的偏僻村落。这个农业社会在其鼎盛时期(1050—1150 年)人口数量可能多达 1 万至 2 万。

　　卡俄基亚土丘历史遗址作为昔日的文化、宗教和经济中心,是保存密西西比河区域文化传统最为成功的案例,亦是一个史前城市建筑的特殊案例,这恰好佐证了史前城市社会的存在,为人类研究某一类型的社会组织提供了原始素材,有效填补了书面资料的空白,它是对密西西比河流域前哥伦布时期文明的全面认定。

　　其他古建筑还包括一个重建的栅栏墙和"巨木阵",许多木桩围成一圈,里面是一个硕大的中心柱,太阳从这里升起后会与某个木桩形成直线,据此确定这一年的季节和时间。1964 年卡俄基亚土丘历史遗址被定为国家级历史地标和国家级保护遗址。

Vocabulary

1. woodhenge *n* 史前木栅;巨木阵

By the way, there is more than one woodhenge in this world. The Native Americans also built woodhenges.

顺便提一下,世界上并非只有一个巨木阵,美国土著人也曾建过巨木阵。

2. cedar *n.* 雪松;香柏;西洋杉木

For me, the lotus and blue cedar dominate, but they work well together.

对我来说,她的芳香以莲花和蓝色雪松为主,几种香味完美融合。

3. alignment *n.* 队列,排成直线

As I say in the article, center alignment should be a last resort, not a first.

正如我在文章里所说,居中对齐应该是下下策而非首选。

4. solstices *n.* 至,至日;至点

Winter solstice is the shortest day of the year in the Northern Hemisphere and marks the official beginning of winter.

在北半球,冬至是一年里最短的一天,同时也标志着冬天正式开始。

5. equinox *n.* 春分;秋分

Twice a year, at the spring and fall equinoxes, the sun rises due east.

一年两次,春分和秋分,太阳从正东方升起。

6. Sunpriest *n.* 太阳祭司

The Sunpriest could feel the life within the crashed celestial city, he could hear strange alien voices and sense the purity of a yet unknown magic.

太阳祭司可以感受到坠毁天体城市的生命,他能听到奇怪的外星人的声音,感觉到一种完全未知的魔法。

7. pigment *n.* 色素;颜料

The pigment absorbs the radiation and protects cells from damage.

黑色素可以吸收辐射,保护你的细胞不受损伤。

扩展阅读

Cahokia Mounds

Fascinating information about the people who once built the great prehistoric city of

Cahokia was revealed accidentally during excavations in the early 1960s. Archaeologists were trying desperately to save archaeological information which was to be destroyed by the construction of an interstate highway, which was later rerouted.

After a summer of intense excavation, Dr. Warren Wittry was studying excavation maps when he observed that numerous large oval-shaped pits seemed to be arranged in arcs of circles. He theorized that posts set in these pits lined up with the rising sun at certain times of the year, serving as a calendar, which he called WOODHENGE. After further excavations by Wittry and other archaeologists, more post pits were found where predicted, and evidenced that there were as many as five woodhenges at this location. These calendars had been built over a period of 200 years (900—1100). Fragments of wood remaining in some of the post pits revealed red cedar had been used for the posts, a sacred wood.

The first circle (date unknown), only partially excavated, would have consisted of 24 posts; the second circle had 36 posts; the third circle (1000), the most completely excavated, had 48 posts; the fourth, partially excavated, would have had 60 posts. The last woodhenge has only 12, or possible 13 posts, along the eastern sunrise arc(if it had been a complete circle, it would have had 72 posts). Building only the sunrise arc might indicate that red cedar trees had become scarce.

It is not known why the size and location of the circles, and the number of posts was constantly changed—perhaps to include more festival dates or to improve and increase alignments.

Only three posts are crucial as seasonal markers—those marking the first days of winter and summer (the solstices), and the one halfway between marking the first days of spring and fall (the equinoxes). Viewing was from the center of the circle, and several circles had large "observation posts" at that location, where it is likely the Sunpriest stood on a raised platform. Other posts between the solstice posts probably marked special festival dates related to the agricultural cycle. The remaining posts around the circle have no known function, other than symbolically forming a circle and forming an enclosure to hold the sacred woodhenge ceremonies. There have been suggestions some posts had alignments with certain bright stars or the moon, or were used in predicting eclipses, and others have suggested woodhenge was used as an engineering "aligner" to determine mound placements, but none of the above has been proven convincing.

The most spectacular sunrise occurs at the equinoxes, when the sun rises due east. The post marking these sunrises aligns with the front of Monks Mound, where the leader resided, and it looks as though Monks Mound gives birth to the sun. A possible offertory pit near the winter solstice post suggests a fire was burned to warm the sun and encouraged it to return northward for another annual cycle and rebirth of the earth. This probably marked the start of the new year.

The third circle (1000) was reconstructed in 1985 at the original location. The circle is 410 feet in diameter, had 48 posts spaced 26.8 feet apart (9 are missing on the west side, removed by a highway borrow pit). The posts were 15—20 inches in diameter and stood about 20 feet high. Red ocher pigment found in some of the post pits suggests the posts may have been painted. The post pits averaged 7 feet long and just over 2 feet wide, sloping from the surface at one end to a depth of 4 feet at the other, forming a ramp to slide the posts down to facilitate their raising.

（资料来源：http://www.crystalinks.com/observa.html.）

Questions

1. According to Dr. Warren Wittry, what were woodhenges built for?

2. Why dose the last woodhenge consist of only 12 or 13 posts instead of 72 in theory?

3. Explain the reasons why only three posts are crucial as seasonal markers?

Pre-Hispanic City of Teotihuacán
特奥蒂瓦坎

简介

所属国家：墨西哥（Mexico）

入选时间：1987

入选标准：(i)(ii)(iii)(iv)(vi)

The holy city of Teotihuacán (the place where the gods were created) was a pre-Columbian Mesoamerican city, located 50km northeast of modern day Mexico City. Built between the 1st and 7th centuries, Teotihuacán was characterized by the vast size of the most architecturally significant Mesoamerican pyramids—in particular, the Temple of Quetzalcoatl and the Pyramids of the Sun and the Moon, laid out on geometric and symbolic principles. Apart from the pyramids, Teotihuacán is also anthropologically significant for its complex, multi-family residential compounds, the Avenue of the Dead, and the small portion of its vibrant murals that have been exceptionally well-preserved. Teotihuacán and its valley bear unique testimony to the pre-urban structures of ancient Mexico. The influence of the first of the great Mesoamerican classic civilizations was exerted over the whole of the central region of Mexico.

The location of the first sanctuary, the Pyramid of the Sun (built on a cave discovered in 1971), was calculated on the position of the Sun at its zenith, and applied astronomical logic to determine the organization of the space: the Avenue of the Dead was drawn out perpendicularly to the principal axis of the solar temple. The Pyramid of the Moon, to the north the "Citadel" and the Temple of Quetzalcoatl to the south east

244

became one by one the borders of a processional avenue 40m wide and 2km long. Pyramids in Teotihuacán were ceremonial platforms that were topped with temples.

圣城特奥蒂瓦坎（"众神诞生之地"）是一个曾经存在于现今墨西哥境内的古印第安文明遗址，位于墨西哥城东北部 50 千米处，该城建于公元 1—7 世纪。其建筑物按照几何图形和象征意义布局，以建筑物（特别是羽蛇神庙、月亮神金字塔和太阳神金字塔）的庞大气势而闻名于世。除了金字塔，复杂的多户型住宅建筑区、死亡大道及一小部分保存完好的壁画使特奥蒂瓦坎还具有重要的人类学研究价值。特奥蒂瓦坎遗迹及其山谷是古代墨西哥城市结构独特的见证，早期伟大的古印第安经典文明始终影响着整个墨西哥中心地区。

第一个避难所的位置，即太阳神金字塔（建在洞穴之上，发现于 1971 年），是按照太阳最高时的位置计算的，用天文逻辑决定空间的构造；死亡大道是以太阳庙为主轴，并与之垂直；月亮神金字塔以"城堡"的北部为主轴；羽蛇神庙以东南部为主轴。四者形成一个边界相互连接、宽 40 米、长 2000 米的游行大道。圣城特奥蒂瓦坎金字塔是用于祭祀的。

Vocabulary

1. plaza *n.* 广场

The place of relaxation and communication for people was provided by the plaza.

广场为人们提供休闲交往的场所。

2. meditation *n.* 冥想

Meditation can be a great stress reliever because we naturally let go of everything when we settle into the meditative state.

冥想可以有效地释放压力，因为进入冥想时，大脑会自然而然地处于放空的状态。

3. manifest *v.* 证明

He easily manifested the truth of his statement.

他很容易地证明了他说的是真话。

4. altar *n.* 祭坛；圣坛

Bless the altar and bless your child.

请神赐福于圣坛并保佑你的孩子。

5. vortex *n.* 旋涡；（动乱，争论等的）中心

It's the largest known vortex in the solar system.

它是太阳系中已知旋涡中最大的一个。

6. divinity *n.* 神；神性；神学

Sexuality and divinity are very closely entwined in the Hindi faith. Religion is closely linked to sexuality and beauty.

在北印度人的信念中，性欲、神性紧密地联系在一起，宗教和性欲、美息息相关。

7. enchiladas and tacos *n.* 辣酱玉米饼和炸玉米饼

Mexican cuisine, including burritos, enchiladas and tacos are now being blended with Thai, Chinese, Vietnamese and other influences to create new delicacies for western gourmands.

包括炸卷饼、辣酱玉米饼和玉米饼的墨西哥烹饪如今融合了泰国、中国、越南及其他美食元素，为西方的饕餮者们创造出了新奇的美味佳肴。

扩展阅读

A Spiritual Journey Through Teotihuacán

The ultimate surrender at the Pyramid of the Sun

A visit to "heaven" is the best way to follow your ceremony at the Pyramid of the Moon, and to prepare you for the Pyramid of the Sun! As you enter the Plaza of the Butterflies, you feel the soft presence of pure love. You are drawn to the center, and stand absorbing the sacred energy there. Your fellow travelers join you in a circle. There is nothing to say, and nothing to do—only to feel the presence of love in the place of heaven at Teo, and in your own heart.

As you continue in this special place, you are opening your heart and connecting with the sun. In the Toltec tradition, the sun is the source of all life on the earth, and you are on your way to merge with it. When you know it is time, you walk back out onto the Avenue of the Dead, and toward the towering Pyramid of the Sun. You walk once again in meditation, opening and preparing yourself for the ultimate surrender: the leap to the black sun.

The black sun: The hole in the veil

A Toltec mythology describes the sun as the light messenger of creation. Every ray of the sun's light carries the message of a different form of life, which manifests itself as DNA. Every living being has its own unique ray of light from the sun, and its own unique DNA. The dream of the humans reflects back to the sun, and as the dream evolves, the sun changes its message. This is the time of the sixth sun, an important stage in the evolution of the human dream.

Manifested creation is the result of the sun dreaming. The unlimited potential for the dream is behind a veil, in the unmanifested side of the universe. There is a hole, through which the unmanifested becomes the manifested—this is the black sun. As you walk toward the pyramid, you set your intent to leap out of this dream into the black sun, where you will experience the ultimate expansion of pure potentiality.

Preparing yourself, preparing the pyramid

You climb the many steps slowly, contemplating your intent. As you walk around each level of the stepped pyramid, you connect with the pyramid, the sun, and the black sun beyond. You climb higher and around, higher and around. You are awakening the pyramid, creating the spiral of the DNA, releasing any last attachments, and calling down your ray of the sun.

As you climb the last steps and approach the center of the pyramid, you find once again that an altar has been prepared, and a powerful vortex is waiting for your energy. You sit down with your companions gathered there, and pour your personal intent into the vortex. You continue to release attachments that might hold you to the earth, and your body begins to shake with the energy of the vortex. You are not sure what to expect, and that is good.

The leap of surrender into the infinite

Suddenly, someone yells "now!" and you throw yourself into the vortex energy and leap to the sun. You do not know it yet, but there is no you. As you pass through the hole in the veil, you instantly expand into the totality of all that is, pure consciousness, absolute divine presence. The "lack of you" drifts there forever, until it is time to return to human form.

As your body stirs, you sit up and look around slowly. You have never seen this world before. It is brighter and more colorful than you remember. Your DNA is tingling from the update into the sixth sun. Your mind is more peaceful than you ever imagined possible. You have nowhere to go, and nothing to do, but to be right where you are in this moment.

Your heart sings in gratitude for the ancient artists of the spirit who created this place for you to experience this moment. You feel their presence, and their gratitude that you are here, a human awakening, and remember your divinity. You are a Toltec artist of the spirit now, and Teotihuacán is part of you. A butterfly appears, and lands on your hand. It is the absolute perfect expression of what you are feeling.

In time, you notice that your human self is very hungry, and you remember that there are great enchiladas and tacos waiting for you back in another world. You gather up this new dream of heaven on the earth, and as you walk back down the pyramid, you carry the dream in your heart—where it stays for the rest of your life.

（资料来源：http://www. netplaces. com/toltec-wisdom/a-spiritual-journey-through-teotihuacan/.）

Questions

1. Why a visit to the Pyramid of the Sun is called "A Spiritual Journey"?

2. How does unmanifested creation get manifested?

3. How do you feel when reading the passage "The Leap of Surrender into the Infinite". Do you have similar experience? Share it with your classmates.

Historic District of Old Québec
魁北克古城区

🖙 简介

所属国家：加拿大（Canada）

入选时间：1985

入选标准：（iv）（vi）

Québec, the former capital of New France in the seventeenth century, illustrates one of the major stages in the European settlement of the colonization of the Americas by Europeans. It is the only North American city to have preserved its ramparts, together with the numerous bastions, gates and defensive works which still surround Old Québec.

Old Québec is a historic neighbourhood of Quebec City, the capital of the province of Québec. Old Québec is comprised of two parts: the Upper Town, defended by fortified ramparts, citadel, and other defensive works; the Lower Town, which developed around the Place Royale and the harbour. The Upper Town, built on the cliff, has remained the religious and administrative centre, with its churches, convents and other monuments like the Dauphine Redoubt, the Citadel and Château Frontenac. Together with the Lower Town and its ancient districts, it forms an urban ensemble which is one of the best examples of a fortified colonial city. A well-preserved integrated urban ensemble, the historic district is a remarkable example of a fortified city of the colonial era, and unique north of Mexico.

The oldest quarters are located in the Lower Town in the vicinity of the Place Royale, which along with the Rue Notre Dame lined with old 17th-and 18th-century houses. Construction of the Notre-Dame-des-Victoires Church started in 1687 at this location and was completed in 1723. and was rebuilt during the English domination. Of the 700 old civil or religious buildings remaining, 2% date back to the 17th century, 9% to the 18th century and 43% to the first half of the 19th century.

魁北克,17 世纪新法兰西的首府,是欧洲人在北美殖民化进程的重要历史见证之一。是北美唯一保存有城墙以及大量的堡垒、城门、防御工事的城市,这些工程至今仍环绕着魁北克古城。

魁北克古城区是魁北克省省府、魁北克市历史上著名的城区,古城遗址分上城区和下城区两大部分,古城标志性建筑魁北克古堡(1892 年建立),坚固的城墙和其他防御工事坐落于上城区。上城区建立在悬崖上,至今仍然是宗教和行政中心。城区内有教堂、女修道院和一些建筑物,如王妃城堡、要塞和弗隆特纳克堡(Dauphine Redoubt)。下城是围绕着皇家广场和海港建设的。上城区、下城区和老城区一起构成了城市的整体,这是具有最完备防御系统的殖民城市之一。

最古老的街区集中在下城区,皇家广场四周和圣母街两旁均为 17 和 18 世纪建筑群。其中有维多利亚圣母教堂(始建于 1687 年,竣工于 1723 年,并于英国统治时期重建)。在本区 700 余座古老的民用及宗教建筑中,2% 可以追溯到 17 世纪,9% 属于 18 世纪的作品,另有 43% 建于 19 世纪上半叶。作为保存完好的城乡集合体,古城遗址是北美堡垒式殖民城市的完美典范,是北部墨西哥的绝佳代表。

Vocabulary

1. advent *n.* 到来;出现

Since the advent of jet aircraft, travel has been speeded up.

自从喷气式飞机出现以来,旅行的速度大为提高。

2. exude *n.* 充分显示，显露（喜、怒等）

Somehow pink can be incorporated seamlessly into any wedding theme and exude a style with unequal romantic touch.

粉色似乎可以与任何婚姻主题无缝连接并且洋溢着独特的浪漫气息。

3. culminate *v.* 达到高潮；以……告终

The Christmas party culminated in the distribution of presents.

圣诞晚会在分发礼物时达到最高潮。

4. cede *v.* 放弃；割让（领土）

This island was ceded to Spain more than one hundred years ago.

这个岛屿在一百多年以前就割让给西班牙了。

5. referendum *n.* 公民投票权

The date of "divorce referendum" on May 28 is approaching, and the controversy of whether to introduce divorce legislation peaks.

随着马耳他 28 日全国"离婚公投"的日益临近，关于该国是否引进离婚法的争论也达到顶峰。

6. repository *n.* 贮藏库

This option enables you to specify the list of repositories that users can access.

选择了这一项，您就可以指定用户能够访问的资料库列表。

7. testimonial *n.* 证明；证据

Davis said one segment would feature a testimonial of McCain's years spent as a prisoner of war during the Vietnam War.

戴维斯说，其中一个部分可作为证明麦凯恩在越战期间被囚禁多年的凭据。

扩展阅读

Portrait of Québec

Unique in North America!

Québec boasts a multi-faceted geography and diverse landscapes, vegetation and climate. Four very distinct seasons put their stamp on this vast territory—Canada's largest province.

After 12,000 years of Native American habitation, Jacques Cartier took possession of this land on behalf of the King of France, beginning an era of colonization that would endure until the advent of the industrial age and the challenges of the modern world.

Exuding enthusiasm and determination, Québecers today are creatively and passionately preserving the vitality of their culture within North America!

Québec Over Time

A Brief History

Sent on an expedition by Francis I, King of France, Jacques Cartier arrived at Gaspé in 1534, taking possession of lands that had been inhabited for thousands of years by Amerindians and the Inuit. In 1608, Samuel de Champlain made landfall on the north shore of the St. Lawrence River at a spot that the Aboriginals called Kébec. In 1642, Paul Chomedey de Maisonneuve founded a Catholic mission that he named Ville-Marie and which would become Montréal at the end of the 18th century.

Old Crown, New Crown

New France expanded rapidly between 1660 and 1713. During the Seven Years' War, the army of General Wolfe laid siege to Québec, and the Battle of the Plains of Abraham culminated in the defeat of the French General Montcalm on September 13, 1759. Four years later, with the signing of the Treaty of Paris, the King of France ceded to the British crown "Canada and all its dependencies". This led to significant immigration on the part of English, Irish and Scottish settlers.

In 1791, the Constitutional Act established two provinces in British North America: Upper Canada (Ontario), with an English-speaking majority, and Lower Canada (Québec), which had a French-speaking majority. The Lower Canada Rebellion, in 1837 and 1838, was put down decisively by the British army. In 1867, the British North America Act established a federation of provinces that became known as Canada.

On the Road to Modern Times

Until the early 20th century, Québec's economic life was heavily dependent on agriculture and the forest industry. With subsequent rapid industrialization and urbanization, there was a huge migration of people from the countryside to the cities. The 1960s was marked by the advent of the Quiet Revolution, crystallizing a decade later in debates on the predominant role of the French language. In 1976, the Parti Québécois, led by René Lévesque, was swept to power. In referendums held in 1980, and again in 1995, the people of Québec voted against a proposal for sovereignty-association with the rest of Canada.

Living History

Québec's roads and waterways echo with countless reminders of the often rustic life led by the province's first settlers: ancestral homes, historic churches and chapels, covered bridges, mills, and lighthouses—all repositories for the collective memories of current and future generations.

The addition of the historic district of Québec City to UNESCO's World Heritage List recognizes the efforts made to preserve and enhance the value of one of the most remarkable historical sites on Québec soil. This recognition also encourages initiatives that aim to protect an architectural heritage that dates back more than three centuries and is a testimonial to the day-to-day lives of Québecers in North America.

Family Trees

Numerous visitors from North America and Europe come to Québec to research branches of their family tree, examining records from both the recent and more remote past. A unique opportunity for family reunions and occasionally surprising discoveries!

（资料来源：http://www. webproxy. ca/browse. php? u ＝ 4SQh1aDcMqa％2FYgf2zDomqlEZ1TXlO01rQLyd3tPHxRnt0XQQI2Itw7LXIwvGavZ42KDZ&b＝29.）

Questions

1. In what way is Québec "Unique in North America"?
2. What does the word "Crown" mean in the phrase "Old Crown, New Crown"?
3. What event that marked the turning point of Québec in modern times?

Mesa Verde National Park
梅萨维德国家公园

⇨ 简介

所属国家：美国（America）

入选时间：1978

入选标准：（iii）

Mesa Verde National Park is located in south west Colorado plateau at an altitude of more than 2,600 m. The park occupies 211 square kilometers and features 4,400 ancient sites of homes and villages built on the Mesa top by the ancient Pueblo people, from the 6th to the 12th century. It is best acknowledged for several spectacular cliff dwellings built of stone and comprising more than 100 rooms while Cliff Palace is thought to be the largest cliff dwelling in in Mesa Verde and also in North America. The Spanish term "Mesa Verde" translates into English as "green table".

The exceptional archaeological sites of the Mesa Verde landscape provide eloquent testimony to the ancient cultural traditions of Native American tribes. They represent a graphic link between the past and present ways of life of the Puebloan Peoples of the American south west.

On June 29, 1906, President Roosevelt signed a bill creating Mesa Verde National Park, and it became the first National Park designed to protect the works of humans. Mesa Verde National Park occupies twenty-one thousand hectares of land. However, only about ten percent of the area has been explored. Today, from a distance, Mesa Verde appears as it did centuries ago.

梅萨维德国家公园坐落在科罗拉多州西南部高原，海拔 2600 多米。梅萨维德高原上发现了大量建于公元 6 世纪至 12 世纪的古代印第安人村落遗址，占地面积 211 平方千米。该遗址共有 4400 多处古普韦布洛人修建的岩壁建筑群，其中包括建在梅萨最高处的村落。当地还有许多壮观的悬崖村落，全都用石头砌成，共有超过 100 间房屋，其中悬崖宫是梅萨维德国家公园也是北美最大的悬崖村落。Mesa Verde 为西班牙语，意为"绿色台地"。

　　梅萨维德国家公园景观罕见的考古遗址为古老的印第安部落文化传统提供了令人信服的证据,他们代表着美国西南部普韦布洛印第安民族古往今来生活方式的延续。

　　1906 年 6 月 29 日,罗斯福总统签署了一项法案,建立梅萨维德国家公园,这是第一个旨在保护人类遗迹的国家公园。梅萨维德国家公园占地面积 21000 公顷,然而,已探索面积只有约 10％。今天,从远处看,梅萨维德像数世纪以前一样保有其原貌。

Vocabulary

　　1. panoramas *n.* 全景图

We flew up Taylor Glacier, with a breath-taking series of panoramas up and down the immense river of ice.

　　我们飞跃泰勒冰川,下方冰河如巨龙盘桓,一幅幅惊心动魄的南极全景图闯入眼帘。

　　2. vista *n.* 远景

The release of this stunning vista celebrates the 21st anniversary of the Hubble Space Telescope in orbit.

　　这张震撼人心的远景图是在庆祝哈勃太空望远镜入轨 21 周年时发表的。

　　3. perch *n.* 栖息;就位;位于

The birds like to perch on rooftops, but none have flown away.

　　火鸡喜欢在房顶栖息,但没有一只飞走。

　　4. rock ledge 岩架;岩礁

The park is a beautiful spot that juts into the Mediterranean and is surrounded by rocky ledges that the waves crash up against.

　　这是一个伸入到地中海中的美丽公园,四周的嶙峋岩礁被海浪不断地冲刷着。

　　5. soot *n.* 煤烟,烟灰

The doors and windows were blurred with soot.

　　那些门窗被煤烟熏得很脏。

　　6. vestige *n.* 遗迹

The upright stone in wild place is the vestige of ancient religion.

　　荒原上那直立的石块是古老宗教的遗迹。

　　7. indigenous *adj.* 本土的;土著的,原住民的

Indigenous Australians migrated from Africa to Asia around 70,000 years ago and arrived in Australia around 50,000 years ago.

　　7 万年前,澳洲原住民由非洲迁徙到亚洲,并于 5 万年前抵达澳洲。

扩展阅读

This Is Mesa Verde Country

Welcome to a land rich in culture history and breath-taking panoramas.

Mesa Verde Country—America's premier archaeological wonder.

The Real West—the authentic drives, and horseback mountain trail rides.

Year-Round Fun—hiking, biking, fishing, boating, golf, skiing, snowmobiling.

Elegant Beauty—red-rock canyons, aspen forests, spectacular mesas.

Land of Plenty—farmer markets, you-pick orchards, vineyards, farms and ranches.

Whether your passion is exploring the past, enjoying spectacular wide open vistas, or hiking rugged canyon or mountain trails, you're guaranteed the vacation of a lifetime in Mesa Verde Country.

Mesa Verde Country is a cradle of ancient civilizations. Our landscape—rolling sage plains rimmed by towering mountains and mesas—has inspired and nurtured people for thousands of years. Like a richly textured Navajo rug, the threads of our histories weave together around these canyons and cliffs to create a living history of native people, Spanish explorers, modern ranchers, archaeologists, and outdoor adventurers. Through the centuries, we have wandered the same paths and trails, and we have wondered at the same endless skies.

Join us to explore ancient villages and western towns, browse through trading posts and galleries, experience the agricultural bounty of the area, hike and bike and ski through silent forests and stunning canyons.

Step back in time

To explore Mesa Verde Country is to travel back through time. Great crumbled villages on wide plains and tiny, vulnerable homes perched high on rocky ledges equally stun and intrigue us. Step into a room and smell centuries-old soot. Look out of the window, and appreciate the same views the original architects enjoyed. Small handprints with open fingers seem to wave at us from high canyon walls, spanning the millennia(a thousand years) with our shared human warmth. You want to connect, to wave back.

Throughout Mesa Verde Country questions abound. Who were these people? How did they build such magnificent homes? Why did they leave? Curiosity bubbles forth as purely as canyon waters, fed by the immediacy—the accessibility—of this culture. The vestiges of the past here offer us clues to possible answers and fascinate us with their possibilities, one spectacular site after another.

The culture continues

The spectacular mountains, mesas, and canyons of Mesa Verde Country communities for thousands of years. The Mesa Verde area represents the ancestral homeland of the current-day Pueblo People, whose nations are now located in Arizona and New Mexico. These Pueblo People are descendants that has established itself over many centuries.

Around 1280, the Pueblo People migrated from the Mesa Verde area in Colorado to New Mexico and Arizona. Some groups founded new settlements; others may have dispersed or joined relatives in southern villages. Oral histories recount a series of migrations en route to a new homeland, and many stories relate the reason for leaving this area as simply as "it was time".

Many changes took place from AD together as clans, and some may have adopted new languages. Villages became larger and more enclosed than before. Katsinas became central to Pueblo ceremonial life. Three centuries later, Spanish explorers found the Pueblo People living in the same regions as today—an arc stretching from the Hopi villages in Arizona to the Pueblos along the upper Rio Grande in New Mexico. These people are represented by the Laguna, Nambe, Picuris, Pojoaque, Owingeh, Santa Ana, Santa Clara, Santo Domingo, Taos, Tesuque, Zia, Zuni and The Hopi Tribe.

Today the history and vibrancy of these people lives on in their traditions, dances and artistic expressions. Trading posts and festivals, including the Mesa Verde Country to view traditional dances and experience timeless artistic traditions as well as artists who are diverting from tradition and exploring new media. Another way to experience the life of today's Pueblo People is to visit their tribal cultural centers and museums, or to observe one of their annual Feast Days.

American Indian land in or near Mesa Verde Country today include those of the Ute Mountain Ute Tribe, the Southern Ute Tribe, and the Navajo Nation, who share the landscape of the Ancestral Puebloan People. All of these indigenous people are connected to their past because they consider relationships to their ancestors to be sacred. Please visit all archaeological lands with respect.

（资料来源：http://www. swcolo. org/. ）

Questions

1. What is the difference between the italicized part and the rest of the text in writing style?

2. How do you interpret the meaning of the sentence "You want to connect, to wave back"?

3. Why do we say "The Culture Continues"?

Independence Hall
独立大厅

简介

所属国家：美国（America）

入选时间：1979

入选标准：（vi）

Independence Hall is the centerpiece of Independence National Historical Park in Philadelphia, Pennsylvania, the United States. It is known primarily as the location where both *The Declaration of Independence* (1776) and the framing of *Constitution of the United States of America* (1787) were both debated, drafted and signed in this fine

18th building. The universal principles of freedom and democracy set forth in these documents are of fundamental importance to American history and have also had a profound impact on law-makers and political thinkers around the world. They became the models for similar charters of other nations, and may justly be considered to have heralded the modern era of government.

It was notable among the documents' many innovative features is the separation of powers among the legislative (Congress), executive (President), and judicial branches of government. Also important is that the Congress was split into two houses, the upper house (originally in the upper floor of adjoining Congress Hall), and the lower house (main floor of Congress Hall); the first gave equal power to all the states regardless of size and the second gave proportional representation according to size.

Independence Hall is recognized as the birthplace of the United States of America, a symbol of the independence of the nation and one of America's most important historic landmarks. Independence Hall is one of the major attractions of Independence National Historic Park, which also includes the Liberty Bell Center.

独立大厅位于美国宾夕法尼亚州费城的国家独立历史公园独立大厦内。1776年《独立宣言》和1787年《美利坚合众国宪法》都是在费城这座独立大厅里讨论、起草和签署的，这两份以自由和民主为原则的文件不仅在美国历史上发挥重要作用，同时也对世界各国法律的制定产生了深远影响。这些形成美国民主政治制度的重要文件成为其他国家制定类似宪章的范本，人们有理由认为它们已经预示着现代社会政府时代的到来。

文件中最为著名的革命性特征是"三权分立"制度的确立——立法部门（国会）、行政部门（总统）、司法部门相互独立，另一个重要之处是将议会分为上议院和下议院。由于上议院最初位于议会大厅的上层，而下议院最初位于议会大厅的下层，这就是上下议院之分的由来。前者不分大小赋予每个州平等的权利，后者则是按照各州的大小分配名额。

独立大厅被公认为是美利坚合众国的诞生地、美国独立的象征，也是美国最重要的历史地标之一。独立大厅，包括自由钟中心，是国家独立历史公园一个主要的景点。

Vocabulary

1. articulate *v.* 明确有力地表达

Articulate how the responsible person can resolve your concern, being as specific as possible.

尽可能清楚地表达相关负责人员可以如何解决你的问题。

2. inherent *adj.* 固有的，内在的，与生俱来的，遗传的

In accepting the Nobel Prize, President Obama spoke about the need to build a world in which peace rests on the inherent rights and dignities of every individual.

在接受诺贝尔奖时，奥巴马总统讲到需要建设这样一个世界——让和平建立在每一个人固有的权利和尊严之上。

3. unanimous *adj.* 全体一致的，意见一致的，无异议的

With its combination of wit, timeliness, cutting-edge direction and near-unanimous backing from critics' groups, it was a firm favourite for both Best Picture and Director awards.

该片风格诙谐时尚,影像技术尖端前沿,获得了评论界的一致好评,最佳影片和最佳导演两项大奖似乎如囊中之物。

4. condemnation *n.* 谴责;定罪

We express our firm opposition and strong condemnation to that.

我们对这种行径予以坚决反对和强烈谴责。

5. preamble *n.* 前言,序文,绪论,导言

The preamble stressed that "all persons are equal before the law", and forbade discrimination on the basis of race, color, sex, religion, and other factors.

前言中强调,"法律面前人人平等",禁止基于种族、肤色、性别、宗教以及其他原因的歧视。

6. theology *n.* 神学;宗教体系

For consumers at the bottom of the pyramid, microfinance has become a form of liberation theology.

对在金字塔底层的消费者来说,微观经济已经变成解放神学的一种形式。

7. expositor *n.* 解释者,说明者,评注者

We want to follow the principle of making the Bible its own expositor.

我们应该遵循这个原则:使圣经成为它自己的解释者。

扩展阅读

The Declaration of Independence

The Declaration of Independence is the founding document of the American political tradition. It articulates the fundamental ideas that form the American nation: All men are created free and equal and possess the same inherent, natural rights. Legitimate governments must therefore be based on the consent of the governed and must exist "to secure these rights".

As a practical matter, *The Declaration of Independence* announced to the world the unanimous decision of the thirteen American colonies to separate themselves from Great Britain. But its true revolutionary significance—then as well as now—is the declaration of a new basis of political legitimacy in the sovereignty of the people. The Americans' final appeal was not to any man-made decree or evolving spirit but to rights inherently possessed by all men. These rights are found in eternal "Laws of Nature and of Nature's God". As such, the *Declaration's* meaning transcends the particulars of time and circumstances.

The circumstances of the *Declaration's* writing make us appreciate its exceptionalist claims even more. The war against Britain had been raging for more than two years when the Continental Congress, following a resolution of Richard Henry Lee on June 7, 1776, appointed a committee to explore the independence of the colonies from Great

Britain. John Adams, Benjamin Franklin, Roger Sherman, and Robert Livingston turned to their colleague Thomas Jefferson to draft a formal declaration which they then submitted, with few corrections, to Congress. On July 2 Congress voted for independence and proceeded to debate the wording of the *Declaration*, which was, with the notable deletion of Jefferson's vehement condemnation of slavery, unanimously approved on the evening of July 4. Every Fourth of July, America celebrates not the actual act of independence (proclaimed on July 2) but rather the public proclamation of the principles behind the act.

The *Declaration* has three parts—the famous Preamble, a list of charges against King George III, and a conclusion. The Preamble summarizes the fundamental principles of American self-government. The list of charges against the king presents examples of the violation of those principles. The stirring conclusion calls for duty, action, and sacrifice.

Almost fifty years later, Jefferson described the *Declaration* as "an expression of the American mind… All its authority rests… on the harmonizing sentiments of the day…" The *Declaration* weaves together philosophy, theology, and political history, both the American mind and American experience. A secular document, the *Declaration* nonetheless needs religion for its authority. Thus, God is mentioned or referred to four times, in three capacities: Legislator (Laws of Nature and of Nature's God), Creator (or executive), Supreme Judge of the world, and Guardian (divine Providence).

The first of the four organic laws of the United States, the *Declaration* may lack legal force but remains nonetheless the source of all legitimate political authority. No wonder the *Declaration's* greatest expositor, Abraham Lincoln, referred to it as more than "a merely revolutionary document". For the first time a nation constituted itself on what it has in common with all other people throughout geographic place and history and thus gave hope and inspiration to the whole world. The *Declaration* created America and with it a "new order of the ages(novus ordo seclorum)" in the history of human self-government.

（资料来源：http://www. heritage. org/initiatives/first-principles/primary-sources/the-declaration-of-independence. ）

Questions

1. What are the fundamental ideas of *The Declaration of Independence*?

2. What is the unanimous decision that *The Declaration of Independence* announced to the world?

3. How did the third president Jefferson comment on the *Declaration* fifty years later?

Statue of Liberty

自由女神像

→ 简介

所属国家：美国（America）

入选时间：1984

入选标准：（i）（vi）

The Statue of Liberty National Monument is located on Liberty Island in the middle of New York Harbor, in Manhattan, New York City. This towering monument to liberty was given to the U. S. as a token of friendship by the French on the centenary of American independence in 1886.

Miss Liberty is tall and heavy coming in at 305 feet, 6 inches high and weighing in at 225 tons. There are seven rays on Liberty's crown, symbolizing the seven seas and seven continents. She holds a torch aloft in her right hand, representing a burning passion for freedom and carries in her left a book of law inscribed "July 4, 1776" (in Roman numerals), which acknowledges and commemorates *The Declaration of Independence*. The broken shackles at the base of Lady Liberty's feet represent freedom from oppression.

This colossal statue is a masterpiece of the human spirit in the production of a technological wonder that brings together art and engineering in a new and powerful way. The Statue of Liberty is one of the most recognized symbols of American freedom, democracy, and justice.

Standing at the entrance to New York Harbor, the Statue has since welcomed millions of immigrants from many countries into the United States for almost 120 years.

自由女神铜像国家纪念碑矗立在美国纽约市曼哈顿区纽约港内的自由岛上。这座象征着自由的高耸的雕塑是法国于 1886 年赠予美国的，以祝贺美国独立 100 周年。

自由女神像高 305 英尺 6 英寸，重 225 吨。女神头戴光芒四射的冠冕，七道尖芒象征世界七大洲。右手高举象征自由的火炬，左手捧着刻有"1776 年 7 月 4 日"字样的法典，象征着《独立宣言》签署日；脚下是打碎的手铐、脚镣和锁链，象征着挣脱压迫的约束，获得自由。

这座巨大的雕像是人类精神的杰作，它的诞生以一种新奇的令人震撼的方式创造了艺术与工程完美结合的科学奇迹。自由女神像是世人公认的美国自由、民主和正义的象征。

近 120 年来，矗立在纽约港入口处的自由女神像表达了美国对来自许多国家数以百万计的移民的欢迎。

Vocabulary

1. splurge *n. /v.* 挥霍

When your income goes up, it's fine to splurge a little.

如果你的收入增加了,当然可以稍微挥霍一下。

2. chaos *n.* 混乱,纷乱

The local government was taking emergency measures to rectify the state of chaos.

地方政府正在采取紧急措施整顿这种混乱局面。

3. hub *n.* 中心

All data passes through this central hub but it provides less than 20% of the total compute capacity.

所有数据都将通过这一中央枢纽,但它只提供总共不到20%的计算能力。

4. vault *n.* [美语](银行等的)保险库;金库

Burglars drilled through the concrete ceiling of the bank vault to reach the coins.

窃贼凿穿了混凝土天花板,直抵贮存钱币的银行金库。

5. din *n.* 喧嚣;喧闹声

The din from the commodity pits on the Chicago exchanges is growing louder.

芝加哥商品交易所商品交易厅的喧嚣声越来越大。

6. Beaux-Arts *n.*【法语】美术;艺术

The Musee des Beaux-Arts (museum of fine arts), was a stylish place to wander among paintings and sculptures.

美术馆,是一个可以徜徉在绘画和雕塑之中的时尚的地方。

7. ferris wheel 摩天轮

Yes, it's a giant ferris wheel, and, yes, it's for tourists—but it's a worth a spin.

就是这个巨大的摩天轮,对所有观光客来讲,去转一圈是非常值得的。

8. photo ops【美语】＝photo opportunity

A valley below the falls has many photo ops, a trail along its southwest side overlooks the Gooseberry River, and at the end of the valley, you reach Lake Superior.

瀑布下方的峡谷中有很多拍摄景点,一条西南走向的小径可以用来俯瞰古兹伯里河流,蜿蜒出谷可以直抵苏必利尔湖。

扩展阅读

New York City's Best Free Landmarks and Attractions

Central Park

Some of New York City's best attractions and landmarks are free to visit. With the cost of hotels, restaurants and more, visiting some free attractions and landmarks will help you stretch your travel budget (& maybe even save something for a splurge-worthy treat!)

With 843 acres of gardens, open spaces, water and pathways, Central Park is a great place to escape from the tall buildings and chaos of New York City streets. Designed by Frederick Law Olmsted and Calvert Vaux, Central Park was the first landscaped public park in the United States and was inspired by public parks in London and Paris.

Of course you can walk around the park, admire its many sculptures and gardens for free, but you might be surprised to discover that the Central Park Conservancy's walking tours are free and offer a great way to get acquainted with Central Park. There are many other ways to enjoy Central Park, including having a picnic and wandering around on your own with the help of a Central Park Map.

The Staten Island Ferry

The commuter ferry that runs from Battery Park to Staten Island may not be fancy, but it offers riders a chance to experience amazing views of Lower Manhattan, the Statue of Liberty, Ellis Island and the New York Harbor for free.

The Staten Island Ferry runs 24 hours a day and each leg of the journey takes about 30 minutes and covers 6.2 miles. Of course, this isn't a "sightseeing cruise" so you'll need to consult your map (or ask a friendly New Yorker) if you want to identify some of the less obvious landmarks.

Grand Central Terminal

First built in 1913, Grand Central Terminal was saved from destruction by New York's landmark laws and vocal New Yorkers, including Jacqueline Kennedy Onassis and Brendan Gill, who wanted to see Grand Central Terminal restored. Extensive efforts to restore and revive this National Historic Landmark lead to its re-dedication on October 1, 1998 when Grand Central Terminal had been restored to its original glory.

Today, Grand Central Terminal is not only a transportation hub for travelers using the subway and Metro-North trains, but it is also a destination in itself. This beautiful example of Beaux-Arts architecture, is home to numerous restaurants, great shopping and even a beautiful cocktail bar, The Campbell Apartment.

The New York Public Library

Free daily tours of the New York Public Library offer visitors a great way to see and explore the Library. This Beaux-Arts building, designed by John M. Carrere and Thomas Hastings, was the largest marble building in the U.S. at the time of its construction in 1911. In addition to beautiful architecture and an impressive book collection, the museum features temporary exhibits on a variety of topics that are also free and open to the public.

Bank of New York

You'll get to see a gold vault, a trading desk, and a multimedia trading exhibit when you tour this neo-Renaissance building erected in 1924. The tour offers a great introduction to what the Federal Reserve does and the role it plays in the economy.

If you want to see the gold vault, you'll have to reserve a guided tour in advance, but you can visit the bank's museum and its two self-guided exhibits without taking a tour. Both the tour and museum exhibits are free and open Monday through Friday (except bank holidays when they are closed).

Times Square

Over 39 million people visit Times Square each year, some to attend the area's many Broadway shows, some to shop or dine, and all to experience the glowing lights and energy of this famed area. The best time to experience Times Square is after sunset when the glowing lights and din are at their most impressive.

In recent years they have closed off many areas to cars, giving pedestrians much greater freedom in the neighborhood. The streets can be pretty crowded, so keep an eye on your belongings and travel companions. The area is filled with chain stores and restaurants, but most have something special to offer visitors at their Times Square location—for example Toys "Я" Us has a ferris wheel inside, many interactive experiences and numerous photo ops.

（资料来源：http://gonyc. about. com/od/bestofnewyorkcity/ss/New-York-Citys-Best-Free-Landmarks-And-Attractions. htm. ）

Questions

1. Among all the famous landmarks in New Yok City, which is the first landscaped public park in the Unite States? How did it come into being?

2. What is so special about the Bank of New York building?

3. What attracts people all over the world come to visit Times Square again and again?

第二节　北美洲的世界自然遗产

Yellowstone National Park
黄石国家公园

🔈 **简介**

所属国家：美国（America）

入选时间：1978

入选标准：(vii)(viii)(ix)(x)

Yellowstone National Park is the world's first national park and it's also one of the most spectacular parks. Yellowstone National Park is located in America's Middle West, covering nearly 9,000 km; 96% of the park lies in Wyoming, 3% in Montana and 1% in Idaho. Yellowstone Lake, the Grand Canyon, and waterfalls are notable features on the Yellowstone River, which crosses the park. Yellowstone contains half of all the world's known geothermal features, with more than 10,000 examples. It has many types of ecosystems, with the subalpine forest dominant. It also has the world's largest concentration of geysers (more than 300 geysers, or two thirds of all those on the planet).

Rivers and lakes cover five percent of the land area, with the largest water body being Yellowstone Lake at 87,040 acres (35,220 ha; 136.00 sq mi). Yellowstone Lake is up to 400 feet (120 m) deep and has 110 miles (180 km) of shoreline. At an elevation of 7,733 feet (2,357 m) above sea level, Yellowstone Lake is the largest high altitude lake in North America. Forests comprise 80 percent of the land area of the park; most of the rest is grassland. Yellowstone is known for its wildlife, such as grizzly bears, wolves, bison and wapitis.

黄石国家公园是美国乃至全世界第一个国家公园,也是世界上最壮观的国家公园之一。园中广袤的自然森林占地面积约 9000 平方千米,其中 96% 位于怀俄明州,3% 位于蒙大拿州,还有 1% 位于爱达荷州。黄石河、黄石湖纵贯其中,有峡谷、瀑布、温泉及间歇喷泉等。黄石国家公园拥有已知地球地热资源种类的一半,共有 1 万多处。国家公园还是世界上间歇泉最集中的地方,共有 300 多处间歇泉,约占地球总数的 2/3。

公园内 5% 的面积为河流和湖泊,其中最大的黄石湖有 35220 公顷。黄石湖最深处有 120 米,湖岸线长 180 千米,海拔高度约为 2357 米,是整个北美高海拔地区最大的湖。公园中 80% 的陆地面积是森林,其余大部分是草原。黄石国家公园建于 1872 年,它也因为其生物多样性而闻名于世,其中包括灰熊、狼、野牛和麋鹿等。

Vocabulary

1. -clad *adj.* (in compounds) ……覆盖的
snow-clad hills 白雪皑皑的山峦
2. magma *n.* 岩浆
All magma consists basically of a variety of silicate minerals.
所有的岩浆基本上都由各种硅酸盐矿物质构成。
3. geyser *n.* 间歇喷泉
Minerals, algae, and cyanobacteria give this geyser in Nevada's Black Rock Desert its brilliant colors.
矿物质、水藻和蓝绿色细菌使内华达黑石沙漠中的这些间歇喷泉色彩绚丽斑斓。
4. scalding *adj.* 滚烫的,灼热的
The scalding water burst forth from the eyes.
滚烫的泪水夺眶而出。
5. algae *n.* [植]水藻;藻类
The only plants to be found in Antarctica are algae, mosses, and lichens.
在南极洲发现的植物只有藻类、苔藓和地衣。
6. vie *vi.* 竞争
Law firms vie with each other to hire the best students.
律师事务所竞相聘用最优秀的学生。

7. iridescent *adj.* 彩虹色的

A close-up of a mounted blue morpho butterfly shows its unique iridescent sheen.

特写镜头拍摄的蓝色大闪蝶显示了其独特的梦幻色彩。

扩展阅读

Yellowstone National Park

In the northwest corner of Wyoming lies Yellowstone National Park, the oldest, largest and most popular National Park in the continental United States. Few places on earth offer so much scenic and scientific interest in one area. Yellowstone is in the heart of the Rockies, a land of pine-clad mountains and broad, grassy valleys. The countryside is laced with lakes and streams of exquisite beauty.

Madison River

The popular West Entrance to Yellowstone parallels the winding Madison River, a route followed by the earliest pioneers into the park. It leads to the Grand Loop Road that will take you to all of the park's major features.

In addition to superb mountain scenery, the park is one of the world's principle wildlife preserves. Many visitors eagerly await the opportunity to photograph wildlife in its native environment. Yellowstone is a photographers' paradise.

Firehole Falls

Traveling south on the Grand Loop Road towards Old Faithful, a side road leads to Firehole River Cascades. Here water pours through an 800-foot canyon, climaxing at roaring Firehole Falls.

The Firehole River is our introduction to the most famous and certainly the most popular section in all of Yellowstone. Our route takes us through a series of thermal basins, beginning with Lower Geyser Basin. The road brings us close to the popular Fountain Paint Pots, pools of colorful, hot mud that bubble and sputter like pudding boiling in a pan. The mud is a mixture of silica, clay and water.

Fountain Paint Pots

Bubbles are formed by super-heated gases rising from magma and molten rock deep within the earth. A stroll around Fountain Paint Pots reveals a variety of small geysers, pools and springs.

Grand Prismatic Spring

Midway, Biscuit and Black Sand basins lie adjacent to each other with the Firehole River serving as a common boundary. Runoff from many of the geysers in these basins drains into the nearby river. Each year Excelsior Geyser alone pours an incredible 5 million gallons of scalding water into the river.

At Midway Basin, Grand Prismatic Spring is the most spectacular feature. From above, its splendid array of deep colors is stunningly visible. At 370 feet in diameter, it is believed to be the largest spring in Yellowstone. Clearly marked boardwalks and paved trails offer visitors a safe and exciting means of exploring the thermal features of Midway Basin.

Cliff Geyser

In the Black Sand Geyser Basin, Cliff Geyser is interesting because it sits on the edge of Iron Spring Creek. Its eruptions can go as high as 50 feet.

Rainbow Pool

Rainbow Pool is a large hot spring with an intensely blue centre. The water at the pool's edge is cooled sufficiently to permit the growth of algae, producing a rainbow of colors. Nearby Sunset Lake vies with Rainbow Pool for beauty and iridescent color.

To many visitors, Upper Basin, the Old Faithful area, is the heart and sole of Yellowstone Park. Unique Old Faithful Inn is one of America's finest lodges. Today, its immense rustic lobby and huge stone fireplace yet posses the grandeur of earlier times.

Old Faithful Geyser

No visit to Yellowstone is complete without witnessing one or more eruptions of Old Faithful Geyser. This iconic geyser is the most famous in the world and is one of America's greatest natural wonders. There are geysers that erupt higher and for longer periods of time, but rarely is the tremendous power of nature so inseparably combined with Old Faithful's innate beauty. This superb spectacle, once you've actually witnessed it in person, will stay in your memory forever.

（资料来源：http://www. webproxy. ca/browse. php? u ＝ 4SQh27LHcKunfxn21y15sVEPnw％3D％3D&b＝29.）

Questions

1. What is Yellowstone National Park famous for?
2. Please briefly describe one of the beautiful sceneries that impresses you most.
3. State the characteristics of Firehole Falls in your own words.

Great Smoky Mountains National Park
大烟雾山国家公园

🔖 简介

所属国家：美国（America）

入选时间：1983

入选标准：（vii）（viii）（ix）（x）

Great Smoky Mountains National Park straddles the ridgeline of the Great Smoky Mountains, part of the Blue Ridge Mountains, which are a division of the larger Appalachian Mountain chain. Encompassing over 500,000 acres of forest land, Great

Smoky Mountains National Park is situated in western North Carolina and eastern Tennessee. Stretching over more than 200,000 ha, this exceptionally beautiful park is home to more than 3,500 plant species, including almost as many trees (130 natural species) as in all of Europe. Many endangered animal species are also found there, including what is probably the greatest variety of salamanders in the world. Since the park is relatively untouched, it gives an idea of temperate flora before the influence of humankind.

The existence of the Great Smoky Mountains is of 1 billion years of history, and is one of the oldest mountains in the world. The National Park is of world importance as an example of temperate deciduous hardwood forest and thus an outstanding example of the diverse Arcto-Tertiary geoflora era, having a high number of temperate species with some rich mixed stands.

Great Smoky Mountains National Park is of exceptional natural beauty with scenic vistas of characteristic mist-shrouded (smoky) mountains, vast stretches of virgin timber, and awesome waterfalls, cool mountain rivers, floral and fauna. The autumn is extremely gorgeous as the tree leaves change to brilliant colors of red, orange, and gold. Autumn's pageantry of colors in the Smoky Mountains usually peaks in mid-October.

大烟雾山国家公园位于美国东部的阿巴拉契亚山系南端的蓝岭山脉上,从行政区位来说,属于北卡罗来纳州西部和田纳西州南部交界处。占地20万公顷,园内生长有超过3500种植物,其中树木约130种,这个数目与整个欧洲的树木种类基本持平。在大烟雾山国家公园中还有许多种濒危动物,其中蝾螈的种类可能是世界上最多的。由于大烟雾山国家公园基本未受到人类破坏,所以在这里可以看到未受人类影响的温带植物生长情况。

大烟雾山脉已存在10亿年了,是世界上最古老的山脉之一。大烟雾山国家公园拥有大量的温带物种和一些丰富的混合林,作为温带落叶阔叶林的典范和北极第三纪古植物区系多样化时期的范例,它的重要性不言而喻。

大烟雾山国家公园的自然美景,具有其罕见的景观特征:云雾缭绕的山脉,一望无垠的原始森林,令人震撼的瀑布群,花卉和动物,以及清冽的山间溪流。大烟雾山国家公园的秋天是异常绚丽多彩的,树叶颜色变成了灿烂的红色、橙色和金色,通常在10月中旬,大烟雾山五彩缤纷的秋日盛典达到巅峰时期。

Vocabulary

1. flair *n.* 眼光;天分;鉴别力

His business skill complements her flair for design.

他的经营技巧和她的设计才能相辅相成。

2. tram *n.* 缆车;电车

How often does the tram run?

这电车多久一班?

3. barbeque *n.* 户外烧烤

A barbeque is organized on an uninhabited island once a week.

一周组织一次荒岛野炊。

4. grill *n.* 烤架

She carried a piping hot grill of oysters and bacon.

她端出一盘滚烫的烤牡蛎和咸肉。

5. bagpipe *n.* 风笛

This is a kind of Scottish bagpipe.

这是一种苏格兰风笛。

6. collie *n.* 苏格兰长毛牧羊犬

On the left is a profile of a collie.

左边是一只苏格兰长毛牧羊犬的轮廓。

7. haggis *n.* 将羊的心、肺、肝等内脏和燕麦粉煮成的食物

Would you like some more haggis?

再来点苏格兰羊杂碎吧？

扩展阅读

Springfest in Great Smoky Mountains National Park

During the three-month Springfest celebration that begins in March and continues through the second week in June, visitors witness the Smoky Mountain area's transformation into spring when city streets overflow with baskets of beautiful blooming flowers and plants. Pansies, daffodils, tulips, mandevillas, bougainvilleas, lantanas, scaveolas and wave petunias are among the many varieties of flowers seen throughout the towns surrounding the national park.

Live entertainment can be found along sidewalks in downtown Gatlinburg, adding a festive flair to the time-honored Downtown Parkway stroll.

Members of Great Smoky Arts & Crafts Community display unique handcrafted wares as they gather at the Gatlinburg Convention Center to host their annual Easter Arts & Crafts show on the Easter weekend. On Easter morning, join in the local tradition and attend Ober Gatlinburg's Annual Easter Sunrise Service enhanced by the beauty of the Smokies. Free tram rides to the mountain top begin at 5:45 a. m. and continue in 15 minute intervals until the service begins. Complimentary parking at the resort will be provided for those who prefer to drive. A breakfast buffet will be waiting and available at the Ober Gatlinburg Restaurant from 7 a. m. until 11 a. m.

The smell of hickory-smoked barbeque fills the air as folks roll up sleeves and dive in to sample their secret sauces on delectable ribs and wings from more than 30 vendors from all over the Southeast in April at Gatlinburg's Ribfest & Wings. This festive street party features live blues entertainment, lots of fun and barbeque ribs and wings on the open grill just for your tasting.

The Annual Spring Wildflower Pilgrimage is another great event, especially for hikers and nature lovers who love to see delicate wildflowers in bloom. Hosted by Great Smoky Mountains National Park, University of Tennessee Botany Department and Gatlinburg Garden Club, this seven-day program offers more than 150 different hiking tours of trails ranging from easy to strenuous, exhibitions, demonstrations, classroom lectures and delightful motor excursions into the wonderful season of spring in the Smokies.

Spring events continue with Gatlinburg's Scottish Festival & Games Grand Parade in May in downtown Gatlinburg. All Scots are invited to march or ride in the parade. Mills Park in Gatlinburg becomes competitive ground for the Annual Scottish Festival & Games where clans meet and feature Highland athletics, bagpipe competitions, highland dancing, border collie demonstrations, haggis hurling, entertainment and whiskey tasting, along with food and merchandise vendors.

Gatlinburg's Fine Arts Festival, a family-oriented fine arts festival featuring juried artists from around the country, delicious cuisine and music takes place on Aquarium Plaza and River Road usually the third Saturday and Sunday in May. Proceeds benefit Arrowmont School of Art and Sevier County Arts Council.

In June, enjoy fun-filled days of bluegrass and genuine mountain music with crafters and demonstrations at the kick-off of Gatlinburg's MountainFest—A Celebration of Our Heritage. Local crafters will be demonstrating their skills passed down from generation to generation. Enjoy local foods such as beans and cornbread, fried potatoes and onions and fried green tomatoes by the areas favorite restaurants. Get a taste of some of the areas talent with the Mountain Strings Competition. Fiddles, banjos, and guitar players are invited to compete for awards and cash prizes.

Beginning in early June and continuing through mid-August during Mountain Fest is Gatlinburg's Smoky Mountain Tunes and Tales. You can experience numerous entertainment mini-performances every evening featuring costumed musical performers, storytellers and artisans portraying various time periods from the 1800s to today as you stroll in downtown Gatlinburg. Nearly a dozen acts involve the audience as they each perform in simultaneous ten-minute performances throughout the night.

（资料来源：http://www.mountains.org/.）

Questions

1. What is Yellowstone National Park famous for?
2. Please briefly describe one of the beautiful sceneries that impresses you most.
3. State the characteristics of Firehole Fall in your own words.

Grand Canyon National Park
大峡谷国家公园

⇨ 简介

所属国家：美国（America）

入选时间：1979

入选标准：（vii）（viii）（ix）（x）

Created on 26 February 1919, Grand Canyon National Park is located in the northwest of Arizona, southwest of the United States. Carved out by the Colorado River, the Grand Canyon is the most spectacular gorge and considered one of the Seven Natural Wonders of the World. With its length of 277 miles (446 km), width of 18 miles (29 km) and depth of over a mile (nearly 1,500 m deep), it cuts across the Grand Canyon National Park. The park covers 1,217,262 acres (1,902 sq mi; 4,926 km^2) of unincorporated area of the Kaibab Plateau, part of the larger Colorado Plateau. Its horizontal strata retrace the geological history of the past 2 billion years. There are also prehistoric traces of human adaptation to a particularly harsh environment.

The canyon is famous for its vastness, richness and colorfulness. The most important reason it is included in the World Heritage List also lies in its geological significance: well preserved and fully exposed rock stratum, from the bottom up neatly lined with rocks from the proterozoic to the Cenozoic of different geological eras in North America, containing rich representative fossils. It is known as "a live geologic history textbook", which recorded the vicissitudes of life changes and biological evolution process of the North American continent.

大峡谷国家公园成立于 1919 年 2 月 26 日,是美国西南部的国家公园,位于美国亚利桑那州的西北角。著名的科罗拉多大峡谷横贯整个公园。大峡谷可分为南缘和北缘,宽度从最窄的 6 千米到 25 千米,深约 1500 米,总长 446 千米,由科罗拉多河长年侵蚀而成,是世界上最为壮观的峡谷,亦是世界七大自然奇景之一。整个国家公园总面积为 1217262 英亩。大峡谷国家公园属于高原地貌,大峡谷的水平层次结构展示了 20 亿年来地球的地质变迁,同时它也保留了大量人类适应当时恶劣环境的遗迹。

科罗拉多大峡谷以其规模巨大、丰富多彩而著称。它被列入《世界遗产名录》的最重要原因,还在于其地质学意义:保存完好并充分暴露的岩层,从谷底向上整齐地排列着北美大陆从元古代到新生代不同地质时期的岩石,并含有丰富的具有代表性的生物化石,俨然是一部"活的地质史教科书",它记录了北美大陆的沧桑巨变和生物演化进程。

Vocabulary

1. asbestos *n.* 石棉

Asbestos fibers remain trapped in your lungs for life.

石棉纤维将终生滞留在肺脏。

2. grueling *adj.* 繁重而累人的，使人精疲力尽的

Hikers begin the long, grueling trek up Kilimanjaro, Africa's highest peak.

旅行者们向着非洲的最高峰——乞力马扎罗山开始了漫长的跋涉。

3. spruce *n.* 针枞，云杉

The pine, cedar and spruce are evergreens.

松树、雪松、云杉都是常青树。

4. recess *n.* (山脉，海岸等的)凹处；深处

He approached imperceptibly the gloomy recess.

他不知不觉地走到了幽暗的山坳。

5. foliage *n.* (集合名词)(树的)叶子

The ancient tree blots out the sky and covers the sun with luxuriant foliage.

这棵古树，枝繁叶茂，遮天蔽日。

6. sparse *adj.* 稀疏的

The beautiful sparse shadows of the arching willows were like a picture etched on the lotus leaves.

柳树弯弯稀疏的倩影，好似一幅镌刻在荷叶上的图画。

7. shale *n.* 页岩，泥板岩

Thin layers of sandy shale, and carbonaceous fragments are locally present.

局部出现砂质页岩薄层和碳质碎屑。

扩展阅读

The Unmatched Grand Canyon

Grand Canyon is unmatched throughout the world for the vistas it offers to visitors on the rim. It is not the deepest canyon in the world. Both the Barranca del Cobre in northern Mexico and Hell's Canyon in Idaho are deeper. But Grand Canyon is known for its overwhelming size and its intricate and colorful landscape. Geologically it is significant because of the thick sequence of ancient rocks that are beautifully preserved and exposed in the walls of the canyon. These rock layers record much of the early geologic history of the North American continent. Grand Canyon is also one of the most spectacular examples of erosion in the world.

Grand Canyon was largely unknown until after the Civil War. In 1869, Major John Wesley Powell, a one-armed Civil War veteran with a thirst for science and adventure, made a pioneering journey through the canyon on the Colorado River. He accomplished this with nine men in four small wooden boats. Though only six men completed the journey, his party was, as far as we know, the first ever to make such a trip.

In the late 19th century there was interest in the region because of its promise of mineral resources, mainly copper and asbestos. The first pioneer settlements along the rim came in the 1880s. Early residents soon discovered that tourism was destined to be more profitable than mining, and by the turn of the century Grand Canyon was a well known tourist destination. Many of the early tourist accommodations were not much different from the mining camps from which they developed. Most visitors made the grueling trip from nearby towns to the South Rim by stagecoach.

In 1901 the railroad was extended from Williams, Arizona to the South Rim, and the development of formal tourist facilities increased dramatically. By 1905 the El Tovar Hotel stood where it does today, a world class hotel on the canyon's edge. The Fred Harvey Company, known throughout the west for hospitality and fine food, continued to develop facilities at Grand Canyon, including Phantom Ranch, built in the Inner Canyon in 1922.

Although first afforded Federal protection in 1893 as a Forest Reserve and later as a National Monument, Grand Canyon did not achieve national park status until 1919, three years after the creation of the National Park Service. Today Grand Canyon National Park receives about five million visitors each year, a far cry from the annual visitation of 44,173 in 1919.

No dams exist within Grand Canyon National Park, although dams bordering the park have a profound effect on the canyon. At the upper end of the canyon, 15 miles / 24 km above Lees Ferry, is Lake Powell, formed by the waters behind Glen Canyon Dam. This dam was completed in 1963. At the lower end of the canyon is Lake Mead, formed by the waters behind Hoover Dam. This dam was completed in 1936.

The controlled release of water from Glen Canyon Dam at the upstream end affects the water that flows through Grand Canyon. Waters from Lake Mead flood the lower 40 miles / 64 km of Grand Canyon when the lake is full.

The Colorado River rushes at the bottom of the canyons, about 1,850 feet above sea level. The sides of the canyons are made of rocks, cliffs, ridges, hills and valleys of every form. Many of the ridges have weather carved lines which make them resemble Chinese temples. Thick forests of blue spruce, fir, oaks as well as Ponderosa pines cover the canyon rim. Deep in the canyon's recesses, the foliage grows sparse and shorter. Pinon pines and juniper growing along the cliffs give way to dry desert scrub on the canyon floor.

The north rim of the Grand Canyon rises about 1,200 feet higher that the south rim. The highest points on the rim are about 9,000 feet above sea level.

Most of the 1,904 square miles of the park are maintained as wilderness. There are three distinct sections of the park; the South Rim, the North Rim and the Inner Canyon. Each section has a different climate as well as different vegetation and different experiences.

The North Rim is the coldest and the wettest. It receives up to 26 inches of precipitation a year. The South Rim only receives around 16 inches of precipitation a year. The Inner Canyon is the closest to a desert as the lower you descend，the hotter and drier it becomes. The floor of the canyon，approximately a mile below the North Rim，is about 35℃ hotter than the temperatures above.

The colorful canyon rocks were formed millions of years ago. Their colors change with the changing light of the sun. Many layers of rock have been bared by the constant cutting force of the rushing river. The first layer of rock through which the Colorado River now cuts is black in color and is called Archean. The second layer，called Algonkian，has a brilliant red color. The next layer is a lavender-brown color and is known as Tapeats sandstone. The forth layer，the Devonian layer，consists of small deposits of lavender stone. Above this，the thick Redwall curves along the canyon. Above the Redwall lies 800 feet of red sandstone called the Supai formation. The Hermit shale，another layer of red rock covers this.

On top of the Hermit shale rests the sand colored Coconino sandstone，a pale bank that lies 350 feet below the rim of the canyon. The top layer of the canyon consists of cream and gray colored Kaibab limestone. This limestone forms a rim known as the Kaibab Plateau on the north side of the canyon，and as the Coconino Plateau on the south.

Scientists still haven't agreed on the how's and why's of the creation of the Grand Canyon，but there is always one constant，the Colorado River. It always was and always will be the catalyst for change in the canyon.

（资料来源：http://www. nps. gov/grca/index. htm. ）

Questions

1. What is so special about the Grand Canyon compared to other canyons in Mexico and Idaho?

2. How many distinct sections are there of Grand Canyon National Park，what are they?

3. What are the characteristics of the canyon rocks in Grand Canyon National Park?

Yosemite National Park
约塞米蒂国家公园

简介

所属国家：美国（America）

入选时间：1984

入选标准：（vii）（viii）

Yosemite National Park lies in the central eastern portion of California，United States. The park covers an area of 1,100 square miles（3,080. 74 km²）and reaches across the western slopes of the Sierra Nevada mountain chain. Yosemite National Park vividly illustrates the effects of glacial erosion of granitic bedrock, creating geologic features that are unique in the world. Repeated glaciations over millions of years have resulted in a concentration of distinctive landscape features: with its 'hanging' valleys, many waterfalls, cirque lakes, polished domes, moraines and U-shaped valleys, it provides an excellent overview of all kinds of granite relief fashioned by glaciation. The Yosemite Valley, the spectacular glaciated topography, is a 914-meter (1/2 mile) deep, glacier-carved cleft with massive sheer granite walls. These geologic features offer a scenic backdrop for mountain meadows and giant sequoia groves, forming a diverse landscape of exceptional natural and scenic beauty.

Almost 95% of the park is designated wilderness. At 600—4,000 m, a great variety of flora and fauna can also be found here.

约塞米蒂国家公园位于美国加利福尼亚州中东部。公园总占地面积约 1100 平方英里，穿越内华达山脉西侧山坡。约塞米蒂国家公园生动地说明了冰川对花岗岩基岩的侵蚀作用，它创造了世界上独一无二的地貌特征。数百万年冰川循环往复的运动导致了今天这一珍奇景观特色的集中体现：呈现在世人面前的是因冰川作用而形成的大量罕见的花岗岩形态，包括"悬空"山谷、瀑布群、冰斗湖、冰穹丘、冰碛及 U 形山谷。约塞米蒂山谷是壮观的冰川地貌，深 914 米，冰川穿凿的大裂谷上布满了无数的花岗岩峭壁。独特的地貌与秀丽的高山草甸、巨大的红杉林相映成辉，构成一幅奇异的、绚丽多姿的大自然的优美画卷。

公园内超过 95% 的土地被指定为原生地域。在约塞米蒂国家公园海拔 600 米至 4000 米的区域内，还可以找到种类繁多的动植物。

Vocabulary

1. battalion *n.* 营（军队单位）；军队；大批

Their mission will be to support combat operations as an artillery battalion.

他们的任务是支援一个炮兵营的作战。

2. grandeur *n.* 伟大；宏伟，壮观；富丽堂皇

I've seen the grandeur of alps.

我曾见识过阿尔卑斯山的壮丽景色。

3. homesteader *n.* 农场所有权者，自耕农

Every farmer, every homesteader in an apple climate, seems to have planted an apple tree.

每一位农民，每一位农场主，似乎都要在气候适宜的时候种一棵苹果树。

4. stagecoach *n.* 公共马车；驿站马车

The stagecoach finally arrived there before sunrise.

日出前这辆公共马车终于到达了那里。

5. grant *n.* 同意；给予

A patent is a governmental grant of an exclusive monopoly as an incentive and a reward for a new invention.

专利权是政府对一项新发明授予的独占权利，以给予该发明以鼓励和奖励。

6. devastating *adj.* 毁灭性的;令人震惊的;强有力的

A smouldering cigarette can kindle a devastating bushfire.

闷燃着的香烟会引起毁灭性的林区大火。

7. grazing *n.* 牧场;草场

Sheep are grazing in the lush green pastures.

羊在青翠葱绿的牧场上吃草。

扩展阅读

Yosemite National Park Cultural History

Yosemite has a long and diverse cultural history that helped to shape the region, country, and even the world.

The History of Yosemite's First People

Yosemite's first residents were Native Americans who may have first inhabited the region as many as 10,000 years ago. The area's most recent tribe (comprised mostly of Miwok, but also Paiute and others) named Yosemite Valley "Ahwahnee" or "place of the gaping mouth", and thus they called themselves the Ahwahneechee. These Native Americans had a rich culture and were frequent traders with tribes from the eastern side of the Sierra.

Pioneers, Conflict, and Yosemite

The discovery of gold in California's foothills brought the first non-native settlers to Yosemite Valley around 1850. Unfortunately, conflict developed between the newcomers and the native population over resources. In 1851, a battalion of troops entered Yosemite during a mission to search for Native Americans and end the conflict. The doctor of the expedition, Lafayette Bunnell, returned with stories of Yosemite Valley's beauty and grandeur, and soon word spread of this inspiring place.

Tourists and Homesteaders of Yosemite's History

In 1855, the first tourists visited Yosemite. As more visitors came to Yosemite via horseback and stagecoach, entrepreneurs saw an opportunity to provide goods and services in this remote destination. Soon, lodging and homes were built and meadows became home to livestock and orchards. By 1864, there were residents living in Yosemite Valley all year long.

Yosemite Grant

Also around 1855, a homesteader in southern Yosemite, came across the Mariposa Grove of Giant Sequoias. The homesteader, Galen Clark, was so impressed with the trees, that he would start a fight to preserve them from logging. Soon after, that fight would include preserving Yosemite Valley. After gathering support from photographer Carlton Watkins, and U. S. Senator John Conness, the *Yosemite Grant* was drafted and submitted to Congress. In 1864, during the heat of the Civil War, Abraham Lincoln signed the Yosemite Grant that protected Yosemite Valley and the Mariposa Grove of Giant Sequoias as the first territory ever set aside by Congress for public use and preservation (although in its initial years it was a California State Park).

Yosemite National Park—Beginnings

In 1889, John Muir, America's most famous and influential naturalist and conservationist, and Robert Underwood Johnson, editor of Century Magazine, had growing concerns about the devastating effects of sheep grazing in the high country. They launched a successful campaign to persuade Congress to set aside this area as a national park in 1890. On October 1, 1890, the U. S. Congress set aside more than 1,500 square miles of reserved forest lands, soon to be known as Yosemite National Park.

Yosemite National Park—The Early Years

In the early 1900s, two dates hold significance for Yosemite. First, in 1906, Yosemite National Park would incorporate the "Yosemite Grant" into its borders. Second, after years of management of our National Parks by the United States Cavalry, in 1916 the newly created National Park Service would take over the role. Today, the NPS oversees over 380 national treasures across the country, including Yosemite.

Yosemite National Park—Today

Yosemite continues to hold the rank as one of the "crown jewels" of the national parks. Yosemite now gets over 3.5 million visitors a year, offering a challenge never experienced in the region's early years—how to protect one of the world's scenic treasures, but also allow for the enjoyment and inspiration of millions of visitors. Delaware North Companies Parks and Resorts proudly embraces our role in helping to meet this challenge head on.

For more information about Yosemite History, please go to the Visitor Center, Yosemite Museum, as well as our numerous bookstores in the park during your stay.

（资料来源：http://www. yosemitepark. com/cultural-history. aspx. ）

Questions

1. What brought the first non-native settlers to California?

2. When and how did the first tourists visit Yosemite?

3. Who signed the *Yosemite Grant* that protected Yosemite Valley and the Mariposa Grove of Giant Sequoias and when was it signed?

Canadian Rocky Mountain Parks
加拿大落基山公园

▷ **简介**

所属国家：加拿大（Canada）

入选时间：1984

入选标准：（vii）（viii）

Renowned for its natural beauty and biological diversity, the Canadian Rocky Mountain Parks is located in the Canadian Rockies, exemplifying the outstanding physical features of the Rocky Mountain Biogeographical Province, classic illustrations of glacial geological processes. The contiguous national parks of Banff, Jasper, Kootenay and Yoho, as well as the Mount Robson, Mount Assiniboine and Hamber provincial parks, studded with the habitats of rare and endangered species and its natural landforms such as mountain peaks, canyons, limestone caves, as well as glaciers, lakes, waterfalls, hot springs and the headwaters of major North American river systems, form a striking mountain landscape. The the unique Burgess Shale fossil site, well known for its fossil remains of soft-bodied marine animals, is also found there.

Banff National Park is Canada's oldest national park, established in 1885. The park encompasses of mountainous terrain, with numerous glaciers and ice fields, dense coniferous forest, and alpine landscapes. The Icefields Parkway extends from Lake Louise, connecting to Jasper National Park in the north. Provincial forests and Yoho National Park are neighbours to the west.

Jasper National Park is the largest national park in the Canadian Rockies including the glaciers of the Columbia Icefield, hot springs, lakes, waterfalls and mountains. Wildlife in the park includes elk, caribou, moose, mule deer, white-tailed deer, mountain goats, bighorn sheep, grizzly bears, black bears, coyotes, beavers, Rocky Mountain pikas, hoary marmots, grey wolves, mountain lions, and wolverines.

Kootenay National Park is located in southeastern British Columbia Canada, The park takes its name from the Kootenay River, one of the two major rivers which flow through the park, the other being the Vermillion River. While the Vermillion River is completely contained within the park, the Kootenay River has its headwaters just outside of the park boundary, flowing through the park into the Rocky Mountain Trench, eventually joining the Columbia River.

Yoho National Park is located along the western slope of the Continental Divide in southeastern British Columbia, covering 1,313 km² and it is the smallest of the four contiguous national parks.

以自然美景和生物多样性而闻名遐迩的加拿大落基山公园坐落于加拿大段落基山脉，彰显了洛基山生物地理学上优异的物理特性，是冰川地质变迁的经典例证。逶迤相连的班夫、贾斯珀、库特奈和约虎国家公园，以及罗布森山、阿西尼博因山和汉伯省级公园构成了一道亮丽的高山风景线，那里栖息着各种珍稀濒危的物种，有丰富多变的自然地形地貌，如山峰、峡谷、石灰石洞穴，还有冰河、湖泊、瀑布、温泉及北美各大水系的众多源头。独特的因海洋软体动物化石而闻名于世的伯吉斯谢尔化石遗址也隐匿其中。

班夫国家公园建于1885年，是加拿大历史最悠久的国家公园，遍布冰川、冰原、松林和高山。冰原公路从路易斯湖开始，一直连接到北部的贾斯珀国家公园。西面是省级森林,与幽鹤国家公园接壤。

贾斯伯国家公园是加拿大落基山脉最大型的国家公园,有哥伦比亚冰原的冰川、温泉、湖泊、瀑布和山脉,有多种野生动植物生长其中,如北美红鹿、小鹿、山羊、驼鹿、大角野绵羊、亚洲黑熊、美洲黑熊、海狸、落基山鼠兔、土拨鼠和驯鹿。

库特尼国家公园位于加拿大不列颠哥伦比亚的东南部,公园的名字源自库特尼河,该河是穿过公园的两条河流之一,另一条为弗米利恩河。库特尼河的上游在公园之外,穿过公园,流到落基山谷,最终流入哥伦比亚河。

幽鹤国家公园坐落于北美洲大陆分水岭的西坡。占地面积 1313 平方千米,是邻近的四个加拿大国家公园中面积最小的一个。

Vocabulary

1. prelude *n.* 序曲,序幕

Some in the media speculated this is a prelude to a presidential run.

一些媒体猜测这是总统竞选的序幕。

2. mogul *n.* 雪坡,雪丘

Whoa! Did you see me catch some air off that mogul?

哇! 你有没有看到我滑过那个雪丘时腾空飞起?

3. trail *n.* 小径

A leisurely walk down this trail will reward the summer visitors with solitude and spectacular scenery.

沿着小径悠闲地散步,避暑游客可尽享幽静和美景。

4. corduroy *adj.* 沼地上用木头铺排成的

corduroy road(road made of tree trunks laid side-by-side across swampy land)

(将树干并排横铺于湿软地面而成的)木排路

5. elevation *n.* 高度,海拔

The house is at an elevation of 2,000 metres.

那幢房子位于海拔两千米的高处。

6. lounge *v.* (酒店、俱乐部或其他公共场所的)休息厅,休息室

The duty free shop is located in the departure lounge.

免税商店设置在出境休息区。

7. terrain *n.* 地带

The terrain changed quickly from arable land to desert.

那个地带很快就从耕地变成了沙漠。

扩展阅读

Olympic Skiing Come and Experience It for Yourself

Come to Calgary on your way to skiing the Canadian Rocky Mountains and you'll discover you can be carving Olympic turns almost immediately.

The city is the gateway to the Canadian Rockies and it boasts two ski and snowboarding facilities with Olympic legacies in less than an hour's drive—actually three Olympic training grounds, if you include cross country skiing.

Olympic Skiing: Nakiska

Nakiska is known as Calgary's closest ski mountain, about a 50-minute drive west of the city into Kananaskis Country, a recreational playground in Alberta. It was home to ski competitions during the 1988 Winter Olympics that were based in Calgary.

Olympic Skiing: Canada Olympic Park

Canada Olympic Park (COP) is right in Calgary and it is a current training ground for World Cup and Olympic athletes as Canada heads toward the 2010 Olympics in Vancouver.

COP has a ski tower used in the 1988 Olympics ski jumping competitions. While you won't be using the COP tower, you can feel the thrill of ski jumping by using the Skyline—North America's fastest zip line. Recreational skiers and snowboarders use COP to train, get in shape and just get out there. Use it as a prelude to the Rockies and it's a quick way to get your snow legs. A new mogul section at the park gives experts a leg-burning playground.

Olympic Skiing: Canmore Nordic Centre Enhanced

If you want to mix up your ski or snowboarding holiday with cross country skiing, the Canmore Nordic Centre was home to competitions at the 1988 Olympics and just hosted a World Cup. The centre remains a training ground and with its close proximity to Calgary—less than an hour's drive away at the recreational mountain town of Canmore—it sits right at the edge of Banff National Park. And it just underwent an almost $26-million makeover with money provided by the Alberta government that extends both the trails and the ski season, while enhancing the day lodge.

Here are overviews of both Nakiska and COP, both of which have reputations as learning hills. You will find challenging areas at each, even if you are an expert skier.

Olympic Skiing: Nakiska's Cruiser Heaven

Nakiska bills itself as the place to learn, and the addition of a new magic carpet at the beginner's area makes learning to ski and snowboard even easier. It's the longest conveyer style lift in Alberta at 350 ft/107 metres long. There is a ski and snowboard school with lessons available for all ages and abilities. This resort is also a place to train for racing. Just drive west of Calgary on the Trans Canada Highway and then south on Highway 40 and you're there.

The resort's ongoing snowmaking enhancements and the addition of a new snowcat ensure that its corduroy runs are enjoyed from December though to spring. Nakiska is scheduled to end the season this year on April 6.

Nakiska has 325 acres of skiable terrain with a summit elevation of 2,260 m/7,415 ft. The longest run is 3.2 km/2 mi. Of the 28 trails, 16% is beginner, 70% is intermediate and 14% is expert. There is a rail park and for Nordic skiing, there are double set trails at Nakiska's base.

"We've had a really great snow year, and with the upgrades to the lounge and the lodge and the snowmaking, we expect another season of great spring skiing," says marketing spokesman Walter Blackstaffe.

The terrain park became a rail park this year with small to large features that provide something for everyone, he says, including the twin tip skiers. "We had our first rail jam in January and it was a huge success."

Family Friendly Layout

Nakiska's layout makes it especially friendly to families. The area is divided by the Bronze, Silver and Gold chairs that take skiers and snowboarders to areas that correspond pretty well to beginner, intermediate and advanced levels, respectively. And all runs lead back to the day lodge, which makes it easy for people to find each other. "Nakiska" is a Greek word which means "to meet".

For A Snack Attack

For dining, you can try the Finnish Line Lounge in the day lodge for pub-style fare and live music on weekends, and there is the day lodge cafeteria that offers breakfast and lunch specials. There is also a small assortment of shops and dining opportunities at the nearby Kananaskis village and the Delta lodge.

History Behind The Skiing

In the late 1940s, coal was discovered at the eastern base of Mt. Allan. But construction began in 1984 on the site now known as Nakiska in preparation for the 1988 Winter Games. In recognition that Alberta was inhabited for 10,000 years before the arrival of the early explorers, names for expert runs were chosen as a salute to Alberta's first nation people. Among others, you can rocket down Walking Buffalo, Alberta's most famous Stoney Chief and leader of the Bearspaw band, or cruise down Eagle Tail, a Peigan chief of the last century.

（资料来源：http://www. webproxy. ca/browse. php？u ＝ 4SQh1aDcMra％2FbwbglCU4qloP0T％2BldVZpGr％2FTlMPAjgyswG8PbWQ1y6rCKA2IKbN5xaPSzBa28tQ％3D&b＝29.）

Questions

1. The city Calgary is so special in its location for two reasons. What are they?

2. What lessons does ski and snowboard school offer and whom is the school for?

3. Why is it said that Nakiska's layout makes it especially friendly to families?

Islands and Protected Areas of the Gulf of California

加利福尼亚湾群岛及保护区

⟳ **简介**

所属国家：墨西哥（Mexico）

入选时间：2005

入选标准：（vii）（ix）（x）

Islands and Protected Areas of the Gulf of California are located in the Gulf of California in north-eastern Mexico. It comprises 244 scattered desert islands, islets and coastal areas. The Sea of Cortez and its islands, described as "the world's aquarium", harbors 39％ of the world's total number of species of marine mammals and a third of the world's marine cetacean species, 891 species of fish (90 of them are endemic), a great diversity of macro-invertebrates, reptiles, cacti, etc. It is home to 695 vascular plant species, more than in any marine and insular property on the World Heritage List. Consequently, it is one of the most ecologically intact ecosystems in the world, valuable both to science and for its fisheries, and has been called a natural laboratory for the investigation of speciation.

The serial property is of striking natural beauty in a dramatic setting formed by rugged islands with high cliffs and sandy beaches, contrasting with the brilliant reflection from the desert and the surrounding turquoise waters. The rich variety of forms and colours is complemented by a wealth of birds and marine life. The diversity and abundance of marine life associated with spectacular submarine forms and high water transparency makes the property a diver's paradise.

加利福尼亚湾群岛及保护区位于墨西哥东北部的加利福尼亚群岛，包括 244 个分散的沙漠岛屿、小岛和海岸区。有"世界水族馆"美誉的科斯特海及其群岛栖息着占世界总数 39％的海生哺乳动物和世界上 1/3 的鲸种类，891 种鱼类（其中 90 种是地方特有的），及大量种类繁多的大型无脊椎动物、爬行动物、仙人掌等。这里是 695 个动植物物种的产地，它比世界遗产列表中任何的海生和海岛物产都要多，是世界上生态最完整的生态系统之一，无论对科学研究和渔业都弥足珍贵，亦被称为研究物种形成的自然实验室，而且，这里为几乎所有的海洋领域的科学家提供了极其重要的研究场所。

加利福尼亚湾群岛及保护区呈现的是一幅妩媚动人的自然美景，众多崎岖的岛屿、高耸的悬崖、沙质海滩是其生动的背景，与流光溢彩的沙漠及周边蓝绿色的海水交相辉映。缤纷的形态和色彩、丰富的鸟类和海洋生物相映成趣，形成壮观的水下美景，高透明度的海水使这里成为潜水者的天堂。

Vocabulary

1. snorkeling *n.* 潜水（运动）

—Let's go snorkeling. —OK. I'll get my mask and flippers.

—我们去潜水吧。—好的。我去拿潜水面罩和橡皮脚蹼。

2. flora & fauna *n.* (某地区或某时期的)植物群 & 动物群

This national park is an area with unique fauna and flora.

该国家公园区域内具有独特的动物种群和植物种群。

3. aquatic *adj.* 水上的；水中(进行)的

Swimming and water skiing are both aquatic sports.

游泳和滑水两项都是水上运动。

4. kayaking *n.* 【体】皮艇运动

Floating, drifting and speeding down rivers is all part of kayaking.

漂浮、漂移和急速冲下河流都是皮艇运动的一部分。

5. sanctuary *n.* 鸟兽类保护区

This island is maintained as a sanctuary for endangered species.

这座岛屿仍然是濒危物种保护区。

6. marina *n.* 小艇船坞

Marbella also has two yachting marinas.

马尔贝拉有两个游艇船坞。

7. moray *n.* 海鳗，欧洲海鳗；海鳝

Known to grow as long as about 5 feet (1.5 meters), moray species generally lack pectoral fins, unlike most other eel species.

众所周知，这种欧洲海鳗最大能长到 5 英尺(1.5 米)长，与大多数其他鳗鱼物种不同的是：它们通常没有胸鳍。

扩展阅读

Main Attractions in San Carlos Bay

Los Algodones Beach—San Carlos Bay's Most Spectacular Beach

This beach is called Algodones (Cotton in English) because the dunes in the areas appear to be balls of cotton. This beautiful beach has smooth swells, transparent water and smooth sand of white tones and fine texture. This beach is the ideal place for diving, fishing, snorkeling, windsurfing, swimming, horse back riding and sports like volleyball or football.

The average temperature ranges from 88F in the spring to 65F in the winter. The flora is desert-based and includes spiny thickets, sahuaros and palm trees. The fauna is made of many ornamental birds.

During high season, such as Spring Break and summer, the beach is perfect for camping and practicing aquatic sports. Along the sands are attractive hotels and residential resorts.

Las Barajitas Canyon—An Ecological Paradise to Discover

Only 12 miles north of San Carlos Bay exists a magical and isolated place ready to be discovered for those lovers of nature, exploring and adventure. Las Barajitas Canyon is an untamed area home of 3 different ecosystems that can only be reached by boat, ferry or yacht. Many Sonoran Desert species of flora & fauna are found in their natural state in this wild & untouched canyon bordering the Cortes Sea.

Considered a "sacred place" by the Seri Indians, Las Barajitas is a paradise for nature lovers and adventurer alike. Check for lodging facilities in this beautiful area or visit our Business Directory for tours & expeditions availability.

Other activities in this area are kayaking, sailing, scuba diving, snorkeling and boat & seashore fishing. Also you can enjoy cave exploring or take a boat charter to San Pedro Nolasco Island, a sanctuary for sea lions. Other alternative is to visit the Barajitas Canyon observatory for astronomical observations.

Panoramic Lookout—The Most Spectacular View of the Sea of Cortez

This is the perfect place to come and watch a sunshine, take spectacular photos and observe the majesty of Tetakawi Hill (the symbol of San Carlos Bay), which is located to one side of this outlook. A few meters before arriving to this site you can observe one of the touristic marinas in town, some hotels, trailer parks and residential resorts. This outlook has its own security wall of rock about 1.5 meters height that covers all of the potentially dangerous spots of the lookout. To make your trip more pleasant, you may enjoy the dainty articles that mobile vendors offer. The police of San Carlos have implemented a 6 a.m. to 8 p.m. visitation policy to this area.

Tetakawi Hill—Cave Paintings

This majestic hill borders the shores of the Sea of Cortes, also known as the Gulf of California. Its name means Tits of Goat in the ancient Yaqui tribe language (if you turn the Tetakawi Mountain upside down it looks like tits of goat), however some stories say that this name come from the Spanish explorers using Yaqui words. From this hill you can appreciate the beautiful view of the beaches, mountains and marinas of San Carlos Bay. The hill itself is slightly more than 600 ft high. Tetakawi Hill has become a must for visitors from throughout Mexico and abroad.

The flora and fauna in the Tetakawi includes sahuaros, palm trees and ornamental birds like cenzontles, huitlacoches, cardinals, wood peckers, bats (in the caves) and a great number of sea birds. The hill can be accessed from either the north or west. The mountain is kind of a challenge and it has been climbed by a lot of people. We strongly recommend (for those who try to climb it) carry adequate supplies including suntan lotion, ample water, a first-aid kit & long pants (for the brush).

These Cave Paintings are located 69 km north of San Carlos Bay on Highway 15 and were created by local Indians in geometric figures representing religious beliefs and depicting daily activities. The Paintings made of mineral and natural colors are high in the caves, suggesting this area may have been underwater or the Indians had very long ladders.

La Pintada is about 3 km into the desert so you better take appropriate clothes. You may be able to hire a guide but the way is fairly well marked. There's a large ranch part-way there. The owner speaks fluent English & for a low fee he will show you the caves and other interesting aspects of the desert.

San Pedro Nolasco Island—A Sea Lions Paradise

San Pedro Nolasco Island is located only 17 miles away from San Carlos Bay，is the perfect place for diving & fishing out of San Carlos. The island is the year round residence for a large population of California Sea Lions so you may able to watch and interact with them when snorkeling and diving.

The underwater landscape consists of sheer cliffs and boulders and you may see lots of morays，angels，puffers，parrot fish and dozens of other species everywhere. Big pelagic fish，manta rays and hammerhead sharks are occasionally seen as well.

Recently the Mexican Federal Government declares the San Pedro Nolasco Island and all its surrounding area as a Federal Ecological Reserve so we encouraged all visitors to protect the area and respect all the species and environment elements.

（资料来源：http://www. webproxy. ca/browse. php? u ＝ 4SQh0bbFf6WiYALq2yku8VcU3XmqLFZ0Dq6KmtnHmUfq120O&b＝29.）

Questions

1. What is so popular and attractive about Los Algodones Beach?
2. Why is Panoralmic Lookout the most spectacular view of the Sea of Cortez?
3. Who created the Cave Paintings in Tetawaki Hill，and what did they represent?

第三节　北美洲的世界文化和自然双重遗产

The Papahānaumokuākea Marine National Monument
帕帕哈瑙莫夸基亚国家海洋保护区

简介

所属国家：美国（America）

入选时间：2010

入选标准：(iii)(vi)(viii)(ix)(x)

Papahānaumokuākea's globally significant natural attributes incorporate its living, indigenous, cultural connections to the sea. The Papahānaumokuākea Marine National Monument is a World Heritage listed, the U. S. National Monument encompassing 140,

000 square miles (360,000 km²) of ocean waters, including ten islands and atolls of the Northwestern Hawaiian Islands, roughly 250 km to the northwest of the main Hawaiian Archipelago and extending over some 1931 km. Much of the monument is made up of pelagic and deepwater habitats, with notable features such as seamounts and submerged banks, extensive coral reefs and lagoons. It is one of the largest marine protected areas (MPAs) in the world.

The area has deep cosmological and traditional significance for living Native Hawaiian culture, as an ancestral environment, as an embodiment of the Hawaiian concept of kinship between people and the natural world. In Hawaiian traditions, the Northwestern Hawaiian Islands are considered a sacred place, a region of primordial darkness from which life springs and spirits return after death. The first discoverers of the Hawaiian Archipelago, Native Hawaiians, have continued to inhabit these islands for thousands of years prior to Western contact. On two of the islands, Nihoa and Makumanamana, there are archaeological remains relating to pre-European settlement and use.

帕帕哈瑙莫夸基亚国家海洋保护区,面积达 36 万平方千米,是一连串孤立的岛屿、珊瑚礁的总和,距离夏威夷群岛西北约 250 千米。帕帕哈瑙莫夸基亚主要由远洋和深海生物的栖息地所组成,其中包括海底山脉和海底沙滩、广阔的珊瑚礁和大面积的潟湖等,保护区涵盖了 14 万平方英里的海域,除了中途岛外皆隶属夏威夷州。区名是由夏威夷创造女神和其丈夫的名字合成。2010 年 7 月 30 日被纳入《世界遗产名录》,它是世界上最大的海洋保护区之一,也是北美地区唯一一个自然与文化结合的双重世界遗产。

对现存的夏威夷原住民来说,该遗址作为祖先生存的环境,蕴含着宇宙精髓与传统意义。帕帕哈瑙莫夸基亚的夏威夷土著文化充分反映了当地人与自然界的亲缘关系,保护区原住民相信这里是神圣的生命摇篮,也是死后灵魂回归之所。尼华岛和马库马纳马纳岛上至今还保留着欧洲殖民者到来之前人们居住和生活的遗迹。

Vocabulary

1. solidify *v.* (使)团结,巩固

He made great efforts to solidify his position as chairman.

他为巩固自己的主席地位做出很大的努力。

2. incorporate *v.* 包含;吸收;合并;混合

We shall try to incorporate some of your ideas in our future plan.

我们将尽力把你的一些想法纳入未来的计划中。

3. indigenous *adj.* 本土的;生来的,固有的

Indians were the indigenous inhabitants of America.

印第安人是美洲的土著居民。

4. canoe *n.* 皮划艇;独木舟

The canoe shot the rapids.

独木舟飞速地冲入急流。

5. inscription *n.* (赠书上的)题词;题赠

The inscription reads: "To Emma, with love from Harry".

题赠写着:"献给爱玛,爱你的哈里"。

6. archipelago *n.* 群岛

Koh Larn (coral island) is the largest of Pattaya's archipelago.

琅岛(珊瑚岛)是芭堤雅群岛中最大的一个岛屿。

7. trustee *n.* 受托人

Her request for money was turned down by the trustees.

她的提款请求被受托人拒绝了。

扩展阅读

Papahānaumokuākea Marine National Monument Becomes First Mixed UNESCO World Heritage Site in the U.S.

Delegates to the United Nations Educational, Scientific and Cultural Organization's (UNESCO) 34th World Heritage Convention in Brasilia, Brazil, agreed July 30, 2010 to inscribe Papahānaumokuākea Marine National Monument as one of only 28 mixed (natural and cultural) World Heritage Sites in the World. Globally, Papahānaumokuākea is also one of only 47 marine sites. Inscription of this remote oceanic expanse is a win for the United States on its first nomination of a site in 15 years. The vote also establishes the first mixed World Heritage Site in the nation, which covers an area of nearly 140,000 square miles, the official decision on the Papahānaumokuākea Inscription.

"Inscription confirms what we feel in our hearts every day," said Susan White, former U. S. Fish and Wildlife Service superintendent for the Monument. "We thank the UNESCO delegates for their recognition that Papahānaumokuākea is a profoundly wonderful place for wildlife, for our host culture, and now for humanity. As a nation, we've solidified our promise to the world that we will continue to protect it."

Where Nature and Culture Are One

Papahānaumokuākea's globally significant natural attributes incorporate its living, indigenous, cultural connections to the sea—where modern Hawaiian wayfinders (non-instrument navigators) still voyage for navigational training on traditional double-hulled sailing canoes; an aspect of inscription unique to Papahānaumokuākea. Additionally, World Heritage status places this traditional skill, which was used to navigate across the world's largest ocean—one of the greatest feats of human kind—onto the world stage.

"This inscription, a first natural and cultural inscription for Hawaii, and a first inscription in 15 years for the United States, elevates Hawaii in the eyes of the world and underscores our responsibility to protect our culturally, naturally and spiritually significant places for future generations, as our ancestors would want," said Haunani Apoliona, chairperson of the Office of Hawaiian Affairs Board of Trustees.

'Aulani Wilhelm, NOAA superintendent for the Monument agreed. "We hope

Papahānaumokuākea's inscription will help expand the global view of culture and the contributions of Oceanic peoples to World Heritage and underscore that for so many indigenous people, nature and culture are one," Wilhelm said.

Hawaii's Second World Heritage Site

Papahānaumokuākea is the second World Heritage Site in the State; Hawaii Volcanoes National Park was inscribed in 1987. Together, the two sites emphasize one of the six criteria for which the Monument was designated. The small islands, reefs, and shoals of Papahānaumokuākea represent the longest, clearest, and oldest example of island formation and atoll evolution in the world, spanning 28 million years, which contrasts strikingly with Hawaii Island's continued volcanic growth at the southeastern end of the Hawaiian Archipelago.

ʻĀina Momona—Place of Abundance

The near pristine remote reefs, islands, and waters of Papahānaumokuākea provide refuge and habitat for a wide array of threatened and endangered species and is one of the last predator-dominated coral reef ecosystems on the planet; manō (sharks) and ʻulua (jacks) dominate the underwater landscape. The region also provides critical nesting and foraging grounds for 14 million seabirds making it the largest tropical seabird rookery in the world.

Management and Visitation

World Heritage designation does not change the Monument's cooperative federal-state management mission, plan or structure, nor does it impose, change or add regulations or restrictions. The Monument's management philosophy and regulations have always been designed to "bring the place to the people" through education, virtual exposure, and extremely limited visitation. Although inscription has increased tourism at other World Heritage Sites, for Papahānaumokuākea, the situation is quite different. All human access and activity will remain by permit only, with visitation by the public restricted to Midway Atoll under strict carrying-capacity guidelines.

Sharing Papahānaumokuākea with the World

Laura Thielen, chairperson of the Hawaii Department of Land and Natural Resources, summarized: "World Heritage inscription for Papahānaumokuākea allows us to share her stories, obtain global recognition of Hawaii's special attributes, and bring the place to our residents, visitors and to people around the world." Papahānaumokuākea is cooperatively managed to ensure ecological integrity and achieve strong, long-term protection and perpetuation of Northwestern Hawaiian Islands ecosystems, native Hawaiian culture, and heritage resources for current and future generations. Three co-trustees—the Department of Commerce, Department of the Interior, and State of Hawaii-joined by the Office of Hawaiian Affairs, protect this special place.

（资料来源：http://www. webproxy. ca/browse. php? u ＝ 4SQh1aDcMrSxfAzx2CY2qlkU2yOqM0dnQaqRhZneggzwynQDJW52&b＝29. ）

Questions

1. In what aspect is Papahānaumokuākea so special?

2. Why do we say in Papahānaumokuākea *Nature and Culture Are One*?

3. What is the goal of the Papahānaumokuākea Monument's management philosophy and regulations?

第四节　北美洲的世界文化景观遗产

Landscape of Grand Pré
格朗普雷景观

⇨ **简介**

所属国家：加拿大（Canada）

入选时间：2012

入选标准：（v）（vi）

Grand Pré is a Canadian rural community in Kings County，Nova Scotia. Its French name translates to "Great Meadow" and the community lies at the eastern edge of the Annapolis Valley several kilometers east of the town of Wolfville on a peninsula jutting into the Minas Basin，framed by the Gaspereau and Cornwallis Rivers. The community was made famous by Henry Wadsworth Longfellow's poem *Evangeline* and is today home to the Grand Pré National Historic Site.

The Landscape of Grand Pré is an outstanding and enduring model of the human capacity to overcome extraordinary natural challenges and cultural ordeals. Its marshland and archaeological sites constitute a cultural landscape bearing testimony to the development of agricultural farmland using dykes and the aboiteau wooden sluice system，started by the Acadians in the 17th century and further developed and maintained by the Planters and present-day inhabitants.

Over 1,300 ha，the cultural landscape encompasses a large expanse of polder farmland and archaeological elements of the towns of Grand Pré and Hortonville，which were built by the Acadians and their successors. The landscape is an exceptional example of the adaptation of the first European settlers to the conditions of the North American Atlantic coast. It is also a powerful symbolic landscape for the Acadians who lived in harmony with the native Mi'Kmaq people，were dispersed by the Grand Derangement，and symbolically re-appropriated it in a spirit of peace and cultural sharing with the English-speaking community.

On June 30, 2012, the Landscape of Grand Pré was named a World Heritage Site by UNESCO.

加拿大格朗普雷景观是由位于新斯科舍省米纳斯盆地南部的格朗普雷沼泽地和考古遗址构成的文化景观,是此地农耕文明发展的见证。2012 年 6 月 30 日,格朗普雷景观被列入《世界遗产名录》。

从 17 世纪开始,阿卡迪亚人就在农业耕地中开始使用排水沟及被称作"阿瓦托"的木制水闸系统。后来,木制水闸系统由普兰特人及当地居民传承下来并得到进一步的发展和维护。这一遗产地也是世界上潮差最大的地区,平均潮差达 11.6 米,是承载着阿卡迪亚人生活方式的标志性地区。

遗址占地超过 1300 公顷,包括一个巨大的低洼地农田和格朗普雷城的考古遗迹。格朗普雷和霍顿维尔城最早由阿卡迪亚人成立,后来由英国的后继者建造。这里的景观是早期欧洲定居者在北美大西洋沿海地区调整自己适应当地环境的最好例证,也是纪念阿卡迪亚人自 1755 年起遭到放逐——史称"大动荡"——的历史纪念场所。

Vocabulary

1. domaine *n.* 酒庄;葡萄园

The owner of the domaine—Mrs. Nicole Bott—will be present to introduce her wines.

酒庄所有人尼科尔·博特女士将向大家介绍她酿造的葡萄酒。

2. indulge *v.* 沉迷;放纵

Cherish today than indulge in yesterday is more meaningful!

珍惜今天要比沉湎于昨天更有意义!

3. rejuvenate *v.* (使)变得年轻;(使)恢复精神

His new job seemed to rejuvenate him.

他的新工作似乎使他焕发了青春。

4. pergola *n.* 绿廊,藤架

The newly married couple sat close together in the sequestered pergola.

新婚夫妇拥坐在幽静的藤架下。

5. venue *n.* 场地;会场

Birmingham's International Convention Centre is the venue for a three-day arts festival.

为期 3 天的艺术节在伯明翰的国际会议中心举办。

6. limousine *n.* 豪华轿车,大型豪华轿车

They drove in a black limousine, past groves of birch trees and endless rows of identical new buildings.

他们驾驶着一辆黑色豪华轿车,穿过片片白桦林和鳞次栉比的新建筑物。

7. fondue *n.* 乳酪火锅(瑞士菜,蘸面包吃)

Eat it as a meal in itself simply as is, or baked in the oven and served as a fondue.

食用时,单独将它作为一道美餐,或者在烤箱中烤成乳酪火锅。

扩展阅读

Weddings

A Winery Wedding

—Make Domaine de Grand Pré the perfect place for your "I Do's!"

The Perfect Outdoor Wedding Location in Nova Scotia

Our mission at Domaine de Grand Pré is to offer you and your guests the perfect venue within our unique setting for your wedding.

We offer a memorable experience in a place where all your senses are indulged and rejuvenated. A stroll around the grounds takes you past the vineyards, along cobblestone walkways, among lovely gardens, all with the soothing sound of our basalt fountain trickling in the background.

The grapevine-canopied pergola provides a beautiful ceremony and reception space, while our vast courtyard is ideal for larger groups.

For smaller and more intimate wedding parties, Le Caveau Restaurant—with its rounded moldings and textured walls—offers a cozy and exceptionally welcoming environment. The arched windows and rich woods give Le Caveau an inimitable brightness and warmth for an inviting and relaxing atmosphere.

In this picturesque private setting, we help you transform your dreams and ideas into a reality!

Testimonials

We both agree it was a perfect day and it was so perfect because of your hard work and attention. I have heard nothing but praise from our guests about the food, service and venue.

I learned the next day that two of our older guests were actually walked back to the Evangeline Inn by one of your staff. We're truly touched at that level of service and dedication.

From producing shooters to accommodating food requests, you and your staff truly provide an experience of excellence.

—*Jennifer and Ron, September 2012*

The whole experience of planning this event was so easy and relaxing thanks to you. Everyone thought I was so calm all of these months and I have to thank you for that.

—*Victoria and Jeff, June 2005*

I tend to believe that those [who say that] planning a wedding is stressful didn't choose to get married at the Grand Pré Winery.

—*Shayne Peddle, October 2005*

We are proud to be one of Canada's most beautiful winery wedding sites

Our facility accommodates every detail, from the ceremony and reception to dinner and an evening of dancing. We are able to seat a maximum of 55 guests in our dining room. For larger groups from 80 up to 150 people, our beautiful and private courtyard is the perfect place to set up a tent.

Many first class accommodations are nearby to ensure you have the perfect room to prepare for your special day and to spend the first night as a married couple.

The quality of our site, from food to the friendly staff, delivers an unforgettable and unique experience here in the heart of the Annapolis Valley.

If you are dreaming of a romantic wedding, an elegant dinner, celebrating a birthday or anniversary, or organizing a corporate gathering, we are more than happy to help you choose a limousine service, florist, photographer, musician and even an officiate for your ceremony.

We look forward to helping you plan and organize your special event!

Menu and Drinks

We will meet with you to discuss the menu and drink options for your special day.

For a stand-up reception, we can provide everything from tapas and finger foods to sweets and even a chocolate fondue!

We customize each and every menu according to the couple's wishes. Once you have booked with us, we will set up a meeting and Chef Jason Lynch will meet with you to discuss menu options.

We are also able to provide your wedding cake!

Our award winning wines, as well as wines from around the world and a fully stocked bar, are available for you and your guests to enjoy throughout the event.

To contact us regarding your wedding, please connect with Beatrice or Kyla, our assistant restaurant managers or send an e-mail to Le Caveau Restaurant or call (902) 542-7177.

（资料来源：http://www. webproxy. ca/browse. php? u ＝ 4SQh1aDcMrSxfAzx2CY2qlkU2yOqM0dnQaqRhZneggzwynQDJW52&b＝29. ）

Questions

1. What is Domaine de Grand Pré?

2. Why is it a perfect place for weddings? Explain your reasons.

3. What types of services can they offer to celebrate your special day?

Agave Landscape and Ancient Industrial Facilities of Tequila

龙舌兰景观和特基拉地区的古代工业设施

⇨ 简介

所属国家：墨西哥（Mexico）

入选时间：2006

入选标准：(ii)(iv)(v)(vi)

Agave Landscape and Ancient Industrial Facilities of Tequila sits between the foothills of the Tequila Volcano and the deep valley of the Rio Grande River, in Jalisco State, Mexico. The 34,658 hectares site encloses a living, working landscape of blue agave fields and the urban settlements of Tequila, Arenal, and Amatitan with large distilleries where the agave "pineapple" is fermented and distilled. The expansive landscape of blue agave is characterized by the culture of the plant used since the 16th century to produce tequila spirit and for at least 2,000 years to make fermented drinks and cloth. The architecture of both the factories and haciendas is characterized by brick and adobe construction, plastered walls with ochre lime-wash, stone arches, quoins and window dressings, and formal, neo-classical or baroque ornamentation. The property is also a testimony to the Teuchitlan cultures which shaped the Tequila area from 200—900, notably through the creation of terraces for agriculture, housing, temples, ceremonial mounds and ball courts.

The tradition and culture of making tequila spirit has engrained into the national identity of Mexico. The Agave Cultural Landscape of Mexico is celebrated for the relationship between the people of the region and the natural environment.

墨西哥特基拉城位于特基拉火山脚下和格兰德河河谷之间，面积为 34658 公顷，以盛产墨西哥最具特色的植物龙舌兰著称。自 16 世纪以来，人们用它酿造龙舌兰酒及各种饮料，也用来织布。该处遗产包括龙舌兰种植地、酿酒厂、工厂、酒坊（西班牙统治时期的非法酿酒厂）、小镇和塔木西兰考古遗址。遗产中很多农庄等不动产甚至可以追溯到 18 世纪。工厂遗址和农庄都是石砖和土砖结构，墙上涂有赭色石灰，建筑内有石拱、榫子和窗上装饰物，以及设计整齐的新古典主义风格或巴洛克风格的装饰品。这些建筑反映了前西班牙统治时期龙舌兰酒的传统酿造工艺与欧洲提取工艺的融合，体现了当地技术与欧美引进技术的融合。保护区内的塔栖兰文化遗址见证了从公元 200 年到 900 年，特基拉地区受塔栖兰文化影响而发生的改变，主要表现在为促进农业发展而修造梯田，建造房屋、庙宇，修建用于纪念仪式的土墩及球场。

古老的龙舌兰酒酿造技术和文化已成为墨西哥人国家的象征。墨西哥龙舌兰酒文化景观反映的是当地人民和自然环境之间和谐的亲密关系。

Vocabulary

1. agave nectar 龙舌兰花蜜

Agave nectar comes from the same plant that tequila is made from.

龙舌兰花蜜和龙舌兰酒都是来源于同一种植物。

2. glycemic index 血糖指数

Please avoid foods with a high glycemic index.

请避免吃血糖指数高的食品。

3. vegan *adj.* 严守素食主义的

I'd been vegan for a long time.

我坚持完全吃素已很久了。

4. fructose *n.* 果糖

The simplest include glucose, fructose, and galactose.

成分最简单的糖有葡萄糖、果糖和半乳糖。

5. botulism *n.* 肉毒杆菌中毒

Don't taste the food; even a small amount can cause botulism.

不要尝这食物；即使稍微尝点也会引起肉毒杆菌中毒。

6. daunting *adj.* 令人畏惧的，令人却步的

Occasionally I find the commitment and responsibility daunting.

偶尔我会觉得这一承诺和责任让人望而却步。

7. sap *n.* (植物的)液，汁

The leaves, bark and sap are also common ingredients of local herbal remedies.

树叶、树皮和树汁也是当地草药的常用药材。

扩展阅读

Agave Nectar vs. Liquid Sugars

Agave nectar is most easily substituted for liquid sugars, since it is already in liquid form and the difference in moisture will usually be negligible. Because of its lower glycemic index, it makes an excellent substitute for many natural and refined liquid sugars.

Agave Nectar vs. Honey

A Wider Appeal

Agave syrup has a number of advantages over honey. The light varieties of nectar can have a more neutral flavor than honey, making them less likely to interfere with or mask delicately flavored foods. Many people who find honey distasteful will still like the flavor of agave nectar. Unlike honey, agave syrup is completely vegan, meaning it can be used by individuals who do not wish to use any product associated with animals.

Avoiding Sugar Shock

The primary sugar in agave nectar is a complex form of fructose, which gives it a much lower glycemic index than honey. Depending on the variety, honey's glycemic index usually falls in the 65—85 range. The glycemic index of agave syrup differs with variety and manufacturer, but usually falls between 11 and 30. This makes it less likely to raise blood sugar or trigger the body's fat storage mechanisms.

Ease of Use

There is nothing more inconvenient than getting out a bottle of honey only to find that it has solidified into an unpourable, grainy mass. While the honey crystals can be re-liquefied by heating, it must be done carefully and at a low temperature to avoid scorching the sugars. Agave syrup has a long shelf life and will not crystallize in the bottle. Agave syrup is also thinner than honey, making it easier to measure and pour, and it dissolves well into liquids—even cold drinks.

Safe for Babies

Parents are vigorously warned not to give honey to children in their first year of life. This is because honey frequently contains bacteria that can cause botulism. While this bacteria is harmless to anyone over the age of one year, it can produce toxins in an infant's immature intestinal tract, causing sickness, hospitalization, and in rare cases, death. Agave syrup is not known to cause botulism in babies.

Agave Syrup vs. Maple Syrup

As sugars go, pure maple syrup is one of the least harmful. It has a medium-low glycemic index (54) and a higher degree of sweetness than table sugar for roughly the same number of calories. However, agave nectar still has some advantages.

While maple syrup is delicious in some applications, its strong flavor and sometimes metallic overtones can make it a less versatile ingredient. While the sweetness of agave and maple is comparable (and agave's caloric count is higher), agave still has the lower glycemic index (between 11 and 30). The most daunting property of maple syrup may be its price. Because it takes approximately 40 gallons of raw maple sap to produce a single gallon of finished syrup, the cost of pure maple syrup can be easily twice that of agave syrup, making it prohibitively priced for regular use.

Agave Syrup vs. Brown Rice Syrup

Brown rice syrup is a liquid sweetener often found in natural foods stores and recipes. Though it is said to have a low glycemic index (20), it is not recommended for diabetics, since its sweetness comes from maltose, which is known to cause spikes in blood sugar. While the caloric count of brown rice syrup is similar to agave syrup, agave is close to three times as sweet as brown rice syrup, so one can use much less agave to achieve the same level of sweetness.

Agave Syrup vs. Corn Syrup

Corn syrup has a glycemic index similar to white table sugar (mid 60s), but it is only about sixty-five percent as sweet. Corn syrup is frequently used in recipes because it is an inert sugar, meaning that it will not crystallize. Agave syrup bears this same property, yet it is over twice as sweet as corn syrup and has half the glycemic index.

（资料来源：http://www. webproxy. ca/browse. php? u = 4SQh1aDcMrSxfAzx2CY2qlkU2yOqM0dnQaqRhZneggzwynQDJW52&b=29.）

Questions

1. In what aspect is agave nectar superior to honey?
2. The glycemic index in agave syrup and honey, which is higher?
3. Why honey is so dangerous to small babies at their very early stage?

The Prehistoric Caves of Yagul and Mitla in the Central Valley of Oaxaca
瓦哈卡州中央谷地的亚古尔与米特拉史前洞穴

⇨ 简介

所属国家：墨西哥（Mexico）

入选时间：2010

入选标准：（iii）

The prehistoric caves of Yagul and Mitla are archaeological sites associated with the Zapotec civilization and much earlier primitive farmers.

Lying on the northern slopes of the Tlacolula valley in subtropical central Oaxaca, the property consists of two pre-Hispanic archaeological complexes and a series of prehistoric caves and rock shelters. Some of these shelters offer archaeological and rock-art evidence of the transition of nomadic hunter-gathers to incipient farmers. Corn cob fragments from one cave in this zone are believed to be the earliest documented evidence for the domestication of maize, and ten thousand-year-old seeds found here are considered the earliest known evidence of domesticated plants on the continent. The cultural landscape of the prehistoric caves of Yagul and Mitla demonstrates the link between man and nature that gave origin to the domestication of plants in North America, thus allowing the rise of Mesoamerican civilizations.

瓦哈卡州中央谷地的亚古尔与米特拉史前洞穴是关于萨波特克文明和更早的原始农民的考古遗址。此文化景观遗产坐落在亚热带气候的瓦哈卡州特拉科卢拉山谷中，由两处西班牙统治前的考古遗址以及一系列史前洞穴和人类居住的岩石庇护所组成。在一些庇护所中发现的考古证据与岩刻艺术，见证了史前人类从游牧式的打猎采集者向定居农业人口的转变进程。在吉拉纳蒂兹洞穴中发现的一万年前的葫芦种子,被认为是美洲大陆上最早进行植物栽培的证据,而同一洞穴发现的玉米穗残粒则被看作最早的人工栽培玉米的证据。亚古尔与米特拉洞穴的文化景观展现了人与自然之间的联系,这一纽带不仅促成了北美洲人工种植的产生,并且推动了中美洲文明的发展。

Vocabulary

1. alpha and omega 首尾,始终;全部

He knows the alpha and omega of his job.

他非常精通本职工作。

2. imperceptibly *adv.* 不知不觉地,难以察觉地

The disease develops gradually and imperceptibly.

这种疾病的发展缓慢且难以察觉。

3. ambience *n.* 气氛

This restaurant has a very romantic ambience.

这间餐厅很有浪漫的气氛。

4. cantina *n.* 小酒店,酒吧

In the cantina sequences filmed in England, John has large fin-like hands.

在英格兰拍摄的小酒馆镜头里,约翰有双像鳍一样的大手。

5. raffle *n.* 抽彩售物

First prize in the raffle is a holiday for two in Paris.

抽奖销售的头奖是巴黎度假双人游。

6. bohemian *adj.* (艺术家)波希米亚风格的,不拘于传统的

This is the bohemian lifestyle of the French capital.

这就是法国首都随性的生活方式。

7. tortilla *n.* 墨西哥玉米薄饼

Tortillas are made from finely ground corn or flour.

玉米饼是用细玉米面和面粉做的。

扩展阅读

Nightlife in Oaxaca, Mexico: Nightclubs, Dance Clubs & More

If you have ever been to Oaxaca's Zocalo, you know that this town square is not only the city's downtown plaza. It is the city's heart by day and its nervous system by night, its alpha and omega. Imperceptibly, lunch turns a nice talk around the table into a dinner with some drinks. All around, you can find a bit of everything: bands, pedestrians, improvised musicians, balloons, craft makers, toasted grasshoppers and shoe polishers.

But nightlife in Oaxaca does not end there. In addition to the many different cultural options, Oaxaca features an unexpected variety of options to start, continue or wrap up the party. The city is so safe at all times that the habitual thing to do is hop from one bar to the other, greeting friends here and there. Around midnight, the very famous Alcala Street becomes a corridor for night owls, in search of the perfect party-ambience and lively Oaxaca nightclubs.

Trova, salsa, techno, trios, and pop are just some of the alternatives to the most traditional and fun atmosphere of the cantinas. It is hard to believe that, despite its conservative looks, Oaxaca nightlife usually carries on until the hours of the morning. This widespread schedule may be the heritage of the legendary 3-day long town parties, which exist to this day.

The Zocalo Gateways

Under the surrounding areas of Zocalo, there are many famous cafes offering an extensive traditional menu. After dinner, they are quite popular gathering spot for locals and foreigners, turning them into enjoyable outdoor bars. The usual drink is either a beer or mezcal and the traditional snacks are peanuts or toasted grasshoppers with lime. The ambience is lively.

La Cantinita

Discover the rich Mexican folklore, vibrant party atmosphere, and delicious cuisine at La Cantinita. Here you can enjoy live bands, have your fortune told by a "lucky bird", and shake your body to the thumping beats of the music. It's a great place to celebrate your birthday with the waiters dressed in costume, and they also have raffles for bottles of liquor, while the DJ spins a fantastic range of music.

Cafe Borgo

Cafe Borgo is very popular among resident foreigners for its exceptional coffee, as it is homegrown and prepared in genuine Italian style. At some point, between 8:00 p.m. and 10:00 p.m., the music starts to pump and then the mezcal starts to pour among the backpackers and avant-garde locals. The cosmopolitan atmosphere is complemented by exhibitions of work by young artists.

La Nueva Babel

Whether you like poetry readings, jazz music, the main characteristic of this cozy bar is the bohemian atmosphere, where the spontaneous playing or singing is always welcome. It features a covered area and a quaint candlelit patio under the bright stars. Its beverage menu includes draft beer, excellent wines and mezcal.

El Decano

This Oaxaca nightclub is devoted to alternative live music. Guest artists go from acoustic trova duets to urban rock bands. This place reaches its climax around midnight. Don't forget to check out its exotic cocktail menu. There will always be one to quench your thirst. If you haven't dined yet, the sandwiches and big tortillas are deliciously famous.

Txalaparta

This pleasant bar is set in an old mansion in downtown Oaxaca, offering a relaxing cantina, a lounge area and a billiard room. In each of these spaces, you'll find an incredible traditional atmosphere, great music and a variety of drinks and cocktails. Make sure to try some of the delicious mezcal.

La Divina

Heavy Metal has its place in Oaxaca and the live guitar jams can't be missed. Year after year, La Divina gets new clients and welcomes its regular customers from all over the world with the same frenzy. In its surreal interior you will find, distributed in several rooms, the bar, tables, dance floor and stage, where the frenetic home band or eventual guest bands play.

La Tentacion

Sooner rather than later, the flow will bring you here. The first notes of the salsa band will start around 10:00 p.m. and it will alternate its show with a DJ who will mix the best Mexican and international pop music. There's always a moment in the middle of the night when it feels like the whole city is in La Tentacion, socializing at the bar, learning the latest salsa steps on the dance floor, chatting in the hallways or standing in line to get in.

Bar Central

When it comes to art, music and fashion, you will find the classiest at El Central, as it is popularly known. Before midnight enjoy a pleasant lounge ambience with soft lights and chill out music. Afterwards, the place fills in with a pagan multitude that easily dances salsa music as well as techno Hindu or the Backstreet Boys hits. The retro style decoration combined with the original art of Oaxacan artists is praiseworthy.

（资料来源：http://www. webproxy. ca/browse. php? u = 4SQh1aDcMrSxfAzx2CY2qlkU2yOqM0dnQaqRhZneggzwynQDJW52&b=29.）

Questions

1. What impresses you most about nightlife in Oaxaca, Mexico?

2. If you were in Oaxaca, Mexico, which place would you want to go first, and why?

3. What special food, drinks and dances can enjoy in Oaxaca?

世界遗产概论

第六章　大洋洲的世界遗产

Introduction to the World Heritage

第一节　大洋洲的世界文化遗产

Australian Convict Sites
澳大利亚监狱遗址

⟱ **简介**

所属国家：澳大利亚（Australia）

入选时间：2010

入选标准：（iv）（vi）

The Australian Convict Sites consists of a selection of 11 penal sites，among the thousands established by the British Empire in the 18th and 19th centuries across Australia，from Fremantle in the west to Kingston and Arthur's Vale in the east，and from areas around Sydney in the north to sites located in Tasmania in the south. Around 166,000 convicts，including men，women and children，were sent to Australia over 80 years between 1787 and 1868，condemned by British justice to transportation to the convict colonies. Each of the sites had a specific purpose，in terms both of punitive imprisonment and of rehabilitation through forced labour to help build the colony. The Australian Convict Sites constitutes the best surviving examples of large-scale convict transportation and the colonial expansion of European powers through the presence and labour of convicts.

　　18 世纪和 19 世纪时，当时的大英帝国在澳大利亚建立了数千所监狱，用于流放本国的"罪犯"。"澳大利亚监狱遗址"选取了其中的 11 座殖民监狱，遗址主要位于悉尼附近地区、塔斯马尼亚岛、亚瑟港、诺福克岛和弗里曼特尔市。其所在地大多是原住民已被驱逐了的、肥沃的海岸地区。这些监狱关押过被英国法院放逐到澳洲殖民地的成千上万名"罪犯"，不仅有成年男女，而且有儿童。每座监狱都有自身的用途，它们或是用于惩罚性的监禁，或是用于让犯人通过劳动教养协助殖民地建设。"澳大利亚监狱遗址"是大规模驱逐罪犯出境以及欧洲列强通过流放犯人和强制劳动进行殖民扩张的现存最佳例证。

Vocabulary

1. penal *adj.* 刑法上的；作为刑罚场所的

Many of them were imprisoned on an island that has served as a penal colony since Roman Times.

他们中有许多人被关押在自罗马时代以来就一直作为罪犯流放地的小岛上。

2. convict *n.* 罪犯

I'd rather die than be a convict.

我宁愿死也不愿做个囚犯。

3. condemn *v.* 判处（某人刑罚）

He was condemned to life imprisonment.

他被判终身监禁。

4. justice *n.* 司法制度，法律制度

Many in Toronto's black community feel that the justice system does not treat them fairly.

多伦多的黑人群体中有很多人觉得司法制度对待他们有失公正。

5. punitive *adj.* 处罚的，惩罚性的

Other economists say any punitive measures against foreign companies would hurt the interests of the U. S.

其他经济学家说任何针对外国公司的惩罚性措施都会损害美国的利益。

6. rehabilitation *n.* 修复；复兴

The prison service has the twin goals of punishment and rehabilitation.

监狱有惩罚和改造双重目的。

7. constitute *v.* 被视为；可算作

Testing patients without their consent would constitute a professional and legal offence.

未经患者同意而对其进行检查被视为违反职业操守并触犯法律。

扩展阅读

Convict Life

The Port Arthur penal settlement began life as a small timber station in 1830. Originally designed as a replacement for the recently closed timber camp at Birches Bay, Port Arthur quickly grew in importance within the penal system of the colonies.

The initial decade of settlement saw a penal station hacked from the bush, and the first manufactories—such as ship building, shoemaking, smithing, timber and brick making—established. The 1840s witnessed a consolidation of the industrial and penal nature of the settlement as the convict population reached over 1,100. In 1842 a huge flour mill and granary (later the penitentiary) was begun, as well as the construction of a hospital.

1848 saw the first stone laid for the Separate Prison, the completion of which brought about a shift in punishment philosophy from physical to mental subjugation. Port Arthur also expanded geographically as the convicts pushed further into the encircling hills to extract the valuable timber.

After the American War of Independence Britain could no longer send her convicts to America, so after 1788 they were transported to the Australian colonies. These men and women were convicted of crimes that seem trivial today, mostly stealing small articles or livestock, but they had been convicted at least once before and Britain's policy was to treat such re-offenders harshly.

The convicts sent to Van Diemen's Land were most likely to be poor young people from rural areas or from the slums of big cities. One in five was a woman. Numbers of children were also transported with their parents. Few returned home.

Of all the laborious occupations some convicts were forced to carry out during their time at Port Arthur, timber-getting was to be the most punishing, yet also the most profitable. From the very early days of settlement gangs of convicts cut timber from the bush surrounding the settlement. The saws of the convicts supplied a steady stream of building materials to fulfill the needs of works both on and off the peninsula.

The trees were enormous, much larger than the ones we find today. When felled, a sawpit was dug under or near the log, so that it could be cut up into smaller lengths of wood. Two convicts used a pitsaw to cut the wood. One convict stood on top the log, whilst the other worked in the pit at the other end of the saw. His job was extremely uncomfortable, as his eyes and ears were filled with sawdust.

When the log was cut into a rough beam, a gang of up to 50 convicts, nicknamed the "centipede gang", hefted the great weight upon their shoulders and carried the timber back to the main settlement. Here, in larger sawpits constructed near the water, the timber was cut up into the planks, beams, boards and spars needed for building.

In 1841 the old Assignment system was replaced by that of Probation. This saw the Tasman Peninsula settled with five new stations, each of which had up to 600 convicts working at agriculture or merely serving time. One probation station, Cascades, was settled with the primary focus of extracting timber from the north side of the peninsula. By 1846 Cascades had replaced Port Arthur as the main timber-producer on the peninsula.

In 1850 the erection of a steam-powered sawmill and the laying of iron tramways increased production to such an extent that, by 1856, the area around Cascades had been completely stripped of useful timber. With the closure of Cascades, operations reverted back to Port Arthur.

The sawmill and tramway rails were removed to Port Arthur and a great bank of covered sawpits built next to the Penitentiary. The tramways and log-slides (long log-lined channels which allowed timber to be slid down from a hill) meant that the centipede gangs were no longer needed, enabling the convict gangs to cut timber further from the settlement.

Sawpits were dotted throughout the hillsides surrounding Port Arthur, cutting the logs into smaller pieces of timber, which were then sent back to the main settlement by the tramway. At the settlement the timber was further cut up in the noisy sawmill and sawpits.

The decade after 1856 was the busiest time for Port Arthur. However, the convicts were getting older and sicker. In the late 1860s they could no longer work as well in the bush as they had once been able. As at Cascades, the area had also been stripped of all its useful timber. Up until the closure of Port Arthur in 1877, the old convicts were used to cut firewood, but no longer did they cut down the massive trees to feed the sawmill.

From 1877 the area was given over to private interests, as individuals and companies began logging the area, often using the old convict tracks for transport. Today chainsaws have replaced the pitsaws, mechanical haulers the tram carts.

（资料来源：http://www.portarthur.org.au/index.aspx? id=12731）

Questions

1. Who were the convicts sent to Port Arthur?
2. What did the convicts do at Port Arthur?
3. Why did the Britain send convicts to Australia?

Kuk Early Agricultural Site
库克早期农业遗址

⇨ 简介

所属国家：巴布亚新几内亚（Papua New Guinea）

入选时间：2008

入选标准：(iii)(iv)

Kuk Early Agricultural Site, consisting of 116 ha of swamps, is situated in the western highlands of Papua New Guinea 1,500 metres above sea level. Archaeological excavation has revealed the evidence that the landscape is of wetland reclamation worked almost continuously for 7,000, and possibly for 10,000 years. The well-preserved archaeological remains at the site demonstrate the technological leap which transformed plant exploitation to agriculture around 6,500 years ago. The site shows clearly the transformation of agricultural practices over time, from cultivation mounds to draining the wetlands through the digging of ditches with wooden tools. Kuk is one of the few places in the world where archaeological evidence suggests independent agricultural development and changes in agricultural practice over such a long period of time.

库科早期农业遗址位于巴布亚新几内亚南高地省，是一片面积为116公顷的湿地，海拔超过1500米。考古挖掘发现，该区域景观为当年的湿地改造，存留时间长达7000至10000年之久。其保存良好的考古遗迹，充分展现了约6500年前将植物采集转化为农业活动的一次技术性飞跃。遗址有力地证明了农业实践的历史变迁，即从最初的土丘耕种发展成为用木制工具挖掘沟渠以排干湿地积水的农耕方式,反映了那段漫长岁月中独立的农业发展与农业实践转变,库克是能证明在如此长时间段内大洋洲原住民独立进行农业实践,取得农业发展的世界上为数不多的考古证据。

Vocabulary

1. excavation *n.* 挖掘,开凿

The excavation of the site is likely to take several years.

这个地点的挖掘可能要花几年的工夫。

2. reveal *v.* 显露,揭露

A survey of the British diet has revealed that a growing number of people are overweight.

对英国人饮食进行的一项调查显示有越来越多的人超重。

3. reclamation *n.* 开垦;开拓

Excess waste discharge and land reclamation are worsening pollution in China's shallow coastal waters, *China Daily* reported last week.

《中国日报》上周报道说,过度的废弃物排放和土地开垦在加剧中国浅水海域的污染状况。

4. work *v.* 使工作,使运作,操作

I know how to work the machine.

我知道如何开动机器。

5. demonstrate *v.* 证明,证实

The study also demonstrated a direct link between obesity and mortality.

该研究还表明了肥胖症和死亡率之间存在直接的联系。

6. exploitation *n.* 开发;利用

The government has a monopoly of oil exploitation in that country.

在那个国家,政府独占石油开采权。

7. transformation *n.* 转型,转化,改造

Transformation is not only a choice, but also a strategy.

转型不仅是选择,更是战略。

8. cultivation *n.* 耕作

Intensive cultivation has impoverished the soil.

集约耕作使土壤变得贫瘠。

扩展阅读

Kuk Swamp (New Guinea): Early Evidence for Agriculture

Kuk Swamp is the collective name of several archaeological sites in the upper Wahgi Valley of the New Guinea highlands. Identified sites at Kuk Swamp include the Manton site, where the first ditch system was identified in 1966; the Kindeng site; and the Kuk site, where the most extensive excavations have been concentrated. Scholarly research refers to Kuk or the Kuk Swamp, in referring to the complex of evidence for early agriculture.

Kuk Swamp, as its name implies, is located on a wetland margin, and its importance for understanding the development of agriculture in the region cannot be overstated. The earliest occupations at Kuk Swamp are dated to ~10,220—9910 cal BP, although whether these levels represent true agriculture is as yet controversial.

Unequivocal evidence for the planting and tending of crops in mounds including banana, taro and yam is dated to 6590—6440 cal BP, and ditched cultivation beginning 4350—3980 cal BP.

An extensive network of ditches constructed for drainage and cultivation is in evidence in the Wahgi Valley as well, dated beginning c6000 BP and continuing up until 100. The ditches represent a long series of wetland reclamation and abandonment, where Kuk's residents struggled with developing a reliable agricultural method.

The oldest human occupations associated with agriculture at the swamp edge are pits, stake—and post-holes and man-made channels associated with levees near a paleo-channel. A paleochannel is a waterway that has since been abandoned, and charcoal from the channel and from a feature on the adjacent surface returned dates between 10,200—9910 cal BP. Scholars interpret this as evidence of planting, digging and tethering of plants in a cultivated plot.

Phase 2 contains the bases of circular mounds, and more stake—and post-holes, evidence strongly supporting the creation of mounds for planting crops. These features date to 6950—6440 cal BP.

Phase 3 consists of a network of drainage channels, some rectilinear others curved, built between ~4350—2800 cal BP.

Identification of the crops being cultivated at Kuk Swamp was accomplished by examining plant residues on stone tools and within sediments at the site. Stone cutting tools (flaked scrapers) and grinding stones (mortars and pestles) recovered from Kuk Swamp were examined by researchers, and starch grains and opal phytoliths of taro (*Colocasia esculenta*), yams (*Dioscorea* spp), and banana (*Musa* spp) were identified. Other phytoliths of grasses, palms and possibly gingers were also identified.

Exploitation of early wild forms of bananas has been noted at the Beli-Lena site of Sri Lanka by c11,500—13,500 BP, Gua Chwawas in Malaysia by 10,700 BP, and Poyang Lake, China by 11,500 BP. Kuk Swamp, in Papua New Guinea, so far the earliest unequivocal evidence for banana cultivation, had wild bananas there throughout the Holocene, and banana phytoliths are associated with the earliest human occupations at Kuk Swamp, between ~10,220—9910 cal BP.

Bananas have been cultivated and hybridized a number of times over several thousand years, so we'll concentrate on the original domestication, and leave the hybridization to botanists. All edible bananas today are hybridized from *Musa acuminata* (diploid) or *M. acuminata* crossed with *M. balbisiana*(triploid). Today, *M. acuminata* is found throughout mainland and island southeast Asia including the eastern half of the Indian subcontinent; *M. balbisiana* is mostly found in mainland southeast Asia. Genetic changes from *M. acuminata* created by the domestication process include the suppression of seeds and the development of parthenocarpy: the ability of humans to create a new crop without the need for fertilization.

Archaeological evidence from the Kuk Swamp of the highlands of New Guinea indicates that bananas were deliberately planted by at least as long ago as 5000—4490 BC (6950—6440 cal BP). Additional evidence indicates that *Musa acuminata* ssp banksii F. Muell was dispersed out of New Guinea and introduced into eastern Africa by ~3000 BC (Munsa and Nkang), and into south Asia (the Harappan site of Kot Diji) by 2500 cal BC, and probably earlier.

（资料来源：http://archaeology.about.com/od/kterms/qt/Kuk-Swamp.htm, http://archaeology.about.com/od/baterms/qt/Banana-History.htm.）

Questions

1. What evidence have the authors given to prove the early agricultural site?
2. Why do the authors mention the banana domestication?

Royal Exhibition Building and Carlton Gardens
皇家展览馆和卡尔顿园林

⇨ 简介

所属国家：澳大利亚（Australia）

入选时间：2004

入选标准：（ii）

The Royal Exhibition Building and its surrounding Carlton Gardens, located at Nicholson Street, Melbourne, were designed for the great international exhibition of 1880—1881 in Melbourne. The building is constructed of brick and timber, steel and slate, with combined elements from the Byzantine, Romanesque, Lombardic and Italian Renaissance styles. Its scale and grandeur demonstrates the values and aspirations attached to industrialization and its international face. The property has witnessed over 50 exhibitions staged between 1851 and 1915 in venues including Paris, New York, Vienna, Calcutta, Kingston (Jamaica) and Santiago (Chile). All shared a common theme and aims: To chart material and moral progress through displays of industry from all nations.

澳大利亚皇家展览馆及其周边的卡尔顿园林，位于墨尔本尼科尔森街 9 号，是为 1880—1881 年墨尔本的盛大国际展览而特别设计的。整个展馆和园林由砖、木头、钢和石板等材料建成,风格则融合了拜占庭式、罗马式、伦巴第式和意大利文艺复兴风格。其气势雄伟的建筑、壮丽的园林美景不仅洋溢着国际化气息,更充分体现了展馆所蕴含的工业化价值和精神。从 1851 年至 1915 年,有 50 余场来自巴黎、纽约、维也纳、加尔各答、牙买加金斯敦、智利圣地亚哥等地的展览在此处举办。所有活动有一个共同的主题和目的:通过各国工业的展示,记录物质和精神的进步。

Vocabulary

1. surrounding *adj.* 周围的,附近的

Carefully detach the surrounding section from the rear window.

小心地将包围部分从后窗上分开。

2. design *v.* 设计

Computer security systems will be designed by independent technicians.

计算机安全系统将由独立的技师来设计。

3. construct *v.* 建造,修建

The French constructed a series of fortresses from Dunkirk on the Channel coast to Douai.

法国人在从敦刻尔克到杜埃的英吉利海峡沿岸修筑了一系列要塞。

4. element *n.* 元素;要素

The exchange of prisoners of war was one of the key elements of the UN's peace plan.

交换战俘是联合国和平计划的一个重要部分。

5. aspiration *n.* 强烈的愿望

There remains a sizable gap between aspiration and accomplishment.

愿望与成果之间仍有相当大的差距。

6. chart *v.* 记录;记述;跟踪(进展或发展)

Bulletin boards charted each executive's progress.

公告牌显示了每个主管人员的工作进展情况。

扩展阅读

Royal Exhibition Building

The Royal Exhibition Building was built to host the Melbourne International Exhibition in 1880—1881 and later hosted the opening of the first Parliament of Australia in 1901. Throughout the 20th century smaller sections and wings of the building were subject to demolition and fire; however, the main building, known as the Great Hall, survived.

It received restoration throughout the 1990s and in 2004 became the first building in Australia to be awarded UNESCO World Heritage status, being one of the last remaining major 19th-century exhibition buildings in the world. It sits adjacent to the Melbourne Museum and is the largest item in Museum Victoria's collection. Today, the building hosts various exhibitions and other events and is closely tied with events at the Melbourne Museum.

The Royal Exhibition Building was designed by the architect Joseph Reed, who also designed the Melbourne Town Hall and the State Library of Victoria. According to Reed, the eclectic design was inspired by many sources. The dome was modeled on the Florence Cathedral, while the main pavilions were influenced by the style of Rundbogenstil and several buildings from Normandy, Caen and Paris.

The foundation stone was laid by Victorian governor George Bowen on 19 February 1879 and it was completed in 1880, ready for the Melbourne International Exhibition. The building consisted of a Great Hall of over 12,000 square metres and many temporary annexes.

In the 1880s, the building hosted two major international exhibitions: The Melbourne International Exhibition in 1880 and the Melbourne Centennial Exhibition in 1888 to celebrate a century of European settlement in Australia. The most significant event to occur in the Exhibition Building was the opening of the first Parliament of Australia on 9 May 1901, following the inauguration of the Commonwealth of Australia on 1 January. After the official opening, the Federal Parliament moved to the Victorian State Parliament House, while the Victorian Parliament moved to the Exhibition Building for the next 26 years.

On 3 September 1901, the Countess of Hopetoun, wife of the Governor-General, announced the winners of a competition to design the Australian National Flag. A large flag, 5.5 metres by 11 metres, was unfurled and flown over the dome of the Royal Exhibition Building.

The period after this time saw the building used for many purposes. It was a venue for the 1956 Summer Olympics, hosting the basketball, weightlifting, wrestling, and the fencing part of the modern pentathlon competitions. As it decayed, it became known derogatively by locals as *The White Elephant* in the 1940s and by the 1950s, like many buildings in Melbourne of that time it was earmarked for replacement by office blocks. In 1948, members of the Melbourne City Council put this to the vote and it was narrowly decided not to demolish the building. The wing of the building which once housed Melbourne's aquarium burnt down in 1953. During the 1940s and 1950s, the building remained a venue for regular weekly dances. Over some decades of this period it also held boat shows, car shows and other regular home and building industry shows. It was also used during the 1950s, 1960s and 1970s for State High School Matriculation and for the Victorian Certificate of Education examinations, among its various other purposes. Nevertheless, the grand ballroom was demolished in 1979, leaving the main structure in place along with annexes constructed in the 1960s and 1970s. Following the demolition of the grand ballroom, there was a public outcry which prevented the main building from also being demolished.

On 13 August 1980, The Hon Norman Lacy, Minister for the Arts in the Hamer Government, unveiled the place (located at the eastern entrance) that commemorates the centenary of the opening to the general public of the Exhibition Building on 29 May 1880.

During a visit to Victoria in 1984, Princess Alexandra (Queen Elizabeth II's cousin) bestowed the royal title on the building and it has been referred to as the Royal Exhibition Building ever since. This title, and the first conservation assessment of the building undertaken by Alan Willingham, sparked a restoration of the interiors of the building in the late 1980s and 1990s, and the construction of a mirror glass annexe (which was later demolished). In 1996, the then Premier of Victoria, Jeff Kennett, proposed the location and construction of Melbourne's State Museum on the adjacent site. Temporary annexes built in the 1960s were removed and in 1997 and 1998, the exterior of the building was progressively restored.

The location of the Melbourne Museum close to the Exhibition Building site was strongly opposed by the Victorian State Labor Party, the Melbourne City Council and the local community. Due to the community campaign opposing the museum development, John Brumby, then State opposition leader, with the support of the Melbourne City Council, proposed the nomination of the Royal Exhibition Building for world heritage listing. The world heritage nomination did not progress until the election of the Victorian State Labor Party as the new government in 1999.

On 1 July 2004, the Royal Exhibition Building and Carlton Gardens was granted listing as a World Heritage Site, the first building in Australia to be granted this status. The heritage listing states that "The Royal Exhibition Building is the only major extant nineteenth-century exhibition building in Australia. It is one of the few major nineteenth-century exhibition buildings to survive worldwide".

In October 2009, Museum Victoria embarked upon a major project to restore the former German Garden of the Western Forecourt. The area had been covered by asphalt in the 1950s for car parking.

The Royal Exhibition Building is still in use as a commercial exhibition venue, hosting many events on a regular basis such as the Melbourne International Flower and Garden Show. Regular tours are also offered by the Melbourne Museum.

The Royal Exhibition Building is used as an exam hall for the University of Melbourne, Royal Melbourne Institute of Technology, Melbourne High School, Nossal High School, Mac. Robertson Girls' High School and Suzanne Cory High School.

However, it is no longer Melbourne's largest commercial exhibition centre. The modern alternative to the Royal Exhibition Building is the Melbourne Exhibition and Convention Centre, located in Southbank to the south of the central city area.

（资料来源：http://en. wikipedia. org/wiki/Royal_Exhibition_Building. ）

Questions

1. For what reason was the Royal Exhibition Building fixed ?
2. What other functions has the building performed besides hosting exhibition?
3. Why is this building referred to as the Royal Exhibition Building?

Sydney Opera House
悉尼歌剧院

▷ **简介**

所属国家：澳大利亚（Australia）

入选时间：2007

入选标准：（i）

The Sydney Opera House, inaugurated in 1976, is situated on Bennelong Point in Sydney Harbour and occupies a land of 1.84 ha, with 183 m in length, 118 m in width and 67 m in height. A great urban sculpture set in a remarkable waterscape, at the tip of a peninsula projecting into Sydney Harbour, the building has had an enduring influence on architecture and constitutes a masterpiece of 20th century architecture that brings together multiple strands of creativity and innovation in both architectural form and structural design. The Sydney Opera House comprises three groups of interlocking vaulted "shells" which roof two main performance halls and a restaurant. It was conceived and largely built by Danish architect Jørn Utzon. As one of the busiest and famous performing arts centres in the world, hosting over 1,500 performances each year attended by some 1.2 million people, the Sydney Opera House provides a venue for many performing arts companies and presents a wide range of productions on its own account. It is also one of the most popular visitor attractions in Australia, with more than seven million people visiting the site each year, 300,000 of whom take a guided tour.

悉尼歌剧院位于澳大利亚悉尼市贝尼朗岬角，整个建筑占地 1.84 公顷，是 20 世纪最具特色的建筑之一，已成为澳大利亚的象征性建筑，也是世界著名的表演艺术中心。该歌剧院 1973 年正式落成，设计者为丹麦设计师约恩·乌松。整个歌剧院分为三个部分：歌剧厅、音乐厅和贝尼朗餐厅。音乐厅是悉尼歌剧院最大的厅堂，共可容纳 2679 名观众，通常用于举办交响乐、室内乐、歌剧、舞蹈、合唱、流行乐、爵士乐等多种表演。每年在悉尼歌剧院举行的表演大约有 1500 场，约 120 万观众前往共襄盛举，是世界上最大的表演艺术中心之一。那些濒临水面的巨大的白色壳片群，像是海上的船帆，又如一簇簇盛开的花朵，在蓝天、碧海、绿树的映衬下，婀娜多姿，轻盈皎洁。这座建筑已被视为世界的经典建筑，载入史册。

Vocabulary

1. inaugurate *v.* 为……举行开幕式(或落成典礼)

The mayor inaugurated a new bridge.

市长为一座新桥举行落成典礼。

2. at the tip of 在……的尖端

Singapore is at the southern tip of this important waterway.

新加坡是在这条重要水道的南端。

3. project *v.* 投射

The team tried projecting the maps with two different projectors onto the same screen.

这个小组想用两台不同的投影仪把这些地图投射到同一个屏幕上。

4. enduring influence 深远的影响

Francis Schaeffer's enduring influence upon evangelicals and evangelicalism cannot be overlooked.

弗朗西斯·薛华对福音派信徒和福音派教义的深远影响是不可忽视的。

5. constitute *v.* 等同于

Testing patients without their consent would constitute a professional and legal offence.

未经患者同意而对其进行检查被视为违反职业操守并触犯法律。

6. strand *n.* (思想等的)一个组成部分,(计划或理论的)一部分

He's trying to bring together various strands of radical philosophic thought.

他正试图把各种激进的哲学思想综合在一起。

7. interlock *v.* (使)相互扣住

Joyce sits with her fingers interlocked under her chin.

乔伊斯坐在那里,十指相扣撑着下巴。

8. conceive *v.* 构思

He conceived a new plan very quickly.

他很快就想出一个新的计划方案。

9. venue *n.* 场地

The first thing to do is to book a venue.

第一件要做的事就是预定场地。

10. on its own account 依靠自己

This company buys a product on its own account and resells it with a reasonable makeup.

公司自行进货并以合理的差价卖出。

An Overview of the Sydney Opera House

The Sydney Opera House (1957—1973) is a masterpiece of late modern architecture. It is admired internationally and proudly treasured by the people of Australia. It was created by a young architect who understood and recognised the potential provided by the site against the stunning backdrop of Sydney Harbour. Denmark's Jørn Utzon gave Australia a challenging, graceful piece of urban sculpture in patterned tiles, glistening in the sunlight and invitingly aglow at night. Jørn Utzon died in Copenhagen in November 2008 aged 90.

In its short lifetime, the Sydney Opera House has earned a reputation as a world-class performing arts centre and become a symbol of both Sydney and the Australian nation.

World Heritage Listed

The Sydney Opera House was inscribed in the World Heritage List in June 2007: "The Sydney Opera House is a great architectural work of the 20th century. It represents multiple strands of creativity, both in architectural form and structural design, a great urban sculpture carefully set in a remarkable waterscape and a world famous iconic building."

The expert evaluation report to the World Heritage Committee stated: "…it stands by itself as one of the indisputable masterpieces of human creativity, not only in the 20th century but in the history of humankind."

Design/Structure

The distinctive roof comprises sets of interlocking vaulted "shells" set upon a vast terraced platform and surrounded by terrace areas that function as pedestrian concourses.

The two main halls are arranged side by side, with their long axes, slightly inclined from each other, generally running north-south. The auditoria face south, away from the harbour with the stages located between the audience and the city. The Forecourt is a vast open space from which people ascend the stairs to the podium. The Monumental Steps, which lead up from the Forecourt to the two main performance venues, are a great ceremonial stairway nearly 100 metres wide.

The vaulted roof "shells" were designed by Utzon in collaboration with internationally renowned engineers Ove Arup & Partners with the final shape of the "shells" derived from the surface of a single imagined sphere. Each "shell" is composed of pre-cast rib segments radiating from a concrete pedestal and rising to a ridge beam. The "shells" are faced in glazed off-white tiles while the podium is clad in earth-toned, reconstituted granite panels. The glass walls are a special feature of the building, constructed according to the modified design by Utzon's successor architect, Peter Hall.

History of the Design

The history surrounding the design and construction of the building became as controversial as its design. In 1956 the NSW Government called an open-ended international design competition and appointed an independent jury. The competition brief provided broad specifications to attract the best design talent in the world; it did not specify design parameters or set a cost limit. The main requirement of the competition brief was a design for two performance halls, one for opera and one for symphony concerts. Reputedly rescued from a pile of discarded submissions, Jørn Utzon's winning entry created great community interest and the NSW Government's decision to commission Utzon as the sole architect was unexpected, bold and visionary.

Construction

Design and construction were closely intertwined. Utzon's radical approach to the construction of the building fostered an exceptional collaborative and innovative environment. The design solution and construction of the "shell" structure took eight years to complete and the development of the special ceramic tiles for the "shells" took over three years. The project was not helped by the changes to the brief. Construction of the "shells" was one of the most difficult engineering tasks ever to be attempted. The revolutionary concept demanded equally revolutionary engineering and building techniques. Baulderstone Hornibrook (then Hornibrook Group) constructed the roof "shells" and the interior structure and fitout. At the behest of the Australian Broadcasting Commission (ABC) the NSW Government changed the proposed larger opera hall into the concert hall because at the time, symphony concerts, managed by the ABC, were more popular and drew larger audiences than opera.

Completion and Opening

Cost overruns contributed to populist criticism and a change of government resulted in 1966 to Utzon's resignation, street demonstrations and professional controversy. Peter Hall supported by Lionel Todd and David Littlemore in conjunction with the then NSW Government Architect, Ted Farmer, completed the glass walls and interiors including adding three previously unplanned venues underneath the Concert Hall on the western side. Opened by Queen Elizabeth II in 1973, new works were undertaken between 1986 and 1988 to the land approach and Forecourt under the supervision of the then NSW Government Architect, Andrew Andersons, with contributions by Peter Hall.

For the Future

In 1999, Jørn Utzon was re-engaged as the Sydney Opera House architect to develop a set of design principles to act as a guide for all future changes to the building. These principles reflect his original vision and help to ensure that the building's architectural integrity is maintained.

Utzon Room

Utzon's first major project was the refurbishment of the Reception Hall into a stunning, light filled space which highlights the original concrete "beams" and a wall-length tapestry designed by him which hangs opposite the harbour outlook. Noted for its excellent acoustics, it is the only authentic Utzon-designed space at Sydney Opera House and was renamed the Utzon Room in his honour in 2004.

Modern Alterations

This project was followed by the first alteration to the exterior of the building with the addition of a new Colonnade along the western side, which shades nine new large glass openings into the previously solid exterior wall. This Utzon-led project, which was completed in 2006, gave the theatre foyers their first view of Sydney Harbour. The foyers' interiors are now being renovated to Utzon's specifications, to become a coherent attractive space for patrons. The design also incorporates the first public lift and interior escalators to assist less mobile patrons.

Utzon was working on designs to renovate the ageing and inadequate opera theatre. On all projects, he worked with his architect son Jan, and Sydney-based architect Richard Johnson of Johnson Pilton Walker.

Architecture Prize

In 2003 Utzon received the Pritzker Prize, international architecture's highest honour.

（资料来源：http://www.sydneyoperahouse.com/about/house_history_landing.aspx.）

Questions

1. What does "The Sydney Opera House (1957—1973)" in the first sentence mean?
2. What account for Utzon's resignation?
3. What is the most difficult task in the building of the Sydney Opera House?
4. Are there any other designers working with Utzon? If "Yes", who are they?

第二节　大洋洲的世界自然遗产

Great Barrier Reef
大堡礁

⇨ **简介**

所属国家：澳大利亚（Australia）
入选时间：1981

入选标准：(vii)(viii)(ix)(x)

Covering an area of 348,000 square kilometres, the Great Barrier Reef is the world's most extensive coral reef ecosystem on the north east coast of Australia. Within the GBR there are some 2,500 individual reefs of varying sizes and shapes, and over 900 islands, with 400 types of coral, 1,500 species of fish, 4,000 types of mollusc and some 240 species of birds. It also holds great scientific interest as the habitat of species such as the dugong ("sea cow") and the large green turtle, which are threatened with extinction. A rich variety of landscapes and seascapes, including rugged mountains with dense and diverse vegetation and adjacent fringing reefs, provide spectacular scenery.

大堡礁位于澳大利亚东北海岸,总面积达348000万平方千米,有2500个大小珊瑚礁岛,是世界上最大、最长的珊瑚礁群,也是世界七大自然景观之一。这里生存着形状、大小、颜色都极不相同的400种珊瑚礁,其中有世界上最大的珊瑚礁。珊瑚栖息的水域颜色从白、青到靛蓝,绚丽多彩。大堡礁有着得天独厚的科学研究条件,因为这里有鱼类1500种,软体动物4000余种,鸟类240种,这里还是某些濒临灭绝的动物物种(如儒艮和巨型绿龟)的栖息地。在落潮时,部分珊瑚礁露出水面形成珊瑚岛。在礁群与海岸之间是一条极方便的交通海路。风平浪静时,游船在此间通过,船下连绵不断的多姿多彩的珊瑚景观,就成为吸引世界各地游客来观赏的海底奇观。

Vocabulary

1. extensive *adj.* 广阔的,广大的

When built, the palace and its grounds were more extensive than the city itself.

建成时,宫殿及其庭园比城市本身面积还要大。

2. ecosystem *n.*【生】生态系统

Madagascar's ecosystems range from rainforest to semi-desert.

马达加斯加生态系统类型多样,从雨林到半荒漠等不一而足。

3. habitat *n.* (动物的)栖息地,住处;产地

Few countries have as rich a diversity of habitat as South Africa does.

几乎没有哪个国家像南非那样拥有如此多样化的动植物栖生地。

4. extinction *n.* 熄灭;消灭,灭绝

An operation is beginning to try to save a species of crocodile from extinction.

一项努力拯救某一鳄鱼物种、使其免于灭绝的行动已经开始。

5. adjacent *adj.* 邻近的,毗邻的

When you first try this, you will feel like you are going to hit the ball to an adjacent court.

当你最初尝试这么做的时候,你将感觉好像你要将球打到毗连的球场上。

6. fringe *v.* 作为……的边缘,围绕着

A line of palm trees fringes the swimming pool.

游泳池边缘围了一圈棕榈树。

7. spectacular *adj.* 壮观的,壮丽的,令人惊叹的

A leisurely walk down this trail will reward the summer visitors with solitude and spectacular scenery.

沿着这条小道悠闲地散散步,避暑客可尽享幽静和胜景。

扩展阅读

Whale Watching

Discover the joy and exhileration of Whale Watching.

Spotting different whale species along the Great Barrier Reef and coast is a common occurence.

Humpback whales and minke whales are two most common species of whale to be seen along the coast.

Going on a whale watching cruise is one of the most exhilarating things you can do. It is an undescribable experience and something you really have to experience first hand.

Between the months July and November the magnificent humpback whales migrate in Pods (groups), moving out of the cold southern waters of the Antartica into the warmer, tropical ocean of the Great Barrier Reef. That's about the time that many tourists book their airline tickets for a whale watching holiday! The whales are simply enchanting and they enjoy their time in the warm Australian waters. Here they spend the Australian winter where they mate, calve and frolic before returning to the south for summer.

One of the best places to experience whale watching is from Hervey Bay, on the Fraser Coast, towards the southern end of the reef.

From here you can catch whale watching cruises and experience the whales up close and personal. And with more than 7,000 humpback whales migrating each year, you are sure to experience them.

Whales measuring from 12 to 16 metres (36 to 48 ft.) in length, and weighing up to 45 tonnes will swim in close to take a look at you. These enormous but gentle creatures will frolic and play, quite happy for you to watch.

Watch out for a spray of water. The whales will spirt water from their blowhole (nostril on the top of their heads), as they break the surface of the ocean for fresh air. Then be amazed at their power as they propel themselves out of the water and crash back down into the ocean again.

If you are planning a trip to the Great Barrier Reef then you must put whale watching at the top of your list of things to do and see.

For more information about the marine animals of the Great Barrier Reef take a look at our pages on the Dangerous Great Barrier Reef Animals; the Endangered Animals of the Reef; and the Hammerhead Shark.

（资料来源：http://www. the-great-barrier-reef-experience. com/whale-watching. html. ）

Great White Shark Expedition

Come with us and experience the world's most famous, most feared and most spectacular shark—the great white shark.

To see a great white shark in the wild is a very special and rare experience but to come face to face with one underwater is one of the most exciting experiences available to divers today!

This tour takes place around the scenic offshore islands of South Australia and has been described as the ultimate adventure that Australia has to offer.

To reliably expect to see great white sharks in South Australia, we need to travel out into the clear blue offshore waters of Australia's largest seal colony, the famous Neptune Islands. These remote offshore islands are reliably accessible only to larger ocean going live-aboard boats such as "Princess Ⅱ".

Even though "the majority" of our initial inquiries request shorter length tours, we feel that it is unrealistic to expect success with only a day or two spent on location. Despite the huge number of people willing to part with good money and gamble on doing a shorter trip, we strongly recommend a minimum of 3 days on location to maximize the potential success of each expedition date.

Our various 3—5 day length tour agendas are designed to firstly allow us time to get out to our viewing locations and back, while also allowing for finding productive spells of weather and reliable shark action. This agenda gives passengers a more realistic chance of enjoying at least one extraordinary magical day when all the conditions favourably come together.

More time spent onboard allows expedition members to spend more quality time with this spectacular animal. These precious moments always seem to go way too fast, and many photographers or passengers, who are travelling from overseas to make this trip the focus of their entire travel to Australia, often do consecutive back-to-back tours to maximize their exposure.

During our days at sea, we also encourage shore parties, and always look for an opportunity to stop off at a special place to snorkel with Australian sea lions on the way out. There are many options to fill our days with interesting activities.

（资料来源：http://www.mikeball.com/great-white-shark-expedition.）

Questions

1. How many whale species are mentioned in the first article? What are they?

2. When will tourists go to Australia for a whale watching holiday?

3. According to the second article could a tourist have a face-to-face experience with a great white shark in the wild?

4. Where should tourists go if they want to see great white sharks?

5. How many days are suggested to stay for the view of great white sharks?

Greater Blue Mountains Area

大蓝山山脉地区

👉 **简介**

所属国家：澳大利亚（Australia）

入选时间：2000

入选标准：(ix)(x)

Blue Mountains

Situated in New South Wales, the Greater Blue Mountains Area consists of 1.03 million hectares of sandstone plateaux, escarpments and gorges dominated by temperate eucalypt forest. The area is called "Blue Mountains" because when atmospheric temperature rise, the essential oil of various Eucalyptus species evaporates and disperses in the air, and then visible blue spectrum of sunlight propagates more than other colours. Therefore the reflected landscape from mountains seems bluish by human eyes. The site with 91 eucalypt groups is outstanding for its representation of the evolutionary adaptation and diversification of the eucalypts in post-Gondwana isolation on the Australian continent. Besides, the area also contains ancient, relict species of global significance. The most famous of these is the recently discovered Wollemi pine, a "living fossil" dating back to the age of the dinosaurs. The attractions of the area like the Three Sisters, Wentworth Falls and Jenolan Caves are breathtaking beauties.

澳大利亚的大蓝山山脉地区位于东南部的新南威尔士州，拥有103万公顷的砂岩平原、陡坡峭壁和峡谷，由三叠纪块状坚固砂岩积累而成。山区到处生长着各种桉树，其挥发的油滴在空气中经过阳光折射呈现蓝光，因而得名蓝山。曾经是当时欧洲移民向西推进的障碍。这里有114类具有明显地域特征的植物和120种国家稀有植物和濒危植物。大蓝山有91个桉叶植物种类，展示了澳洲大陆在冈瓦纳分离后桉树种群进化的适应性和多样性；占有世界数量10%的维管植物以及大量珍稀濒危物种，包括当地堪称活化石的物种，如生存范围非常有限的瓦勒迈松，更加充分展示了澳大利亚的生物多样性。著名旅游景点有三姐妹峰、大瀑布、钟乳洞等，风景绝美；三姐妹峰是蓝山的标志性景观。

Vocabulary

1. situated *adj.* 位于……的

His hotel is situated in one of the loveliest places on the Loire.

他下榻的旅馆位于卢瓦河畔最漂亮的地方之一。

2. dominate *v.* 控制；在……中占首要地位

The book is expected to dominate the best-seller lists.

这本书预计会占据各大畅销书排行榜的榜首。

3. evaporate *v.* 蒸发

The movement of the sea breaks up the oil so that much of it evaporates.

海洋运动也可以分解石油，让其中大部分蒸发。

4. disperse *v.* 分散，散开

When the rain came down the crowd started to disperse.

下雨时人群开始分散。

5. propagate *v.*【物】通过媒介传送，扩大

Very-high-energy gamma rays may be slowed down as they propagate through the quantum turbulence of space-time.

超高能伽马射线在时空的量子乱流中传播时，其速度可能会降低。

6. date back to 追溯到

The stone circle is said to date back to 3200 BC and is a vision in itself.

据说石圈的历史可以追溯至公元前 3200 年，位于其中便能看到一番美景。

扩展阅读

Five Ways to Experience Blue Mountains Beauty

You'll love the blue-hazed beauty of the Blue Mountains World Heritage Area—more than one million hectares of tall forests, sandstone cliffs, canyons, waterfalls and bushland. Take in the breathtaking panoramas on a bushwalk, mountain bike, climbing rocks, canyoning or abseiling. Marvel at natural attractions like Wentworth Falls and the Three Sisters—a trio of rocky pinnacles named after an Aboriginal legend. Explore the underground rivers and chambers of Jenolan Caves, then walk the historic Six Foot Track to Katoomba. Amongst the sandstone outcrops and eucalypt forests you'll find great dining, luxury retreats, the world's steepest railway and a vibrant community of artists.

Go Walkabout with an Aboriginal Guide

Discover a rich Aboriginal heritage in the Blue Mountains—from the legend of the Three Sisters to ancient art and ceremonial sites. Visit the shallow cave of Lyrebird Dell, an Aboriginal campsite around 12,000 years old. See fine hand stencils and prints at Red Hands Cave near Glenbrook. You can reach the cave on a walking trail past Camp Fire Creek, where many years ago an Aboriginal tribe left axe-grinding grooves on volcanic rock. Go walkabout with a local Darug guide and learn about the songlines that connect sacred sites. See bark and body painting demonstrations, taste bush tucker and swim in a crystal clear billabong under a rainbow waterfall. Get up close to wildlife, explore sandstone caves and listen to the Dreamtime stories that wove this wilderness.

Walking, with Great Gulps of Mountain Air

Soak up the Blue Mountains scenery—streams, waterfalls, forested valleys, dark ravines and sheer cliffs—on one of the many well-marked walking trails. Follow the original 1884 horse track from Katoomba to Jenolan Caves on the three-day Six Foot Track. Or follow the easy Princes Rock Walk to a lookout over Wentworth Falls, Kings Tableland and Mount Solitary. You can wade and boulder-hop your way down the Glenbrook Gorge on the Glenbrook Gorge Track. Or creep up the sheer cliffs around Wentworth Falls on the challenging National Pass. Trek the Pulpit Rock Track past swamps, eucalypt forests and open heathland to be rewarded with a 280-degree panorama of the blue gum forest of Grose Valley.

Next to Natural Attractions

You'll marvel at nature's majestic statements in the Blue Mountains. Pay homage to the Three Sisters from Katoomba. Then visit Wentworth Falls, a picturesque waterfall on the edge of the Jamison Valley. Watch it plunge almost 300 metres and check out the valley views from the walks that circle it. Stand on the top of the narrow sandstone outcrop of Hanging Rock and hear your voice echo through the enormous, forested valley below. Don't miss the underground rivers, prehistoric formations and huge chambers of Jenolan Caves, the world's oldest open underground cave system. Get goosebumps on a ghost tour or enjoy a monthly cave concert with natural acoustics and fairytale ambience. In Mount Tomah Botanic Gardens, you can step back in time with the Wollemi Pine, one of the world's oldest and rarest plants.

With High Tea or a Hot Dinner

The Blue Mountains is a place to eat, drink and indulge. Lunch on Leura's pretty tree-lined streets, then browse the galleries, boutiques and bric-a-brac stores. Fine dine in front of a roaring fire or do coffee and cake in an art deco café in Katoomba. Shop for gourmet food at Blackheath or take high tea in a majestic, historic home at Jenolan Caves. During June, July and August, you can embrace the Yulefest celebrations with a Christmas roast and pudding around a roaring fire. Wherever you eat and drink, you'll love the food prepared with care and the seductive mountain settings.

On a Long, Leisurely Drive

Take on adventure on the Greater Blue Mountains Drive—a series of linked drives and discovery trails that circle the 10,000 square kilometer Blue Mountains World Heritage area. You can journey to surrounding regions such as Macarthur and the Southern Highlands, Mudgee, the Hunter Valley and the Hawkesbury. Or explore magical places within the Blue Mountains—including Kurrajong, The Mounts, Blackheath and Megalong—on 18 discovery trails. If you tire of being behind the wheel, jump on the Zig Zag Railway, a vintage steam train that follows the original line from Bell to Lithgow.

（资料来源：http://www.australia.com/explore/icons/blue-mountains.aspx.）

Questions

1. What can a traveler get if he goes walkabout with an Aboriginal guide?

2. How many attractions are mentioned in the passage? What are they?

3. Will you travel the Greater Blue Mountains Area on foot, by bike or vehicle? Why?

New Zealand Sub-Antarctic
新西兰次南极区群岛

简介

所属国家：新西兰（New Zealand）

入选时间：1998

入选标准：（ix）（x）

Covering a total land area of 76,458 ha, the New Zealand Sub-Antarctic Islands consist of five island groups (the Snares, Bounty Islands, Antipodes Islands, Auckland Islands and Campbell Island) in the Southern Ocean south east of New Zealand. The Snares and Bounty Islands are groups of islands formed of predominately granitic rock and the rest three are eroded remnants of Pliocene volcanoes. These islands have a high level of productivity, biodiversity, wildlife population densities and endemism among plants, invertebrates and birds. Of 126 species of bird on the islands, five breed nowhere else in the world. The Snares and two of the Auckland Islands are especially important in that their vegetation has not been modified by human or alien species. With the exception of the Bounty Islands where some scientists work at the weather station, the remaining islands are not inhabited by human beings.

位于新西兰南岛的东南海面上的新西兰次南极区群岛（占地76458公顷）包括五组群岛：邦地群岛、安蒂鲍迪斯群岛、斯纳尔斯群岛、奥克兰群岛和坎贝尔岛。这些漂亮岛屿是许多稀有动物的栖息地，如南半球的皇家信天翁、黄眼企鹅及新西兰胡克海狮等。在此生息繁衍的126种鸟类中，有5种在世界任何其他地方从未见到过。斯奈尔斯群岛、安蒂波德斯群岛及奥克兰群岛的两个岛的植物从来没有被人类或者外来动物影响过。邦提岛和斯奈尔斯群岛是在花岗岩和变质岩基底上形成的，另外三个群岛位于其南部，是在火山岩构造上发展形成的。奥克兰群岛和坎贝尔岛上有大规模冰川发育的证据，拥有许多海湾和深水港。除了坎贝尔岛上的气象站有科学研究人员外，其他岛都无人定居。

Vocabulary

1. erode v. 腐蚀，侵蚀

Once exposed, soil is quickly eroded by wind and rain.

一旦暴露在外，土壤很快就会被风雨侵蚀。

2. remnants n. 剩余部分（remnant 的名词复数）；残余

Beneath the present church were remnants of Roman flooring.

在现在的教堂下面是古罗马时期地面的遗存。

3. endemism *n.* 地方特殊性；(动植物的)特有分布；地方性生长

There are basically two types of endemism.

特有现象基本有两种类群。

4. breed *v.* 繁殖，旺盛生长

The area now attracts over 60 species of breeding birds.

这一地区现在吸引了 60 多种鸟类到此繁育后代。

5. modify *v.* 改变

Established practices are difficult to modify.

既定的惯例是很难改变的。

6. with the exception of 除……以外

All his novels are set in Italy with the exception of his last.

除了最后一部小说，他的所有作品都以意大利为背景。

7. inhabit *v.* 居住

Wild tribes still inhabit part of the Philippines.

菲律宾部分地区仍然居住着一些原始部落。

扩展阅读

Sub-Antarctic Islands

Why Visit

The far-flung Sub-Antarctic islands are southward from New Zealand，crossing six degrees of latitude. Isolated and life-rich，they are considered one of the world's biodiversity hotspots. For nature lovers，birders，photographers，and travelers whose inner explorer beg to venture where few have gone before，this UNESCO World Heritage site is indeed a paradise found.

Five island clusters belong to New Zealand. Macquarie，also part of the Sub-Antarctic collection，is an Australian territory. The islands offer you a chance to explore a wide array of volcanic and glaciated geography—including cave-riddled basalt cliffs，pristine sugar-sand beaches，wind-and-water-chiseled monolithic rock formations，and windswept grassy headlands. Walk through impressively tall stands of rata trees，among giant ferns and into the twisted world of elfin forests—home to melodious songbirds and stunning botanicals found nowhere else on the globe. Along the shoreline，search for the Hooker sea lions，their adorable pups piling atop one another. Snap a group portrait of huge elephant seals lolling about on the beach，and witness the awkward flight forays of young albatross and the graceful soar of their elders.

Cross off an additional eight species from your must-see penguin list on a single voyage to the Sub-Antarctic Islands. Two are found nowhere else in the world：the extremely rare yellow-eyed penguin of Enderby and the endemic Snares-crested penguin，which only nests on Snares Island. On Macquarie，the sight of over one million royal penguins and 200,000 pairs of kings will simply knock your socks off.

Whether surveying wild and scenic vistas from the deck of your ship, zipping past craggy cliffs on Zodiac inflatable boats, stepping onto shores only a lucky few have explored, or hiking through forests rooted in the beginning of time, a Sub-Antarctic cruise allows the intrepid traveler a truly privileged glimpse into a magical world.

Note: *For travelers wishing to continue the adventure, a Ross Sea expedition travels deep into the Antarctic continent, offering the rare opportunity to observe emperor penguins in their natural habitat at certain times of year. For information, visit the Ross Sea page of our Research section.*

History

No single discoverer can put his name on the collective Sub-Antarctics, and the distance between the widely spread islands is too great for sailors to simply happen upon them. The captain of a whaling vessel made the first European record of the islands on August 18, 1806, thanks to a new shipping route established between Australia and Cape Horn that passed between the five archipelagos. But prehistoric artifacts found on the islands prove that early seafaring Polynesians were there far earlier.

Hundreds of sealers and a few whalers worked on the islands, making them the main sealing station in the Pacific until 1812, when the ocean's seal populations nearly ran out. In addition to the marine plunder, the sealers brought pigs, goats, cattle, cats, rats and dozens of more animals, introducing them to the native species of the islands with a deadly result—the unmaking of which is still ongoing.

In 1907, the Sub-Antarctic Islands Scientific Expedition conducted magnetic surveys and collected rare and unique botanical and zoological specimens, piquing the world's interest in these outposts. In 1941, New Zealand sent a contingent of four men to Campbell Island for coastwatching (i. e. keeping an eye on the Germans in the area). Until 1945 they gathered meteorological information that proved so useful that, after the war, permanent bases were established on Campbell and the Auckland Islands became part of New Zealand's forecasting network.

Geologically the islands are all volcanic in origin, distinguished by dramatic cliffs, caves, winding fjordlike waterways and offshore seastacks. From the harsh yet nutrient-rich terrain grows a mind-boggling array of unique and endemic botanicals—first described by British naturalist Joseph Hooker while sailing with Captain James Ross on his epic Antarctic expeditions. Named "megaherbs" by Ross, the remarkable species of herbaceous perennials include the Ross lily, which can reach six feet in height, and the Campbell Island daisy, whose leaves can extend to four feet across.

The avian statistics alone are reason enough to travel to the Sub-Antarctics—even if you're not a birder at heart. Millions of seabirds comprise some 40 different species. Most live here permanently; others come from across the world to breed and raise their young. Snares Island alone boasts more nesting seabirds than the entire realm of the

British Isles. Almost half of the world's albatross and penguin species also reside here, including the rare yellow-eyed penguin of Enderby and the southern royal albatross with its impressive wingspan of ten feet. Other penguin species include rockhoppers, erect-crested, Snares, gentoos, kings and royals—about three million of which call Macquarie home.

Each island offers its own lovely habitats and wildlife that thrive in the rarified conditions. In the elfin forests of Enderby, colorful birds—red-crowned parakeets and bellbirds—offer a special soundtrack for hikers. Walking in rata forests and among lofty ferns on Campbell recalls a primeval world lost in time. Its beaches resonate with the barking of Hooker's sea lions and elephant seals.

Under the protection of UNESCO, the New Zealand Sub-Antarctics (the Snares, Bounty, Antipodes, Auckland and Campbell Islands) along with Australia's Macquarie Island are being restored to their natural origins. The introduced species of animals are mostly gone now. Though some plants, marine life and wildlife will never be restored, the environment is beginning to resemble its former pristine conditions. Cruise travel to the Sub-Antarctic is the perfect way to enjoy this unique natural wonderland—and to recognize the need to shelter and protect this fragile, exquisite corner of the globe.

（资料来源：http://www.expeditiontrips.com/sub-antarctic-islands-cruises/.）

Questions

1. List 3 reasons for visiting Sub-Antarctic Islands.
2. What is the result of introducing aliens to the islands?
3. How many bird species are mentioned here? Please name some.

Shark Bay
西澳大利亚鲨鱼湾

简介

所属国家：澳大利亚（Australia）

入选时间：1991

入选标准：（vii）（viii）（ix）（x）

Shark Bay which lies on the westernmost point of Australia covers an area of 10,000 km², with an average depth of 10 metres. It is the site of the first recorded European landing in western Australia. Shark Bay is an area of importance for life diversity and abundance. It is home to about 10,000 dugongs (around 12.5% of the world's population), many Indo-Pacific bottlenose dolphins, 26 threatened Australian mammal species, over 230 species of bird, and nearly 150 species of reptile as well as fish, crustaceans, and coelenterates. It has over 4,800 km² of seagrass meadows, including the 1,030 km^2 Wooramel Seagrass Bank, the largest seagrass bank in the world. Twelve species have been found here, with up to nine occurring together in some places. Hamelin Pool contains the most diverse and abundant examples of living stromatolite forms in the world and are considered to be a "classic site" for the study and classification of stromatolitic microbiolites, as the morphology and biology of diverse living types can be studied through a range of environments.

鲨鱼湾位于西澳大利亚洲的加斯科因,是全澳大利亚第一个与欧洲建立联系的地方。海洋公园里有各种不同的地形和生物的栖息地,有崎岖的海边悬崖、安静的礁湖,还有沙子和贝壳堆积成的海滩。海湾里狭长的水域维持着多样的生态系统,包括艳丽的珊瑚和丰富的水生生物,如海龟、鲸鱼、海豚、儒艮、海蛇和鲨鱼等;12 种不同的海草覆盖了大约 4800 平方千米的区域,包括世界上最大的海草沙洲;在海湾南边的哈美林池是由微生物组成的、种类丰富的叠层岩,是世界上最古老、最伟大的活化石。关于它的起源的秘密,吸引了世界各地的科学家进行研究。

Vocabulary

1. diversity *n.* 多样化,多样性

It is vital to stress the diversity of Asia.

强调亚洲的多样性至关重要。

2. abundance *n.* 丰富

But the report has evidence in abundance.

但是报告显示的证据十分充足。

3. classic *adj.* 典型的

The debate in the mainstream press has been a classic example of British hypocrisy.

主流媒体上的辩论是英国式虚伪的典型例子。

4. classification *n.* 分类;(动植物等的)分类学

Classification has been widely applied to many areas, such as medical diagnosis and weather prediction.

分类学被广泛应用在许多领域,例如医学的诊断和天气预测。

5. morphology *n.* 形态学(尤指动植物形态学或词语形态学)

They usually differ markedly in morphology.

它们在形态学上是有明显不同的。

扩展阅读

Why Shark Bay Is a World Heritage Area

Shark Bay World Heritage Area covers 2.2 million hectares on the coast of Western Australia. Its colourful and diverse landscapes are home for a profusion of animals and plants, including some found nowhere else on Earth. Its vast seagrass meadows feed and shelter globally endangered species. Complex interactions among these plants, the climate and the marine environment have allowed unusual "living fossils", stromatolites, to thrive, much as they did at the dawn of time. Shark Bay's extraordinary natural riches are of outstanding global significance.

Shark Bay was inscribed on the World Heritage List in 1991 for its natural heritage values. To be inscribed, properties must be of outstanding universal value and meet at least one of ten selection criteria set by the United Nations Educational, Scientific and Cultural Organisation (UNESCO). Shark Bay satisfied all four of the natural criteria for World Heritage listing.

Natural Beauty

Shark Bay is renowned for its stunning scenery. It is a place of colour and texture, drama and peace: of bright white beaches and blood-red headlands, shallow bays and plunging cliffs.

Shark Bay's vast seagrass meadows pattern the aquamarine waters with dark dapples, ripples and swirls. The coasts are peppered by rocky islands and fringed with sweeping beaches of glittering sand and shells. The spectacular rolling red sands of the Peron Peninsula, interspersed by oddly shaped claypans called birridas, create a dramatic backdrop to the surrounding seas. Closer to the coast, some birridas have been inundated with seawater, forming tranquil turquoise lagoons.

The western peninsula, Edel Land, is white and rocky. Here limestone outcrops give way to soaring sand dunes, rubble prongs and the knife-edge Zuytdorp Cliffs. Giant surf smashes against the seaward coast of Edel Land and Dirk Hartog, Bernier and Dorre Islands. Humpback whales skirt this coast on their annual migrations. Shark Bay's inner waters teem with other life, including dugongs, dolphins, turtles, sharks and rays. Back on shore, the heath and shrublands burst into bloom each spring, and wildflowers carpet the sands.

Earth's History

Shark Bay is home to a community of life forms representing a major stage in Earth's history. They are stromatolites, rock-like structures built by microbes (single-celled cyanobacteria). Shark Bay's stromatolites are similar to life forms found on Earth up to 3.5 billion years ago! Hamelin Pool in Shark Bay has the most diverse and abundant examples of living marine stromatolites in the world.

For 2.9 billion years microbes were the only life on Earth. They modified the Earth's atmosphere by producing oxygen, developed the ability to respire oxygen, emerged from the sea to colonize the land, and evolved most of the survival techniques used by life on Earth today. The only present day evidence of their activities can be found in fossilised stromatolites which have preserved the biology of these unique organisms and shows what the environment was like when they were alive. Shark Bay's stromatolites are "living fossils", providing a unique, modern-day insight into the nature and evolution of Earth's biosphere, and the history of life on Earth.

Ecological Processes

Shark Bay is a place where it is possible to see evolution in action. This includes not only the development of different plant and animal communities, but also an entire marine ecosystem!

Shark Bay is the transition zone between major ecological provinces, marine and terrestrial, and has a high number of endemic species and others at the limit of their range. Living at the extreme, these plants and animals have stretched their survival capabilities to adapt to their environment. Shark Bay's isolation means some animals and plants have evolved into distinct subspecies of species found in other parts of Australia. These ongoing ecological processes are important for the scientific study of species distribution, adaptation, diversity and abundance.

Shark Bay's vast seagrass meadows have influenced the physical, chemical, biological and geomorphic evolution of the region's marine environment. Sediments trapped by seagrasses have formed banks and sills, affecting tidal flow which, combined with the hot dry climate, have created areas of super-concentrated salinity. This has not only led to the emergence of genetically distinct, salt-tolerant animals, but has allowed the proliferation of cyanobacteria and creation of stromatolites—which are themselves a World Heritage value!

Biological Diversity

Shark Bay is a refuge for numerous rare and threatened plants and animals. Largely spared the habitat destruction and introduced predators that wreaked havoc on mainland Australia, it is the last stronghold for five critically endangered mammals—four of which occur in the wild nowhere else on Earth. Shark Bay's sheltered coves and lush seagrass beds are a haven for vulnerable animals such as the humpback whale and green turtle. The world's largest dugong population grazes in its sheltered waters, and it is one of Australia's most important nesting areas for the endangered loggerhead turtle.

The meeting point of three climatic zones and two botanical provinces, Shark Bay is home for at least 100 species of reptile and amphibian, 240 bird species, 320 fish, 80 corals, 218 bivalves and 820 species of plant. At least 70 of these species are endemic—from emu-wrens to eucalypts, featherflowers to frogs. Found nowhere else in the world, these species secure Shark Bay's status as a place vital for the conservation of the Earth's biological diversity.

（资料来源：http://www.sharkbay.org/WHA_values.aspx.）

Questions

1. Please describe the natural beauty of Shark Bay within 80 words.
2. Why do scientists consider Shark Bay's stromatolites "living fossils"?
3. How many endangered animals are mentioned here? What are they?

Te Wāhipounamu—South West New Zealand
蒂瓦希普纳穆—新西兰西南部地区

⇨ **简介**

所属国家：新西兰(New Zealand)

入选时间：1990

入选标准：(vii)(viii)(ix)(x)

Te Wāhipounamu is situated in south-west New Zealand and covers an area of 2.6 million hectares with the inclusion of Fiordland, Mount Aspiring, Mount Cook and Westland. The landscape in this park has been shaped by successive glaciations into fjords, rocky coasts, towering cliffs, lakes and waterfalls. Two-thirds of the park are covered with southern beech and podocarps, some of which are over 800 years old. The kea, the only alpine parrot in the world, lives in the park, as does the rare and endangered takahe, a large flightless bird. As the largest and least modified area of New Zealand's natural ecosystems, it contains the best modern representation of the ancient flora and fauna of Gondwanaland, including Podocarpus species, genera of beech, flightless kiwis, "bush" moas and carnivorous Powelliphanta land snails.

蒂瓦希普纳穆位于新西兰的西南部，占地 2.6 万平方千米，主要由峡湾国家公园、库克峰国家公园、韦斯特兰国家公园和阿斯派灵山国家公园四部分构成。其景观在冰川的持续作用下形成，有海滩、石头海岸、悬崖、湖泊和瀑布，这个地区在其自然生态环境中保存了古冈瓦纳的动物群和植物群。公园从北向南跨越了三个纬度带，形成了沼泽地、草地、灌木丛和森林群落显著的交错现象，其中有 2/3 被南部的山毛榉树和罗汉松覆盖，有的树龄已超过 800 年。公园里的大鹦鹉是世界上仅有的高山鹦鹉，这里还有一种巨大的不会飞的南秧鸟，也属于濒危品种。

Vocabulary

1. inclusion *n.* 包含；内含物

He admired the inclusion of so many ideas in such a short work.

他羡慕在这简短的工作中包含如此多的思想。

2. successive *adj.* 连续的，相继的

Jackson was the winner for a second successive year.

杰克逊已经是连续两年获胜了。

3. modify *v.* 修改，改变

The industrial revolution modified the whole structure of English society.

工业革命改变了整个英国的社会结构。

4. flora *n.* (某地区或某时期的)植物群

fauna *n.* 动物群

No other country has flora and fauna more various and beautiful.
没有其他国家的动植物比巴西的种类更繁多，外形更美丽。

扩展阅读

Family Fun at Fox Glacier

Glacier country is a great place for a family holiday. Experience New Zealand's wilderness at its very best. Expand your family's horizons as you experience nature together. Here you will find suggestions of family friendly adventures, attractions as well as tips on fun things for families to do in and around Fox Glacier villages to help you create an unforgettable holiday in the glacier region.

Glacier Valley Walks

There are a range of short walks in Fox Glacier. In the Fox Glacier Valley alone there are four family friendly walks. Take a picnic lunch and see if you can complete the Fox Glacier Valley Walk, River Walk, Moraine Walk, and the Chalet Lookout Track, all in one day.

Gillespie's Beach: Epic Views & Mining Relics

Drive down the Cook Flat Road to Gillespie's Beach. Enjoy the most spectacular "Mountains to the Sea" views of the Southern Alps. The lagoon walk allows you to examine the rusty mining relics and the Department of Conservation information boards along the way. Skipping stones in the waves is fun too. It's a great place to practice—the beach is covered with perfectly shaped stones!

Mountain Bike Hire

Use some pedal power. Hire a bike from Fox Glacier Bike Rental, Fox Glacier Lodge or Lake Matheson Motel. Enjoy the new cycle way up the Fox Glacier valley, or ride down Cook Flat Road to Lake Matheson, or all the way to the Peak View Lookout. The view is well worth the effort!

Lake Matheson Walk

This is home to one of the most iconic images of New Zealand. Take a camera, and go on a photographic excursion around Lake Matheson. Walk through the podocarp rainforest. Keep an eye out for native birds and see if you can spot eels in the water at the "View of Views" lookout.

Glow Worm Search

After dark, take a flashlight and wander the Minnehaha Walk. You can see glow worms creating their own galaxies hidden in old tree stumps and along the river bank. The track is wheelchair and pushchair friendly, and takes about 20 minutes return.

DOC South Westland Weheka Field Centre

From Monday to Friday you can check out the informative displays on the glaciers, geology, local tracks and walks, Westland Tai Poutini National Park. The rangers have up to date weather forecasts and information on the many walks to do in the Fox Glacier/Weheka area.

Scenic Flights

An unforgettable family experience. Share the thrill of a scenic flight and discover the beauty of the glacier country's high alpine environment together. See rugged westcoast rainforests, cascading waterfalls, spectacular glaciers and New Zealand's highest peaks from the air. The awe inspiring views of New Zealand's iconic scenery will be a lasting family memory. There are a range of flight-seeing options available in Fox Glacier.

Hunts Beach

Drive past Fox Glacier village, to the Hunts Beach turn off just before Jacobs River Makaawhio. Enjoy the rugged, untouched coastline, and search for shiny pebbles on the beach. You may even find a small piece of Aotea stone.

Feed the Salmon

There is something meditative about feeding the salmon at the Salmon Farm Cafe, just north of Lake Paringa. Use your loose change to buy a bag of fish food and watch the greedy fat salmon fight for their treats.

Postcards

Look for the NZICESCAPE postcards created by our talented local photographer Petr Hlavacek. Keep one for your own memoirs, and send someone special an image from Fox Glacier. The Hobnail Shop in the Fox Glacier Guiding Building is the local NZ Post agent where you can buy stamps, and post your treasures home.

Peak View Lookout

Drive to Fox Glacier village, then go down Cook Flat Road to the Peak View Lookout. Enjoy the picnic area. The plane table mounted on a stone plinth can be used to identify the peaks of the Southern Alps Kä Tiritiri o Te Moana.

Family Camping

Spend a night out in the open air and enjoy the Department of Conservation campsites at Gillespie's Beach or Lake Paringa. At Gillespie's you can camp near old gold mining sites and walk to a seal colony. At Lake Paringa the lakeside campground offers boating, fishing and swimming in the lake.

Cafe Crawl

Try a Fox Glacier "Cafe Crawl". Start at the Salmon Farm Cafe near Lake Paringa, drive to Fox Glacier Village, Lake Matheson, and Franz Josef Glacier Village. Finish your journey Okarito Nature Tours at the small seaside village of Okarito.

Children's Adventure Playground

Outside of normal school hours visitors are welcome to use the fantastic adventure playground at the Fox Glacier School. There is also a brand new adventure playground for guests' use at the Fox Glacier Top 10 Holiday Park and Motels.

Souvenir Hunt

See who can buy the most intriguing Glacier Country souvenir for only ＄5. Go hunting in The Hobnail Shop, ReflectioNZ Gifts ＆ Gallery: Lake Matheson, Fox Glacier Store, and Fox Glacier Motors.

（资料来源：http://glaciercountry. co. nz/directory. asp？ ItineraryTypeID＝14.）

Questions

1. What would you choose to do if you have three days in Fox Glacier?

2. Will you take walks if you go to Fox Glacier for travel? Why?

3. What would you do if you want to have some souvenir for your travel to Fox Glacier?

Wet Tropics of Queensland
昆士兰湿热带地区

▷ **简介**

所属国家：澳大利亚（Australia）

入选时间：1988

入选标准：（vii）（viii）（ix）（x）

Covering some 894,420 hectares of mostly tropical rainforest, the Wet Tropics of Queensland stretches along the northeast coast of Australia for some 450 kilometres. This stunningly beautiful area presents an unparalleled record of the ecological and evolutionary processes that shaped the flora and fauna of Australia, containing the relics of the great Gondwanan forest that covered Australia and part of Antarctica 50 to 100 million years ago. The property is extremely important for its rich and unique biodiversity, because all of Australia's unique marsupials and most of its other animals originated in rainforest ecosystems, and their closest surviving relatives occurred in the Wet Tropics. These living relics of the Gondwanan era and their subsequent diversification provide unique insights to the process of evolution in general. The Aboriginal Rainforest People of the Wet Tropics of Queensland have lived continuously in the rainforest environment for at least 5,000 years and this is the only place in Australia where Aboriginal people have permanently inhabited a tropical rainforest environment.

由许多国家公园组成的昆士兰热带雨林位于澳大利亚东北海岸，占地894420公顷，已有一亿三千万年历史，是世界上为数不多的尚未被人类开发的地区之一。雨林与大堡礁相连，这种雨林与礁石相连的地形在全世界是屈指可数的。崎岖的山路、茂密的热带雨林、湍急的河流、深邃的峡谷、白色的沙滩、绚丽的珊瑚礁、活火山和火山湖，构成了昆士兰雨林独特的美景。许多奇特的动植物生活在这里，其中有些可追溯到澳大利亚还是古冈瓦那大陆一部分的时代。至少有483种稀有动物和83种面临灭绝的动物在这里繁衍生息,其中有25种为特别稀有动物。几千年前,土著人就开始在这个热带雨林里生活,但如今仅存500人左右。他们至今仍讲本民族特有的语言,保持着本民族的文化习俗。

Vocabulary

1. stretch *v.* 伸展

The procession stretched for several miles.

游行队伍长达数英里。

2. stunningly *adv.* 绝妙地,极好地

The video is filmed in stunningly beautiful countryside.

这段录像拍摄于景色无比优美的乡村。

3. unparalleled *adj.* 无比的,无双的,空前的

The 18 years to 2000 witnessed an unparalleled bull market for shares and bonds.

2000年之前的18年,股票和债券达到了空前高涨的牛市。

4. relicts *n.* 残余物

More than any other of the crack relicts of the old navy who now serve under him, Raeder has always been a man of one idea:The navy must be rebuilt,must again fight on(and not only under) the sea.

他比他所率领的从旧海军出来的同僚有一种更强烈的愿望:海军必须重建,必须再次屹立在水面之上,而不仅仅是在水下逞威。

5. biodiversity *n.* 生物多样性

There are many measures of biodiversity.

有许多方法可以测量生物多样性。

6. subsequent *adj.* 后来的,随后的

Those concerns were overshadowed by subsequent events.

随后发生的事使之前所关注的那些问题显得无足轻重。

扩展阅读

Rainforest Aboriginal History

The First Australians

Aboriginal people have been living in the rainforests of the Wet Tropics Region for many thousands of years. Some stories handed down over the generations relate to times of most recent volcanic activities, while archeological evidence indicates occupation of the region for at least 40,000 years.

Before European settlement, the Wet Tropics rainforests were one of the most populated areas of Australia, and the only area where Aboriginal people of Australia lived permanently in the rainforest.

Rainforest Aboriginal people's environment provided everything—spirituality, identity, social order, shelter, food and medicine. Aboriginal people also had an excellent economic system in place that involved the bartering of resources amongst different tribal groups.

The Arrival of Europeans

For Rainforest Aboriginal people, the rugged rainforest mountains and inaccessible coastal wetlands provided some protection when Europeans arrived in the mid-nineteenth century. Rainforest Aboriginal people continued to practice their cultures and languages, and their knowledge of ecology, native foods, and access routes was invaluable to the newcomers. However, as more land was cleared, competition became fierce between the settlers and the people of the rainforest.

Many Rainforest Aboriginal people died from introduced diseases like the common cold. Others starved when they could not access their traditional country and their food resources. Many were also shot and poisoned when they were found hunting the introduced cattle and horses that new settlers had brought. This aggression from the early settlers was not met with passivity. Rainforest Aboriginal people fought for their land and continue to this day campaigning to get their land back.

To visitors, many of the Wet Tropics waterfalls are places of extraordinary beauty, but for many Rainforest Aboriginal people, apart from often being important story places, they can also be places of immense sorrow—places their people were driven over and massacred.

Rainforest Aboriginal people had to survive on the margins of the new society that brought with it many foreign laws and government policies that were often directly in conflict with traditional lores and customs. Great restrictions were imposed on Aboriginal peoples' lives and the new laws were quite often discriminatory on the basis of their race.

Many Aboriginal people from this region worked unpaid for rations such as sugar, flour, tea and tobacco. They worked as maids, farm labourers, stockmen and timber cutters, and played a key role in helping to shape the rural landscape you see today.

Many more Rainforest Aboriginal people were forcibly removed to Christian missions across the region at Mission Beach, Mona Mona, Murray Upper, Palm Island, Yarrabah and Wujal Wujal, and some were even sent out of the region to other missions. In addition, Aboriginal people from other parts of Queensland were removed from their families and their traditional lands to live in missions in the Wet Tropics region. They all suffered hardships through the splitting up of their families, being forced to forget their languages, and being stopped from practising their cultures.

Cultural Survival

Today over 20,000 Aboriginal people live in the urban centres, country towns, Aboriginal communities (some are former missions) both outside the Wet Tropics World Heritage Area, and small settlements within the World Heritage Area.

In spite of the imposition of a Government land ownership（tenure）system and significant changes to land management brought about by European settlement and development，Rainforest Aboriginal people continue to maintain and care for the country through their traditional beliefs，knowledge and practices. Their cultures continue to live and grow，and lifestyles today contain a mix of traditional and contemporary knowledge and practices that continues to be handed down from one generation to the next.

While they have endured massive upheaval and loss，Rainforest Aboriginal people's stories，languages and cultures have survived and people continue to have a strong sense of their connection to，and relationship with，their traditional country. These relationships are mapped out in shared stories and places.

Some shared stories connect and identify tribal groups. Other story places are personal，connected to individuals when they are born—a practice which continues today. Like the forests，Rainforest Aboriginal cultures survive in the landscape features that remain.

In this way，the Wet Tropics continues to hold the key to indigenous culture and identity. It tells the story of complex traditional cultures and also of the tragedy，hardship and the strength and resilience of Rainforest Aboriginal people over a hundred and fifty years of change.

（资料来源：http://www. wettropics. gov. au/rainforest-aboriginal-history. ）

Questions

1. What would Aboriginal people do，when they fell ill?
2. What caused the competition between Europeans and Aboriginal people?
3. How do Aboriginal people maintain their cultures and identity?

第三节　大洋洲的世界文化和自然双重遗产

Kakadu National Park
卡卡杜国家公园

简介

所属国家：澳大利亚（Australia）

入选时间：1981 年入选，1987 年、1992 年扩大

入选标准：(i)(vi)(vii)(ix)(x)

Kakadu National Park, a land typical of the ecological balance in the world, covers an area of 20,000 km² in the Northern Territory of Australia. The region inhabited for over 40 thousand years has been little affected by European settlement. Hence the natural vegetation remains extensive in area and relatively unmodified, and its faunal composition is largely intact. The park contains many Aboriginal archaeological, sacred and art sites. The cave paintings, rock carvings and archaeological sites record the skills and way of life of the region's inhabitants, from the hunter-gatherers of prehistoric times to the Aboriginal people of contemporary times. For the historian, they constitute a fund of documentary evidence of primordial importance and a source which is unique. For the ethnologist, Kakadu offers a privileged field of exploration and observation, as the Aborigines who continue to inhabit this site contribute to the maintenance of the balance of the ecosystem.

卡卡杜国家公园位于澳大利亚北领地,占地约 2 万平方千米,是一个典型的生态平衡的地区。公园内有大面积的植被和基本未受侵扰的动物区系祖。有的物种在这里已经延续 4 万多年。由于没有受到现代社会的影响,没有引进物种,公园许多地方仍保存着罕见的原始澳大利亚生态系统。岩画、石刻和考古遗址记载了从史前时代到现在仍然居住在这里的土著居民的生活内容和方式,以及某些飞禽走兽的形象,反映了澳大利亚土著对世界的独特认识,为澳大利亚的考古学、艺术史学和人类史学提供了珍贵的研究资料。

Vocabulary

1. ecological balance 生态平衡

Some scientists, however, warn that encouraging bacterial growth could upset a beach's ecological balance.

然而有些科学家警告,如果任由细菌生长,可能会破坏海滩的生态平衡。

2. inhabite v. 居住于,栖居于

South Korea is inhabited by almost 50 million people.

韩国居住人口有近 5000 万。

3. hence adv. 因此,所以

The trade imbalance is likely to rise again in 1990. Hence a new set of policy actions will be required soon.

贸易失衡可能会在 1990 年再次加剧,因此需要尽快采取一系列新的政策行动。

4. faunal composition 区系组成

The *faunal composition* and economic value of Cleoninae in Xinjiang Uygur Aut will be introduced in the next chapter.

下一章将介绍新疆方喙象亚科的区系组成及经济意义。

5. contemporary adj. 当代的

She writes a lot of contemporary music for people like Whitney Houston.

她给像惠特尼·休斯顿这样的人写了很多当代音乐作品。

6. a fund of 大量

He is possessed of an extraordinary fund of energy.

他的精力异常充沛。

7. documentary *adj.* 记录的；文书的；纪实的

We have documentary evidence that they were planning military actions.

我们有书面证据证明他们正在策划军事行动。

8. primordial *adj.* 初生的，初发的，原始的

It is the primordial force that propels us forward.

它是推动我们前进的原始动力。

扩展阅读

Aboriginal Rock Art

Rock art shows our life.

Rock art is an important part of Aboriginal people's lives.

Mimi spirits were the first of the Creation Ancestors to paint on rock.

They taught some Aboriginal people how to paint and other Aboriginal people learned by copying Mimi art. At the end of their journeys, some Creation Ancestors put themselves on rock walls as paintings and became djang (dreaming places). Some of these paintings are andjamun (sacred and dangerous) and can be seen only by senior men or women; others can be seen by all people.

The escarpment, gorges, and rock outliers of Kakadu hold one of the world's greatest concentrations of rock art sites: Approximately 5,000 art sites have been recorded and a further 10,000 sites are thought to exist.

The paintings, estimated to range in age from 20,000 years to the recent present, constitute one of the longest historical records of any group of people in the world. The rock art sites of Kakadu are recognized internationally for their cultural value and are one of the reasons that Kakadu is inscribed on the United Nations list of World Heritage properties.

Aboriginal people in the Kakadu area paint rock images rarely now. Among the reasons for this are the facts that Aboriginal people no longer live in rock shelters and there are fewer people with the necessary knowledge to allow them to paint at certain sites. Nevertheless, Aboriginal artists continue to paint on bark, paper and other materials. In recent years printing traditional designs onto fabric has become a popular art form, particularly among women.

Rock art remains relevant to Bininj/Mungguy as the works depict objects still used, animals still hunted, and activities people still do. The rock art in Kakadu was painted for a number of reasons:

Hunting

Animals were often painted to increase their abundance and to ensure a successful hunt by placing people in touch with the spirit of the animal.

Religious Significance

At some sites paintings depict aspects of particular ceremonies.

Stories and Learning

Stories associated with the Creation Ancestors, who gave shape to the world were painted.

Sorcery and Magic

Paintings could be used to manipulate events influence people's lives, fun-for play and practice.

Some sites and paintings could be painted only by people with the requisite knowledge. Sorcery paintings could be painted only by the holder of magic knowledge, for instance. Other paintings, particularly at sites depicting stories of Creation Ancestors, were often repainted. Again, only people with knowledge of the stories could repaint them. The act of painting put artists in touch with their Creation Ancestors—a powerful experience.

Generally, the act of painting was more important than the painting itself. At many sites in Kakadu images have been painted over each other: The artist was not concerned about preserving an image for posterity but simply wanted to paint to tell a story.

The stories and knowledge associated with many paintings often have a number of levels. Younger people and non-Aboriginal people are told the first level, known as the "public story". Access to the "full story" depends on an individual's progression through ceremonial life, their interest, and their willingness to take on the responsibilities that go with that knowledge.

As with European art, different Aboriginal art styles have developed over time. Researchers have identified about 11 main artistic styles of rock art in Kakadu. At many sites paintings are layered on top of each other, often in a number of different styles. "Art on art" sites are used to determine which styles came first. It is important to remember that style itself is not enough to determine the age of a painting, since styles were not necessarily exclusive to one period; some styles developed a long time ago are still used today.

By studying the subjects and art styles and then comparing them with climatic, geological and archaeological evidence, researchers have been able to estimate the age of a number of paintings. Paintings of animals now extinct on the Australian mainland can be assumed to have been done before, or shortly after, these animals disappeared: The long-beaked echidna is thought to have become extinct 15,000 years ago; the thylacine and Tasmanian devil became extinct more recently, probably about 2,000 to 3,000 years ago. Paintings of other animals are linked to specific environmental conditions: Estuarine conditions are thought to have begun about 6,000 years ago, so paintings of estuarine fish are probably less than 6,000 years old; the freshwater floodplains developed more recently, so paintings of freshwater birds such as magpie geese are probably less than 1,500 years old.

（资料来源：http://www.environment.gov.au/parks/kakadu/culture/art/index.html.）

Questions

1. Where can people find rock art in Kakadu?
2. Who is allowed to see sacred and dangerous paintings?
3. Why was rock art painted?
4. How can researchers tell the age of a painting?

Tasmanian Wilderness
塔斯马尼亚荒原

简介

所属国家：澳大利亚（Australia）

入选时间：1982 年入选，1989 年扩大，2010 年、2012 年微调

入选标准：（iii）（iv）（vi）（vii）（viii）（ix）（x）

Covering an area of over 1 million hectares, the Tasmanian Wilderness constitutes one of the three largest temperate wilderness areas remaining in the Southern Hemisphere. It has the country's largest river, the deepest lake and the most spectacular mountains, and the rocks here tell each geological period, the oldest rocks formed about 110 million years ago in the Precambrian. The region is renowned for its diversity of flora, and some of the longest lived trees and tallest flowering plants in the world grow in the area. It is also a stronghold for several animals that are either extinct or threatened on mainland Australia. Surveys and excavations demonstrate that human existence here can be dated back to as early as twenty thousand years ago. The earliest settlement of Europeans in the Tasmania Wilderness is during the 18th and 19th centuries when they used this area as a penal colony.

澳大利亚的塔斯马尼亚荒原占地 138 万公顷，是南半球仅存的三个温带荒原之一，有该国最大的河系、最深的湖泊和最壮观的山脉，这里能发现各个地质时期的岩石，最古老的岩石形成于约 11 亿年前的前寒武纪。这里生长着种类繁多的植物，已被世界保护联合会确立为"国际植物多样性中心"，世界上一些最古老的树种生长于此。塔斯马尼亚荒原还为在澳大利亚大陆早已灭绝或濒危的几种动物提供了最后的栖身之所。考古中发现的遗迹可以证明早在两万多年前就曾有人类在这里居住过。欧洲人在塔斯马尼亚荒原的最早开发是把此地当作罪犯的流放地。18—19 世纪时世界人口迁移的重要一页是大批欧洲的罪犯被强制运往偏僻的流放地。

Vocabulary

1. temperate *adj.* (气候)温和的

The Nile Valley keeps a temperate climate throughout the year.

尼罗河谷一年四季气候温和。

2. spectacular *adj.* 场面富丽的,壮观的

Scotland is famous for its spectacular countryside.

苏格兰以其壮丽的乡间景观闻名于世。

3. renowned *adj.* 著名的

British education is renowned for concerning itself with the development of the whole personality.

英国教育以其对个人整体个性发展的关注而闻名。

4. diversity *n.* 多样性,多元化

It is vital to stress the diversity of Asia.

强调亚洲的多样性至关重要。

5. stronghold *n.* (某种动物的)主要栖息地

Shetland is the last stronghold of otters in the British Isles.

设得兰群岛是水獭在不列颠群岛上最后的栖息地。

6. penal colony 流放地

The island was a penal colony during imperial times for officials who fell out of favor with the emperor.

在封建时代,该岛是失去皇帝恩宠的官员们的流放地。

扩展阅读

Threats to the Tasmanian Wilderness

Illegal activities

Especially the illegal cutting and removal of Huon pine and other valuable timbers; the illegal introduction of trout into trout-free lakes; arson and other unlawful lighting of fires; removal of mineral specimens, and unauthorised track cutting into remote areas.

Wildfires

Unmanageable wildfires are probably the greatest realistic threat that could cause rapid, large-scale major ecological impacts to the World Heritage Area. In addition, inappropriate fire regimes (e. g. fires being too frequent, too infrequent, or too hot, etc.) can cause significant long-term changes to the nature and extent of vegetation communities, as well as giving rise to serious risks to public safety, built assets, and adjacent lands. The frequency and intensity of wildfires, especially the risk of unmanageable "landscape-scale fires", is likely to increase as a result of human-induced climate change.

Drought and Human-induced Climate Change

The effects of climate change and sea level rise may be slow and difficult to identify with certainty but potential changes include the degradation and loss of alpine environments and associated communities (alpine communities contain many endemic species) which are limited in distribution in Australia; increased coastal erosion through rising sea levels (with associated loss of significant coastal Aboriginal midden sites); alteration to natural rates and magnitudes of change in the region's drainage system and alteration in the erosive potential of the area's rivers and streams. Over the past decade, there has been a widespread lack of regeneration of the fire-sensitive endemic pencil pine (Athrotaxis cupressoides) within the coniferous woodlands of the Central Plateau. In addition, throughout Tasmania (including the World Heritage Area) there has been a decline in the health of eucalypt woodlands. Drought and/or global warming are considered possible causes for these observations. In addition, there appears to be some evidence that coastal dune systems (which are very sensitive to sea level change) are having foredunes truncated for the first time in the last 3,000 years. This may be a result of depleted sediment supply and/or a result of rising sea levels.

Devil Facial Tumour Disease: Since the mid-1990s, there has been a widespread outbreak of Devil Facial Tumour Disease in Tasmanian devil populations in the northern and eastern regions of Tasmania. Devils affected by the disease grow obvious facial cancers and die within about three to five months. Research findings suggest that the disease is an infectious cancer spread by physical contact between devils e. g. through fighting and biting.

Plant diseases and dieback: Especially the root rot disease Phytophthora. Phytophthora cinnamomi is an introduced plant pathogen that causes root rot disease in susceptible plant communities. The disease is spread by water, with human activities accelerating the spread e. g. through the movement of infected soil. Walking boots and vehicle tyres are the main carriers.

Weeds: Especially marram grass, sea spurge, Spanish heath, gorse, ragwort, broom, blackberries, Canadian pond weed and holly.

Introduced animals: Already established introduced species in the WHA include trout, starlings, goats, rabbits, wasps and bumblebees. Potential new establishments in the WHA include the European red fox, red fin perch, carp and Mesopotamia deer.

Increasing tourism and visitor activities and use: Especially ecologically unsustainable levels or types of use. The number of visitors to the World Heritage Area has grown strongly over the past decade and the level of tourism development within and adjacent to the World Heritage Area has also increased. While tourism is an important component of the state's economic future, a key issue for management of the WHA is how increasing tourism and visitation can be managed in ways that are ecologically sustainable, and that do not degrade the area's special natural and cultural heritage values. Below are some examples of how tourism and visitor activities and use in the WHA are being carefully managed and monitored to achieve sensitive and sustainable use.

Walker impacts: As the number of walkers in the WHA increases, a variety of environmental and social impacts can arise. These include track erosion, braiding, damage to sensitive vegetation communities, as well as social impacts such as visitors feeling the place is becoming too crowded.

Riverbank erosion on the lower Gordon River: Wake waves from vessels (especially commercial cruise boats) can cause erosion of the riverbanks.

Development of new facilities and other infrastructure: Construction of new developments can involve the removal of vegetation, habitat and/or changes in human use which can cause direct and/or indirect impacts to reserve values.

Coastal erosion: Wind and wave erosion along Tasmania's coastline has resulted in the loss of some coastal Aboriginal heritage sites in the southwest. While much of this erosion is due to natural processes, dune blowouts can also be initiated or made worse by human disturbance e. g. by camping, quad bike use, and fires. Climate change predictions also foreshadow sea level rises which would see an increase in the rate of coastal erosion.

（资料来源：http://www.parks.tas.gov.au/index.aspx? base＝667.）

Questions

1. Do human beings constitute a threat to the Tasmanian Wilderness? Give your reasons to support your answer.

2. What do you suggest people do to help keep the area's special natural and cultural heritage values?

Willandra Lakes Region
威兰德拉湖区

⇨ 简介

所属国家：澳大利亚（Australia）

入选时间：1981

入选标准：（iii）（viii）

The Willandra Lakes Region covers a land of 2,400 km² in the Murray Basin area of far south western New South Wales, including the entire lake and river system from Lake Mulurulu, the latest to hold water, to the Prungle Lakes, dry for more than 15,000 years. It is a semi-arid region. The vegetation here consists of semi-arid plant community, characterized by scattered shrubs, grassland and woodland. About 20 species of mammals live here. The Willandra Lakes provide excellent conditions for recording the events of the Pleistocene epoch (when man evolved into its present form). Archaeological discoveries made here reveal a 26,000-year-old cremation site (the oldest known in the world), a 30,000-year-old ochre burial, the remains of giant marsupials in an excellent state of conservation, and grindstones from 18,000 years ago used to crush wild grass for flour whose age is comparable with that claimed for the earliest seed-grind economies. The region also contains the remains of hearths, some dated to 30,000 years ago. It is a unique landmark in the study of human evolution on the Australian continent.

占地 240000 公顷的威兰德拉湖区位于新南威尔士西南部的墨累河盆地,由一系列干湖组成,有世界少见的地层分界。湖区流域由小到池塘、大到占地 500 平方千米深 10 米的加纳朋湖等大小不一的湖组成。威兰德拉湖区属于雨量少、半干旱气候。这里的植被由半干旱植物群落组成,特征为稀疏分散的灌木丛、草地和林地零星点缀着沙原和沙丘。约 20 种哺乳动物生活在这里。该地区的许多人类文化遗迹表明人类至少在 3 万年以前就开发这个地区了。人们在这里发现了 26000 年前的火葬遗址(世界上最早的火葬遗址),3 万年前的赭石墓葬遗址和 18000 年前的磨石和灰泥,大型有袋动物的遗迹。这些对研究澳洲大陆人类进化史有着里程碑式的意义。

Vocabulary

1. semi-arid *adj.* 半干旱的

Dryland farming is a system of producing crops in arid and semi-arid regions without the use of irrigation.

旱地耕作法是一种在干旱或半干旱土地上不使用灌溉方法生产作物的耕作制度。

2. vegetation *n.* 植物,植被

Forests and jungles have thick vegetation.

森林和热带雨林中有茂密的植被。

3. epoch *n.* 【地质】世;时代

These aquifers were created during the Pleistocene epoch, between 12,000 and 2.5 million years ago, and lack the organic carbon that is needed for arsenic to leach into water.

这些蓄水层是在更新世形成的,它们形成于 1.2 万至 250 万年之前,并且缺少能够使砷渗入水中的有机碳。

4. cremation *n.* 火葬

Obama's New Delhi stop officially begins with a wreath-laying ceremony at the Rajghat, the site of Mahatma Gandhi's cremation in 1948.

奥巴马的新德里之行正式开始于在圣雄甘地墓举行的敬花圈仪式,这里也是 1948 年甘地遗体火化的地方。

5. conservation *n.* 保护

One method of soil conservation is the use of windbreaks.

其中一种土壤保护的方法就是使用防风林。

6. date to 追溯到

Fragments of primitive loom can also be seen from the sites of Hemudu culture in Yuyao, Zhejiang, dated to about 4000 BC.

原始的织机碎片也能在浙江余姚的大约公元前 4000 年的河姆渡遗址上看到。

扩展阅读

Direction：Read the following reviews by travelers and answer the questions listed below.

1. "Walk in History's Footsteps"

Reviewed March 12, 2013

Mungo NP is a great place to visit for our country's heritage. Indigenous Australians lived here for more than 50,000 years.

Visit the "Walls of China" at sunset to watch the landscape colors change with the setting sun—just magical! I learned more about the Aboriginal culture from talking to a local for 15 minutes than I have ever learnt from any history book.

Make sure you drive the 70km self drive tour with its many stops along the way for short walks and exploring (do it nice and early before the heat sets in).

Explore the Visitors Centre and make sure you do the short walks from there.

Don't forget extra water and insect repellant!

2. "Isolated, beautiful and not for the feint hearted but well worth the final reward!"

Reviewed November 30, 2012

The first thing you notice about the place is that it's a long way from anything and everything is a dirt road away. Not just any dirt road but sandy, red earth that can be difficult to navigate in places. For several years I had promised myself a trip to this famous spiritual landscape and only now made it. It requires effort and perseverance to make the trip but it's more than worth it. Take a tour with the indigenous guides at the national park. These are called the "discovery tours" and they are tag-a-long, which means you follow in your own car. The only accommodation is either in the camping grounds or at the shearers quarters and if you're staying at the shearers quarters you had better book ahead. There are only 4 rooms. Payment is via an honor system with the forms, etc. at the visitors centre. I loved it, but it was stiflingly hot when I was there. Bring lots of water and food because you are miles from anywhere. There is no "shop" on the park. That means no fuel, no food, no water. Religiously follow the instructions from the park personnel to ensure you have a safe stay out there. Snakes are not uncommon, as are emus and kangaroos as well as all the smaller desert wildlife. Most people don't make the effort but this wild landscape is not to be missed. I have a NSW national parks annual pass but if you don't have one entry to the park is approx $7 and then you have to pay for your accommodation. I stayed overnight so I could get one sunrise, sunset and night shots for my photography.

3. "Amazing, we are so privileged to be able to visit"

Reviewed November 22, 2008

We took a long weekend trip to Mildura (to eat at Stefanos) and spent an afternoon/evening at Mungo. We had no idea that it was World Heritage listed. We were totally blown away. We joined a tour as there is about 1. 5 hrs worth of dirt road to drive on before reaching the park from Mildura and we didn't have a 4WD. It is much more informative to join a tour rather than go by yourself so that you get a sense of the importance of the area, to the Aboriginals as well as to anthropology history. The first stop is the visitor's centre and next to it is the Woolshed, dating back to the 1,800s. A 15 min drive further down the road is the Walls of China, which are sand/rock formations as a result of erosion over many years. What makes this place so special is that the remains of the oldest known human (not neandathal) was found here, dating back 60,000 years from memory (the visitors dislay centre says 23,000 years or so but apparently that was reported to appease other scientists—apparently there was a lot of controversy when the remains were found). Subsequent remains of 2 more bodies were also found, confirming the age of the remains. Apparently this dispelled all myths about humans coming from apes in Africa. The beauty about Mungo is that there are no fences, no barriers, so we could walk anywhere and find bones of all sorts of things that were revealed by the wind and rain. What the rangers do is place sticks around it, divert water flow and let the bones and fossils return back to the earth (at the request of the original owners of the land). The Aboriginals and the rangers work closely together with the scientists. They don't allow excavation so whatever is found is revealed by mother nature.

Definately worth a visit, particularly at sunset. It is just awe inspiring. And definately go before 2010, when Toursim Australia put this destination on their list of must sees, along with Uluru and the Great Barrier Reef. You know what will happen next, a board of tourists will come and it just won't be the same anymore.

（资料来源：http://www. tripadvisor. com/ShowUserReviews-g504275-d497500-r22076470-Mungo_National_Park-Wentworth_New_South_Wales. html. ）

Questions

1. According to the first review, what is the advantage of travel?

2. According to the second review, what must you take with, if you go to Mungo NP?

3. What is the Walls of China?

第四节 大洋洲的世界文化景观遗产

Tongariro National Park
汤加里罗国家公园

⇨ **简介**

所属国家：新西兰（New Zealand）

入选时间：1990 年入选，1993 年扩大

入选标准：（vi），（vii），（viii）

Tongariro National Park，approximately 795.98 km², is situated at the heart of the North Island of New Zealand. The mountains in the center of the park have cultural and religious significance for the Maori people and symbolize the spiritual links between this community and its environment. The park has 15 volcanoes and 3 of them—Tongariro, Ngauruhoe and Ruapehu—have been active for some 20,000—230,000 years. The park has a diverse range of ecosystems and some spectacular landscapes as well as a land of strong contrasts. Chaotic, barren lava flows, winter snowfields, hot springs and active craters can be seen side by side. Its plants too vary considerably, from alpine herbs to thick swathes of tussocks and flax, from the hardy, low-growing shrubs of the Rangipo gravel-field to dense beech forests. It is home to many creatures native to New Zealand, including the short-tailed bat, kereru (New Zealand's native pigeon), fantails and parakeets.

汤加里罗国家公园位于新西兰北岛中部，面积约 795.98 平方千米。中心地带的山脉对于毛利人来说具有文化和宗教上的象征意义，标志着这个部落与其环境在精神上的联系。公园内有 15 座火山，其中最著名的 3 座火山（汤加里罗、鲁阿佩胡和瑙鲁霍伊）都在距今约 200 多万年前开始喷发，后来仍不断活动，直到现在；由火山灰铺成的银灰色大道蜿蜒在山间，呈现一片火山园林风光。整个国家公园里森林茂密，高山雪景，溪水流淌，生物种类繁多，生态环境变化万端，风景十分秀丽。

Vocabulary

1. situated *adj.* 位于……的，坐落在……的

His hotel is situated in one of the loveliest places on the Loire.

他下榻的旅馆位于卢瓦河畔最漂亮的地方之一。

2. symbolize *v.* 象征

They symbolize immortality and longevity.

它们象征着不朽和长寿。

3. diverse *adj.* 不同的,多种多样的

Since then,she has played a diverse range of roles.

从那时起,她出演了各种不同的角色。

4. side by side 肩并肩地;一起

The couple walked side by side on the pavement.

这一对肩并肩地走在人行道上。

5. considerably *adv.* 相当,非常,颇

Children vary considerably in the rate at which they learn these lessons.

孩子们学习这些课文的速度大不相同。

6. spectacular *adj.* 场面富丽的,壮观的

The cruise provided us with some spectacular views.

一路驶去,壮丽的景色不绝于目。

扩展阅读

Challenges and Preservation Efforts

Like many other indigenous sacred places worldwide, Tongariro National Park faces the flattering threat of being "loved to death" as increasing numbers of visitors—currently about a million each year—come to partake of its natural beauty and recreation opportunities. Skiiers have been enjoying the slopes of the park since the early 1900s, and hiking, biking, camping and mountaineering are other big recreational draws. But these activities require facilities and infrastructure, hence the park contains roads, parking lots, trails, ski lifts, viewing platforms, trekking huts and the like. Unlike many other national parks, Tongariro has a village within it. Whakapapa Village, which provides lodging and amenities, was established early in the park's history, before ideas about conservation shifted to discourage such practices.

The primary problems created by the large numbers of visitors to the park are high quantities of garbage; erosion caused by hikers taking shortcuts between trails; pollution from heavy car traffic; and an overburdened and outdated sewage system that releases low-quality waste water into streams. There is also concern about the growth of nonnative plant species, possibly brought in by foreign materials used in roads and parking lots. In addition, the active volcanic nature of the park poses threats to public safety.

Nevertheless, because of the management system in place, which actively incorporates Maori concerns and emphasizes preservation of the World Heritage values that enabled the park's designation, these challenges are not insurmountable. The New Zealand Department of Conservation manages the park and a Conservation Board prepares the Tongariro Park Management Plan, which was reviewed in 2003. The Maori tribes of the Tongariro region—the Ngati Rangi, Ngati Tuwharetoa and Ngati Tahu *iwi*—are consulted on all significant management issues within the park, especially where cultural values are involved, and there are several Maori members on the Conservation Board.

The current Park Management Plan prohibits extension of the amenity areas—Whakapapa Village, the commercial ski fields and a smaller ski village—and defines what development can take place within those areas. For example, no further accommodations can be built within amenity areas, and ski fields are restricted to three percent of the total area of the park. Outside the amenity areas, priority is being placed on restoring hiking trails, and all toilets are being converted to ecologically friendly dry-vault toilets. There are two small wilderness areas ensuring that parts of the park are free from any sort of facilities.

New considerations from the 2003 review include implementing measures to limit visitor numbers on Mount Tongariro; new sewage treatment efforts; limiting the impact of aircraft and commercial filming; and whether to permit commercial guiding. The issue of commercialization in the park is of particular concern to Maori tribes. Additional outside recommendations include moving parking and accommodation facilities outside the park and providing bus service into the park; trucking and disposing of all sewage outside of the park; and encouraging ecotourism operations.

With so much tradition, history and culture tied to the mountain, the Maori want to see these values, as well as the park's physical integrity, preserved for future generations. Since the designation of Tongariro National Park as a cultural landscape, awareness and understanding of Maori cultural values have increased. Maori have been involved in the redevelopment and creation of new displays at the visitor centers that explain the cultural and natural significance of the park and help foster respect for its careful management and conservation. They have also taken part in planning World Heritage celebrations, developing education resources and biodiversity programs, and assessing concession applications.

A good example of the collaboration between park management and local Maori tribes is the handling of a safety threat after a series of volcanic eruptions in 1995 and 1996 emptied Mount Ruapehu's Crater Lake and built an accumulation of ash deposits at the lake's outlet. Because of the threat of a volcanic mudflow once the lake refilled, the Department of Conservation undertook an environmental and cultural assessment, in consultation with local tribes, of the options to minimize risks to public safety. One option, which entailed bulldozing a trench into the summit of the mountain, was opposed by the local tribes, who felt it would "challenge the indigenous integrity and strength of the cultural World Heritage status". The conservation minister decided against such work and instead opted to install a state-of-the-art alarm and warning system and construct a protective bank along the Whangaehu River to prevent a mudflow from overflowing onto the highway—a decision that received commendation from the World Heritage Committee for its ethical and cultural sensitivity.

（资料来源：http://www. sacredland. org/tongariro/. ）

Questions

1. What are the major problems Tongariro National Park is facing?

2. What do visitors come to the park for?

3. Why do the Maori want to preserve the park?

4. What measures would the government take to preserve the world heritage?

Uluru-Kata Tjuta National Park
乌卢鲁-卡塔曲塔国家公园

⇨ **简介**

所属国家：澳大利亚（Australia）

入选时间：1987 年入选，1994 年扩大

入选标准：（v）（vi）（vii）（viii）

Uluru-Kata Tjuta National Park is located in Australia's Red Center and comprises extensive sand plains, dunes and alluvial desert, punctuated by the Uluru monolith and Kata Tjuta. Uluru is composed of hard red sandstone which has been exposed as a result of folding, faulting and the erosion of surrounding rock. It is 9. 4 km in circumference and 340 m in height. Kata Tjuta comprises 36 steep-sided rock domes of gently dipping Mount Currie conglomerate consisting of phenocrysts of fine-grained acid and basic rocks, granite and gneiss in an epidote-rich matrix. There are 22 native mammals and 5 major categories of vegetation found in the park. The park, and in particular the Uluru monolith, is one of several equally important and interconnected centers of local and religious significance scattered throughout the extensive area of western central Australia occupied by Aborigines.

乌卢鲁-卡塔曲塔国家公园位于澳大利亚的红土中心，这里具有一系列奇异的地质与地貌特点，其中包括雄伟壮观的独体巨石乌卢鲁和卡塔·丘达石岩。乌卢鲁巨石由长石砂岩构成，高度达 340 米，圆周有 9.4 千米，底部有一些浅洞穴，被某些原住民部落视为圣地，洞内有雕刻和绘画；卡塔曲塔是由 36 个巨大的远古岩石形成的石阵，其形状和颜色皆是美丽独特的红色风化砂岩圆顶。公园显示了干旱的生态系统所独具的生物多样化现象。整个国家公园，尤其是乌卢鲁巨石，一直是西部沙漠地区土著人宗教、文化、地域和内部经济关系的中心之一。

Vocabulary

1. comprise *v.* 包含，包括；由……组成；由……构成

The task force is comprised of congressional leaders, cabinet heads and administration officials.

工作小组由国会领导人、内阁首脑和行政官员组成。

2. extensive *adj.* 广泛的；大量的；广阔的

I have benefited a lot from extensive reading.

广泛的阅读使我受益匪浅。

3. punctuate *v.* 不时打断

The silence of the night was punctuated by the distant rumble of traffic.

夜晚的宁静不时被远处车辆的隆隆声打断。

4. expose *v.* 使暴露

Lowered sea levels exposed the shallow continental shelf beneath the Bering Sea.

海平面下降使白令海底部的浅层大陆架暴露出来。

5. category *n.* 种类

Designer wedding dresses make wedding fashion a separate category from mainstream fashion.

著名设计师设计的婚纱使得婚纱时尚有别于主流服装时尚。

6. in particular 尤其，特别

In particular, it can enhance transparency and accountability.

特别是它能提高透明度，巩固问责制。

7. interconnect *v.* 使互相连接；使互相联系

The regions are interconnected by an excellent highway system.

那些地区通过完善的公路系统相互连接。

扩展阅读

Attractions of Uluru—Kata Tjuta National Park

Most tourists visit Uluru in the mornings and Kata Tjuta (the Olgas) in the afternoon. Reverse the order (do the Valley of the Winds walk in the morning and Uluru in the afternoon), and you'll likely find both spots a little more silent and spiritual.

The peak time to catch the Rock's beauty is sunset, when oranges, peaches, pinks, reds, and then indigo and deep violet creep across its face. Some days it's fiery, and other days the colors are muted. A sunset-viewing car park is on the Rock's western side. Plenty of sunset and sunrise tours operate from the resort.

At sunrise, the colors are less dramatic, but many people enjoy the spectacle of the Rock unveiled by the dawn to birdsong. You'll need an early start—most tours leave about 75 minutes before sunup.

A paved road runs around the Rock. The easy 9.4-km (6-mile) Base Walk circumnavigating Uluru takes about 2 hours (the best time is early morning), but allow time to linger around the water holes, caves, folds, and overhangs that make up its walls.

The Pitjantjatjara people refer to tourists as minga—little ants—because that's what they look like crawling up Uluru. Climbing this sacred rock is a fraught subject, and one which Australians fall into two camps over. Those who have or want to and those who never will. I fall into the latter category. Climbing Uluru is against the wishes of the traditional owners, the Anangu ("the people", a term used by Aboriginal people from the Western Desert to refer to themselves), because of its deep spiritual significance to them. The climb follows the trail the ancestral Dreamtime Mala (rufous hare-wallaby) men took when they first came to Uluru, something you will hear about when you visit. While tourists are still allowed to climb, the traditional owners strongly prefer that they don't, and you will see signs and information to this effect.

Apart from respecting Uluru as a sacred place, there are several good practical reasons for resisting the temptation to become one of the more than 200,000 people each year who complete the 348 m (1,142-ft.) hike. The Rock is dangerously steep and rutted with ravines about 2.5 m (8 1/4 ft.) deep; and 35 people have died while climbing—either from heart attacks or falls—in the past 4 decades. Anangu feel a duty to safeguard visitors to their land, and feel great sorrow and responsibility when visitors are killed or injured. The climb, by all accounts, is tough. There are sometimes strong winds, the walls are almost vertical in places (you have to hold onto a chain), and it can be freezing cold or maddeningly hot. Heat stress is a real danger. If you're unfit, have breathing difficulties, heart trouble, high or low blood pressure, or are scared of heights, don't do it. The climb takes at least 1 hour up for the fit, and 1 hour down. The less sure-footed should allow 3 to 4 hours. The Rock is closed to climbers during bad weather; when temperatures exceed 97°F (36°C), which they often do from November to March; and when wind speed exceeds 25 knots. It is closed at 8 am daily in January and February because of the extreme heat.

The Australian government recognized the existence of the traditional Aboriginal owners in 1979 and created a national park to protect Uluru and Kata Tjuta. In 1983, the traditional owners were granted ownership of the land and the park was leased to the Australian National Parks and Wildlife Service for 99 years, with the agreement that the public could continue to climb it. The current (at press time) Australian government has a 10-year management plan for Uluru that decrees the climb will close permanently if climber numbers drop to below 20% of all visitors to Uluru. In any case, visitors will be given 18 months' warning of any planned closure.

While it would be worth coming all the way to Central Australia just to see Uluru, there is a second unique natural wonder to see, just a 50 km (31-mile) drive away. Kata Tjuta, or the Olgas, consists of 36 immense ochre rock domes rising from the desert, rivaling Uluru for spectacular beauty. Some visitors find it lovelier and more mysterious than Uluru. Known to the Aborigines as Kata Tjuta, or "many heads", the tallest dome is 200 m (656 ft.) higher than Uluru, and Kata Tjuta figures more prominently in Aboriginal legend than Uluru.

This part of Australia's red heart was first discovered in the 1870s by English explorers. Ernest Giles named part of Kata Tjuta "Mount Olga" after the reigning Queen Olga of Wurttemberg, while William Gosse gave Uluru the name "Ayers Rock" after Sir Henry Ayers, the Chief Secretary of South Australia.

Two walking trails take you in among the domes: the 7.4-km (4.6-mile) Valley of the Wind walk, which is fairly challenging and takes 3 to 5 hours, and the easy 2.6-km (1.6-mile) Gorge walk, which takes about an hour. The Valley of the Winds trail is the more rewarding in terms of scenery. Both have lookout points and shady stretches. The Valley of the Winds trail closes when temperatures rise above 97°F (36°C).

（资料来源：http://www.frommers.com/destinations/uluru-katatjutanationalpark/1403010029.html#ixzz2Nzc5gjZg.）

Questions

1. What can people see when they visit Uluru?
2. Why do Aboriginal people resist the idea of climbing Uluru?
3. Will you climb Uluru, if you go there?
4. What other names do Uluru and Kata Tjuta have?